OFFICIAL TOURIST BOARD GUIDE

New 40th Edition

Camping, Touring & Holiday Parks

Britain's quality-assessed holiday parks

2015

Welcome to Britain, a country brimming with awe-inspiring heritage, iconic culture, stunning landscapes and buzzing cities. Whether you're planning to cycle through our gorgeous countryside, hike along the coast, shop till you drop or savour some local delicacies, we are delighted you've chosen to spend your precious holiday time in Britain. You won't regret it.

Britain offers unique holiday experiences for every taste, budget and age. If you're after a culture-filled city break, head to vibrant Newcastle or historic Edinburgh. Or if you fancy a quieter, off-the-beaten path experience, you can explore remote corners of Britain by caravan, car or bicycle. One of Britain's strengths as a destination is the ease of accessibility around the country, so you can reach magical destinations in a matter of hours.

We hope you will revisit your favourite spots in Britain again, or explore new places you've wanted to experience. Always dreamt of learning to surf? Cornwall and Devon offer world-class surfing for beginners and pros alike, coupled with excellent beachside camping sites and holiday parks. The Wales Coast Path is one of the most striking areas of the country and a favourite with hikers. Or take a road trip around Inverness, visiting the glistening Scottish lochs and majestic castles dotted around the Highlands.

Timing your visit to include a gig or festival is a must for any music fans - there's something for everyone, in all corners of the country. If you're into sports, don't miss the opportunity to experience a Barclays Premier League football game or the Rugby World Cup, which is being hosted across England and Wales in 2015.

Whatever your destination, activity or budget, this guide is an indispensable source for visitors looking to make the most out of their holiday time in Britain.

Joss Croft
Marketing Director, VisitBritain

Contents

Further Information

Useful Indexes

How to use this guide

This official VisitBritain guide is packed with information from where to stay, to how to get there and what to see on arrival. In fact, this guide captures everything you need to know when exploring Britain.

Choose from a wide range of quality-assessed places to stay to suit all budgets and tastes. This guide contains a comprehensive listing of touring, camping and holiday parks and holiday villages participating in the British Graded Holiday Parks Scheme.

Each park is visited annually by professional assessors, who apply nationally agreed standards, so that you can book with confidence knowing your accommodation has been checked and rated for quality.

Check out the places to visit in each region, from towns and cities to spectacular coast and countryside, plus historic homes, castles and great family attractions! Maps show accommodation locations, selected destinations and some of the National Cycle Networks. For even more ideas go online at www.visitbritain.com.

Regional tourism contacts and tourist information centres are listed in each of the regional sections of this guide. Before booking your stay, why not contact them to find out what's going on in the area? You'll also find events, travel information, maps and useful indexes that will help you plan your trip, throughout this guide.

Accommodation entries explained

Each accommodation entry contains detailed information to help you decide if it is right for you. This has been provided by proprietors and our aim is to ensure that it is as objective and factual as possible.

① ② ③ ④ ⑤

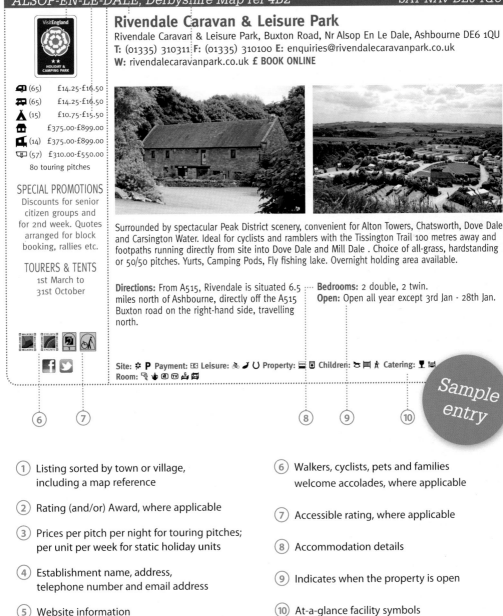

ALSOP-EN-LE-DALE, *Derbyshire Map ref 4B2*   *SAT NAV DE6 1QU*

★★
HOLIDAY &
CAMPING PARK

🚐 (65)   £14.25-£16.50
🚏 (65)   £14.25-£16.50
⛺ (15)   £10.75-£15.50
🏠   £375.00-£899.00
🚚 (14)   £375.00-£899.00
🛏 (57)   £310.00-£550.00
80 touring pitches

SPECIAL PROMOTIONS
Discounts for senior citizen groups and for 2nd week. Quotes arranged for block booking, rallies etc.

TOURERS & TENTS
1st March to
31st October

Rivendale Caravan & Leisure Park

Rivendale Caravan & Leisure Park, Buxton Road, Nr Alsop En Le Dale, Ashbourne DE6 1QU
T: (01335) 310311 **F:** (01335) 310100 **E:** enquiries@rivendalecaravanpark.co.uk
W: rivendalecaravanpark.co.uk **£ BOOK ONLINE**

Surrounded by spectacular Peak District scenery, convenient for Alton Towers, Chatsworth, Dove Dale and Carsington Water. Ideal for cyclists and ramblers with the Tissington Trail 100 metres away and footpaths running directly from site into Dove Dale and Mill Dale . Choice of all-grass, hardstanding or 50/50 pitches. Yurts, Camping Pods, Fly fishing lake. Overnight holding area available.

Directions: From A515, Rivendale is situated 6.5 miles north of Ashbourne, directly off the A515 Buxton road on the right-hand side, travelling north.

Bedrooms: 2 double, 2 twin.
Open: Open all year except 3rd Jan - 28th Jan.

Site: ❀ P **Payment:** ▨ **Leisure:** ⅋ ♩ ☋ **Property:** ▦ 🖥 **Children:** 🛝 🛏 🚼 **Catering:** 🍽 🍴
Room: 🍵 🍶 🖨 📺 🛗 📠

Sample entry

① Listing sorted by town or village, including a map reference

② Rating (and/or) Award, where applicable

③ Prices per pitch per night for touring pitches; per unit per week for static holiday units

④ Establishment name, address, telephone number and email address

⑤ Website information

⑥ Walkers, cyclists, pets and families welcome accolades, where applicable

⑦ Accessible rating, where applicable

⑧ Accommodation details

⑨ Indicates when the property is open

⑩ At-a-glance facility symbols

There are hundreds of "Green" places to stay and visit in England from small bed and breakfasts to large visitor attractions and activity holiday providers. Businesses displaying this logo have undergone a rigorous verification process to ensure that they are sustainable (green) and that a qualified assessor has visited the premises.

We have indicated the accommodation which has achieved a Green award... look out for the symbol in the entry.

Information about many of the accommodation services and facilities is given in the form of symbols.

Pitches/Units

- Caravans (number of pitches and rates)
- Motor caravans (number of pitches and rates)
- Tents (number of pitches and rates)
- Caravan holiday homes (number of pitches and rates)
- Log cabins/lodges (number of units and rates)
- Chalets/villas (number of units and rates)

Site Features

- Parking next to pitch
- Public house/Inn

Booking & Payment Details

- Booking recommended in summer
- Euros accepted
- Visa/Mastercard/Switch accepted

Leisure Facilities

- Tennis court(s)
- Swimming pool – outdoor
- Swimming pool – indoor
- Games room
- Riding/pony-trekking nearby
- Golf available (on site or nearby)
- Fishing nearby
- Cycles for hire

Children

- Childrens outdoor play area
- Children welcome

Catering

- Foodshop/Mobile foodshop
- Restaurant on site

Park Facilities

- Showers available
- Public telephone
- Laundry facilities
- Wi-Fi/Internet access
- Regular evening entertainment
- Dogs/Pets welcome by arrangement

Camping & Touring Facilities

- Water/waste hookup
- Electrical hook-up points
- Calor Gas/Camping Gaz purchase/ exchange service
- Chemical toilet disposal point

Visitor Attraction Quality Assurance

Participating attractions are visited by a professional assessor. High standards in welcome, hospitality, services, presentation; standards of toilets, shop and café, where provided, must be achieved to receive these awards.

Visitor Attraction Quality Scheme Accolades

For top-scoring attractions where visitors can expect a really memorable visit.

For 'going the extra mile', ensuring that visitors are really well looked after.

For small, well-run attractions that deserve a special mention.

For particularly innovative and effective interpretation or tour, telling the story to capture visitors' imaginations.

For attractions with cafes and restaurants that consistently exceed expectations.

 Pets Come Too - accommodation displaying this symbol offer a special welcome to pets. Please check for any restrictions before booking.

 VisitScotland Thistle Award for Excellence. Award winning parks listed in this guide show the logo on their entries.

Businesses displaying this logo have undergone a rigorous verification process to ensure that they are sustainable (green). See page 20 for further information.

National Accessible Scheme

The National Accessible Scheme includes standards for hearing and visual impairment as well as mobility impairment – see pages 10-11 for further information.

Welcome Schemes

Walkers, cyclists, families and pet owners are warmly welcomed where you see these signs – see page 9 for further information.

Motorway Service Area Assessment Scheme

The star ratings cover over a wide range of aspects of each operation including cleanliness, the quality and range of catering and also the quality of the physical aspects, as well as the service provided. – See page 272 for further information.

A special welcome

To help make booking your accommodation easier, VisitEngland has four special Welcome schemes which accommodation in England can be assessed against. Owners participating in these schemes go the extra mile to welcome walkers, cyclists, families or pet owners to their accommodation and provide additional facilities and services to make your stay even more comfortable.

Families Welcome

If you are searching for the perfect family holiday, look out for the Families Welcome sign. The sign indicates that the proprietor offers additional facilities and services catering for a range of ages and family units. For families with young children, the accommodation will have special facilities such as cots and highchairs, storage for push-chairs and somewhere to heat baby food or milk. Where meals are provided, children's choices will be clearly indicated, with healthy options also available. They'll have information on local walks, attractions, activities or events suitable for children, as well as local child-friendly pubs and restaurants. However, not all accommodation is able to cater for all ages or combinations of family units, so do remember to check for any restrictions before confirming your booking.

Welcome Pets!

Do you want to travel with your faithful companion? To do so with ease make sure you look out for accommodation displaying the Welcome Pets! sign. Participants in this scheme go out of their way to meet the needs of guests bringing dogs, cats and/or small birds. In addition to providing water and food bowls, torches or nightlights, spare leads and pet washing facilities, they'll buy in pet food on request and offer toys, treats and bedding. They'll also have information on pet-friendly attractions, pubs, restaurants and recreation. Of course, not everyone is able to offer suitable facilities for every pet, so do check if there are any restrictions on the type, size and number of animals before you confirm your booking.

Walkers Welcome

If walking is your passion, seek out accommodation participating in the Walkers Welcome scheme. Facilities include a place for drying clothes and boots, maps and books for reference and a first-aid kit. Packed breakfasts and lunches are available on request in hotels and guesthouses, and you have the option to pre-order basic groceries in self-catering accommodation. On top of this, proprietors provide a wide range of information including public transport, weather forecasts, details of the nearest bank, all night chemists and local restaurants and nearby attractions.

Cyclists Welcome

Are you an explorer on two wheels? If so, seek out accommodation displaying the Cyclists Welcome symbol. Facilities at these properties include a lockable undercover area, a place to dry outdoor clothing and footwear, an evening meal if there are no eating facilities available within one mile and a packed breakfast or lunch on request. Information is also available on cycle hire, cycle repair shops, maps and books for reference, weather forecasts, details of the nearest bank, all night chemists and much much more.

National Accessible Scheme

Finding suitable accommodation is not always easy, especially if you have to seek out rooms with level entry or large print menus. Use the National Accessible Scheme to help you make your choice.

Proprietors of accommodation taking part in the National Accessible Scheme have gone out of their way to ensure a comfortable stay for guests with hearing, visual or mobility needs. These exceptional places are full of extra touches to make everyone's visit trouble-free, from handrails, ramps and step-free entrances (ideal for buggies too) to level-access showers and colour contrast in the bathrooms. Members of staff may have attended a disability awareness course and will know what assistance will really be appreciated.

Appropriate National Accessible Scheme symbols are included in the guide entries (shown opposite). If you have additional needs or specific requirements, we strongly recommend that you make sure these can be met by your chosen establishment before you confirm your reservation. The index at the back of the guide gives a list of accommodation that has received a National Accessible Scheme rating.

'Holiday in the British Isles' is an annual guidebook produced by Disability Rights UK. It lists NAS rated accommodation and offers extensive practical advice to help you plan your trip.

£12.99 (inc. P&P),
www.disabilityrights.uk.org

England

Mobility Impairment Symbols

Older and less mobile guests
Typically suitable for a person with sufficient mobility to climb a flight of steps but who would benefit from fixtures and fittings to aid balance.

Part-time wheelchair users
Typically suitable for a person with restricted walking ability and for those who may need to use a wheelchair some of the time and can negotiate a maximum of three steps.

Independent wheelchair users
Typically suitable for a person who depends on the use of a wheelchair and transfers unaided to and from the wheelchair in a seated position. This person may be an independent traveller.

Assisted wheelchair users
Typically suitable for a person who depends on the use of a wheelchair and needs assistance when transferring to and from the wheelchair in a seated position.

Access Exceptional is awarded to establishments that meet the requirements of independent wheelchair users or assisted wheelchair users shown above and also fulfil more demanding requirements with reference to the British Standards BS8300.

....

Visual Impairment Symbols

Typically provides key additional services and facilities to meet the needs of visually impaired guests.

Typically provides a higher level of additional services and facilities to meet the needs of visually impaired guests.

....

Hearing Loss Symbols

Typically provides key additional services and facilities to meet the needs of guests with hearing loss.

Typically provides a higher level of additional services and facilities to meet the needs of guests with hearing loss.

The criteria VisitEngland has adopted does not necessarily conform to British Standards or to Building Regulations. They reflect what the organisation understands to be acceptable to meet the practical needs of guests with mobility or sensory impairments and encourage the industry to increase access to all.

For more information on the NAS and tips and ideas on holiday travel in England go to:
www.visitengland.com/accessforall

Additional help and guidance on accessible tourism can be obtained from the national charity Tourism for All:

Tourism for All

Tourism for All UK
7A Pixel Mill
44 Appleby Road
Kendal
Cumbria LA9 6ES

Information helpline 0845 124 9971
(lines open 9-5 Mon-Fri)
E info@tourismforall.org.uk
W www.tourismforall.org.uk
   www.openbritain.net

Peace of Mind with Star Ratings

 Most camping and caravan parks in Britain have a star rating from one of the four assessing bodies – VisitEngland, VisitScotland, Visit Wales or the AA. The three national tourist boards assess to the same national standards, so you can expect comparable services, facilities and quality standards at each star rating.

All the parks in this guide are checked annually by national tourist board assessors. So when you see the star rating sign you can be confident that we've checked it out.

The national standards are based on research of consumer expectations. The independent assessors decide the type (classification) of park – for example if it's a 'touring park', 'holiday park', 'holiday village', etc. – and award a star rating based on over fifty separate aspects, from landscaping and layout to maintenance, customer care and, most importantly, cleanliness.

The Quality marque helps you choose with confidence knowing that the park has been thoroughly checked out before you check in.

Accommodation Types

Always look at or ask for the type of accommodation as each offers a very distinct experience. The parks you'll find in this guide are:

Camping Park – these sites only have pitches available for tents.

Touring Park – sites for your own caravan, motor home or tent.

Holiday Park – sites where you can hire a caravan holiday home for a short break or longer holiday, or even buy your own holiday home. Sites range from small, rural sites to larger parks with added extras, such as a swimming pool.

Many of the above parks will offer a combination of these classifications.

Holiday Villages – usually comprise of a variety of types of accommodation, with the majority in custom-built rooms, for example, chalets. The option to book on a bed and breakfast, or dinner, bed and breakfast basis is normally available. A range of facilities, entertainment and activities are also provided, which may, or may not, be included in the tariff. Holiday Villages must meet minimum requirements for provision and quality of facilities and services, including fixtures, fittings, furnishings, décor and any other extra facilities.

Forest Holiday Village – a holiday village situated in a forest setting with conservation and sustainable tourism being a key feature. Usually offering a variety of accommodation, often purpose built and with a range of entertainment, activities and facilities on site, free of charge or at extra cost.

Star ratings are based on a combination of the range of facilities, level of service offered and quality - if a park offers the facilities required to achieve a certain star rating but does not achieve the quality score required for that rating, a lower star rating is awarded.

A random check is made of a sample of accommodation provided for hire (caravans, chalets, etc) and the quality of the accommodation itself is included in the grading assessment.

Holiday Villages in England are assessed under a separate rating scheme (for details see www.qualityintourism.com).

Also included in this guide are Bunkhouses and Camping Barns – safe, budget-priced, short-term accommodation for individuals and groups.

Gold Awards

How can you find those special places to stay? Those that, regardless of the facilities and services, achieve exceptional scores for quality. VisitEngland's Gold Awards highlight this excellence and are given to four and five-star caravan parks that offer the highest level of quality within their particular star rating.

OFFICIAL TOURIST BOARD GUIDES

40th Anniversary Golden Ticket Giveaway!

Are you a winner in our Special 40th Anniversary golden ticket giveaway?

To celebrate the 40th anniversary edition of the Official Tourist Board Guides, we are giving away 6 x UK short breaks worth £500 each. We have randomly inserted 6 golden tickets in copies of the 2015 guides and if this guide contains one then you are a winner!

Check inside this copy of the guide and if you find a Golden Ticket call us on 01733 296910 quoting the reference number from your ticket to claim your prize. You will be asked to provide your ticket, together with the sales receipt for the guide in order to claim your prize.

www.visitor-guides.co.uk

AVAILABLE FROM ALL GOOD BOOKSHOPS AND ONLINE RETAILERS

VisitEngland's unique Gold Awards are given in recognition of exceptional quality in caravan parks.

VisitEngland professional assessors make recommendations for Gold Awards during assessments. They look for aspects of exceptional quality in all areas, in particular, cleanliness, facilities and reception.

While star ratings are based on a combination of quality, the range of facilities and the level of service offered, Gold Awards are based solely on Quality.

Caravan parks with a Gold Award and a detailed entry in this guide are:
• **Ross Park, Ipplepen, Devon**
• **Seafield Caravan Park, Seahouses, Northumberland**

Detailed entries for these properties can be found using the property index on page 300.

VisitEngland Awards for Excellence

In 2014 the annual VisitEngland Awards celebrated 25 years of excellence. Years during which the breadth of tourism experience offered to visitors in England has grown to suit every purse and preference whilst matching, and often exceeding, the quality and choice available on the international stage.

With a history stretching back over 25 years, the VisitEngland Awards for Excellence are firmly established as representing the highest accolade in English tourism. The Awards recognise businesses that incorporate best practice and demonstrate excellence in customer service throughout their operation and celebrate the very best in quality and innovation. The Awards are open to all tourism businesses and tourism support organisations which meet the published criteria for the award category or categories they are entering.

Competition to win one of the 15 categories is hotly contested with the majority of finalists having won their destination heats and truly out to show that they are the best of the best! A panel of expert judges review the entries and this year a total of 76 finalists, 15 gold, 16 silver, 15 bronze and 30 highly commended winners were selected from a total of 368 entries from areas spanning the length and breadth of England. You can find a complete list of winners online at: www.visitenglandawards.org

The hunt for the Caravan Holiday Park or Holiday Village of the Year shone the spotlight onto the wonderful locations and top-notch accommodation offer available within this sector. Highly Commended finalist Hoburne Bashley at New Milton in Hampshire, lies in the heart of the stunning New Forest with the coast close by. At the other end of the country in Northumberland's Kielder Forest Northumbrian Water's Leaplish Waterside Park offers the best of both worlds - peace and tranquillity combined with opportunities to try out new sports and activities as part of a 'Go Active Break'. The second Bronze Award winner,

Waldegraves & Cosways Family Holiday Parks at Mersea Island, Essex, is a family run business that has been trading for over 70 years and continues to achieve a level of service designed to exceed the customer's expectations. The family take pride in constantly identifying and developing new services and facilities. The Silver Award winner is found in a beautiful setting in Cornwall with Gwel an Mor Resort, Portreath, and a team that sets itself the challenge of providing a completely new standard in holiday lodges. The Gold Award winner is Seafield Caravan Park in the much-loved Northumberland village of Seahouses. Over the last decade the multi-award winning owners have been consistent in their commitment to investing in quality and to providing their guests with a holiday to remember.

Caravan Holiday Park of the Year 2014

GOLD WINNER	
Seafield Caravan Park, Northumberland	★ ★ ★ ★ ★

SILVER WINNER	
Gwel an Mor Resort, Portreath	★ ★ ★ ★ ★

BRONZE WINNERS	
Leaplish Waterside Park, Northumberland	★ ★ ★ ★ - ★ ★ ★ ★ ★
Waldegraves & Cosways Family Holiday Parks, Essex	★ ★ ★ ★

HIGHLY COMMENDED	
Hoburne Bashley, Hampshire	★ ★ ★ ★

Award winning holiday park

VisitEngland
Awards for
Excellence
2014

Seafield Caravan Park

It's difficult to imagine a more breathtaking location than Seafield Caravan Park with views of the dramatic Northumberland coastline and the imposing Bamburgh Castle.

Seafield was established in 1960 on a site chosen for its unbeatable position, situated in the seaside resort of Seahouses and overlooking the Farne Islands. Fifty-five years on and the park has developed into an award-winning business still owned by the same family.

Manager Allison Thompson, whose grandfather set up Seafield, says: "We are located in an Area of Outstanding Natural beauty, close to World Heritage Sites, nature reserves including the world-famous Farne Islands, and in the heart of a buzzing seaside village. It's an amazing place.

Seafield has changed a lot over the years. Today it can offer a wide-range of accommodation to suit all tastes – 40 caravans and six lodges which are used for letting purposes and an additional 380 pitches for caravan ownership. There is an impressive private leisure club, The Ocean Club, built at a cost of £2.5 million and completed in 2005. It consists of a 20m swimming pool, separate children's pool, spa, steam room, sauna, gymnasium, health/beauty suite and a licensed coffee shop. Camping is not allowed on the park but there are 18 touring pitches which all have electric hook up, water tap, electric light and waste disposal facilities.

"The peace and tranquility of the park is one of its greatest attractions, which is why we have resisted any temptation to build bars or evening entertainment centres on site."

Apart from the amazing location what sets Seafield apart from the rest? "Delivering excellence is essential to us and is engrained in all we do," says Allison. "Our motto is 'Going far beyond expectations', and is achieved by giving a five-star service in every aspect of our business. We are actively involved on a day-to-day basis, setting the standard for our team to follow. Attention to detail is of the utmost importance, leaving no stone unturned, however minor a problem may appear.

The most critical aspects to our success are the team of people who work on the park. They constantly deliver exceptional service, which encourages our customers to return year after year."

Seafield doesn't rest on its laurels and the owners invest heavily every year so that the park continues to set high standards. For example, a piped gas supply has cut owner fuel bills and removed unsightly bottles. An investment of £25,000 was committed to revamp touring facilities, including the renewal of the shower and toilet block, plus the laundry, dishwasher and meal preparation areas.

"Our motto is 'Going far beyond expectations', "

Allison

An additional 30 pitches are being installed for occupancy in 2015, and the owners are awaiting planning permission for a £700,000 extension to The Ocean Club. The list goes on.

"The biggest challenge is to be one step ahead and thinking of ways to continually improve the facilities and service we offer," adds Allison.

"But our unique selling points are undeniably our location coupled with our high standards. We ensure that excellence begins when you drive onto the park."

Seafield won Gold in the VisitEngland Awards for Excellence 2014, Caravan Holiday Park/Holiday Village of the Year category.

Contact: Seafield Caravan Park, Seahouses, Northumberland NE68 7SP.
T 01665 720628; E info@seafieldpark.co.uk,
www.seafieldpark.co.uk

Sustainable Tourism in England

More and more operators of accommodation, attractions and events in England are becoming aware of sustainable or "green" issues and are acting more responsibly in their businesses. But how can you be sure that businesses that 'say' they're green, really are?

Who certifies green businesses?

There are a number of green certification schemes that assess businesses for their green credentials. VisitEngland only promotes those that have been checked out to ensure they reach the high standards expected. The members of those schemes VisitEngland have validated are truly sustainable (green) businesses and appear amongst the pages of this guide with the heart-flower logo on their entry.

 Businesses displaying this logo have undergone a rigorous verification process to ensure that they are sustainable (green) and that a qualified assessor has visited the premises.

The number of participating green certification scheme organisations applying to be recognised by VisitEngland is growing all the time. At the moment, VisitEngland promotes the largest green scheme in the world - Green Tourism Business Scheme (GTBS) - and the Peak District Environmental Quality Mark.

Peak District Environmental Quality Mark

This certification mark can only be achieved by businesses that actively support good environmental practices in the Peak District National Park. When you buy a product or service that has been awarded the Environmental Quality Mark, you can be confident that your purchase directly supports the high-quality management of the special environment of the Peak District National Park.

Green Tourism Business Scheme

GTBS recognises places to stay and attractions that are taking action to support the local area and the wider environment. With over 2000 members in the UK, it's the largest sustainable (green) scheme to operate globally and assesses hundreds of fantastic places to stay and visit in Britain, from small bed and breakfasts to large visitor attractions and activity holiday providers.

Businesses that meet the standard for a GTBS award receive a Bronze, Silver, or Gold award based on their level of achievement. Businesses are assessed in areas that include management and marketing, social involvement and communication, energy, water, purchasing, waste, transport, natural and cultural heritage and innovation.

How are these businesses being green?

Any business that has been certified 'green' will have implemented initiatives that contribute to reducing their negative environmental and social impacts, whilst trying to enhance the economic and community benefits to their local area.

Many of these things may be behind the scenes, such as energy efficient boilers, insulated lofts or grey water recycling, but there are many fun activities that you can expect to find too. For example, your green business should be able to advise you about traditional activities nearby, the best places to sample local food and buy craft products, or even help you to enjoy a 'car-free' day out.

David Bellamy Conservation Award

2013/14

DAVID BELLAMY CONSERVATION AWARD

GOLD

'These well-deserved awards are a signpost to parks which are making real achievements in protecting our environment. Go there and experience wrap-around nature … you could be amazed at what you find!' says Professor David Bellamy.

573 gold, silver and bronze parks were named in the 2013/14 David Bellamy Conservation Awards, organised in conjunction with the British Holiday and Home Parks Association.

These parks are recognised for their commitment to conservation and the environment through their management of landscaping, recycling policies, waste management, the cultivation of flora and fauna and the creation of habitats designed to encourage a variety of wildlife onto the park. Links with the local community and the use of local materials are also important considerations.

Parks wishing to enter for a David Bellamy Conservation Award must complete a detailed questionnaire covering different aspects of their environmental policies, and describe what positive conservation steps they have taken. The park must also undergo an independent audit from a local wildlife or conservation body which is familiar with the area. Final assessments and the appropriate level of any award are then made personally by Professor Bellamy.

An index of award-winning parks featured in the regional pages of this guide can be found on page 292.

Crafty Camping

With holidaymakers increasingly searching for something different, alternatives to the traditional camping and caravanning holiday continue to flourish. Furniture designer and wood craftsman Guy Mallinson tells Neil Pope how his unique Crafty Camping business, which offers luxury 'glamping' in an adults-only, hand-crafted environment, happened by accident.

Guy trained as a cabinet-maker but now runs green woodwork courses, which offer participants the chance to make things out of wood such as bowls, spoons and chairs.

"Crafty Camping evolved out of our green wood craft courses," says Guy. "Course participants asked if they could camp in our woods. Then they asked if we could put up a tent for them. Then they wanted a bigger tent with more luxury, followed by proper loos and hot showers. Eventually they were asking for electric blankets and heated towel rails and a sauna - we just gave them what they asked for. Crafty Camping was not planned - it evolved due to an expressed need."

"Our yurts are handmade using traditional hand skills"

Guy

perhaps try the shepherd's hut named Bodger. There are three luxury bell tents – Bodkin, Fipple and Twybil – and these have custom-made canvas flysheets to ensure the inner tent is dry whatever the weather.

Crafty Camping can be found in a private woodland area that visitors have described as magical – something akin to Avatar in summer and Narnia in winter! It's tranquil and uncrowded, and nestles in glorious West Dorset countryside.

"Most people now come glamping without doing a course at all" says Guy. "It's a fantastic place to spend some time, and visitors love the unique nature of our yurts. They appreciate the comfort of the accommodation and also the attention to detail.

"We've been able to make Crafty Camping a success through hard work and good luck, and have some exciting plans in place for the future, including building a treehouse."

Contact: Crafty Camping, Woodland Workshop, Yonder Hill, Holditch, West Dorset TA20 4NL. www.mallinson.co.uk

Guy is offering peace and tranquility in a magical woodland setting near to the Jurassic Coast World Heritage Site. Children and noisy groups are strictly forbidden, and you don't even have to attend one of Guy's green wood craft courses to be able to stay in his unique accommodation.

So what is the accommodation really like? "Our yurts are handmade using traditional hand skills – no machines – and coppiced chestnut that needs no preservative," adds Guy. "They are on decks and the bell tents have custom-made flysheets to protect the inner canvas from rot in the woods. Everything is built on stilts above the woodland floor, and is designed to return to nature if we were ever to leave. There is no concrete or foundations - just wood."

All of the accommodation features king-sized beds provided with linen and towels to ensure a comfortable night's sleep. Each tent has its own private clearing or deck to ensure privacy and seclusion. There are private, proper flushing loos and the site has become famous for its 'tree showers'. Each accommodation has been given its own name, you can take your pick between two yurts called Poppet and Coracle and a tipi called Hoppus, or

Don't Miss...

Eden Project

St. Austell, Cornwall PL24 2SG
(01726) 811911
www.edenproject.com

Explore your relationship with nature at the world famous Eden Project, packed with projects and exhibits about climate and the environment, regeneration, conservation and sustainable living. Be inspired by cutting-edge buildings, stunning year round garden displays, world-class sculpture and art, as well as fabulous music and arts events. See all the sights and immerse yourself in nature with a walk among the the treetops on the Rainforest Canopy Walk or a ride on the land train.

Paignton Zoo

Paignton, Devon TQ4 7EU
(0844) 474 2222
www.paigntonzoo.org.uk

One of Britain's top wildilfe attractions, Paignton Zoo has all the usual suspects with an impressive collection of lions, tigers, gorillas, orangutans, rhinos and giraffes. It is also home to some of the planet's rarest creatures and plants too. For a day jam-packed with family fun and adventure there's Monkey Heights, the crocodile swamp, an amphibian ark and a miniature train, as well as the hands-on interactve Discovery Centre.

Roman Bath

Bath, Somerset BA1 1LZ
(01225) 477785
www.romanbaths.co.uk

Bathe in the naturally hot spa water at the magnificent baths built by the romans, indulge in a gourmet getaway, or enjoy a romantic weekend exploring the wealth of historic architecture. You can find all of this in the beautiful city of Bath and attractions such as Longleat Safari Park and Stonehenge are all within easy reach too.

Sherborne Castle & Gardens

Sherborne, Dorset DT9 5NR
(01935) 812072
www.sherbornecastle.com

Built by Sir Walter Raleigh in c1594, the castle reflects various styles from the Elizabethan hall to the Victorian solarium, with splendid collections of art, furniture and porcelain. The grounds around the 50-acre lake were landscaped by 'Capability' Brown and the 30 acres of tranquil lakeside gardens are the perfect place to escape.

Stonehenge

Amesbury, Wiltshire SP4 7DE
(0870) 333 1181
www.english-heritage.org.uk/stonehenge

The Neolithic site of Stonehenge in Wiltshire is one of the most famous megalithic monuments in the world, the purpose of which is still largely only guessed at. This imposing archaeological site is often ascribed mystical or spiritual associations and receives thousands of visitors from all over the world each year.

South West

Cornwall & Isles of Scilly, Devon, Dorset, Gloucestershire, Somerset, Wiltshire

Gloucestershire

Wiltshire

Somerset

Devon   Dorset

Cornwall

A spectacular combination of ancient countryside and glorious coastline, Britain's South West is its most popular holiday area. It stretches from the soft stone and undulating hills of the Cotswolds in the north, through Wiltshire with its historic monuments, to the wild moors, turquoise waters, golden sands and pretty harbours of Dorset, Devon and Cornwall. The beauty of this region and all it has to offer never fails to delight.

Explore – South West

Cornwall

Spectacular turquoise seas and white sands dotted with fishing harbours, beautiful gardens and the remnants of Cornwall's fascinating industrial heritage draw visitors from far and wide. The pounding waves to be found along the coastline attract surfers from all over to the world famous beaches around Newquay and make Cornwall a mecca for watersports enthusiasts of all kinds.

Hotspot: Boardmasters, Europe's largest surf and music festival, takes place at Fistral Beach and Watergate Bay near Newquay in early August.
www.boardmasters.co.uk

The majestic and largely untouched wilderness of Bodmin Moor is only one example of the rich natural environment that can be found here, with miles of walking paths criss-crossing the impressive landscape and offering panoramic views.

The captivating landscape of West Cornwall continues to intrigue and inspire a vibrant art scene centred around St Ives, and Cornwall has a diverse history with prehistoric, Celtic and medieval roots. There are a huge number of heritage attractions, such as Tintagel Castle which overlooks the dramatic windswept Atlantic coast and the Grade I listed Port Eliot House & Gardens, a hidden gem nestling beside a secret estuary near Saltash.

Plymouth is famous for its seafaring heritage, with Plymouth Hoe as the backdrop for Sir Francis Drake's legendary game of bowls, as well as being one of the most beautiful natural harbours in the world. Climb Smeaton's Tower for the incredible views if you're feeling energetic, visit the world-famous Plymouth Gin Distillery at Sutton Harbour, or take the kids to the National Marine Aquarium for an afternoon of fishy fun.

Torquay, gateway to the English Riviera, boasts elegant Victorian villas, iconic palm trees, a sweeping sandy beach and a rich maritime history. Paignton offers great days out including its famous zoo, and the traditional fishing harbour of Brixham is awash with seafood restaurants, waterside pubs and cafés. This whole area is also home to a huge selection of beaches from small, romantic coves to larger, award-winning stretches. The Jurassic Coast is a UNESCO World Heritage Site which stretches for 95 miles along the Devon/Dorset coast, revealing 185 million years of geology and is a must for visitors to the South West.

Devon

Take a hike or a mountain bike and discover the rugged beauty of Exmoor, explore the drama of the craggy coastline, or catch a wave on some of the region's best surf beaches. North Devon is also rich in heritage with many stately homes and historic attractions including Hartland Abbey and the picturesque Clovelly village.

Stunningly beautiful, Dartmoor is perhaps the most famous of Devon's National Parks and offers miles of purple, heather-clad moorland, rushing rivers and stone tors. Walk the length and breadth of the moor or cycle the Drake's Trail, where you'll come across wild ponies and plenty of moorland pubs, perfect for a well earned rest. Head east and discover the imposing Blackdown Hills Area of Outstanding Natural Beauty, stopping off in one of the area's picture-postcard villages for a delicious Devon Cream Tea.

Hotspot: The Dartmouth Steam Railway runs from Paignton along the spectacular Torbay coast and through the wooded slopes bordering the Dart estuary. With stunning scenery and seascapes right across Lyme Bay to Portland Bill on clear days. www.dartmouthrailriver.co.uk

Gloucestershire

Perfect for a relaxing break or as a base for touring the Cotswolds, Cheltenham is an elegant spa town where Regency town houses line the historic promenade and leafy squares. Relax in award-winning gardens or visit one of the impressive range of sporting and cultural events such as The Cheltenham Gold Cup or The Cheltenham Festival of music.

Dorset

Stretching from historic Lyme Regis in the west to Christchurch in the east, and including a number of designated heritage areas, the whole Dorset coastline is a treasure trove of geology. Interesting landforms are plentiful - Durdle Door, Lulworth Cove, the Isle of Portland with the famous Portland Bill lighthouse and the shingle bank of Chesil Beach to name but a few. Weymouth and Portland are two of the best sailing locations in Europe and offer water sports galore, as well as pretty harbours. For traditional English seaside resorts visit Victorian Swanage, or Bournemouth with its fine sandy beach, perfect for families.

Inland, enchanting market towns, quaint villages and rolling countryside play host to delightful shops, museums, family attractions, historic houses and beautiful gardens such as the Sub-Tropical Gardens at Abbotsbury. Explore Dorset's natural beauty on foot or by bicycle at Stoborough Heath and Hartland Moor nature reserves.

Hotspot: Step back in time at Lulworth Castle or the majestic ruins of Corfe Castle, perched above the Isle of Purbeck.

In the North of the Severn Vale, the ancient settlement of Tewkesbury, famous for its fine half-timbered buildings, network of alleyways and 12th Century Norman Abbey, is one of the best medieval townscapes in England. Enjoy a riverside stroll along the River Severn or a boat trip along the Avon. At the centre of the Severn Vale, Gloucester is a vibrant and multicultural city, combining historic architecture with numerous visitor attractions, shops and a collection of mouth watering tea shops, restaurants, bars and pubs. The city, with its impressive cathedral, is linked to Sharpness Docks via the historic 16 mile ship canal and the ancient woodlands of Forest of Dean are only a stone's throw away.

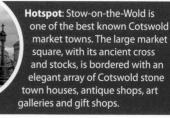

Hotspot: Stow-on-the-Wold is one of the best known Cotswold market towns. The large market square, with its ancient cross and stocks, is bordered with an elegant array of Cotswold stone town houses, antique shops, art galleries and gift shops.

Hotspot: Featuring over 300 flights, world records, special shape balloons from all over the world, nightglows, spectacular fireworks and air displays, the annual Bristol Balloon Fiesta at the beautiful Ashton Court Estate, to the West of Bristol City Centre is an experience not to be missed. www.bristolballoonfiesta.co.uk

Wiltshire

Surrounded by stunning scenery and home to a magnificent Cathedral, a wealth of heritage and cultural, dining and shopping venues, the medieval city of Salisbury is the jewel in the crown of South West England's rural heartland.

Further afield you can find an abundance of quintessential English market towns including Chippenham, Devizes, and the county town of Trowbridge. Marlborough, famed for its charming high street and independent shops, is stylish and sophisticated with a cosmopolitan café culture, while Wilton, the ancient capital of Wessex, is home to Wilton House and a beautiful Italianate Church.

Somerset & Bristol

The maritime city of Bristol is packed with historic attractions, exciting events and fabulous festivals. Cabot Circus offers first class shopping, while stylish restaurants and cafés on the Harbourside serve up locally produced food to tempt and delight. Out and about, Isambard Kingdom Brunel's Clifton Suspension Bridge and the Bristol Zoo Gardens are firm favourites.

Topped by the tower of the ruined 15th Century church, Glastonbury Tor is the stuff of myth and legend, rising high above the Somerset Levels near the delightful town of Glastonbury. Believed to be the site of a Saxon fortress, it has breathtaking views reaching to Wells, the Mendips and the Bristol Channel in the North, Shepton Mallet and Wiltshire in the East, South to the Polden Hills and to the Quantocks and Exmoor in the West.

29

Indulge – South West

Deli on the Quay serves fabulous fudge brownies, ideal with a coffee while the kids indulge in an ice cream. Dolphin Quays, The Quay, Poole. www.delionthequay.com

Enjoy delicious seafood at the fun and quirky **Rum & Crab Shack**, Wharf Road, St Ives, Cornwall www.rumandcrabshack.com

Relax with a sumptuous afternoon tea at **The Salty Monk**, Church Street, Sidford in Devon. T: 01395 513174

Indulge your sweet tooth with handmade luxury chocolates from **Cockington Chocolate Company** at Cockington Court in Devon. www.cockingtonchocolate.co.uk

Visit **Temple Quay Food Market** in Bristol for Jamaican patties, Thai curry, handmade falafel, home-made cakes, artisan breads and cheeses, hearty pies and much more!

Sample the delights and discover the history and heritage of Wadworth brewing at **Wadworth Visitor Centre**, Devizes, Wiltshire. T: (01380) 732277 www.wadworthvisitorcentre.co.uk

Visit – South West

Cornwall

Minack Theatre
Porthcurno, Cornwall TR19 6JU
(01736) 810181
www.minack.com
Cornwall's world famous Minack open-air theatre is carved into the granite cliff and set in glorious gardens with spectacular views.

Blue Reef Aquarium
Newquay, Cornwall TR7 1DU
(01637) 878134
www.bluereefaquarium.co.uk
A dazzling undersea safari through the oceans of the world.

Cornwall Film Festival
November, Cornwall
www.cornwallfilmfestival.com
A month long festival of fabulous films.

Cornwall's Crealy Great Adventure Park
Wadebridge, Cornwall PL27 7RA
(01841) 540276
www.crealy.co.uk/cornwall
Enter the magical land of Cornwall's Crealy and hold on tight for a thrilling ride.

Crantock Bale Push
September, Crantock, nr Newquay
www.balepush.co.uk
Over 100 teams pushing giant hay bales around the village.

Lost Gardens of Heligan
St. Austell, Cornwall PL26 6EN
(01726) 845100
www.heligan.com
An exploration through Victorian Productive Gardens & Pleasure Grounds, a sub-tropical Jungle, pioneering Wildlife Project and more.

National Maritime Museum Cornwall
Falmouth, Cornwall TR11 3QY
(01326) 313388
www.nmmc.co.uk
This multi award-winning museum delivers something for everyone.

National Seal Sanctuary
Helston, Cornwall TR12 6UG
(01326) 221361
www.sealsanctuary.co.uk
The National Seal Sanctuary rescues, rehabilitates and releases over 40 seal pups a year, providing a home for those that can't be released back to the wild.

Newquay Fish Festival
September, Newquay, Cornwall
www.newquayfishfestival.co.uk
Three days celebrating Newquay harbour and delightful fresh local produce.

Newquay Zoo
Newquay, Cornwall TR7 2LZ
(01637) 873342
www.newquayzoo.org.uk
Multi-award winning Newquay Zoo set in sub-tropical lakeside gardens and home to over 130 species of animals.

St Michaels Mount
Marazion, Cornwall TR17 0EF
(01736) 710265
www.stmichaelsmount.co.uk
Explore the amazing island world of St Michael's Mount and discover legend, myth and over a thousand years of incredible history.

Tate St Ives
St. Ives, Cornwall TR26 1TG
(01736) 796226
www.tate.org.uk
Tate St Ives offers an introduction to international Modern and contemporary art, including works from the Tate Collection.

Devon

Bournemouth Air Festival
August, Bournemouth, Devon
www.bournemouthair.co.uk
Free four-day seafront air show.

The Agatha Christie Festival
September, Torquay, Devon
www.agathachristiefestival.co.uk
*Celebrate the world's most
famous crime writer, Dame
Agatha Christie. A literary festival
with a murder mystery twist!*

Brixham Pirate Festival
May, Brixham, Devon
www.brixhampiratefestival.co.uk
*Brixham turns pirate with live music, games,
re-enactments, skirmishes on the Golden Hind.*

Clovelly Village
(01237) 431781
www.clovelly.co.uk
*Most visitors consider Clovelly to be unique.
Whatever your view, it is a world of difference not to
be missed.*

Dartmouth Castle
Dartmouth, Devon TQ6 0JN
(01803) 833588
www.english-heritage.org.uk/dartmouthcastle
*For over six hundred years Dartmouth Castle has
guarded the narrow entrance to the Dart Estuary and
the busy, vibrant port of Dartmouth.*

Escot Gardens, Maze & Forest Adventure
Ottery St. Mary, Devon EX11 1LU
(01404) 822188
www.escot-devon.co.uk
*Historical gardens and fantasy woodland
surrounding the ancestral home of the
Kennaway family.*

Fishstock
September, Brixham, Devon
www.fishstockbrixham.co.uk
*A one-day festival of seafood and entertainment
held in Brixham.*

Hartland Abbey & Gardens
(01237) 441496/234
www.hartlandabbey.com
*Hartland Abbey is a family home full of history in a
beautiful valley leading to a wild Atlantic cove.*

Ilfracombe Aquarium
Ilfracombe, Devon EX34 9EQ
(01271) 864533
www.ilfracombeaquarium.co.uk
*A fascinating journey of discovery into the aquatic life
of North Devon.*

Plymouth City Museum and Art Gallery
Devon PL4 8AJ
(01752) 304774
www.plymouth.gov.uk/museumpcmag.htm
*The museum presents a diverse range of
contemporary exhibitions, from photography to
textiles, modern art to natural history.*

Quay House Visitor Centre
Exeter, Devon EX2 4AN
(01392) 271611
www.exeter.gov.uk/quayhouse
*Discover the history of Exeter in 15 minutes
at the Quay House Visitor Centre on Exeter's
Historic Quayside.*

Dorset

Athelhampton House and Gardens
Athelhampton, Dorchester, Dorset DT2 7LG
(01305) 848363
www.athelhampton.co.uk
One of the finest 15th century Houses in England nestled in the heart of the picturesque Piddle Valley in the famous Hardy county of rural Dorset.

Christchurch Food and Wine Festival
May, Christchurch, Dorset BH23 1AS
www.christchurchfoodfest.co.uk
Celebrity chefs, over 100 trade stands, culinary treats, cookery theatres and some eminent food critics.

Corfe Castle Model Village and Gardens
Corfe Castle, Dorset BH20 5EZ
(01929) 481234
www.corfecastlemodelvillage.co.uk
Detailed 1/20th scale model of Corfe Castle and village before its destruction by Cromwell.

Dorset Knob Throwing Festival
May, Cattistock, nr Dorchester, Dorset
www.dorsetknobthrowing.com
World famous quirky festival.

Forde Abbey & Gardens
Chard, Dorset TA20 4LU
(01460) 221290
www.fordeabbey.co.uk
Founded 850 years ago, Forde Abbey was converted into a private house in c.1649 and welcomes visitors all year round.

Larmer Tree Festival
July, Cranborne Chase, North Dorset
www.larmertreefestival.co.uk
Boutique festival featuring over 70 diverse artists across six stages, a comedy club, 150 free workshops, street theatre, carnival procession, all in front of an intimate crowd of 4,000.

Lulworth Castle & Park
Wareham, Dorset BH20 5QS
0845 450 1054
www.lulworth.com
Walk in the footsteps of Kings & Queens as you enjoy wide open spaces, historic buildings & stunning landscapes. Enjoy the tranquillity of the nearby 18th century Chapel, wander through the park & woodland & bring a picnic.

Lyme Regis Fossil Festival
May, Lyme Regis, Dorset
www.fossilfestival.co.uk
A natural science and arts cultural extravaganza on the UNESCO World Heritage Jurassic Coast.

Portland Castle
Portland, Dorset DT5 1AZ
(01305) 820539
www.english-heritage.org.uk/portland
A well preserved coastal fort built by Henry VIII to defend Weymouth harbour against possible French and Spanish attack.

Sherborne Abbey Music Festival
May, Sherborne, Dorset
www.sherborneabbey.org
Five days of music performed by both nationally acclaimed artists and gifted young musicians.

Sturminster Newton Cheese Festival
September, Sturminster, Dorset
www.cheesefestival.co.uk
A celebration of the region's dairy heritage with quality local food and crafts.

Swanage Regatta
July - August, Swanage, Dorset
www.swanagecarnival.com
The South's premier carnival.

Bristol

At-Bristol
Bristol BS1 5DB
(0845) 345 1235
www.at-bristol.org.uk
21st century science and technology centre, with hands-on activities, interactive exhibits.

Avon Valley Railway
Bristol BS30 6HD
(0117) 932 5538
www.avonvalleyrailway.org
Railway that's much more than your average steam train ride, offering a whole new experience for some or a nostalgic memory for others.

City Sightseeing
The Bristol Tour
Central Bristol BS1 4AH
(03333) 210101
www.citysightseeingbristol.co.uk
Open-top bus tours, with guides and headphones, around the city of Bristol, a service that runs daily throughout the summer months.

Bristol Zoo Gardens
Bristol BS8 3HA
(0117) 974 7300
www.bristolzoo.org.uk
A visit to this city zoo is your passport for a day trip into an amazing world of animals, exhibits and other attractions.

Brunel's SS Great Britain
Bristol BS1 6TY
(0117) 926 0680
www.ssgreatbritain.org
Award-winning attraction showing the world's first great ocean liner and National Brunel Archive.

Gloucestershire

Chavenage
Chavenage, Tetbury, Gloucestershire GL8 8XP
(01666) 502329
www.chavenage.com
Elizabethan Manor Chavenage House, a TV/ Film location is still a family home, offers unique experiences, with history, ghosts and more.

Corinium Museum
Cirencester, Gloucestershire GL7 2BX
(01285) 655611
www.coriniummuseum.org
Discover the treasures of the Cotswolds as you explore its history at this award winning museum.

Forest Food Showcase
October, Forest of Dean, Gloucestershire
www.forestshowcase.org
A celebration of the foods and fruits of the forest. Held annually at Speech House on the first Sunday in October. With many food stalls and demonstrations it's a great opportunity to try what the area has to offer.

Gloucester Cathedral
Gloucestershire GL1 2LR
(01452) 528095
www.gloucestercathedral.org.uk
A place of worship and an architectural gem with crypt, cloisters and Chapter House set in its precincts.

Gloucester Waterways Museum
Gloucester GL1 2EH
(01452) 318200
www.nwm.org.uk
Three floors of a Victorian warehouse house, interactive displays and galleries, which chart the story of Britain's waterways.

Hidcote Manor Garden
Chipping Campden, Gloucestershire GL55 6LR
(01386) 438333
www.nationaltrust.org.uk/hidcote
Famous for its rare trees and shrubs, outstanding herbaceous borders and unusual plants from all over the world.

Painswick Rococo Garden
Painswick, Gloucestershire GL6 6TH
(01452) 813204
www.rococogarden.org.uk
A unique Garden restoration, situated in a hidden valley.

Sudeley Castle Gardens and Exhibition
Winchcombe, Gloucestershire GL54 5JD
(01242) 602308
www.sudeleycastle.co.uk
Award-winning gardens surrounding Castle and medieval ruins.

Westonbirt, The National Arboretum
Tetbury, Gloucestershire GL8 8QS
(01666) 880220
www.forestry.gov.uk/westonbirt
600 acres with one of the finest collections of trees in the world.

Somerset

Glastonbury Abbey
Somerset BA6 9EL
(01458) 832267
www.glastonburyabbey.com
Glastonbury Abbey – Somewhere for all seasons ! From snowdrops and daffodils in the Spring, to family trails and quizzes during the school holidays and Autumn colour on hundreds of trees.

Glastonbury Festival
June, Pilton, Somerset
www.glastonburyfestivals.co.uk
Best known for its contemporary music, but also features dance, comedy, theatre, circus, cabaret and other arts.

Haynes International Motor Museum
Yeovil, Somerset BA22 7LH
(01963) 440804
www.haynesmotormuseum.co.uk
An excellent day out for everyone. With more than 400 vehicles displayed in stunning style, dating from 1886 to the present day, it is the largest international motor museum in Britain.

The Jane Austen Centre
Bath, Somerset BA1 2NT
(01225) 443000
www.janeausten.co.uk
Celebrating Bath's most famous resident.

Number One Royal Crescent
Bath, Somerset BA1 2LR
(01225) 428126
www.bath-preservation-trust.org.uk
The magnificently restored and authentically furnished town house creates a wonderful picture of fashionable life in 18th century Bath.

West Somerset Railway
Minehead, Somerset TA24 5BG
(01643) 704996
www.west-somerset-railway.co.uk
Longest independent steam railway in Britain at 20 miles in length.

Wiltshire

Castle Combe Museum
Castle Combe, Wiltshire SN14 7HU
(01249) 782250
www.castle-combe.com
Displays of life in Castle Combe over the years.

Longleat
Warminster, Wiltshire BA12 7NW
(01985) 844400
www.longleat.co.uk
Widely regarded as one of the best loved tourist destinations in the UK, Longleat has a wealth of exciting attractions and events to tantalise your palate.

Old Sarum
Salisbury, Wiltshire SP1 3SD
(01722) 335398
www.english-heritage.org.uk/oldsarum
Discover the story of the original Salisbury and take the family for a day out to Old Sarum, two miles north of where the city stands now. The mighty Iron Age hill fort was where the first cathedral once stood and the Romans, Normans and Saxons have all left their mark.

Salisbury Cathedral
Salisbury, Wiltshire SP1 2EJ
(01722) 555120
www.salisburycathedral.org.uk
Britain's finest 13th century cathedral with the tallest spire in Britain. Discover nearly 800 years of history, the world's best preserved Magna Carta (AD 1215) and Europe's oldest working clock (AD 1386).

Stourhead House and Garden
Warminster, Wiltshire BA12 6QD
(01747) 841152
www.nationaltrust.org.uk/stourhead
A breathtaking 18th century landscape garden with lakeside walks, grottoes and classical temples.

Wilton House
Wilton House, Wilton, Wiltshire SP2 0BJ
(01722) 746714
www.wiltonhouse.com
Wilton House has one of the finest art collections in Europe and is set in magnificent landscaped parkland featuring the Palladian Bridge.

Tourist Information Centres

When you arrive at your destination, visit the Tourist Information Centre for quality assured help with accommodation and information about local attractions and events, or email your request before you go.

Axminster	The Old Courthouse	01297 34386	touristinfo@axminsteronline.com
Barnstaple	Museum of North Devon	01271 375000 01271 346747	info@staynorthdevon.co.uk
Bath	Abbey Chambers	0906 711 2000	tourism@bathtourism.co.uk
Bideford	Burton Art Gallery	01237 477676	bidefordtic@torridge.gov.uk
Blandford Forum	Riverside House	01258 454770	blandfordtic@btconnect.com
Bodmin	Shire Hall	01208 76616	bodmintic@visit.org.uk
Bourton-on-the-Water	Victoria Street	01451 820211	bourtonvic@btconnect.com
Braunton	The Bakehouse Centre	01271 816688	brauntonmuseum@yahoo.co.uk
Bridport	Bridport Town Hall	01308 424901	bridport.tic@westdorset-weymouth.gov.uk
Bristol : Harbourside	E Shed	0906 711 2191	ticharbourside@destinationbristol.co.uk
Brixham	18-20 The Quay	01803 211 211	holiday@englishriviera.co.uk
Bude	Bude Visitor Centre	01288 354240	budetic@visitbude.info
Budleigh Salterton	Fore Street	01395 445275	info@visitbudleigh.com
Cartgate	South Somerset TIC	01935 829333	cartgate.tic@southsomerset.gov.uk
Chard	The Guildhall	01460 260051	chard.tic@chard.gov.uk
Cheltenham	Municipal Offices	01242 522878	info@cheltenham.gov.uk
Chippenham	High Street	01249 665970	info@chippenham.gov.uk
Chipping Campden	The Old Police Station	01386 841206	info@campdenonline.org
Christchurch	49 High Street	01202 471780	enquiries@christchurchtourism.info
Cirencester	Corinium Museum	01285 654180	cirencestervic@cotswold.gov.uk
Combe Martin	Seacot	01271 883319	mail@visitcombemartin.co.uk
Dartmouth	The Engine House	01803 834224	holidays@discoverdartmouth.com
Dawlish	The Lawn	01626 215665	dawtic@teignbridge.gov.uk
Dorchester	11 Antelope Walk	01305 267992	dorchester.tic@westdorset-weymouth.gov.uk
Exeter	Exter Visitor Information Centre	01392 665700	tic@exeter.gov.uk
Exmouth	Travelworld	01395 222299	tic@travelworldexmouth.co.uk
Falriver	11 Market Strand	0905 325 4534	vic@falriver.co.uk
Fowey	5 South Street	01726 833616	info@fowey.co.uk
Frome	The Library	01373 465757	touristinfo@frome-tc.gov.uk

Glastonbury	The Tribunal	01458 832954	info@glastonburytic.co.uk
Gloucester	28 Southgate Street	01452 396572	tourism@gloucester.gov.uk
Honiton	Lace Walk Car Park	01404 43716	honitontic@btconnect.com
Ilfracombe	The Landmark	01271 863001	marie@visitilfracombe.co.uk
Ivybridge	The Watermark	01752 897035 / 01752 89222	info@ivybridgewatermark.co.uk
Launceston	The White Hart Arcade	01566 772321	info@launcestontic.co.uk
Looe	The Guildhall	01503 262072	looetic@btconnect.com
Lyme Regis	Guildhall Cottage	01297 442138	lymeregis.tic@westdorset-weymouth.gov.uk
Lynton and Lynmouth	Town Hall	01598 752225	info@lyntourism.co.uk
Malmesbury	Town Hall	01666 823748	tic@malmesbury.gov.uk
Minehead	19 The Avenue	01643 702624	minehead.visitor@hotmail.com
Modbury	5 Modbury Court,	01548 830159	modburytic@lineone.net
Moreton-in-Marsh	High Street	01608 650881	moreton@cotswold.gov.uk
Newquay	Municipal Offices	01637 854020	newquay.tic@cornwall.gov.uk
Newton Abbot	6 Bridge House	01626 215667	natic@teignbridge.gov.uk
Ottery St Mary	10a Broad Street	01404 813964	info@otterytourism.org.uk
Padstow	Red Brick Building	01841 533449	padstowtic@btconnect.com
Penzance	Station Approach	01736 335530	beth.rose@nationaltrust.org.uk
Plymouth: Mayflower	Plymouth Mayflower Centre	01752 306330	barbicantic@plymouth.gov.uk
Poole		0845 2345560	info@pooletourism.com
Salcombe	Market Street	01548 843927	info@salcombeinformation.co.uk
Salisbury	Fish Row	01722 342860	visitorinfo@salisburycitycouncil.gov.uk
Shepton Mallet	70 High Street	01749 345258	enquiries@visitsheptonmallet.co.uk
Sherborne	3 Tilton Court	01935 815341	sherborne.tic@westdorset-weymouth.gov.uk
Scilly, Isles Of	Hugh Street, Hugh Town	01720 424031	tic@scilly.gov.uk
Seaton	The Underfleet	01297 21660	visit@seaton.gov.uk
Shaftesbury	8a Bell Street	01747 853514	tourism@shaftesburydorset.com
Sidmouth	Ham Lane	01395 516441	ticinfo@sidmouth.gov.uk
Somerset Visitor Centre	Sedgemoor Services	01934 750833	somersetvisitorcentre@somerset.gov.uk
South Molton	1 East Street	01769 574122	visitsouthmolton@btconnect.com
St Austell	Southbourne Road	01726 879 500	staustelltic@gmail.com
St Ives	The Guildhall	01736 796297	ivtic@stivestic.co.uk
Street	Clarks Village	01458 447384	info@streettic.co.uk
Stroud	Subscription Rooms	01453 760960	tic@stroud.gov.uk
Swanage	The White House	01929 422885	mail@swanage.gov.uk
Swindon	Central Library	01793 466454	infocentre@swindon.gov.uk
Taunton	The Library	01823 336344	tauntontic@tauntondeane.gov.uk
Tavistock	The Den	01626 215666	teigntic@teignbridge.gov.uk
Tetbury	33 Church Street	01666 503552	tourism@tetbury.org
Tewkesbury	100 Church Street	01684 855040	tewkesburytic@tewkesbury.gov.uk
Tiverton	Museum of Mid Devon Life	01884 256295	tivertontic@tivertonmuseum.org.uk
Torquay	The Tourist Centre	01803 211 211	holiday@englishriviera.co.uk
Torrington	Castle Hill	01805 626140	info@great-torrington.com
Totnes	The Town Mill	01803 863168	enquire@totnesinformation.co.uk
Truro	Municipal Building	01872 274555	tic@truro.gov.uk
Wareham	Discover Purbeck	01929 552740	tic@purbeck-dc.gov.uk
Warminster	Central Car Park	01985 218548	visitwarminster@btconnect.com
Wellington	30 Fore Street	01823 663379	wellingtontic@tauntondeane.gov.uk
Wells	Wells Museum	01749 671770	visitwellsinfo@gmail.com
Weston-Super-Mare	The Winter Gardens	01934 417117	westontic@parkwood-leisure.co.uk
Weymouth	The Pavilion	01305 785747	tic@weymouth.gov.uk
Wimborne Minster	29 High Street	01202 886116	wimbornetic@eastdorset.gov.uk
Winchcombe	Town Hall	01242 602925	winchcombetic@tewkesbury.gov.uk
Woolacombe	The Esplanade	01271 870553	info@woolacombetourism.co.uk
Yeovil	Petters House	01935 462781	yeoviltic@southsomerset.gov.uk

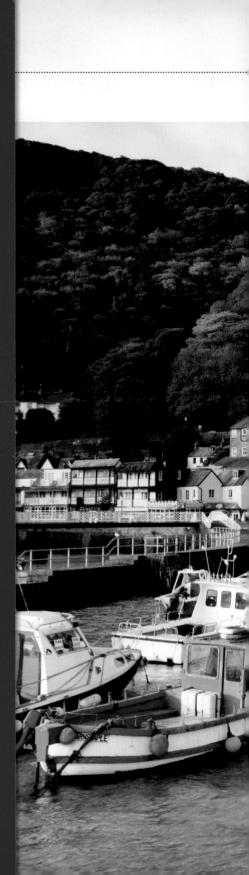

Regional Contacts and Information

For more information on accommodation, attractions, activities, events and holidays in South West England, contact one of the following regional or local tourism organisations. Their websites have a wealth of information and many produce free publications to help you get the most out of your visit.

www.visitsouthwest.co.uk
www.visitdevon.co.uk
www.visitcornwall.co.uk
www.visit-dorset.com
www.visitsomerset.co.uk
www.visitbristol.co.uk
www.visitbath.co.uk
www.southwestcoastpath.org.uk

Entries appear alphabetically by town name in each county. A key to symbols appears on page 7

BLACKWATER, Cornwall   Map ref 1B3

SatNav TR4 8HR

Trevarth Holiday Park

Blackwater, Truro TR4 8HR
T: (01872) 560266 **E:** trevarth@btconnect.com
W: www.trevarth.co.uk **£ BOOK ONLINE**

(30) £13.00-£20.50
(30) £13.00-£20.50
(30) £13.00-£20.50
(20) £180.00-£655.00
30 touring pitches

Luxury caravan holiday homes, touring and camping. A small, quiet park conveniently situated for North and South-coast resorts. Level touring and tent pitches with electric hook-up. Overnight holding area available. Laundry room, games room and play area.

Directions: Leave A30 at Chiverton roundabout (signed St Agnes). At the next roundabout take the road to Blackwater. Park on right after 200m.

Open: April to October 31st.

Payment: ⊡ ☼ Leisure: ♦ Children: ✎ ⚠ Park: ▭ ⊟ ⋒ Touring: ☎ ☝ ⚙

BUDE, Cornwall   Map ref 1C2

SatNav EX23 9HJ

Wooda Farm Holiday Park

Poughill, Bude, Cornwall EX23 9HJ
T: (01288) 352069 **E:** enquiries@wooda.co.uk
W: www.wooda.co.uk **£ BOOK ONLINE**

(80) £19.00-£35.00
(60) £14.00-£35.00
(60) £14.00-£30.00
(55) £273.00-£980.00
200 touring pitches

SPECIAL PROMOTIONS
See our website for special offers.

Stunning views over Bude Bay and countryside; 1.5 miles from safe, sandy beaches. Family-owned and run with excellent facilities for touring and camping and luxury holiday homes for hire. Activities include fishing, sports barn, tennis court, woodland walks and golf. An ideal base for touring the delights of Devon and Cornwall. Overnight holding area available.

Directions: 1.5 miles from Bude, just outside the village of Poughill.

Open: April to October.

Payment: ⊡ Leisure: ♪ ► ♺ ♦ ⚲ Property: ⛺ ▭ ⊟ ⊞ Children: ✎ ⚠ Catering: ✗ ⚞

Juliots Well Holiday Park

Juliots Well, Camelford, Cornwall PL32 9RF
T: (01840) 213302 **F:** (01840) 212700 **E:** holidays@juliotswell.co.uk
W: www.juliotswell.co.uk

🚐	£8.00–£19.00
🚏	£8.00–£19.00
⛺	£8.00–£19.00
🏠 (35)	£325.00–£1065.00
🚐 (26)	£130.00–£790.00
39 touring pitches	

SPECIAL PROMOTIONS
Seasonal Tourers are welcome. For further information please contact the office on 01840 213302.

Juliots Well is a relaxing rural retreat set in 33 acres of Cornish Countryside and is perfect for those looking to get away from it all and unwind, without having to integrate into a holiday-making community. This park is especially popular with couples and small families who want to enjoy each other's company and spend simple, quality time together.

The park has an outdoor heated pool, open mid-May to mid- September. The Coach House Pub serves delicious home cooked food from locally sourced produce and has a fine selection of wines and ales. A children's play area, a launderette and access to the stunning Bowood Golf Club, where holiday guests can receive a great discount on green fees.

Directions: From Exeter follow A30. Right onto A395, left onto A39 to Camelford. Beyond Camelford, right onto B3266, left on sharp bend.

Open: 28th March - 31st October.

Site: 🏕 ⛺🅿 **Payment:** 💷 ☀ **Leisure:** 🏊 ♪ ♭ ♫ ♘ ☌ **Children:** 🐴 ⛰ **Catering:** ✗ 🍴
Park: 🐕 ♬ 🖳 🗐 🅿 **Touring:** 🚐

Penhale Caravan & Camping Park

Penhale Caravan & Camping Park, Penhale Farm, Fowey, Cornwall PL23 1JU
T: (01726) 833425 **F:** (01726) 833425 **E:** info@penhale-fowey.co.uk
W: www.penhale-fowey.co.uk **£ BOOK ONLINE**

🚐 (35)	£15.00–£30.00
🚏 (16)	£15.00–£25.00
⛺ (56)	£8.00–£18.00
🚐 (10)	£195.00–£535.00
56 touring pitches	

Friendly, uncrowded family run park that overlooks unspoilt farmland and lovely views of the sea. In Area of Outstanding Natural Beauty close to sandy beaches, many scenic walks and the Eden Project. David Bellamy Award. Choice of caravans. Touring pitches, electric hook-ups, free showers. Overnight holding area available.

Directions: From A30 west from Lostwithiel, on A390 turn left after 1 mile onto B3269, after 3 miles turn right onto A3082.

Open: Easter or 1st April to End October.

Site: ⛺🅿 **Payment:** 💷 ☀ **Leisure:** ♪ ♭ ♫ ♘ **Children:** 🐴 **Catering:** 🍴 **Park:** 🐕 🖳 🗐 🅿 🏧
Touring: 🚰 ☇ 🚐

FOWEY, Cornwall *Map ref 1B3* *SatNav PL23 1QH*

Polruan Holidays Camping & Caravanning
Polruan-By-Fowey, Cornwall PL23 1QH
T: (01726) 870263 **E:** polholiday@aol.com
W: www.polruanholidays.co.uk

🚐 (7)	£17.00-£26.00
🚏 (15)	£17.00-£26.00
🅰 (25)	£14.00-£23.00
🏚 (10)	£200.00-£500.00

Whether you're looking to stay in one of our Holiday Homes or in our Camping field you will discover Polruan Holidays to be a magical place. An area of tranquility and inspiration, with the sheep and the cows gracefully grazing on the rolling Cornish countryside and headland, the singing of birds and the welcoming nature of wildlife nestling within our hedgerows, you may see a rabbit or two, and a occasional sighting of a fox or a deer, all this with 45 miles of the most magnificent astonishing panoramic sea views.
Open: Easter to September.

Site: 🅰🅿 Payment: 💳 ☼ Children: 🐾 ⛰ Catering: 🍴 Park: 🐕 🖃 🗐 📱 🛒 Touring: 🚰 🕒 🔌

HAYLE, Cornwall *Map ref 1B3* *SatNav TR27 5BL*

Atlantic Coast Holiday Park
53 Upton Towans, Hayle, Cornwall TR27 5BL
T: (01736) 752071 **E:** enquiries@atlanticcoastpark.co.uk
W: www.atlanticcoastpark.co.uk **£ BOOK ONLINE**

🚐 (15)	
🚏 (15)	
🅰 (15)	
🏚 (22)	

15 touring pitches

The park is situated alongside the sand dunes of St Ives bay, bordering Gwithian beach, a fantastic quiet beach ideal for families and surfers. The park is also pet friendly. Please contact us for prices. **Directions:** Leave the A30 at the Hayle exit, turn right onto the B3301, approx 1 mile on left is where we are situated. **Open:** 1st March - January.

Payment: 💳 ☼ Leisure: ♿ ♪ ▶ ∪ Children: 🐾 Catering: 🍴 Park: 🐕 🖃 🗐 📱 🛒 Touring: 🚰 🔌 ♪

HAYLE, Cornwall *Map ref 1B3* *SatNav TR27 5AW*

Beachside Holiday Park
Phillack, Hayle TR27 5AW
T: (01736) 753080 **F:** (01736) 757252 **E:** reception@beachside.co.uk
W: www.beachside.co.uk **£ BOOK ONLINE**

🚐 (80)	£11.00-£40.00
🚏 (80)	£11.00-£40.00
🅰 (80)	£11.00-£40.00
🏠 (29)	£288.00-£1190.00
🚪 (80)	£226.00-£675.00

80 touring pitches

Beachside is a family holiday park, set amidst sand dunes right on the beach in the famous St Ives Bay. With a range of accommodation and touring pitches, our location is ideally situated in West Cornwall for a touring and beach holiday. **Directions:** Travel west on A30 and turn off into Hayle. Turn right, following the sign to Phillack & Beachside. Our entrance is approximately 400m on right. **Open:** Easter to End October.

Site: 🏕 🅰🅿 Payment: 💳 ☼ Leisure: ♪ ∪ 🔍 ⚡ Children: 🐾 ⛰ Catering: 🍴 Park: 🎵 🖃 🗐 📱 🛒 Touring: 🚰 🔌

LANIVET, Cornwall *Map ref 1B2* *SatNav PL30 5HD*

Kernow Caravan Park
Clann Farm, Clann Lane, Lanivet, Bodmin PL30 5HD
T: (01208) 831343
W: www.kernowcaravanpark.co.uk

🏚 (6)	£170.00-£490.00

Kernow Caravan Park is quiet and peaceful, in a tranquil setting run by a Cornish family. An ideal touring location to visit The Eden Project, The Lost Gardens of Heligan, Lanhydrock, Camel Trail, Saints Way or Wenford Steam Railway. A few minutes walk from Lanivet village shop, pub and fish & chip restaurant. **Directions:** Leave A30 Innis Downs roundabout. Follow sign to Lanivet 0.75 miles. Left in village centre, opposite shop. Along Clann Lane 300m left into concrete drive. **Open:** March to October.

Leisure: ♪ ▶ ∪ Property: 🖃 📱 Children: 🐾

MARAZION, Cornwall Map ref 1B3

Mounts Bay Caravan Park

Green Lane, Marazion, Cornwall TR17 0HQ
T: (01736) 710307 **E:** reception@mountsbay-caravanpark.co.uk
W: www.mountsbay-caravanpark.co.uk **£ BOOK ONLINE**

(18) £230.00-£699.00

A small family run park of just 18 caravans with views overlooking the sea & St Michaels Mount. Quiet location, only yards from fine sandy beach & nature reserve. On site swimming pool and a 5 minute walk to Marazion centre. **Directions:** On the western approach to Marazion, look out for us on the seafront by the red river bridge. **Open:** Late March to November.

Payment: ⊞ **Leisure:** ⅄ **Property:** ⊟ ⊞ **Children:** ⅏

MEVAGISSEY, Cornwall Map ref 1B3

Seaview International Holiday Park

Boswinger, Gorran, St. Austell PL26 6LL
T: (01726) 843425 **F:** (01726) 843358 **E:** holidays@seaviewinternational.com
W: www.seaviewinternational.com

(189)	£12.00-£53.00
(189)	£12.00-£53.00
(189)	£12.00-£53.00
(5)	£330.00-£1207.00
(27)	£142.00-£920.00

189 touring pitches

SPECIAL PROMOTIONS
Please visit our website
for special offers.

A 5 star park with everything from camping pitches to lodges with incredible sea views. Set in beautiful grounds with far reaching views. With an outdoor heated pool, play area with equipment and ball games, licensed cafe and shop, plus park wide Wi-Fi. Come and experience why so many families return time and time again.

Directions: From St Austell roundabout take B3273 to Mevagissy, at brow of hill before village, turn right and follow signs for Gorran and then brown Seaview signs.

Open: March 28th to 2nd October (Camping & Touring) 30th October (Statics & Lodges).

Site: ⴲ◨ **Payment:** ⊞ ☼ **Leisure:** ⅍ ♩ ▶ ♨ ⅄ ⚲ **Children:** ⅏ ⚠ **Catering:** ✗ ⴲ **Park:** ⴱ ⌸ ⊟ ⊞ ⋔
Touring: ⴲ ⟳ ⊕ ♪

NEWQUAY, Cornwall Map ref 1B2

Hendra Holiday Park

Newquay, Cornwall TR8 4NY
T: (01637) 875778 **F:** (01637) 879017 **E:** enquiries@hendra-holidays.com
W: www.hendra-holidays.com

(548)	£12.90-£22.25
(548)	£12.90-£22.25
(548)	£12.90-£22.25
	£40.00-£55.00
(307)	£295.00-£1149.00

548 touring pitches

Our five star award-winning holiday park near Newquay, Cornwall offers superb. Caravans, touring, camping, glamping, and motorhome accommodation set in picturesque rural countryside just minutes from golden sand beaches. **Directions:** Please See Website. **Open:** From Easter to end of October.

Site: ⴲ◨ **Payment:** ⊞ **Leisure:** ⅍ ▶ ⚲ ⅄ ⚲ **Children:** ⅏ ⚠ **Catering:** ✗ ⴲ **Park:** ⴱ ♫ ⌸ ⊟ ⊞ ⋔
Touring: ⴲ ⟳ ⊕ ♪

NEWQUAY, Cornwall Map ref 1B2 SatNav TR8 4PE

Riverside Holiday Park

Lane, Newquay TR8 4PE
T: (01637) 873617 **F:** (01637) 877051 **E:** info@riversideholidaypark.co.uk
W: www.riversideholidaypark.co.uk

🚐 (65)   £19.50-£25.50
🏠 (3)   £320.00-£900.00
🏠 (1)   £320.00-£900.00
🚐 (15)   £235.00-£750.00
65 touring pitches

SPECIAL PROMOTIONS
3 or 4 nights short stay
up to 24th July.
Continues from 4th
September.

Welcome to Riverside Holiday Park - Newquay, Cornwall. The park makes an excellent base for exploring the famous seaside resort – just two and half miles away – and the rest of Cornwall too. The park is family owned and run. It's well maintained and caters for families and couples only.

A warm welcome awaits at our reception and information desk which includes a small shop with basic everyday supplies. The park has sheltered, level touring pitches, luxury lodges and caravans. Covered, heated pool and bar.

Directions: Follow A392 for Newquay, at Quintrell Downs go straight over at roundabout, we are first left after Hendra Holiday Park.

Open: Easter to end of October.

Site: 🏕 **Payment:** 💷 ☀ **Leisure:** ♿ ♪ ▶ ♻ ♣ ⚲ **Children:** 🛝 🎠 **Catering:** ✗ 🍴 **Park:** 🐕 🔲 🏚 🏕 **Touring:** 🚿 🚾 🚐

NEWQUAY, Cornwall Map ref 1B2 SatNav TR8 5EW

Trevella Holiday Park

Crantock, Newquay, Cornwall TR8 5EW
T: (01637) 830308 **F:** (01637) 830155 **E:** holidays@trevella.co.uk
W: www.trevella.co.uk

🚐 (137)
🚙 (137)
⛺ (98)
🏠 (2)
🚐 (70)

Trevella Park is an outstanding 5-star holiday park near Newquay. Our incredible setting on the north Cornwall coast is close to the sandy expanse of Crantock Beach and a whole host of fascinating attractions. With an outdoor pool, adventure playground, fishing lakes and free Ranger Adventures, Trevella is a much-loved setting for for camping, touring, glamping and static caravan holidays. Please contact for 2015 rates.

Directions: Please contact for directions.

Open: March - October.

Site: 🏕 **Payment:** 💷 ☀ **Leisure:** ♪ ♣ ⚲ **Children:** 🛝 🎠 **Catering:** ✗ 🍴 **Park:** 🐕 🔲 🏚 🏕 **Touring:** 🚾 🚐 ♪

PAR, Cornwall *Map ref 1B2*   *SatNav PL24 2AS*

⛺ (45)

Par Sands Holiday Park

Par Beach, Par, Cornwall PL24 2AS
T: (01726) 812868 **F:** (01726) 817899 **E:** holidayparsands@parkleisure.co.uk
W: www.parkleisure.co.uk

A quiet family holiday park alongside a large safe sandy beach, next to a wildlife lake with hundreds of visiting birds. The coastal footpath runs through the park. We have a warm indoor heated pool, tennis and badminton court. Please contact for 2015 rates. **Directions:** Please contact for directions. **Open:** All year (excluding 7th January - 13th February).

Payment: 🔢 **Leisure:** ▶ ∪ ⚲ ⚲ **Property:** 🛏 🖥 🔲 **Children:** ⚲ ⚠ **Catering:** ✗ 🍴

PENZANCE, Cornwall *Map ref 1A3*   *SatNav TR20 9AU*

🚐 (20)   £17.00-£26.00
🚏 (20)   £17.00-£26.00
🅰 (40)   £12.00-£26.00
⛺ (7)   £275.00-£555.00
    40 touring pitches

Kenneggy Cove Holiday Park

Higher Kenneggy, Rosudgeon, Penzance, Cornwall TR20 9AU
T: (01736) 763453 **E:** enquiries@kenneggycove.co.uk
W: www.kenneggycove.co.uk

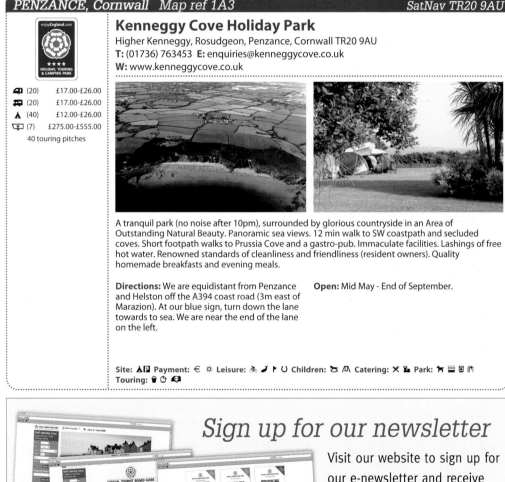

A tranquil park (no noise after 10pm), surrounded by glorious countryside in an Area of Outstanding Natural Beauty. Panoramic sea views. 12 min walk to SW coastpath and secluded coves. Short footpath walks to Prussia Cove and a gastro-pub. Immaculate facilities. Lashings of free hot water. Renowned standards of cleanliness and friendliness (resident owners). Quality homemade breakfasts and evening meals.

Directions: We are equidistant from Penzance and Helston off the A394 coast road (3m east of Marazion). At our blue sign, turn down the lane towards to sea. We are near the end of the lane on the left.

Open: Mid May - End of September.

Site: 🅰🅿 **Payment:** € ☼ **Leisure:** ♿ 🥢 ▶ ∪ **Children:** ⚲ ⚠ **Catering:** ✗ 🍴 **Park:** 🛏 🖥 🔲 ⌂ **Touring:** 🚽 🚰 🔌

Trethiggey Touring Park

Quintrell Downs, Newquay TR8 4QR
T: (01637) 877672 **F:** (01637) 879706 **E:** enquiries@trethiggey.co.uk
W: www.trethiggey.co.uk **£ BOOK ONLINE**

🚐	(70)	£14.00-£21.00
🚍	(30)	£14.00-£21.00
⛺	(86)	£9.00-£21.00
🏕	(14)	£200.00-£785.00

186 touring pitches

SPECIAL PROMOTIONS
Holiday home short breaks available in Spring and Autumn and other offers featured on the park website.

Two miles from Newquay and surf beaches and 15 miles from The Eden Project. A sheltered well landscaped park with beautiful panoramic views. Restaurant and bar, shop, off-licence, childrens' play area and two games rooms. Two modern shower/toilet blocks with disabled facilities. 7 acre recreation field with a small fishing lake and dog walking area. A David Bellamy Gold Award park.

Directions: Leave the A30 at the Newquay exit, follow the A392 to Quintrell Downs. Turn left at roundabout. The park is half a mile on the right.

Open: March 2nd to January 2nd.

Site: 🏠 Payment: 💷 € ☼ Leisure: ♿ ♪ ↑ ∪ ♦ Children: 🐕 ⚠ Catering: ✕ 🍴
Park: ↑ 🔌 🗑 📧 ⚡ Touring: 🚿 🚽 🚐 ♪

Tehidy Holiday Park

Harris Mill, Illogan, Nr Portreath, Redruth TR16 4JQ
T: (01209) 216489 **F:** (01209) 213555 **E:** holiday@tehidy.co.uk
W: www.tehidy.co.uk

🚐	(10)	£14.00-£23.00
🚍	(8)	£14.00-£23.00
⛺	(20)	£14.00-£23.00
🏠	(4)	£350.00-£700.00
🏕	(20)	£240.00-£760.00

30 touring pitches

SPECIAL PROMOTIONS
To celebrate being voted BEST FAMILY SITE in UK 2013, Book a week in the summer and get a 1/2 price (similar type) out of season break. Special offers on our website.

Cottages, holiday caravans, touring/camping and wigwam cabins, on our multi award winning holiday park, including voted Best Caravan and Lodge Site in UK 2014 - Practical Caravan and Best Small Site in UK 2012 - Practical Motorhome. David Bellamy Gold Award 2013. Nestled in a wooded valley, woodland walks, play area and excellent facilities close to beautiful sandy beaches, gardens and cycling.

Directions: Exit A30 to Redruth/Porthtowan. Rigth to Porthtowan. 300m left at corssroads. Straight on over B3300 (Portreath) crossroads. Past Cornish Arms. Site 500m on left.

Open: March to November.

f 🐦

Payment: 💷 Leisure: ↑ ♦ Property: 🗑 📧 Children: 🐕 ⚠ Catering: 🍴

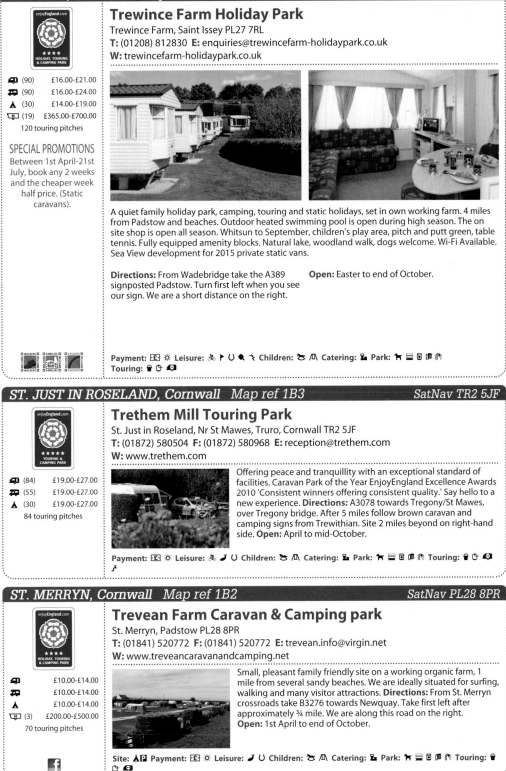

ST. ISSEY, Cornwall   Map ref 1B2

SatNav PL27 7RL

Trewince Farm Holiday Park

Trewince Farm, Saint Issey PL27 7RL
T: (01208) 812830 **E:** enquiries@trewincefarm-holidaypark.co.uk
W: trewincefarm-holidaypark.co.uk

🛏 (90)	£16.00-£21.00	
🚐 (90)	£16.00-£24.00	
⛺ (30)	£14.00-£19.00	
🏠 (19)	£365.00-£700.00	

120 touring pitches

SPECIAL PROMOTIONS
Between 1st April-21st July, book any 2 weeks and the cheaper week half price. (Static caravans).

A quiet family holiday park, camping, touring and static holidays, set in own working farm. 4 miles from Padstow and beaches. Outdoor heated swimming pool is open during high season. The on site shop is open all season. Whitsun to September, children's play area, pitch and putt green, table tennis. Fully equipped amenity blocks. Natural lake, woodland walk, dogs welcome. Wi-Fi Available. Sea View development for 2015 private static vans.

Directions: From Wadebridge take the A389 signposted Padstow. Turn first left when you see our sign. We are a short distance on the right.

Open: Easter to end of October.

Payment: 💳 ☼ **Leisure:** 🦽 ▶ ひ 🍴 🎣 **Children:** 🎠 🎪 **Catering:** 🍴 **Park:** 🐕 🚐 🛢 🛒 📶 **Touring:** 🚰 🛁 📶

ST. JUST IN ROSELAND, Cornwall   Map ref 1B3

SatNav TR2 5JF

Trethem Mill Touring Park

St. Just in Roseland, Nr St Mawes, Truro, Cornwall TR2 5JF
T: (01872) 580504 **F:** (01872) 580968 **E:** reception@trethem.com
W: www.trethem.com

🛏 (84)	£19.00-£27.00
🚐 (55)	£19.00-£27.00
⛺ (30)	£19.00-£27.00

84 touring pitches

Offering peace and tranquillity with an exceptional standard of facilities. Caravan Park of the Year EnjoyEngland Excellence Awards 2010 'Consistent winners offering consistent quality.' Say hello to a new experience. **Directions:** A3078 towards Tregony/St Mawes, over Tregony bridge. After 5 miles follow brown caravan and camping signs from Trewithian. Site 2 miles beyond on right-hand side. **Open:** April to mid-October.

Payment: 💳 ☼ **Leisure:** 🦽 🎣 ひ **Children:** 🎠 🎪 **Catering:** 🍴 **Park:** 🐕 🚐 🛢 🛒 📶 **Touring:** 🚰 🛁 📶 ⚓

ST. MERRYN, Cornwall   Map ref 1B2

SatNav PL28 8PR

Trevean Farm Caravan & Camping park

St. Merryn, Padstow PL28 8PR
T: (01841) 520772 **F:** (01841) 520772 **E:** trevean.info@virgin.net
W: www.treveancaravanandcamping.net

🛏	£10.00-£14.00
🚐	£10.00-£14.00
⛺	£10.00-£14.00
🏠 (3)	£200.00-£500.00

70 touring pitches

Small, pleasant family friendly site on a working organic farm, 1 mile from several sandy beaches. We are ideally situated for surfing, walking and many visitor attractions. **Directions:** From St. Merryn crossroads take B3276 towards Newquay. Take first left after approximately ¾ mile. We are along this road on the right. **Open:** 1st April to end of October.

Site: ⛺🅿 **Payment:** 💳 ☼ **Leisure:** 🎣 ひ **Children:** 🎠 🎪 **Catering:** 🍴 **Park:** 🐕 🚐 🛢 🛒 📶 **Touring:** 🚰 🛁 📶

WADEBRIDGE, Cornwall Map ref 1B2   SatNav PL27 7JQ

★★★★ TOURING & CAMPING PARK

The Laurels Holiday Park
Padstow Road, Whitecross, Wadebridge PL27 7JQ
T: (01209) 313474 **E:** jamierielly@btconnect.com
W: www.thelaurelsholidaypark.co.uk

🚐 £14.00-£26.00
🛖 £14.00-£26.00
42 touring pitches

Touring and camping at The Laurels, near Padstow in North Cornwall offers seclusion and personal space for family holidays or a short break for a couple all year round. Our superbly presented and well maintained pitches offer ample space for many sizes of tents, motorhomes, RV's and caravans. **Directions:** Between Wadebridge (2 ¾ miles) and Padstow (5 ¾ miles). Direct access off the A389 Padstow Road junction on the A39.
Open: All year.

Site: ⚐🅿 **Payment:** 💳 ☼ **Children:** 🐎 ⚠ **Park:** 🐕 🚭 🅿 **Touring:** ☎ 🔌 ♪

WATERGATE BAY, Cornwall Map ref 1B2   SatNav TR8 4AD

★★★★ HOLIDAY, TOURING & CAMPING PARK

Watergate Bay Touring Park
Tregurrian, Newquay, Cornwall TR8 4AD
T: (01637) 860387 **F:** 0871 661 7549 **E:** email@watergatebaytouringpark.co.uk
W: www.watergatebaytouringpark.co.uk

🚐 (200) £11.00-£22.00
🚐 (200) £11.00-£22.00
🛖 (220) £11.00-£22.00
🏠 (2) £250.00-£720.00
200 touring pitches

SPECIAL PROMOTIONS
Outside of the dates
17th July – 31st August,
book 7 nights or more
and receive a 10%
discount.

Half a mile from Watergate Bay's sand, surf and cliff walks. Rural Location in an Area of Outstanding Natural Beauty. Personally run and supervised by resident owners. Heated indoor/outdoor pool, tennis courts, skate park, games room, shop/cafe, licensed clubroom, free entertainment including kids club and kids play area. Overnight holding area available.

Directions: From A30 follow signs for Newquay then airport. After passing the airport, turn left onto the B3276. Park 0.5 miles on the right.

Open: 1st March to the 1st November.

Site: ❀ **Payment:** 💳 ☼ **Leisure:** ♪ ∪ ⚽ 🎯 🏹 🎾 **Children:** 🐎 ⚠ **Catering:** ✗ 🛒
Park: 🐕 🎵 🚭 🅿 🏧 🅿 **Touring:** ☎ 🔌 🔌 ♪

BRAUNTON, Devon   Map ref 1C1

Lobb Fields Caravan and Camping Park

Saunton Road, Braunton EX33 1HG
T: (01271) 812090 **E:** info@lobbfields.com
W: www.lobbfields.com

🚐 (181)   £11.00-£29.00
🚏 (25)   £11.00-£29.00
⛺ (181)   £10.00-£14.00
181 touring pitches

South facing park with great views over the sea. On edge of Braunton, with Saunton beach only 1.5 miles away. Excellent bus service. Ideal for all holiday seaside activities. Surf board hire and snack bar on site. Seasonal pitches available. **Directions:** From Barnstaple to Braunton on A361. Then follow B3231 for 1 mile towards Saunton. Lobb Fields is marked on the right of the road. **Open:** 27th March to 1st November.

Payment: 💷 ☼ **Leisure:** 🚲 🏊 ▶ ☺ **Children:** 🛝 ⚠ **Park:** 🐕 🚮 🔋 🚿 🌊 **Touring:** 🍴 🕐 🔌 🎣

BRIXHAM, Devon   Map ref 1D2

Galmpton Touring Park

Greenway Road, Galmpton, Nr. Brixham TQ5 0EP
T: (01803) 842066 **E:** enquiries@galmptontouringpark.co.uk
W: www.galmptontouringpark.co.uk   **£ BOOK ONLINE**

🚐 (60)   £17.50-£27.50
🚏 (60)   £17.50-£27.50
⛺ (50)   £14.50-£23.50
120 touring pitches

Quiet family park in a stunning location with spectacular views over the River Dart. The perfect base to explore the nearby delights of the South Hams, with ferries, steam railway, beautiful gardens, local pub & shop all a short walk away. **Directions:** South on Ring Road (A380) then straight onto A3022 towards Churston. At lights turn right, then 2nd right, through village 600yds past school. **Open:** 27th March - 31st October.

Site: ⛺🅿 **Payment:** 💷 ☼ **Leisure:** ▶ **Children:** 🛝 ⚠ **Catering:** 🛒 **Park:** 🐕 🚮 🔋 🚿 🌊 **Touring:** 🍴 🕐 🔌 🎣

COMBE MARTIN, Devon   Map ref 1C1

Manleigh Holiday Park

Rectory Road, Combe Martin, Combe Martin, Devon EX34 0NS
T: (03301) 230 374 **E:** enquiries@csmaclubretreats.co.uk
W: www.manleighpark.co.uk

🏠 (3)   £400.00-£833.00
🏠 (9)   £400.00-£770.00
🏕 (14)   £290.00-£672.00

For a great value getaway and an ideal base to explore the beautiful North Devon coast, Manleigh Park is just perfect. Take your pick from Deluxe Static Caravans, Log Cabins and Chalets. **Directions:** From the M5, take exit 27 to Tiverton/Barnstaple (A361) then head for the A399 for Combe Martin. **Open:** From 6th February.

Payment: 💷 € **Leisure:** ⚲ **Property:** 🐕 🔋 🚿

CREDITON, Devon   Map ref 1D2

Yeatheridge Farm Caravan Park

East Worlington, Crediton, Devon EX17 4TN
T: (01884) 860330 **F:** (01884) 860330 **E:** yeatheridge@talk21.com
W: www.yeatheridge.co.uk

🚐 (100) £10.00-£27.00
🚏 (100) £10.00-£27.00
⛺ (80)   £10.00-£24.00
🏕 (4)   £160.00-£580.00
100 touring pitches

Paint a country picture of lush green fields, butterflies, wild flowers, shady trees, lakes calm and still, disturbed only by the plop of rising fish. In the distance, are rolling hills, misty against a blue sky. Placid farm animals nearby, content in the sun. **Directions:** By Road: From From B3137 take B3042 before Witheridge. Site 3.5 miles on left. Alternatively, turn off A377 at Eggesford Station onto B3042. By Public Transport: From Eggesford - 6 miles. **Open:** March 15th to September 30th.

Site: 📷 ⛺🅿 **Payment:** 💷 **Leisure:** ▶ ☺ 🏊 🎣 **Catering:** 🛒 **Park:** 🐕 🔋 🚿 🌊 **Touring:** 🕐 🔌

Cofton Country Holidays

Starcross, Nr Dawlish, Devon EX6 8RP
T: (01626) 890111 **F:** (01626) 890160 **E:** info@coftonholidays.co.uk
W: www.coftonholidays.co.uk **£ BOOK ONLINE**

(450)	£14.50-£42.00
(450)	£14.50-£42.00
(450)	£14.50-£33.00
(17)	£375.00-£1060.00
(70)	£230.00-£955.00

450 touring pitches

SPECIAL PROMOTIONS
Save 25% on touring/ camping in winter, low, mid and high season for advance bookings of 5 or more nights.

A stunning setting surrounded by rolling meadows, mature woods, fishing lakes and just minutes from Dawlish Warren's Blue Flag beach. Superb countryside views. Hardstanding and super pitches available. Fantastic facilities in clean, tidy surroundings with indoor and outdoor swimming pools, play areas, restaurant, bars, park shop, take-away, woodland walks and games room complete with Bowling.

Directions: Leave M5 at junction 30, take A379 towards Dawlish. After passing through harbour village of Cockwood, park is on the left after half a mile.

Open: All year.

Site: 🏕 ▲🅿 **Payment:** 🔲 ☼ **Leisure:** 🏊 ▶ 🔍 ⚲ 🎿 **Children:** 🧸 🎢 **Catering:** ✕ 🍴
Park: ⊼ 🎵 🖥 🔋 📶 🏪 **Touring:** 🚿 🕐 💧 🎶

Lady's Mile Touring and Camping Park

Exeter Road, Dawlish, Devon EX7 0LX
T: (01626) 863411 **F:** (01626) 888689 **E:** info@ladysmile.co.uk
W: www.ladysmile.co.uk **£ BOOK ONLINE**

(480)	£9.50
(200)	£195.00-£1155.00

Lady's Mile is an award winning, family run park designed to please everyone! With a fabulous range of indoor and outdoor sports and leisure facilities, you won't have to leave the site to enjoy a holiday full of family fun, come rain or shine!

Directions: Leave the M5 at Junction 30, take A379 to Dawlish, pass the Cockwood harbour for 2 miles over the Sainsburys roundabout, then take 2nd left.

Open: All year - (except for the outdoor pool).

WALKERS ☑ FAMILIES ☑ CYCLISTS ☑ PETS! ☑
WALKERS ☑ FAMILIES ☑ CYCLISTS ☑ PETS! ☑

Site: 🏕 ▲🅿 **Payment:** 🔲 ☼ **Leisure:** ▶ 🔍 ⚲ 🎿 **Children:** 🧸 🎢 **Catering:** ✕ 🍴 **Park:** 🎵 🖥 🔋 🏪
Touring: 🚿 🕐 💧

DAWLISH, Devon   Map ref 1D2   SatNav EX7 0ND

Oakcliff Holiday Park

Mount Pleasant Road, Dawlish Warren, Dawlish, Devon EX7 0ND
T: (01626) 863347 **F:** (01626) 888689 **E:** info@ladysmile.co.uk
W: www.oakcliff.co.uk **£ BOOK ONLINE**

(50) £145.00-£1005.00

Oakcliff is an 8 acre park laid out in lawns and parkland around an elegant Georgian house, complete with a heated outdoor swimming pool and children's playground. Set in a prime location in Devon's premier holiday resort of Dawlish Warren, 600 yards from a Blue Flag beach and nature reserve. Away from the hustle and bustle, Oakcliff offers more peaceful surroundings with views across the estuary.

Directions: Leave M5 at junction 30, take A379 to Dawlish, continue past Cockwood harbour, pass Sainsburys roundabout, then take the 3rd left to Dawlish Warren for 3/4 mile.

Open: Accommodation - All year . Pool - May to September.

WALKERS FAMILIES CYCLISTS
WALKERS FAMILIES CYCLISTS

Site: **Payment:** **Leisure:** **Children:** **Park:**

DAWLISH, Devon   Map ref 1D2   SatNav EX7 0PH

Welcome Family Holiday Park

Welcome Family Holiday Park, Warren Road, Dawlish Warren, Dawlish, Devon EX7 0PH
T: (0345) 165 6265 **E:** fun@welcomefamily.co.uk
W: www.welcomefamily.co.uk

(60) £230.00-£1020.00
(70) £310.00-£1140.00
(120) £175.00-£815.00

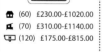

Fantastic entertainment, 4 terrific indoor fun–pools and a truly superb location just a short walk from an award winning Blue Flag beach - these are just a few of the things that make 4* Welcome Family Holiday Park an ideal place for a family seaside holiday. Accommodation is available to suit every taste and pocket and ranges from luxury lodges, to comfortable bungalows and cosy caravans. Welcome Family - Where The Fun Always Shines!
Open: April - January (No park facilities from November to January).

Site: **Payment:** **Leisure:** **Children:** **Catering:** **Park:**

For **key to symbols** see page 7

ILFRACOMBE, Devon Map ref 1C1   SatNav EX34 9RD

Hele Valley Holiday Park

Hele Bay, Ilfracombe, North Devon EX34 9RD
T: (01271) 862460 **F:** (01271) 867926 **E:** holidays@helevalley.co.uk
W: www.helevalley.co.uk **£ BOOK ONLINE**

🚐 (15)	.	£16.00-£33.00
🚏 (15)		£16.00-£33.00
⚊ (40)		£16.00-£33.00
ᴨ (9)		£455.00-£1010.00
⟁ (16)		£310.00-£875.00

Family run holiday park, offering peace and tranquility at the heart of North Devon. Hele Valley offers the perfect holiday choice in beautiful cottages, stunning lodges, luxury caravans and sheltered camping & touring (including cedar pods). The only camping park in Ilfracombe, we are only a stroll away from local inns and Hele beach and walking distance to Ilfracombe centre. Pets are welcome.

Directions: From J27 of the M5 take the A361 to Barnstaple. A39 & then A3230 to Ilfracombe. After 12 miles turn right at traffic lights for Combe Martin (A399). Follow tourist signs for Hele Valley Holiday Park.

Open: 1st April or Easter (if earlier) to 15th January.

f

Site: A🄿 **Payment:** £⊡ ☀ **Leisure:** ▶ **Children:** ⅌ ⚠ **Park:** 🛏 ☷ 🗑 🄵 **Touring:** 🔋 🜩 🅰 ♪

IPPLEPEN, Devon Map ref 1D2   SatNav TQ12 5TT

Ross Park

Park Hill Farm, Moor Road, Ipplepen, Newton Abbot, Devon TQ12 5TT
T: (01803) 812983 **F:** (01803) 812983 **E:** enquiries@rossparkcaravanpark.co.uk
W: www.rossparkcaravanpark.co.uk

🚐 (110)	£15.50-£28.50
🚏 (87)	£15.50-£28.50
⚊ (8)	£14.50-£28.50

110 touring pitches

SPECIAL PROMOTIONS
Weekly rates available except Easter, Whitsun and July, August.

Ross Park is an award winning, family-run park providing excellent facilities in beautiful rural surroundings. Magnificent floral displays, high standards throughout the park with a tranquil atmosphere and friendly service.

Directions: 3 miles from Newton Abbot, 6 miles from Totnes on A381 at Park Hill Cross, follow tourist sign to Ross Park and sign to Woodland.

Open: March - 2nd January.

Site: 🅿 **Payment:** £⊡ ☀ **Leisure:** ♪ ▶ ∪ ⚘ **Children:** ⅌ ⚠ **Catering:** ✕ 🝙 **Park:** 🛏 ☷ 🗑 🖉 🄵 **Touring:** 🔋 🜩 🅰 ♪

IVYBRIDGE, Devon   Map ref 1C2   SatNav PL21 0SH

Moor View Touring Park
California Cross, Modbury, Devon PL21 0SG
T: (01548) 821485 **E:** info@moorviewtouringpark.co.uk
W: www.moorviewtouringpark.co.uk **£ BOOK ONLINE**

🚐 (68)	£12.95-£25.95
🏕 (15)	£14.50-£16.00
🏠 (9)	£315.00-£850.00

A child free sanctuary of peace and relaxation you can enjoy throughout the year. Set in an idyllic location with fantastic views of South Devon and the Moors.

Ideal base for camping and caravans, as well as offering superb luxurious lodges to rent and buy. Member of Tranquil Touring Parks.

Directions: Leave the A38 signposted Modbury, left at the top of the slip road, over the crossroads. Follow the road, after the hamlet of California Cross, travel approx half a mile. We are on the left.

Open: All year.

Site: ▲🅿 Payment: 💳 Park: 🐕 🗑 🌐 🛜 Touring: 🚰 🔌

MORTEHOE, Devon   Map ref 1C1   SatNav EX34 7EG

North Morte Farm Caravan & Camping Park
North Morte Road, Mortehoe, Woolacombe EX34 7EG
T: (01271) 870381 **E:** info@northmortefarm.co.uk
W: www.northmortefarm.co.uk

🚐 (25)	£15.50-£24.00
🚍	£12.00-£24.00
🏕 (150)	£12.00-£19.50
🛖 (21)	£275.00-£670.00
25 touring pitches	

Set in beautiful countryside overlooking Rockham Bay, close to village of Mortehoe and Woolacombe. **Directions:** Take A361 from Barnstaple, turn left at Mullacott roundabout signed Mortehoe and Woolacombe, head for Mortehoe, turn right at Post Office, park 500m on left. **Open:** April to October.

Payment: 💳 ☀ Leisure: 🎵 ⛳ Children: 🛝 🎠 Catering: 🛒 Park: 🐕 🗑 🌐 🛜 Touring: 🚿 🚰 🔌 ♪

NEWTON ABBOT, Devon   Map ref 1D2   SatNav TQ12 6QT

Twelve Oaks Farm Caravan Park
Teigngrace, Newton Abbot TQ12 6QT
T: (01626) 335015 **E:** info@twelveoaksfarm.co.uk
W: www.twelveoaksfarm.co.uk

🚐 (50)	£10.00-£17.50
🚍 (50)	£10.00-£17.50
🏕 (30)	£10.00-£17.50
🛖 (6)	£300.00-£1350.00
50 touring pitches	

A working farm specialising in Charolais beef cattle. Friendly, personal service. Luxury showers and toilets, heated outdoor swimming pool. Coarse fishing. Good dog walks nearby. Children's play park, Overnight holding area available. Wi-Fi Available. **Directions:** Please come via the A38 south bound exit for Teigngrace straight through the village for two miles Twelve Oaks Farm on left. **Open:** All year.

Payment: 💳 ☀ Leisure: 🚲 🎵 ⛳ Children: 🛝 🎠 Catering: 🛒 Park: 🐕 🗑 🌐 🛜 Touring: 🚿 🚰 🔌 ♪

Riverside Caravan and Camping Park

Marsh Lane, North Molton Road, South Molton, North Devon EX36 3HQ
T: (01769) 579269 E: relax@exmoorriverside.co.uk
W: www.exmoorriverside.co.uk

enjoyEngland.com
★★★★
TOURING &
CAMPING PARK

🚐 (42)   £15.00-£25.00
🚚 (42)   £15.00-£25.00
⛺ (40)   £10.00-£24.00
🏠 (2)   £210.00-£485.00
42 touring pitches

SPECIAL PROMOTIONS
For special offers,
please visit our website
for full details.

70 acres of parkland with lakes and rivers for fishing, woods and meadowland for walking. We are a 4 star park with 5 star facilities. Overnight holding area available.

Directions: M5 turn off on junction 27 onto the A361 turn right when you see North Molton and riverside sign.

Open: All year.

Site: 🏕 Payment: 💷 ☼ Leisure: 🏊 ∪ Children: 🧒 🎠 Catering: ✕ 🛒 Park: 🐕 🎵 🖥 📺 🛍 🎣
Touring: 🚰 🔌 🚿 🎣

Sign up for our newsletter

Visit our website to sign up for our e-newsletter and receive regular information on events, exclusive competitions and new publications.

www.visitor-guides.co.uk

OTTERTON, Devon Map ref 1D2   SatNav EX9 7BX

enjoyEngland.com
★★★★
HOLIDAY, TOURING
& CAMPING PARK

Ladram Bay Holiday Park

Otterton, Budleigh Salterton, Devon EX9 7BX
T: (01395) 568398 **F:** (01395) 568338 **E:** info@ladrambay.co.uk
W: www.ladrambay.co.uk **£ BOOK ONLINE**

🚐 (65)   £16.00-£38.00
🚎 (65)   £16.00-£38.00
⛺ (35)   £16.00-£38.00
🏠 (500) £199.00-£1815.00
160 touring pitches

SPECIAL PROMOTIONS
Short Breaks Available.
Over 55s / Under 5s
Discounts, Up to £20
Off. Early Booking
Discounts.

Nestled in the rolling Devon Hills overlooking the unspoilt Jurassic Coast, Ladram Bay is the Holiday Park in Devon that has something to offer everyone. Previously voted as Best in Britain, you can be assured that your holiday is better than ever before! Whether you choose to stay in one of our luxury holiday homes or your own touring caravan or tent, our extensive range of facilities will suit all.

Directions: M5 Junct 30, follow A376 to Clyst St Mary then A3052 to Newton Poppleford, then B3178 and follow signposts to Ladram Bay.

Open: 13th March - 1st November.

Site: 🏕 ⛺📶 **Payment:** 💷 ☀ **Leisure:** 🎵 ▶ ∪ 🔍 ♨ **Children:** 🛝 ⚠ **Catering:** ✕ 🛒
Park: 🐕 🎵 🚮 🚻 🚿 🏧 **Touring:** 🚰 🔌 🚽 🎵

SALCOMBE, Devon Map ref 1C3   SatNav TQ7 3DY

enjoyEngland.com
★★★
HOLIDAY, TOURING
& CAMPING PARK

Bolberry House Farm Caravan & Camping

Bolberry, Malborough, Kingsbridge TQ7 3DY
T: (01548) 561251 **E:** enquiries@bolberryparks.co.uk
W: www.bolberryparks.co.uk

🚐 (20)
🚎 (20)
⛺ (50)
🏠 (10)
70 touring pitches

Friendly family-run park between sailing paradise of Salcombe and Hope Cove (old fishing village). Peaceful, mostly level and good facilities. Children's play area. Good access to coastal footpaths. Sandy beaches nearby. Overnight holding area available. Please contact us for prices. **Directions:** A381 from Totnes, ringroad Kingsbridge to Salcombe. At Malborough sharp right through village, signs to Bolberry approx 1m. Do not follow Sat Nav from Totnes. **Open:** Easter to October.

Site: ⛺📶 **Payment:** ☀ **Leisure:** 🚲 🎵 ▶ ∪ **Children:** 🛝 ⚠ **Catering:** 🛒 **Park:** 🐕 🚮 🚻 🚿 🏧
Touring: 🚰 🔌

SALCOMBE, Devon Map ref 1C3   SatNav TQ7 3BW

enjoyEngland.com
★★★★
TOURING &
CAMPING PARK

Higher Rew Touring Caravan & Camping

Higher Rew, Malborough, Kingsbridge, Devon TQ7 3BW
T: (01548) 842681 **E:** enquiries@higherrew.co.uk
W: www.higherrew.co.uk

102 touring pitches

Higher Rew is a family run park in an area of outstanding natural beauty close to the beautiful Salcombe Estuary. Three generations of the Squire family have, over many years, created a relaxed caravan and camping park for your enjoyment. We are annually inspected by the English Tourism Council, who have awarded our park four stars and have been featured in both the Lonely Planet and Rough Guides. Please contact or see website for 2015 rates. **Directions:** Please see website **Open:** March 27th to Nov 2nd.

Site: ⛺📶 **Leisure:** 🔍 ♨ **Catering:** 🛒 **Park:** 🐕 🚻 🚿 🏧 **Touring:** 🚽 🔌

TAVISTOCK, Devon   Map ref 1C2   SatNav - Do Not Use.

Langstone Manor Holiday Park

Moortown, Tavistock, Devon PL19 9JZ
T: (01822) 613371 **F:** (01822) 613371 **E:** jane@langstonemanor.co.uk
W: www.langstonemanor.co.uk

🚐	(15)	£14.50-£19.50
🚏	(15)	£14.50-£19.50
⛺	(15)	£14.50-£19.50
🏕	(12)	£225.00-£599.00

45 touring pitches

Fantastic location with direct access onto moor, offering great walks straight from the park. Peaceful site with beautiful views of the surrounding moorland. Level pitches, some hardstanding with brand new five star facilities. Camping pods also available. The Langstone Bar provides evening meals. A warm welcome awaits! **Directions:** Take the B3357 Princetown road from Tavistock. After approx 1.5 miles, turn right at x-roads, go over cattle grid, up hill, left following signs. **Open:** March 15th to November 15th.

Site: 🏨 Payment: 💷 ☀ Leisure: 🏊 ▶ ∪ 🔍 Children: 🐾 ⚠ Catering: ✗
Park: 🐕 🚮 🗄 📮 📶 Touring: 📶 🕐 🔌 ♪

TAVISTOCK, Devon   Map ref 1C2   SatNav PL19 8NY

Woodovis Park

Gulworthy, Tavistock, Devon PL19 8NY
T: (01822) 832968 **E:** info@woodovis.com
W: www.woodovis.com **£ BOOK ONLINE**

🚐	(50)	£19.00-£41.00
🚏	(50)	£19.00-£41.00
⛺	(50)	£19.00-£41.00
🏠	(4)	£45.00-£79.00
🏕	(24)	£289.00-£825.00

50 touring pitches

AA Campsite of the Year for the SW 2014. A small and friendly 5 star park, offering peace and quiet. Indoor heated pool, sauna and spa. Excellent facilities, shop baking bread and croissants. Child and pet friendly. **Directions:** From Tavistock take the A390 towards Gunnislake & Callington. After approx. 3 miles, turn right at the roundabout, park is on left after 1.5 miles. **Open:** End of March until end of Oct half term.

Site: ⛺🅿 Payment: 💷 ☀ Leisure: 🏊 ▶ 🔍 🎣 Children: 🐾 ⚠ Catering: 🍴 Park: 🐕 🚮 🗄 📮 📶
Touring: 📶 🕐 🔌 ♪

TOTNES, Devon   Map ref 1D2   SatNav TQ9 6PU

Broadleigh Farm Park

Coombe House Lane, Stoke Gabriel, Totnes TQ9 6PU
T: (01803) 782110 **E:** enquiries@broadleighfarm.co.uk
W: www.broadleighfarm.co.uk

🚐	£12.00-£20.50
🚏	£12.00-£20.50
⛺	£12.00-£20.50

85 touring pitches

Situated in beautiful South Hams village of Stoke Gabriel, close to River Dart and Torbay's wonderful beaches. Local walks. Bus stop at end of lane. Dartmoor within easy reach. Overnight holding area available. **Directions:** Please visit our website for directions. **Open:** Early March - November 15th for non-caravan club members. All year for caravan club members.

Site: ⛺🅿 Payment: 💷 ☀ Leisure: ♪ ▶ ∪ Children: 🐾 Park: 🐕 🚮 🗄 📮 📶 Touring: 📶 🔌 ♪

Book your accommodation online

Visit our websites for detailed information, up-to-date availability and to book your accommodation online. Includes over 20,000 places to stay, all of them star rated.

www.visitor-guides.co.uk

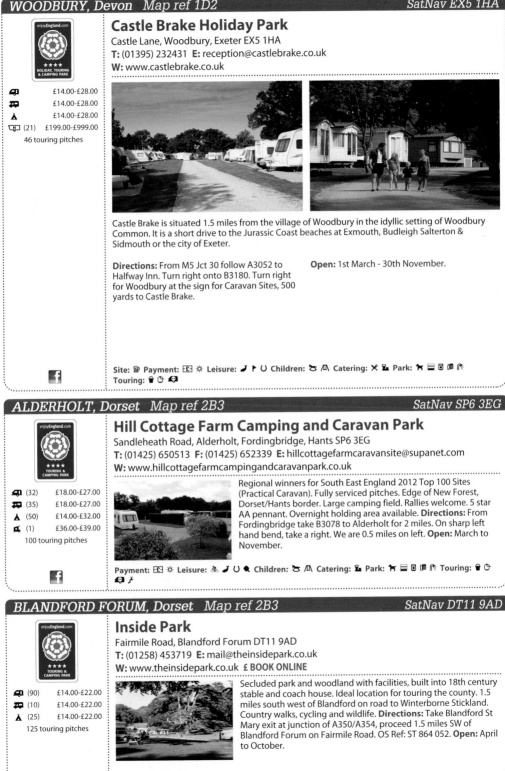

WOODBURY, Devon *Map ref 1D2* *SatNav EX5 1HA*

enjoyEngland.com ★★★★ HOLIDAY, TOURING & CAMPING PARK

£14.00-£28.00
£14.00-£28.00
£14.00-£28.00
(21) £199.00-£999.00
46 touring pitches

Castle Brake Holiday Park

Castle Lane, Woodbury, Exeter EX5 1HA
T: (01395) 232431 **E:** reception@castlebrake.co.uk
W: www.castlebrake.co.uk

Castle Brake is situated 1.5 miles from the village of Woodbury in the idyllic setting of Woodbury Common. It is a short drive to the Jurassic Coast beaches at Exmouth, Budleigh Salterton & Sidmouth or the city of Exeter.

Directions: From M5 Jct 30 follow A3052 to Halfway Inn. Turn right onto B3180. Turn right for Woodbury at the sign for Caravan Sites, 500 yards to Castle Brake.

Open: 1st March - 30th November.

Site: **Payment:** **Leisure:** **Children:** **Catering:** **Park:**
Touring:

ALDERHOLT, Dorset *Map ref 2B3* *SatNav SP6 3EG*

enjoyEngland.com ★★★★ TOURING & CAMPING PARK

(32) £18.00-£27.00
(35) £18.00-£27.00
(50) £14.00-£32.00
(1) £36.00-£39.00
100 touring pitches

Hill Cottage Farm Camping and Caravan Park

Sandleheath Road, Alderholt, Fordingbridge, Hants SP6 3EG
T: (01425) 650513 **F:** (01425) 652339 **E:** hillcottagefarmcaravansite@supanet.com
W: www.hillcottagefarmcampingandcaravanpark.co.uk

Regional winners for South East England 2012 Top 100 Sites (Practical Caravan). Fully serviced pitches. Edge of New Forest, Dorset/Hants border. Large camping field. Rallies welcome. 5 star AA pennant. Overnight holding area available. **Directions:** From Fordingbridge take B3078 to Alderholt for 2 miles. On sharp left hand bend, take a right. We are 0.5 miles on left. **Open:** March to November.

Payment: **Leisure:** **Children:** **Catering:** **Park:** **Touring:**

BLANDFORD FORUM, Dorset *Map ref 2B3* *SatNav DT11 9AD*

enjoyEngland.com ★★★★ TOURING & CAMPING PARK

(90) £14.00-£22.00
(10) £14.00-£22.00
(25) £14.00-£22.00
125 touring pitches

Inside Park

Fairmile Road, Blandford Forum DT11 9AD
T: (01258) 453719 **E:** mail@theinsidepark.co.uk
W: www.theinsidepark.co.uk **£ BOOK ONLINE**

Secluded park and woodland with facilities, built into 18th century stable and coach house. Ideal location for touring the county. 1.5 miles south west of Blandford on road to Winterborne Stickland. Country walks, cycling and wildlife. **Directions:** Take Blandford St Mary exit at junction of A350/A354, proceed 1.5 miles SW of Blandford Forum on Fairmile Road. OS Ref: ST 864 052. **Open:** April to October.

Payment: **Leisure:** **Children:** **Catering:** **Park:** **Touring:**

For **key to symbols** see page 7

BOURNEMOUTH, Dorset   Map ref 2B3   SatNav BH23 2PQ

Meadowbank Holidays

Stour Way, Christchurch BH23 2PQ
T: (01202) 483597 **F:** (01202) 483878 **E:** enquiries@meadowbank-holidays.co.uk
W: www.meadowbank-holidays.co.uk

🚐 (41)
🚎 (41)
🏠 (75)
41 touring pitches

Meadowbank Holidays operate Bournemouth's closest holiday caravan and touring park. We are superbly located on the beautiful River Stour and provide a wonderful relaxing environment for a peaceful, carefree holiday or break. Visit the superb local beaches, New Forest, the famous Jurassic Coast, the Isle of Wight and the lovely town of Christchurch. Please contact us for prices.
Directions: Please see website or contact us for directions.
Open: March to October.

Site: A🅿 **Payment:** 💳 ☀ **Leisure:** 🏊 ♪ ▶ ∪ 🎣 **Children:** 🛝 ⚲ **Catering:** 🍴 **Park:** 🗑 🔋 📮 📶
Touring: 🚽 🚻 🚐 ♨

BRIDPORT, Dorset   Map ref 2A3   SatNav DT6 6AR

Highlands End Holiday Park

Eype, Bridport, Dorset DT6 6AR
T: (01308) 422139 **F:** (01308) 425672 **E:** holidays@wdlh.co.uk
W: www.wdlh.co.uk **£ BOOK ONLINE**

🚐   £16.50-£29.00
🚎   £16.50-£29.00
⛺ (80) £16.50-£22.50
🏠 (21) £259.00-£729.00
120 touring pitches

SPECIAL PROMOTIONS

Half-price holiday – 19th Sep to 12th Dec when full price holiday is taken earlier in year. T&Cs apply.

7 Night Saver – Save £15 on all 7 Night bookings in low + mid season. T&Cs apply.

Please see our website for further offers.

Highlands End Holiday Park is the perfect destination for a family walking holiday or couples retreat, located on the UNESCO World Heritage Jurassic Coast cliff top with panoramic coastal views from Lyme Regis to Portland Bill. The holiday park is a 500 metre coastal walk from Eype Beach and 1.5 miles to the bustling market town of Bridport.

The park has a quality Restaurant & Bar and an exclusive Leisure Club with indoor heated Pool, Sauna, Steam Room & Gym. There is an onsite shop and the barn converted 'Cowshed Café' with stunning views across Eype Downs. Be sure to try our new 2 & 3 bed lodges and our quirky Camping Pods. AA 5 Pennants & TripAdvisor Certificate of Excellence holder.

Directions: Approaching Bridport follow the A35 and take turning signposted Eype. Pass service area and continue until park entance.

Open: March to November for Camping, Touring & Hire Caravans, Year-Round for Lodges, Apartments & Bungalows.

Site: 🐾 A🅿 **Payment:** 💳 ☀ **Leisure:** ♪ ▶ 🎣 🏊 🎾 **Children:** 🛝 ⚲ **Catering:** ✕ 🍴
Park: 🐕 🗑 🔋 📮 📶 **Touring:** 🚽 🚻 🚐 ♨

CHRISTCHURCH, Dorset   Map ref 2B3

Harrow Wood Farm Caravan Park

Poplar Lane, Bransgore, Christchurch BH23 8JE
T: (01425) 672487 **F:** (01425) 672487 **E:** harrowwood@caravan-sites.co.uk
W: www.caravan-sites.co.uk **£ BOOK ONLINE**

🚐 (60)	£17.50-£35.50	
🚐 (60)	£17.50-£35.50	
⛺ (14)	£17.50-£25.00	

60 touring pitches

Quiet site bordered by woods and meadows. Take A35 from Lyndhurst, turn right at Cat and Fiddle pub, site approximately 1.5 miles into Bransgore, first right after school. **Directions:** OS: N=97758 E= 19237 GPS: 50.7719 North 1.72872 West **Open:** 1st March to 6th January.

Payment: 💷 ☀ **Leisure:** 🚲 ♪ ▶ ∪ **Children:** ⊃ **Park:** 🖥 📠 ♟ **Touring:** 🚐 🛉 🔌 ♪

DORCHESTER, Dorset   Map ref 2B3

Brewery Farm

Ansty, Dorchester, Dorset DT2 7PN
T: (01258) 881660 **E:** wallis@breweryfarmansty.co.uk
W: www.breweryfarmdorset.com **£ BOOK ONLINE**

🚐 (10)	£12.00	
🚐 (10)	£12.00	

Quiet 10 pitch camping site situated in beautiful countryside with walks in every direction. Easy distance to coast and Dorchester. Pets and children welcome. We are listed with the Caravan and camping club. **Directions:** Turn towards Milton Abbas off A354 at Milborne St Andrew. 2 miles turn left to Ansty. 3 miles. Opposite Fox Inn. **Open:** All year.

Site: 🅿 **Children:** ⊃ **Catering:** ✗ 🛍 **Park:** 🐕 🖥 **Touring:** 🚐 🛉 🔌

EYPE, Dorset   Map ref 1D2

Eype House Caravan Park Ltd

Eype, Bridport, Dorset DT6 6AL
T: (01308) 424903 **F:** (01308) 424903 **E:** enquiries@eypehouse.co.uk
W: www.eypehouse.co.uk

🚐 (20)	£15.00-£24.00	
⛺ (20)	£15.00-£24.00	
🏠 (1)	£30.00-£45.00	
🏕 (35)	£250.00-£590.00	

20 touring pitches

Small, quiet site, 200 yards from the beach on the Jurassic Coast in Area of Outstanding Natural Beauty. **Directions:** From A35 turn to Eype Take 3rd turn, sign Lower Eype and to the sea, follow lane past pub and hotel, caravan park on right. **Open:** Easter to October.

Site: ⛺🅿 **Payment:** ☀ **Leisure:** ♪ **Children:** ⊃ **Catering:** 🛍 **Park:** 🐕 🖥 📠 ♟ **Touring:** 🚐 🛉

Need more information?

Visit our websites for detailed information, up-to-date availability and to book your accommodation online. Includes over 20,000 places to stay, all of them star rated.
www.visitor-guides.co.uk

LYME REGIS, Dorset Map ref 1D2

SatNav TA20 4NL

Crafty Camping

Woodland Workshop, Yonder Hill, Holditch, Dorset TA20 4NL
T: (01460) 221102 **E:** enquiries@mallinson.co.uk
W: www.mallinson.co.uk £ **BOOK ONLINE**

SPECIAL PROMOTIONS
Yurts, Tipi, Shepherds hut & Bell tents Start from £84/night low season. 'Have a go' woodworking courses start at £42 per person. Please see website for all courses, pricing and availability.

Luxury 'glamping' in an adults-only, hand-crafted environment. Stay with us and our cosy bell tents and beautiful yurts, tipi and shepherds hut can be your home-from-home. Our Wonderful 'glamping' facilities include piping hot 'tree showers', a sauna yurt and games yurt while the 'Out of Africa' kitchen is a fully equipped kitchen with commercial gas oven & a wood fired pizza oven for all to use.

Directions: Google maps link and pdf directions on the information page of our website. **Open:** All year.

Payment: 🖭 **Leisure:** 🚵 🎣 🔦 **Property:** 🖥 **Catering:** 🍴

WAREHAM, Dorset Map ref 2B3

SatNav BH20 5PU

Durdle Door Holiday Park

West Lulworth, Wareham BH20 5PU
T: (01929) 400200 **F:** (01929) 400260 **E:** durdle.door@lulworth.com
W: www.lulworth.com £ **BOOK ONLINE**

🚐 (58)   £18.00-£46.00
🚏 (16)   £18.00-£46.00
 (19)   £295.00-£800.00
    58 touring pitches

SPECIAL PROMOTIONS
Please see website for further details.

Ideally situated between Weymouth and Swanage in one of the most accessible parts of the Jurassic Coast. This delightful park has direct access to the South West Coast path, unspoilt beaches, stunning countryside and Jurassic Coast landmarks.

Fully serviced and seafront pitches for tourers and motor homes, pods and holiday homes available. Close to the picturesque Lulworth Cove and many other family attractions.

Directions: Please see website for details. **Open:** 1st March to 31st October.

Site: 🏢 **Payment:** 🖭 ☀ **Leisure:** ∪ **Children:** 🛝 ⛰ **Catering:** ✗ 🍴 **Park:** 🐕 🎵 🖥 🗄 📱 ⛲ **Touring:** 📶 🚻 💧 🎵

WAREHAM, Dorset Map ref 2B3 — SatNav BH20 5AZ

The Lookout Holiday Park
Corfe Road, Stoborough, Wareham BH20 5AZ
T: (01929) 552546 **F:** (01929) 556662 **E:** lookout@caravan-sites.co.uk
W: www.thelookoutholidaypark.co.uk

(126)	£16.00-£28.00	
	£15.00-£29.50	
(24)	£11.00-£25.00	
(37)	£199.00-£657.00	
140 touring pitches		

This small holiday park is situated 1 mile south of Wareham in the village of Stoborough on A351. At the gateway to the beautiful Purbeck Hills. New Camping Pods. Check out our new website for details. **Directions:** Take the A351 from Poole to Wareham, go through Wareham town, crossing the river Frome, pass through Stoborough village and we are on the left. **Open:** Touring park 23rd March. Static caravan site - All year.

Payment: **Leisure:** **Children:** **Catering:** **Park:** **Touring:**

WOOL, Dorset Map ref 2B3 — SatNav BH20 6HG

Whitemead Caravan Park
East Burton Road, Wool, Wareham BH20 6HG
T: (01929) 462241 **F:** (01929) 462241 **E:** whitemeadcp@aol.com
W: www.whitemeadcaravanpark.co.uk

(95)	£16.00-£23.50	
(95)	£16.00-£23.50	
(95)	£13.00-£20.50	
95 touring pitches		

Within easy reach of beaches and beautiful countryside, this friendly site is maintained to a high standard of cleanliness. Turn west off the A352 near Wool level crossing. Overnight holding area available. **Directions:** Turn west off A352, Wareham-Dorchester Road, along East Burton Road, by Wool level crossing. We are along this road on the right. **Open:** 15th March to 31st October.

Payment: **Leisure:** **Children:** **Catering:** **Park:** **Touring:**

GLOUCESTER, Gloucestershire Map ref 2B1 — SatNav GL2 7BP

Tudor Caravan Park - Slimbridge
Shepherds Patch, Slimbridge, Gloucestershire GL2 7BP
T: (01453) 890483 **E:** info@tudorcaravanpark.co.uk
W: www.tudorcaravanpark.co.uk **£ BOOK ONLINE**

(75)	£13.00-£23.00	
(75)	£13.00-£23.00	
(15)	£8.00-£23.00	
75 touring pitches		

Cotswolds - Caravan and Camping Site of the Year 2014 - Gold. Tudor Caravan Park is one of the best located caravan & campsites in Gloucestershire. A quiet country site alongside the Gloucester-Sharpness canal, 800 yds from Slimbridge WWT. **Directions:** M5 J13 or J14, follow signs to 'WWT Wetlands Centre, Slimbridge', Turn off A38 at Slimbridge, After 1.5 miles turn left after Tudor Arms Pub. **Open:** All Year.

Site: **Payment:** **Leisure:** **Children:** **Catering:** **Park:** **Touring:**

LYDNEY, Gloucestershire Map ref 2A1 — SatNav GL15 4LA

Whitemead Forest Park
Whitemead Forest Park, Parkend, Lydney, Gloucestershire GL15 4LA
T: (03301) 230 374 **F:** (01594) 564174 **E:** enquiries@csmaclubretreats.co.uk
W: www.whitemead.co.uk

(110)	£12.00-£53.00	
(110)	£12.00-£37.00	
(29)	£448.00-£1680.00	

With a range of woodland lodges, log cabins, and apartments, as well as camping and caravanning pitches in the heart of the forest, you can enjoy the free indoor pool, gym, sauna and Jacuzzis; join in with some great activities and entertainment; explore the acres of ancient woodland right on your doorstep, or simply curl up in your cabin and relax. **Directions:** (M5 headling South) Leave at J11 (signposted Gloucester). Take the A40 and then the A48 towards Lydney. **Open:** 23rd January, throughout 2015.

Site: **Payment:** **Leisure:** **Children:** **Catering:** **Park:** **Touring:**

AXBRIDGE, Somerset Map ref 1D1 — SatNav BS26 2TA

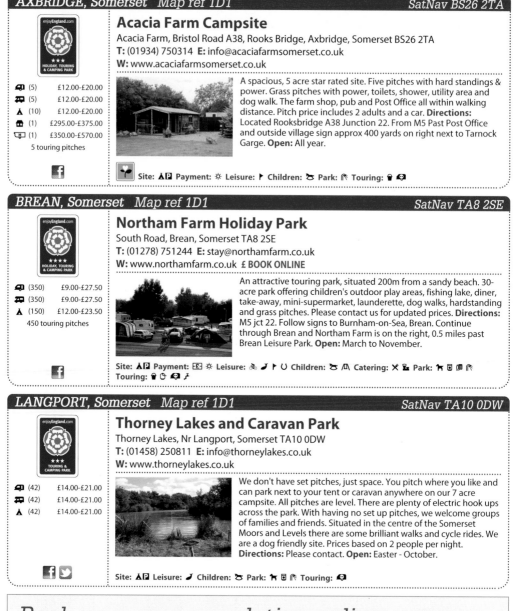

Acacia Farm Campsite

Acacia Farm, Bristol Road A38, Rooks Bridge, Axbridge, Somerset BS26 2TA
T: (01934) 750314 **E:** info@acaciafarmsomerset.co.uk
W: www.acaciafarmsomerset.co.uk

(5)	£12.00-£20.00
(5)	£12.00-£20.00
(10)	£12.00-£20.00
(1)	£295.00-£375.00
(1)	£350.00-£570.00

5 touring pitches

A spacious, 5 acre star rated site. Five pitches with hard standings & power. Grass pitches with power, toilets, shower, utility area and dog walk. The farm shop, pub and Post Office all within walking distance. Pitch price includes 2 adults and a car. **Directions:** Located Rooksbridge A38 Junction 22. From M5 Past Post Office and outside village sign approx 400 yards on right next to Tarnock Garge. **Open:** All year.

Site: Payment: Leisure: Children: Park: Touring:

BREAN, Somerset Map ref 1D1 — SatNav TA8 2SE

Northam Farm Holiday Park

South Road, Brean, Somerset TA8 2SE
T: (01278) 751244 **E:** stay@northamfarm.co.uk
W: www.northamfarm.co.uk £ BOOK ONLINE

(350)	£9.00-£27.50
(350)	£9.00-£27.50
(150)	£12.00-£23.50

450 touring pitches

An attractive touring park, situated 200m from a sandy beach. 30-acre park offering children's outdoor play areas, fishing lake, diner, take-away, mini-supermarket, launderette, dog walks, hardstanding and grass pitches. Please contact us for updated prices. **Directions:** M5 jct 22. Follow signs to Burnham-on-Sea, Brean. Continue through Brean and Northam Farm is on the right, 0.5 miles past Brean Leisure Park. **Open:** March to November.

Site: Payment: Leisure: Children: Catering: Park: Touring:

LANGPORT, Somerset Map ref 1D1 — SatNav TA10 0DW

Thorney Lakes and Caravan Park

Thorney Lakes, Nr Langport, Somerset TA10 0DW
T: (01458) 250811 **E:** info@thorneylakes.co.uk
W: www.thorneylakes.co.uk

(42)	£14.00-£21.00
(42)	£14.00-£21.00
(42)	£14.00-£21.00

We don't have set pitches, just space. You pitch where you like and can park next to your tent or caravan anywhere on our 7 acre campsite. All pitches are level. There are plenty of electric hook ups across the park. With having no set up pitches, we welcome groups of families and friends. Situated in the centre of the Somerset Moors and Levels there are some brilliant walks and cycle rides. We are a dog friendly site. Prices based on 2 people per night. **Directions:** Please contact. **Open:** Easter - October.

Site: Leisure: Children: Park: Touring:

Explore Exmoor!

Book your pitch overlooking the River Barle at **Exmoor House Caravan Club Site** and you'll be perfectly positioned for a holiday exploring Exmoor National Park. Once you've finished wandering the moor why not amble into the quaint town of Dulverton and enjoy a tasty local meal at one of the many restaurants or pubs.

Exmoor House Caravan Club Site

Book now: **01342 488 356**
www.caravanclub.co.uk/visitbritainsites
Lines are open Mon-Fri 8.45am-5.30pm. Calls may be recorded.

THE **CARAVAN CLUB**

PORLOCK, Somerset   Map ref 1D1   SatNav TA24 8HT

Burrowhayes Farm Caravan & Camping Site & Riding Stables

West Luccombe, Porlock, Minehead TA24 8HT
T: (01643) 862463 **E:** info@burrowhayes.co.uk
W: www.burrowhayes.co.uk

(54)	£18.00-£25.00
(54)	£18.00-£25.00
(66)	£14.00-£21.50
(19)	£220.00-£480.00

120 touring pitches

Popular family site in delightful National Trust setting on Exmoor, just 2 miles from the Coast. Surrounding moors and woods provide a walker's paradise. Children can play and explore safely. Riding stables offer pony-trekking for all abilities. Heated shower block with disabled and baby-changing facilities, laundrette and pot wash.

Directions: From Minehead, A39 towards Porlock, 1st left after Allerford to Horner and West Luccombe, Burrowhayes is 0.25 miles along on right before hump-backed bridge.

Open: Mid-March to end of October.

Payment: ▦ ☼ Leisure: ♨ ♪ ∪ Catering: ▦ Park: ⚓ ▤ ▣ ▯ ⚑ Touring: ♀ ♁ ◉ ♪

PORLOCK, Somerset   Map ref 1D1   SatNav TA24 8ND

Porlock Caravan Park

High Bank, Porlock, Somerset TA24 8ND
T: (01643) 862269 **F:** (01643) 862269 **E:** info@porlockcaravanpark.co.uk
W: www.porlockcaravanpark.co.uk

(40)	
(14)	
(7)	

40 touring pitches

Delightful, family run, award winning park situated within walking distance of quaint village of Porlock. Luxury holiday homes for hire. Touring caravans, motor homes and tents welcome. Spotless facilities. Prices on Application. **Directions:** A39 from Minehead, in Porlock village take B3225 to Porlock Weir, site signposted. **Open:** March to October.

Payment: ▦ ☼ Leisure: ♪ ∪ Park: ⚓ ▤ ▣ ▯ ⚑ Touring: ♀ ♁ ◉ ♪

TAUNTON, Somerset   Map ref 1D1

Ashe Farm Caravan and Campsite

Ashe Farm Caravan and Campsite, Thornfalcon, Taunton TA3 5NW
T: (01823) 443764 **E:** info@ashefarm.co.uk
W: www.ashefarm.co.uk

(20)	£12.00-£15.00
(10)	£12.00-£15.00
(10)	£12.00-£14.00
(3)	£170.00-£220.00

30 touring pitches

Quiet farm site, lovely views, easy access. Central for touring. Easy reach coast and hills. Family run and informal. **Directions:** Leave M5 at Jnt 25, take A358 eastwards for 2.5 miles, turn right at Nags Head pub towards West Hatch. Site 0.25 miles on RHS. **Open:** 1st April to 31st October.

Payment: ☼ **Leisure:** ♪ ► ∪ ◕ **Children:** ⛺ ⚲ **Park:** ⌖ ⊟ ⋒ **Touring:** ⚑ ☕

WATERROW, Somerset   Map ref 1D1

Waterrow Touring Park

Wiveliscombe, Nr Taunton, Somerset TA4 2AZ
T: (01984) 623464 **E:** info@waterrowpark.co.uk
W: www.waterrowpark.co.uk £ BOOK ONLINE

(38)	£18.00-£28.50
(38)	£18.00-£28.50
(8)	£18.00-£28.50

46 touring pitches

Attractively landscaped park with good access, situated in beautiful river valley. All pitches are level with hardstanding or grass plus electric. Ideal base from which to explore this unspoilt area. Dog friendly with lots of walks to and from the park. Adults only. Twitter #WaterrowTouring **Directions:** M5 Junction 25, A358 round Taunton. B3227 through Wiveliscombe to Waterrow. Park 500 yds after Rock Inn. Do not use Sat Nav directions. **Open:** All year.

Payment: ⊞ ☼ **Leisure:** ♪ ► ∪ **Park:** ⌖ ⊟ ⊟ ⊞ ⋒ **Touring:** ⚑ ☸ ☕ ♪

WESTON-SUPER-MARE, Somerset   Map ref 1D1

Country View Holiday Park

29 Sand Road, Sand Bay, Weston-super-Mare BS22 9UJ
T: (01934) 627595 **E:** info@cvhp.co.uk
W: www.cvhp.co.uk

(90)	
(90)	
(30)	

120 touring pitches

Country View is surrounded by countryside and just 200yds from Sand Bay Beach. Heated pool, bar, shop and children's play area. Fantastic toilet and shower facilities. Holiday Homes for sale. Please contact us for prices. **Directions:** Exit 21 of M5, follow signs for Sand Bay along Queensway into Lower Norton Lane, take right into Sand Road. **Open:** March to January.

Site: ☏ **Payment:** ⊞ ☼ **Leisure:** ⚲ ♪ ► ∪ ◕ ⋌ **Children:** ⛺ ⚲ **Catering:** ☕ **Park:** ⌖ ⊟ ⊞ ⋒ **Touring:** ⚑ ☸ ☕ ♪

Sign up for our newsletter

Visit our website to sign up for our e-newsletter and receive regular information on events, articles, exclusive competitions and new publications.

www.visitor-guides.co.uk

WESTON-SUPER-MARE, Somerset   Map ref 1D1
SatNav BS24 0JQ

Dulhorn Farm Holiday Park
Weston Road, Lympsham, Weston Super Mare, Somerset BS24 0JQ
T: (01934) 750298 **F:** (01934) 750913 **E:** dfhp@btconnect.com
W: www.dulhornfarmholidaypark.co.uk

🚐 (100)	£14.00-£28.00
🚃 (10)	£14.00-£28.00
⛺ (60)	£8.00-£28.00
🏠 (4)	£192.00-£504.00
🚏 (1)	£242.00-£504.00

100 touring pitches

A family site on a working farm set in the countryside. Between Weston-S-M and Burnham on Sea. Ideal for touring. Close to Cheddar Gorge & Quantock Hills. Secure caravan storage available. S/C Cottages available. Seasonal pitches and statics. Short breaks available. **Directions:** M5 Junction 22, then North on A38, at next roundabout A370 towards Weston-Super-Mare, 1.5 miles on left. **Open:** March to October.

Site: Aᴾ **Payment:** 💳 ☀ **Leisure:** ♪ ▶ ∪ **Children:** 🛝 ⚠ **Catering:** 🍴 **Park:** 🐕 🚮 🗑 ℞ **Touring:** 🚻 ℃ 🚿

WINSFORD, Somerset   Map ref 1D1
SatNav TA24 7JL

Halse Farm Caravan & Tent Park
Halse Farm Caravan & Tent Park, Winsford, Exmoor, Somerset TA24 7JL
T: (01643) 851259 **E:** brit@halsefarm.co.uk
W: www.halsefarm.co.uk

🚐 (22)	£14.00-£19.00
🚃 (22)	£14.00-£19.00
⛺ (22)	£14.00-£19.00

44 touring pitches

Exmoor National Park, small, peaceful, working farm with spectacular views. Walkers and country lovers paradise. David Bellamy Gold Conservation Award. One mile to Winsford with shop, thatched pub and tea gardens. Overnight holding area available. **Directions:** Signposted from A396. In Winsford turn left and bear left past Royal Oak Inn. One mile up hill. Entrance immediately after cattle grid on left. **Open:** 20th March to 31st October.

Site: Aᴾ **Payment:** 💳 **Children:** 🛝 ⚠ **Park:** 🐕 🚮 🗑 💧 **Touring:** 🚻 🚿

LACOCK, Wiltshire   Map ref 2B2
SatNav SN15 2LP

Piccadilly Caravan Park Ltd
Folly Lane (West), Lacock, Chippenham, Wiltshire SN15 2LP
T: (01249) 730260 **E:** info@piccadillylacock.co.uk
W: www.piccadillylacock.co.uk

🚐 (39)	£19.00-£21.00
🚃 (39)	£19.00-£21.00
⛺ (4)	£19.00-£24.50

43 touring pitches

This peaceful site stands in countryside 0.5 miles from the historic National Trust village of Lacock. The site is well screened and beautifully maintained. An ideal location for exploring the West Country. **Directions:** Turn off A350 between Chippenham and Melksham, into Folly Lane West signposted Gastard and with Caravan symbol. **Open:** April to October.

Payment: ☀ **Leisure:** ♪ **Children:** ⚠ **Park:** 🐕 🗑 💧 ℞ **Touring:** 🚻 ℃ 🚿

SALISBURY, Wiltshire   Map ref 2B3
SatNav SP3 4TQ

Stonehenge Campsite & Glamping Pods
Berwick St James, Salisbury SP3 4TQ
T: (07786) 734 732 **E:** stay@stonehengecampsite.co.uk
W: www.stonehengecampsite.co.uk

🚃	£15.00-£25.00
⛺	£10.00-£25.00
🏠	£45.00-£75.00

35 touring pitches

Stonehenge Campsite is the most Beautiful Small Gold & Multi Award Winning Glamping Campsite. It is perfectly situated close to Stonehenge, Longleat Safari Park, Bath, Devizes, Wilton, Salisbury, Stourhead & The New Forest. It is the ideal touring base for South Wiltshire. We are a very friendly, well laid out campsite and have over 500+ positive reviews. We are a secluded, rural campsite in a semi woodland setting, with outstanding walking, woods, streams, 2 pubs and a excellent farm & village shop all close by. **Open:** All year.

Site: 📶 Aᴾ **Payment:** 💳 ☀ **Leisure:** ♪ ▶ **Children:** 🛝 **Park:** 🐕 🚮 🗑 ℞ **Touring:** 🚻 🚿 ♪

Don't Miss...

The Royal Pavilion Brighton

Brighton, East Sussex BN1 1EE
03000 290900
www.brighton-hove-rpml.org.uk/RoyalPavilion
This spectacularly extravagant seaside palace was built for the
Prince Regent, later King George IV, between 1787 and 1823.
Housing furniture, works of art and a splendid balconied tearoom
overlooking the gardens, it is one the most extraordinary and exotic
oriental buildings in the country.

Portsmouth Historic Dockyard

Portsmouth, Hampshire PO1 3LJ
(023) 9283 9766
www.historicdockyard.co.uk
Portsmouth Historic Dockyard offers a great day out for all the
family and spans over 800 years of British Naval history. The state-
of-the-art Mary Rose Museum is home to the remains of Henry
VIII's flagship and an astounding collection of 400 year old artefacts
recovered from the sea.

Beaulieu National Motor Museum, House and Garden

Beaulieu, Hampshire SO42 7ZN
(01590) 612345
www.beaulieu.co.uk
In the New Forest, Beaulieu is one of England's top family days out.
There's lots to enjoy including the world famous National Motor
Museum, home to a stunning and historic collection of automobiles;
Palace House, home of the Montagu family; historic Beaulieu
Abbey founded in 1204 by Cistercian Monks, and World of Top Gear
features vehicles from some of the most ambitious challenges.

Turner Contemporary Art Gallery

Margate, Kent, CT19 1HG
(01843) 233000
www.turnercontemporary.org
Situated on Margate's seafront, Turner Contemporary is a welcoming
space that offers world-class exhibitions of contemporary and
historical art, events and activities. Taking inspiration from Britain's
best-known painter JMW Turner and designed by internationally
acclaimed David Chipperfield Architects, this gleaming structure
hovering over the town is the largest exhibtiion space in the South
East outside of London and admission to the gallery is free.

Windsor Castle

Windsor, Berkshire SL4 1NJ
(020) 7766 7304
www.royalcollection.org.uk
Built by Edward III in the 14th century and restored by later
monarchs, Windsor Castle is the largest and oldest occupied castle
in the world and has been the family home of British kings and
queens for almost 1,000 years. It is an official residence of Her
Majesty the Queen and encapsulates more than 900 years of
English history. St George's Chapel within the Castle Precincts
is the spiritual home of the Order of the Garter, the oldest order
of chivalry in the world.

South East

Berkshire, Buckinghamshire, Hampshire,
Isle of Wight, Kent, Oxfordshire, Surrey, Sussex

Oxfordshire
Buckinghamshire
Berkshire
Surrey Kent
Hampshire
Sussex
Isle of Wight

The Thames sweeps eastwards in broad graceful curves, cutting through the beeches of the Chiltern Hills. Miles of glorious countryside and historic cities offer heritage sites, gardens, parks and impressive architecture for you to visit. In the far south, fun-filled resorts and interesting harbours are dotted along 257 miles of delightful coastline and the Isle of Wight is a only a short ferry ride away. The South East of England is an area of great beauty that will entice you to return again and again.

Explore – South East

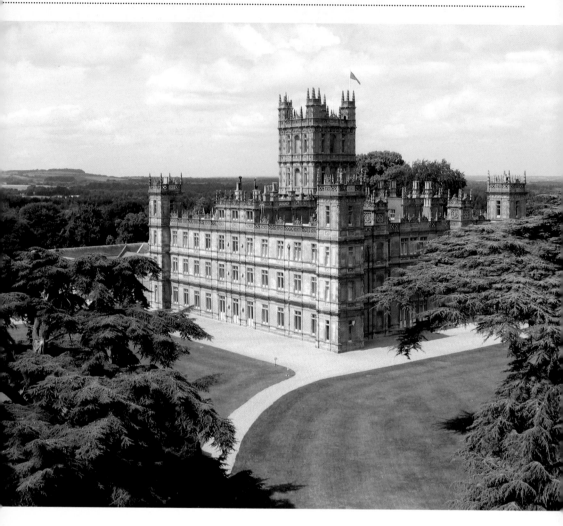

Berkshire

Renowned for its royal connections, the romantic county of Berkshire counts Windsor Castle as its most famous building. Cliveden House, former seat of the Astor family and now a famous hotel, is nearby. Highclere Castle, the setting for Downton Abbey, as well as Eton College and Ascot Racecourse can be found here too.

Hotspot: LEGOLAND® Windsor
Berkshire SL4 4AY (0871) 222 2001
www.legoland.co.uk
With over 55 interactive rides and attractions, there's just too much to experience in one day!

Buckinghamshire

Buckinghamshire, to the north east of the region, is home to the most National Trust properties in the country as well as the magnificent 'Capability Brown' landscape at Stowe, now a famous public school.

The city of Milton Keynes has its infamous concrete cows and the delights of its vast shopping centre but there's plenty more to see and do in the county. Experience a hands-on history lesson at the fascinating Chiltern Open Air Museum or get your adrenalin pumping and test your head for heights with a zip wire adventure at Go Ape Wendover Woods. For a gentler pace, enjoy a tranquil bike ride through beautiful countryside along the meandering Thames.

Hampshire & Isle Of Wight

Historic Winchester is a must-visit for its charming medieval streets, imposing Cathedral, vibrant galleries and stylish, independent shops. The ancient heaths and woodlands of the New Forest National Park were once a royal hunting ground for William the Conqueror and deer, ponies and cattle continue to roam free. Cycle, walk or go horseriding in this tranquil, car-free environment or visit attractions such as the National Motor Museum at Beaulieu and Exbury Gardens & Steam Railway for a great day out.

Coastal Hampshire, with the Solent, Southampton Water and the Isle of Wight, is one of the sailing playgrounds of England. Nearby Portsmouth Harbour has Nelson's Victory, the Mary Rose and the ironclad HMS Warrior. Stroll gently around the picturesque village of Lymington or explore the cliffs along the coast. The Isle of Wight can be reached by ferry and is a great destination for amazing beaches, exciting events such as Bestival, or a step back in time, counting Osborne House and Carisbrooke Castle among its historic gems.

Kent

The Garden of England is a diverse county full of romantic villages and unmissable heritage. The opulent Leeds Castle, surrounded by its shimmering lake and set in 500 acres of spectacular parkland and gardens, has attractions and events aplenty. Take a tour of Kent's rural past with a scenic cruise along the River Medway to Kent Life, a museum and working farm with animals galore and a real sense of nostalgia for bygone days. At the northeast tip of the county, where stunning sea- and sky-scapes famously inspired JMW Turner, Margate is home to the brilliant Turner Contemporary art gallery and the Shell Grotto, a subterranean wonder lined with 4.6 million shells. Broadstairs hosts an acclaimed annual folk festival and Ramsgate is a firm favourite, with its sophisticated café culture, marina and award-winning sandy beach.

Hotspot: Hever Castle in Kent is a romantic 13th century moated castle with magnificently furnished interiors, award winning gardens, miniature Model House Exhibition, Yew Maze and a unique Splashing Water Maze. www.hevercastle.co.uk

Oxfordshire

Oxford's dreaming spires, echoing quads and cloistered college lawns have a timeless beauty. The Ashmolean Museum, Britain's oldest public museum, opened in 1683 and contains gold and jewellery believed to have belonged to King Alfred, the lantern carried by Guy Fawkes and riches from ancient Egypt and Greece. The Bodleian Library, founded in 1596, contains over one million volumes, including a copy of every book published in the UK since 1900. Just north of Oxford at Woodstock sits magnificent Blenheim Palace, the birthplace of Sir Winston Churchill. Oxfordshire's quiet paths and roads are perfect for cycling, and charming picture postcard villages like Great Tew make excellent rest points.

Surrey

Ashdown Forest, now more of a heath, covers 6400 acres of upland, with a large deer, badger and rare bird population. The heights of Box Hill and Leith Hill rise above the North Downs to overlook large tracts of richly wooded countryside, containing a string of well protected villages. The Devil's Punchbowl, near Hindhead, is a two mile long sandstone valley, overlooked by the 900-ft Gibbet Hill. Farnham, in the west of the country, has Tudor and Georgian houses flanking the 12th century castle. Nearby Aldershot is the home of the British Army and county town Guildford is a contemporary business and shopping centre with a modern cathedral and university. The north of the county borders Greater London and includes the 2400 acre Richmond Park, Hampton Court Palace and Kew Gardens.

Sussex

Sussex is a popular county for those wanting a short break from the hustle and bustle of London. Cosmopolitan Brighton, surely the capital of East Sussex, oozes culture, boutique hotels, marina, shops and 'buzz'. The eccentric Royal Pavilion testifies to its history as the Regency summer capital of Britain.

Hotspot: The Brighton Festival in May is a sensational programme of art, theatre, dance, music, literature and family shows starting with a Children's Parade winding its way through the city. www.brightonfestival.org

To the west is the impressive Arundel Castle, with its famous drama festival, nearby popular marinas and Wittering sands. Bognor Regis is a traditional seaside resort with a blue flag beach and the usual attractions. To the east the impressive Beachy Head and Seven Sisters cliffs provide a dramatic backdrop for Eastbourne. The Sussex section of the South Downs National Park stretches from Beachy Head to Harting Down with miles of open chalk grassland, lush river valleys and ancient forests to explore.

If heritage is your thing then Sussex has a plethora of historic houses and gardens and three of the historic cinque ports. Rye in particular, with its cobbled streets, transports the visitor back three centuries. The 1066 Story is told at Battle, near Hastings and Groombridge Place, Great Dixter and Borde Hill all feature stunningly beautiful heritage gardens.

The world famous **Blackbird Tea Rooms** in Brighton is a treat to be savoured, evoking the charm of a bygone era with delicious breakfasts and home-made cakes served on original vintage china in an elegant pre-war setting.
www.blackbirdtearooms.com

For retro-style sweet treats in Kent, **Morelli's ice** cream parlour on Victoria Parade in Broadstairs can't be beaten.

The Grapes in George Street, Oxford is the sole surviving Victorian pub in the city centre and is a fabulous example of a traditional pub with a contemporary approach.

Take a tour of the **Chiltern Brewery**, the oldest independent brewery in the Chiltern Hills and Buckinghamshire, and test its award-winning range of bottle conditioned and draught ales.
www.chilternbrewery.co.uk

For sheer luxury, book a visit to the Elizabethan **Ockenden Manor Hotel & Spa** in Cuckfield near Haywards Heath and enjoy full use of the spa facilities and dinner in the Michelin starred restaurant. Tel (01444) 416111
www.hshotels.co.uk/ockenden-manor-hotel-and-spa

Barefoot Books in Oxford is the perfect place to browse and experience live storytelling, educational games, music, arts, crafts and more.
www.barefootbooks.com

Visit – South East

Attractions with this sign participate in the Visitor Attraction Quality Assurance Scheme.

Berkshire

French Brothers Ltd
Windsor, Berkshire SL4 5JH
(01753) 851900
www.boat-trips.co.uk
Large range of public trips on weather-proof vessels from Windsor, Runnymede and Maidenhead.

Go Ape! Bracknell, Swinley Forest
Berkshire RG12 7QW
(0845) 643 9215
www.goape.co.uk
Go Ape! and tackle a high-wire forest adventure course of rope bridges, Tarzan swings and zip slides up to 35 feet above the forest floor.

Ascot CAMRA Beer Festival
Ascot Racecourse, October
An action packed day of flat racing and an array of over 240 real ales, ciders and perries at the Ascot CAMRA Beer Festival.

Highclere Castle and Gardens
Newbury, Berkshire RG20 9RN
(01635) 253210
www.highclerecastle.co.uk
Visit the spectacular Victorian Castle which is currently the setting for Downton Abbey. Splendid State Rooms, Library and Egyptian Exhibition in the Castle Cellars, plus gardens inspired by Capability Brown.

The Look Out Discovery Centre
Bracknell, Berkshire RG12 7QW
(01344) 354400
www.bracknell-forest.gov.uk
A hands-on, interactive science exhibition with over 80 exhibits, set in 1,000 hectares of Crown woodland.

Reading Festival
August, Reading, Berkshire
www.readingfestival.com
The Reading and Leeds Festivals are a pair of annual music festivals that take place simultaneously.

REME Museum of Technology
Reading, Berkshire RG2 9NJ
(0118) 976 3375
www.rememuseum.org.uk
The museum shows the developing technology used by the Royal Electrical and Mechanical Engineers in maintaining and repairing the army's equipment since 1942.

Buckinghamshire

Aerial Extreme Milton Keynes
Milton Keynes, Buckinghamshire MK15 0DS
0845 652 1736
www.aerialextreme.co.uk/courses/willen-lake
Amaze yourself as you take each of the challenges head on.

Bekonscot Model Village and Railway
Beaconsfield, Buckinghamshire HP9 2PL
(01494) 672919
www.bekonscot.co.uk
Use your imagination in this unique world of make-believe that has delighted generations of visitors.

Gulliver's Land
Milton Keynes, Buckinghamshire MK15 0DT
(01908) 609001
www.gulliversfun.co.uk
Family theme park with 40 rides aimed at children between 2 and 12 years.

Kop Hill Climb
September, Princes Risborough, Buckinghamshire
www.kophillclimb.org.uk
In the 1900s Kop Hill Climb was one of the most popular hill climbs in the country for cars and motorcycles. Now the spirit of the climb is revived.

Marlow Regatta
June, Eton Dorney, Buckinghamshire
www.themarlowregatta.com
Marlow Regatta is one of the multi-lane regattas in the British Rowing calendar.

National Trust Stowe
Buckinghamshire MK18 5DQ
(01280) 817156
www.nationaltrust.org.uk/stowe
Over 40 temples and monuments, laid out against an inspiring backdrop of lakes and valleys.

Reading Real Ale and Jazz Festival
June, Reading, Buckinghamshire
www.readingrealalejazzfest.co.uk
This year's festival is going to be the biggest and best yet, featuring some of the best jazz acts on the circuit.

Roald Dahl Festival
July, Aylesbury Town Centre, Buckinghamshire
www.aylesburyvaledc.gov.uk/dahl
An annual celebration of the famous author, including a 500-strong parade of pupils, teachers and musicians with puppets and artwork based on the Roald Dahl stories.

Roald Dahl Museum and Story Centre
Great Missenden, Buckinghamshire HP16 0AL
(01494) 892192
www.roalddahl.com/museum
Where Roald Dahl (1916-1990) lived and wrote many of his well-loved books.

Waddesdon Manor
Aylesbury, Buckinghamshire HP18 0JH
(01296) 653226
www.waddesdon.org.uk
This National Trust property houses the Rothschild Collection of art treasures and wine cellars. It also features spectacular grounds with an aviary, parterre and woodland playground, licensed restaurants, gift and wine shops.

Xscape
Milton Keynes, Buckinghamshire MK9 3XS
01908 397007
www.xscape.co.uk
Xscape, Milton Keynes offers a unique combination of extreme sports and leisure activities for all ages.

Hampshire & Isle Of Wight

Alton Summer Beer Festival
May, Alton, Hampshire
www.altonbeerfestival.co.uk
Celebrating the cultural heritage of Alton as a traditional area for brewing, based on the clear waters rising from the source of the River Wey, and locally grown hops.

Blackgang Chine
Chale, Isle of Wight PO38 2HN
(01983) 730330
www.blackgangchine.com
Great family fun in over 40 acres of spectacular cliff-top gardens.

Cowes Week
August, Cowes, Isle of Wight
www.aamcowesweek.co.uk
Cowes Week is one of the longest-running regular regattas in the world.

Dinosaur Isle
Sandown, Isle of Wight PO36 8QA
(01983) 404344
www.dinosaurisle.com
In a spectacular pterosaur shaped building on Sandown's blue flag beach walk back through fossilised time and meet life sized replica dinosaurs.

Exbury Gardens and Steam Railway
Beaulieu, Hampshire SO45 1AZ
(023) 8089 1203
www.exbury.co.uk
World famous woodland garden, home to the Rothschild Collection of rhododendrons, azaleas, camellias, rare trees and shrubs, with its own steam railway.

Isle of Wight Festival
June, Newport, Isle of Wight
www.isleofwightfestival.com
Annual music festival featuring some of the UK's top acts and bands.

Isle of Wight Walking Festival
May, Isle of Wight
www.isleofwightwalkingfestival.co.uk
The festival boasts 16 days of unbeatable, informative and healthy walks.

Marwell Zoo
Winchester, Hampshire SO21 1JH
(01962) 777407
www.marwell.org.uk
A chance to get close to the wonders of the natural world – and play a big part in helping to save them.

New Forest and Hampshire Show
July, New Park, Brockenhurst, Hampshire
www.newforestshow.co.uk
The show attracts, on average, 95,000 visitors every year and brings together a celebration of traditional country pursuits, crafts, produce and entertainment.

Osborne House
East Cowes, Isle of Wight PO32 6JX
(01983) 200022
www.english-heritage.org.uk/daysout/properties/osborne-house
Step into Queen Victoria's favourite country home and experience a world unchanged since the country's longest reigning monarch died here just over 100 years ago.

Paultons Family Theme Park
Romsey, Hampshire SO51 6AL
(023) 8081 4442
www.paultonspark.co.uk
A great family day out with over 60 different attractions and rides included in the price!

Shanklin Chine
Shanklin, Isle of Wight PO37 6BW
(01983) 866432
www.shanklinchine.co.uk
Historic gorge with dramatic waterfalls and nature trail.

Southampton Boat Show
September, Southampton, Hampshire
www.southamptonboatshow.com
See the best boats and marine brands gathered together in one fantastic water-based show.

Ventnor Botanic Gardens
St. Lawrence, Isle of Wight PO38 1UL
(01983) 855397
www.botanic.co.uk
The Botanic Garden on the Isle of Wight is a place where the pleasure of plants can be enjoyed to the fullest.

Winchester Hat Fair
July, Winchester, Hampshire
www.hatfair.co.uk
Named after the tradition of throwing donations into performer's hats, it's Britain's longest running festival of street theatre and outdoor arts.

Oxfordshire

Blenheim Palace

Woodstock, Oxfordshire OX20 1PX
(0800) 849 6500
www.blenheimpalace.com
Birthplace of Sir Winston Churchill and home to the Duke of Marlborough, Blenheim Palace, one of the finest baroque houses in England, is set in over 2,000 acres of landscaped gardens.

Didcot Railway Centre

Oxfordshire OX11 7NJ
(01235) 817200
www.didcotrailwaycentre.org.uk
Living museum recreating the golden age of the Great Western Railway. Steam locomotives and trains, Brunel's broad gauge railway, engine shed and small relics museum.

Kent

Bedgebury National Pinetum & Forest

Cranbrook, Kent TN17 2SL
(01580) 879820
www.forestry.gov.uk/bedgebury
Visit the world's finest conifer collection at Bedgebury National Pinetum.

Deal Festival of Music and the Arts

June/July, Deal, Kent
(01304) 370220
www.dealfestival.co.uk
Experience great classical and contemporary music from some of the world's finest music-makers, as well as theatre, opera, cinema and dance – in the beautiful and historic surroundings of Deal and Dover on England's south coast.

The Historic Dockyard Chatham

Kent ME4 4TZ
(01634) 823807
www.thedockyard.co.uk
A unique, award-winning maritime heritage destination with a fantastic range of attractions, iconic buildings and historic ships to explore, plus a fabulous programme of touring exhibitions.

Kent & East Sussex Railway

Tenterden, Kent TN30 6HE
(01580) 765155
www.kesr.org.uk
England's finest rural light railway enables visitors to experience travel and service from a bygone age aboard beautifully restored Victorian coaches and locomotives.

Rochester Castle

Kent ME1 1SW
(01634) 335882
www.visitmedway.org/site/attractions/rochester-castle-p44583
One of the finest keeps in England. Also the tallest, partly built on the Roman city wall. Good views from the battlements over the River Medway.

Henley Royal Regatta

July, Henley, Oxfordshire
www.hrr.co.uk
Attracting thousands of visitors over a five-day period and spectators will be thrilled by over 200 races of international standard.

Oxford Official Guided Walking Tour

owtours@visitoxfordshire.org
The Official Guided Walking Tours are a fascinating and entertaining way to explore and learn about this unique city, its history, University, famous people and odd traditions. Covering a wide range of topics from an introduction to the city and its University to Inspector Morse, Harry Potter, J.R.R. Tolkien and more.

Surrey

British Wildlife Centre

Lingfield, Surrey RH7 6LF
(01342) 834658
www.britishwildlifecentre.co.uk
The best place to see and learn about Britain's own wonderful wildlife, with over 40 different species including deer, foxes, otters, badgers, pine martens and red squirrels.

Guildford Cathedral
Surrey GU2 7UP
(01483) 547860
www.guildford-cathedral.org
New Anglican Cathedral, the foundation stone of which was laid in 1936. Notable sandstone interior and marble floors. Restaurant and shops.

Investec Derby
June, Epsom Racecourse, Surrey
www.epsomderby.co.uk
The biggest horse race in the flat-racing calendar.

Loseley Park
Guildford, Surrey GU3 1HS
(01483) 405120
www.loseleypark.co.uk
A beautiful Elizabethan mansion, set in stunning gardens and parkland. Built in 1562 it has a fascinating history and contains a wealth of treasures.

RHS Garden Wisley
Woking, Surrey GU23 6QB
(0845) 260 9000
www.rhs.org.uk/wisley
Stretching over 240 acres of glorious garden.

RHS Hampton Court Palace Flower Show
July, Hampton Court, Surrey
www.rhs.org.uk
One of the biggest events in the horticulture calendar.

Thorpe Park
Chertsey, Surrey KT16 8PN
(0871) 663 1673
www.thorpepark.com
Thorpe Park Resort is an island like no other, with over 30 thrilling rides, attractions and live events.

Wings & Wheels
August, Dunsfold Aerodrome, Surrey
www.wingsandwheels.net
Outstanding variety of dynamic aviation, motoring displays and iconic cars.

Sussex

1066 Battle Abbey and Battlefield
East Sussex TN33 0AD
(01424) 775705
www.english-heritage.org.uk
An abbey founded by William the Conqueror on the site of the Battle of Hastings.

Arundel Festival
August, Arundel, Sussex
www.arundelfestival.co.uk
Ten days of the best music, theatre, art and comedy.

Arundel Wetland Centre
West Sussex BN18 9PB
(01903) 883355
www.wwt.org.uk/visit/arundel
WWT Arundel Wetland Centre is a 65-acre reserve in an idyllic setting, nestled at the base of the South Downs National Park.

Brighton Digital Festival
September, Brighton, Sussex
www.brightondigitalfestival.co.uk
With a month of exhibitions, performances, workshops and outdoor events, Brighton & Hove is certainly a leading digital destination. There will be workshops, interactive demonstrations and displays throughout the city.

Brighton Fringe
May, Brighton, Sussex
www.brightonfestivalfringe.org.uk
One of the largest fringe festivals in the world, offering cabaret, comedy, classical concerts, club nights, theatre and exhibitions, as well as street performances.

Brighton Marathon
April, Brighton, Sussex
www.brightonmarathon.co.uk
Having grown enormously in just two years, the Brighton Marathon is now one of the top 12 running events in the UK.

Chichester Cathedral

West Sussex PO19 1RP
(01243) 782595
www.chichestercathedral.org.uk
A magnificent Cathedral with treasures ranging from medieval stone carvings to world famous 20th century artworks.

Denmans Garden

Fontwell, West Sussex BN18 0SU
(01243) 542808
www.denmans-garden.co.uk
Beautiful 4 acre garden designed for year round interest through use of form, colour and texture. Beautiful plant centre, award-winning and fully licensed Garden Café.

Eastbourne Beer Festival

October, Winter Gardens, Eastbourne, Sussex
www.visiteastbourne.com/beer-festival
Eastbourne's annual beer festival features over 120 cask ales, plus wines, international bottled beers, ciders and perries. Each session features live music.

Eastbourne Festival

July, Eastbourne, Sussex
www.eastbournefestival.co.uk
Eastbourne Festival is an Open Access Arts Festival which takes place annually for three weeks. It has become recognised as an annual showcase for local professional and amateur talent.

England's Medieval Festival

August, Herstmonceux Castle, Sussex
www.englandsmedievalfestival.com
A celebration of the Middle Ages.

Fishers Adventure Farm Park

Billingshurst, West Sussex RH14 0EG
(01403) 700063
www.fishersfarmpark.co.uk
Award-winning Adventure Farm Park and open all year. Ideally suited for ages 2-11 years. Huge variety of animals, rides and attractions from the skating rink, to pony rides, toboggan run, bumper boats, theatre shows and more!

Glorious Goodwood

July, Chichester, Sussex
www.goodwood.com
Bursting with fabulous fashions, succulent strawberries, chilled Champagne and top horse racing stars, as well as music and dancing.

Glyndebourne Festival

May - August, Lewes, Sussex
www.glyndebourne.com
An English opera festival held at Glyndebourne, an English country house near Lewes.

Great Dixter House and Gardens

Rye, East Sussex TN31 6PH
(01797) 252878
www.greatdixter.co.uk
An example of a 15th century manor house with antique furniture and needlework. The house is restored and the gardens were designed by Lutyens.

London to Brighton Bike Ride

June, Ends on Madeira Drive, Brighton, Sussex
www.bhf.org.uk/london-brighton
The annual bike ride from the capital to the coast in aid of the British Heart Foundation. The UK's largest charity bike ride with 27,000 riders.

Pashley Manor Gardens

Wadhurst, East Sussex TN5 7HE
(01580) 200888
www.pashleymanorgardens.com
Pashley Manor Gardens offer a blend of romantic landscaping, imaginative plantings, fine old trees, fountains, springs and large ponds plus exciting special events.

Petworth House and Park

West Sussex GU28 0AE
(01798) 342207
www.nationaltrust.org.uk/petworth
Discover the National Trust's finest art collection displayed in a magnificent 17th century mansion within a beautiful 700-acre park. Petworth House contains works by artists such as Van Dyck, Reynolds and Turner.

RSPB Pulborough Brooks

West Sussex RH20 2EL
(01798) 875851
www.rspb.org.uk
Set in the scenic Arun Valley with views to the South Downs, the two mile circular nature trail leads around this beautiful reserve.

Tourist Information Centres

When you arrive at your destination, visit the Tourist Information Centre for quality assured help with accommodation and information about local attractions and events, or email your request before you go.

Aldershot	Prince's Hall	01252 320968	aldershotvic@rushmoor.gov.uk
Ashford	Ashford Gateway Plus	01233 330316	tourism@ashford.gov.uk
Aylesbury	The Kings Head, Kings Head Passage	01296 330559	tic@aylesburyvaledc.gov.uk
Banbury	Within Castle Quay Shopping Centre	01295 753752	banbury.tic@cherwell-dc.gov.uk
Battle	Yesterdays World	01797 229049	battletic@rother.gov.uk
Bexley (Hall Place)	Central Library	0208 3037777	touristinfo@bexleyheritagetrust.org.uk
Bicester	Unit 86a Bicester Village	01869 369055	bicestervisitorcentre@valueretail.com
Bracknell	The Look Out Discovery Centre	01344 354409	thelookout@bracknell-forest.gov.uk
Brighton	Brighton Centre Box Office	01273 290337	visitor.info@visitbrighton.com
Buckingham	The Old Gaol Museum	01280 823020	buckinghamtic@touismse.com
Burford	33a High Street	01993 823558	burford.vic@westoxon.gov.uk
Burgess Hill	Burgess Hill Town Council	01444 238202	touristinformation@burgesshill.gov.uk
Canterbury	The Beaney House	01227 378100	canterburyinformation@canterbury.gov.uk
Chichester	The Novium	01243 775888	chitic@chichester.gov.uk
Deal	The Landmark Centre	01304 369576	info@deal.gov.uk
Dover	Dover Museum and VIC	01304 201066	tic@doveruk.com

Eastbourne	Cornfield Road	0871 663 0031	tic@eastbourne.gov.uk
Fareham	Westbury Manor	01329 221342	farehamtic@tourismse.com
Faringdon	The Corn Exchange	01367 242191	tic@faringdontowncouncil.gov.uk
Faversham	Fleur de Lis Heritage Centre	01795 534542	ticfaversham@btconnect.com
Folkestone	20 Bouverier Place Shopping Centre	01303 258594	chris.kirkham@visitkent.co.uk
Fordingbridge	Kings Yard	01425 654560	fordingbridgetic@tourismse.com
Gosportq	Gosport TIC, Bus Station Complex	023 9252 2944	tourism@gosport.gov.uk
Gravesend	Towncentric	01474 337600	info@towncentric.co.uk
Guildford	155 High Street	01483 444333	tic@guildford.gov.uk
Hastings	Queens Square	01424 451111	hic@hastings.gov.uk
Hayling Island	Central Beachlands	023 9246 7111	tourism@havant.gov.uk
Henley-On-Thames	Town Hall,	01491 578034	vic@henleytowncouncil.gov.uk
High Wycombe	High Wycombe Library	01494 421892	tourism_enquiries@wycombe.gov.uk
Horsham	9 The Causeway	01403 211661	visitor.information@horsham.gov.uk
Lewes	187 High Street	01273 483448	lewes.tic@lewes.gov.uk
Littlehampton	The Look & Sea Centre	01903 721866	jo-lhvic@hotmail.co.uk
Lymington	St Barbe Museum	01590 676969	office@stbarbe-museum.org.uk
Lyndhurst & New Forest	New Forest Visitor Centre	023 8028 2269/ 023 8028 5492	info@thenewforest.co.uk
Maidenhead	Maidenhead Library	01628 796502	maidenhead.tic@rbwm.gov.uk
Maidstone	Maidstone Museum	01622 602169	tourism@maidstone.gov.uk
Marlow	55a High Street	01628 483597	tourism_enquiries@wycombe.gov.uk
Midhurst	North Street	01730 812251	midtic@chichester.gov.uk
Newbury	The Wharf	01635 30267	tourism@westberks.gov.uk
Oxford	Oxford Information Centre	01865 252200	info@visitoxfordshire.org
Petersfield	County Library	01730 268829	petersfieldinfo@btconnect.com
Portsmouth	D-Day Museum	023 9282 6722	vis@portsmouthcc.gov.uk
Princes Risborough	Tower Court	01844 274795	risborough_office@wycombe.gov.uk
Ringwood	Ringwood Gateway	01425 473883	town.council@ringwood.gov.uk
Rochester	95 High Street	01634 338141	visitor.centre@medway.gov.uk
Romsey	Museum & TIC	01794 512987	romseytic@testvalley.gov.uk
Royal Tunbridge Wells	Unit 2 The Corn Exchange	01892 515675	touristinformationcentre@ tunbridgewells.gov.uk
Rye	4/5 Lion Street	01797 229049	ryetic@tourismse.com
Sandwich	The Guildhall	01304 613565/ 617197	tourism@sandwichtowncouncil.gov.uk
Seaford	37 Church Street	01323 897426	seaford.tic@lewes.gov.uk
Sevenoaks	Stag Community Arts Centre	01732 450305	tic@sevenoakstown.gov.uk
Swanley	Swanley Library	01322 614660	touristinfo@swanley.org.uk
Tenterden	Tenterden Gateway	08458 247 202	
Thame	Town Hall	01844 212833	oss@thametowncouncil.gov.uk
Thanet	The Droit House	01843 577577	visitorinformation@thanet.gov.uk
Tonbridge	Tonbridge Castle	01732 770929	tonbridge.castle@tmbc.gov.uk
Winchester	Guildhall	01962 840500	tourism@winchester.gov.uk
Windsor	Old Booking Hall	01753 743900	windsor.tic@rbwm.gov.uk
Witney	Welsh Way	01993 775802/ 861780	witney.vic@westoxon.gov.uk
Worthing	The Dome	01903 239868	tic@adur-worthing.gov.uk

Regional Contacts and Information

For more information on accommodation, attractions, activities, events and holidays in South East England, contact one of the following regional or local tourism organisations. Their websites have a wealth of information and many produce free publications to help you get the most out of your visit.

www.visitsoutheastengland.com
email enquiries@tourismse.com or
call (023) 8062 5400.

www.visitnewbury.org.uk
www.visitbuckinghamshire.org
www.visit-hampshire.co.uk
www.visitisleofwight.co.uk
www.visitkent.co.uk
www.visitoxfordandoxfordshire.com
www.visitsurrey.com
www.visitbrighton.com

Entries appear alphabetically by town name in each county. A key to symbols appears on page 7

HURLEY, Berkshire   Map ref 2C2

Hurley Riverside Park

Hurley, Near Henley-on-Thames SL6 5NE
T: (01628) 824493 **E:** info@hurleyriversidepark.co.uk
W: www.hurleyriversidepark.co.uk **£ BOOK ONLINE**

🚐 (138)	£15.00-£30.00
🚎 (138)	£15.00-£30.00
⛺ (130)	£13.00-£26.00
🏠 (10)	£300.00-£550.00
200 touring pitches	

SPECIAL PROMOTIONS

Touring Park Loyalty Card. Membership Card. Giveaways and offers on Facebook and Twitter. Short breaks available in Hire Caravan Holiday Homes and ReadyTents one week prior to arrival.

Family-run park alongside the River Thames, ideal for visiting LEGOLAND® Windsor, Henley-on-Thames, Oxford & London. Tents, tourers, motorhomes & RVs are welcome. Caravan Holiday Homes and ReadyTents for hire. Heated shower blocks, laundry, shop, nature trail, children's play area , riverside picnic grounds, slipway, fishing in season and Wi-Fi. 2 day LEGOLAND® tickets available at a great rate.

Directions: M4 J8/9 or M40 J4, onto A404(M), third exit to Henley (A4130). Past Hurley Village, turn right into Shepherds Lane.

Open: March to October.

Payment: 💳 ☀ **Leisure:** ♩ ► ∪ **Children:** 🛝 🎢 **Catering:** 🛒 **Park:** 🐕 🚃 🚿 📶 📷
Touring: 🚿 🚰 🔌 ♩

READING, Berkshire   Map ref 2C2

Wellington Country Park - Touring Caravan & Campsite

Odiham Road, Riseley, Nr Reading RG7 1SP
T: (0118) 932 6444 **F:** (0118) 932 6445 **E:** info@wellington-country-park.co.uk
W: www.wellington-country-park.co.uk **£ BOOK ONLINE**

🚐 (57)	£36.00
🚎 (57)	£17.00-£36.00
⛺ (30)	£15.50-£29.50
87 touring pitches	

Set within beautiful woodlands, fees include 2 people and free unlimited access to Country Park with nature trails, animal farm, play areas, miniature railway, sand pits and mini golf. Easy access from both M3 & M4. **Directions:** Hampshire/Berkshire border between Reading/Basingstoke. Do not use Sat Nav. M4 junction 11 A33 to Basingstoke. M3 junction 5 B3349 to Reading. **Open:** March to November.

Payment: 💳 ☀ **Leisure:** 🚲 ∪ **Children:** 🛝 🎢 **Catering:** ✕ 🛒 **Park:** 🐕 🚃 🚿 📶 📷 **Touring:** 🚿 🚰 🔌

LYMINGTON, Hampshire   Map ref 2C3

Downton Holiday Park

Shorefield Road, Milford-on-Sea, Lymington SO41 0LH
T: (01425) 476131 **F:** (01590) 642515 **E:** info@downtonholidaypark.co.uk
W: www.downtonholidaypark.co.uk

🏠 (74)	£150.00-£685.00

Downton Holiday Park is a small, peaceful park, close to the New Forest and less than 5 minutes drive from the beach at Milford-on-Sea. **Directions:** By road, leave the M27 at Junction 1 and follow the A337 to Lyndhurst. Keeping on the A337, drive through Brockenhurst and Lymington and on to Downton. **Open:** March to October.

Payment: 💳 **Leisure:** 🚲 🎣 **Property:** 🐕 🚃 🚿 📶 **Children:** 🛝 🎢

AA
▶▶▶▶

🛏 (142) £119.00-£1559.00

Shorefield Country Park

Shorefield Road, Milford-on-Sea, Hampshire SO41 0LH
T: (01590) 648331 F: (01590) 645610 E: holidays@shorefield.co.uk
W: www.shorefield.co.uk

A fabulous AA 4 Pennants rated holiday park set in 100 acres of delightful landscaped parkland. The perfect setting to relax in or explore the rural surroundings. Shorefield Country Park has a wide variety of accommodation to suit all tastes and budgets including chalets, caravans, lodges as well as our Signature properties which all have luxury hot tubs and private decking.

Close to the coast at Milford-on-Sea and just 3 miles from the New Forest National Park, home to the famous ponies and deer. Bournemouth and its famous beaches are only 7 miles away.

Directions: Please see website.

Open: All year.

Site: 🏕 Payment: 💳 Leisure: ♪ ▶ ☯ ⚲ ⚓ ⚲ ⚲ Property: ⌖ 🎵 🖥 🖨 📶 Children: 🐴 ⛰ Catering: ✗ 🛍

---

enjoyEngland.com
★★
TOURING & CAMPING PARK

🚐 £19.00-£24.00
🚍 £19.00-£24.00
⛺ £14.00
100 touring pitches

Green Pastures Caravan Park

Green Pastures Farm, Whitemoor Lane, Romsey SO51 6AJ
T: (023) 8081 4444 E: enquiries@greenpasturesfarm.com
W: www.greenpasturesfarm.com

Located on the outskirts of the New Forest, Green Pastures Farm is ideal for families as there is plenty of space for children to play in full view of the caravans and tents. However, it is also peaceful enough to be able to unwind after a busy working week. Directions: Drive Off A3090 between Romsey and Cadnam. From M27 junction 2 follow signs for Salisbury until our own brown signs are seen at big roundabout. Open: 15th March - 3rd November.

Site: ⛺🄿 Payment: 💳 ☀ Leisure: 🚲 ♪ ▶ ☯ Children: 🐴 Catering: 🛍 Park: ⌖ 🖨 🄿 Touring: 🚽 ⚲ 🚰

---

enjoyEngland.com
★★★★
HOLIDAY, TOURING & CAMPING PARK

🚐 (70) £15.00-£35.00
🚍 (70) £15.00-£35.00
⛺ (30) £15.00-£35.00
🛏 (6) £280.00-£550.00
100 touring pitches

Hill Farm Caravan Park

Branches Lane, Sherfield English, Romsey SO51 6FH
T: (01794) 340402 E: gjb@hillfarmpark.com
W: www.hillfarmpark.com

In countryside on the edge of the New Forest, our quiet family-run site provides an ideal base for mature visitors and families with younger children to visit the area. Directions: Please see our website. Open: Touring & camping: March to October Statics: February to December.

Site: ⛺🄿 Payment: 💳 ☀ Leisure: 🚲 ♪ ▶ ☯ Children: 🐴 ⛰ Catering: ✗ 🛍 Park: ⌖ 🖨 🖨 🄿 Touring: 🚽 ⚲ 🚰 🎵

RYDE, Isle of Wight   Map ref 2C3 — SatNav PO33 1QJ

Whitefield Forest Touring Park

Brading Road, Ryde PO33 1QJ
T: (01983) 617069 E: pat&louise@whitefieldforest.co.uk
W: www.whitefieldforest.co.uk

🚐 (50)	£17.00-£25.00	
🚍 (50)	£17.00-£25.00	
⛺ (50)	£17.00-£25.00	
100 touring pitches		

Award winning campsite in the picturesque woodland of Whitefield Forest. Near to the sandy beaches of Ryde & Sandown on a good bus route, ideal for caravans, motor homes and tents. Special offers available on ferry travel & for over 50's. **Directions:** Just off A3055 follow to Brading, at Tesco's roundabout straight across, site approx half mile on left hand side. **Open:** 27th March - 5th October.

Payment: 💷 ☼ **Leisure:** ♪ ↾ ∪ **Children:** 🐴 ⚠ **Catering:** 🍴 **Park:** 🐕 🖳 🗑 🏧 **Touring:** ☎ ⚙ 🔌 ♪

ST. HELENS, Isle of Wight   Map ref 2C3 — SatNav PO33 1YN

Carpenters Farm Campsite

Carpenters Road, St Helens PO33 1YN
T: (01983) 874557 E: info@carpentersfarms.co.uk
W: www.carpentersfarm.co.uk

100 touring pitches

Family campsite with beautiful views in picturesque rural setting, adjacent to RSPB Reserve and SSSI. Close to beaches and attractions. Relaxed atmosphere on site. Family groups and pets very welcome. Overnight holding area available. Electric hookup, bookings advised for high season, please check our website for up to date tariffs. **Directions:** Please contact us for directions. **Open:** May - September.

Site: ⏏🅿 **Payment:** 💷 ☼ **Leisure:** 🚲 ♪ ↾ ∪ 🎣 **Children:** 🐴 ⚠ **Catering:** 🍴 **Park:** 🐕 🖳 🗑 🏧 🔌 **Touring:** ☎ ⚙ 🔌

WROXALL, Isle of Wight   Map ref 2C3 — SatNav PO38 3EP

Appuldurcombe Gardens Holiday Park

Appuldurcombe Road, Wroxall, Nr. Ventnor, Isle of Wight PO38 3EP
T: (01983) 852597 F: (01983) 856225 E: info@appuldurcombegardens.co.uk
W: www.appuldurcombegardens.co.uk

🚐 (70)	£16.45-£32.95	
🚍 (30)	£16.45-£32.95	
⛺ (30)	£16.45-£28.45	
🏕 (40)	£215.00-£860.00	

Picturesque holiday park within Area of Outstanding Natural Beauty. Situated within 14 acres of lush secluded grounds & only minutes by car to glorious beaches and attractions. 40 static caravans within a walled orchard and 130 pitches with a selection of pitch options. **Directions:** Head to Newport and take A3020 towards Shanklin and Ventnor. Travel through Blackwater onto Rookley, Godshill & Sandford. Reaching Whiteley Bank roundabout, turn right towards Wroxall. **Open:** February-November.

Site: 🏠 ⏏🅿 **Payment:** 💷 ☼ **Leisure:** 🚲 ♪ ↾ ∪ 🎣 ⚓ **Children:** 🐴 ⚠ **Catering:** ✕ 🍴 **Park:** 🐕 🎵 🖳 🗑 🏧 **Touring:** ☎ ⚙ 🔌 ♪

KINGSDOWN, Kent   Map ref 3C4 — SatNav CT14 8EU

Kingsdown Park Holiday Village

Upper Street, Kingsdown, Deal CT14 8EU
T: (01304) 361205 E: info@kingsdownpark.net
W: www.kingsdownpark.net

🏠 (30)	£229.00-£770.00	

This picturesque park provides the perfect base for exploring Kent. Comfortable lodges and excellent leisure facilities ensure you are not disappointed. Short breaks are available on request, starting from £139. Please note facilities are only open between March-October and 20th December - 2nd January. **Directions:** Please see our website. **Open:** Accommodation available all year.

Site: 🏠 **Payment:** 💷 **Leisure:** 🚲 ♪ ↾ ∪ 🎣 ⚓ **Property:** 🎵 🖳 🗑 🏧 **Children:** 🐴 ⚠ **Catering:** ✕

SANDWICH, Kent   Map ref 3C3

SatNav CT13 0AA

Sandwich Leisure Park

Woodnesborough Road, Sandwich, Kent CT13 0AA
T: (01304) 612681 E: info@sandwichleisurepark.co.uk
W: www.caravansandcampingkent.co.uk £ BOOK ONLINE

🚐	£22.00-£28.00
🚎	£22.00-£28.00
⛺	£22.00-£28.00
🏠	£45.00-£60.00
	£350.00-£550.00
	£350.00-£550.00

Sandwich Leisure Holiday Park is a 5-Star Caravan and Camping holiday park in the historic Medieval Cinque Port of Sandwich, Kent. Find your sanctuary in tranquil picturesque surroundings but with the town of Sandwich on your doorstep, where you will find pubs, restaurants and curiosity shops a plenty. Ideally situated close to historic Canterbury, the seaside towns of Deal, Ramsgate, Margate & Broadstairs and only a few miles from the cross channel Port of Dover. Directions: Please see website. Open: March - October.

Site: 🏕 Payment: 💷 Property: 🐕 🔲 📶 Children: 🧸 ⛰

BANBURY, Oxfordshire   Map ref 2C1

SatNav OX17 1AZ

Anita's Touring Caravan Park

The Yews, Church Farm, Banbury OX17 1AZ
T: (01295) 750731 / 07966 171959 F: (01295) 750731 E: bookings@anitascampsite.co.uk
W: www.oxfordshirecamping.com

🚐	(36)	£18.00-£20.00
🚎	(36)	£18.00-£20.00
⛺	(20)	£14.00-£17.00
🏠		£30.00-£50.00

Anita's is a friendly family run site in North Oxon on the edge of Mollington village. Clean facilities, shop, reception, hard and grass pitches, camping, camping pods and cottages. Directions: M40 Junction 11 Banbury take 3rd roundabout to Southam for 4 miles, 150yds past Mollington, turn-off on left. Brown signs. Open: All year.

Site: ⛰🅿 Payment: 💷 Leisure: 🎵 ▶ ∪ Children: 🧸 Catering: 🛒 Park: 🐕 🔲 📶 Touring: 🔵 🔄 🔵

STANDLAKE, Oxfordshire   Map ref 2C1

SatNav OX29 7PZ

Hardwick Parks

Downs Road, Standlake, Witney OX29 7PZ
T: (01865) 300501 F: (01865) 300037 E: info@hardwickparks.co.uk
W: www.hardwickparks.co.uk £ BOOK ONLINE

🚐	(214)	£16.00-£26.50
🚎	(214)	£16.00-£26.50
⛺	(214)	£11.00-£19.00
	(7)	£295.00-£600.00

214 touring pitches

Rural park near Witney with lakes and river. Licensed clubhouse serving food and drinks. Shower/toilet block and shop. Tents, caravans and motorhomes welcome. Holiday caravans for hire and sale. Watersports available. Dogs on leads welcome. Directions: Four and a half miles from Witney, signposted from the A415. Open: April to October.

Site: 🏕 ⛰🅿 Payment: 💷 ☀ Leisure: 🎵 Children: 🧸 ⛰ Catering: ✕ 🛒 Park: 🐕 🔲 🔲 📶 Touring: 🔵 🔄 🔵 🎵

WITNEY, Oxfordshire   Map ref 2C1

SatNav OX29 7RH

Lincoln Farm Park Oxfordshire

High Street, Standlake, Witney, Oxon OX29 7RH
T: (01865) 300239 F: (01865) 300127 E: info@lincolnfarmpark.co.uk
W: www.lincolnfarmpark.co.uk £ BOOK ONLINE

🚐	(90)	£18.30-£33.80
🚎	(44)	£18.30-£33.80
⛺	(16)	£18.30-£30.80

90 touring pitches

Set in eight acres of beautiful Oxfordshire countryside, Lincoln Farm park offers you the opportunity to explore, or simply relax. Open: 6th February to Mid November.

Site: 🏕 ⛰🅿 Payment: 💷 € ☀ Leisure: 🎵 ▶ ∪ 🎯 Children: 🧸 ⛰ Catering: 🛒 Park: 🐕 🔲 🔲 📶 Touring: 🔵 🔄 🔵 🎵

For **key to symbols** see page 7

EASTBOURNE, Sussex Map ref 2D3
SatNav BN24 5NG

enjoyEngland.com
★★★★
TOURING & CAMPING PARK

Fairfields Farm Caravan & Camping Park

Eastbourne Road, Westham, Pevensey BN24 5NG
T: (01323) 763165 F: (01323) 469175 E: enquiries@fairfieldsfarm.com
W: www.fairfieldsfarm.com

🚐 (60) £17.00-£25.00
🚎 (60) £17.00-£25.00
⛺ (60) £17.00-£25.00
60 touring pitches

SPECIAL PROMOTIONS
Special promotions available throughout the season, please contact us for more details.

A quiet country touring site on a working farm. Clean facilities, lakeside walk with farm pets and free fishing for campers. Close to the beautiful seaside resort of Eastbourne, and a good base from which to explore the diverse scenery and attractions of South East England. Overnight holding area available. Free Wi-Fi is also available on site.

Directions: From A27 Pevensey roundabout, travel through Pevensey towards castle, then through Westham. Turn left (B2191) towards Eastbourne. Over level crossing and we are on left.

Open: April to October.

Site: ⛺🅿 Payment: 💳 ☀ Leisure: 🎵 ▶ ☋ Children: 🐎 Catering: 🍴 Park: 🐕 🖥 📖 🎧
Touring: 🚰 🚻 ♿ 🚮 ♪

f

HASTINGS, Sussex Map ref 3B4
SatNav TN35 5DX

enjoyEngland.com
★★★★
HOLIDAY PARK

Shearbarn Holiday Park

Barley Lane, Hastings, East Sussex TN35 5DX
T: (01424) 423583 F: (01424) 718740 E: holidays@shearbarn.co.uk
W: www.shearbarnholidaypark.co.uk

🏠 (26) £646.00-£819.00
🚐 (3) £420.00-£672.00

A holiday at Shearbarn offers something for everyone. Our guests return year after year, to explore the majestic cliffs and beaches, cafes and bars in Hastings Old Town, and to enjoy the dramatic and rich history of 1066 Country. All of our holiday homes are designed and built to the highest specification by the UK's leading manufacturers and are available in an array of styles, sizes and layouts with state of the art features, fixtures and fittings and sumptuous furnishings. Short breaks available. **Open:** March - Jan.

f 🐦

Site: 🛈 ⛺🅿 Payment: 💳 ☀ Leisure: 🎵 ✿ Children: 🐎 ⛰ Catering: ✗ Park: 🐕 🎵 🖥 📖 🎧
Touring: 🚮

SELSEY, Sussex Map ref 2C3
SatNav PO20 9EJ

enjoyEngland.com
★★★★★
HOLIDAY PARK

Green Lawns Holiday Park (Bunn Leisure)

Paddock Lane, Selsey, Chichester, West Sussex PO20 9EJ
T: (01243) 606080 F: (01243) 606068 E: holidays@bunnleisure.co.uk
W: www.bunnleisure.co.uk £ BOOK ONLINE

🏠 (1) £690.00-£1650.00
🚐 (20) £168.00-£1055.00

Offers leafy lanes, duck ponds and open green spaces for privacy, peace and quiet but with access to all Bunn Leisure's facilities and a courtesy bus to take you around. Open 10 months of the year from March to January. **Directions:** From A27 Chichester by-pass take B2145 to Selsey. Green Lawns is clearly signed on right once you are in town. **Open:** March to January.

f 🐦

Site: 🛈 Payment: 💳 Leisure: ♨ 🎵 ▶ ☋ ✿ ✈ ✿ Property: 🐕 🎵 🖥 📖 🎧 Children: 🐎 ⛰
Catering: ✗ 🍴

South East - Sussex

SELSEY, Sussex Map ref 2C3 — SatNav PO20 9EL

enjoyEngland.com
★★★★★
TOURING PARK

Warner Farm Camping & Touring Park

Warner Lane, Selsey, Chichester, West Sussex PO20 9EL
T: (01243) 604499 E: touring@bunnleisure.co.uk
W: www.warnerfarm.co.uk

🚐 (80) £20.00-£45.00
🚐 (50) £20.00-£45.00
⛺ (120) £18.00-£33.00
250 touring pitches

Great value, quality, fun filled family camping & touring holidays. Well maintained standard, electric & full service pitches. Stay here & enjoy all Bunn Leisure's great facilities and entertainment. Overnight holding area available. **Directions:** From A27 Chichester by-pass take B2145 to Selsey. Warner Farm is clearly signed on the right once you are in town. **Open:** March to January.

Site: Payment: Leisure: Children: Catering: Park: Touring:

SELSEY, Sussex Map ref 2C3 — SatNav PO20 9BH

enjoyEngland.com
★★★★
HOLIDAY PARK

West Sands Holiday Park (Bunn Leisure)

Mill Lane, Selsey, Chichester, West Sussex PO20 9BH
T: (01243) 606080 F: (01243) 606068 E: holidays@bunnleisure.co.uk
W: www.bunnleisure.co.uk

🏠 (5) £440.00-£1600.00
🏕 (150) £168.00-£1055.00

The liveliest of our parks on the South Coast offering family fun in a fantastic seaside location. Famous for the best entertainment with top acts, live performances and kids entertainment. **Directions:** From A27 Chichester by-pass take B2145 to Selsey. West Sands is clearly signed on right once you are in the town. **Open:** March to January.

Site: Payment: Leisure: Property: Children: Catering:

SELSEY, Sussex Map ref 2C3 — SatNav PO20 9EJ

enjoyEngland.com
★★★★
HOLIDAY PARK

White Horse Holiday Park (Bunn Leisure)

Paddock Lane, Selsey, Chichester, West Sussex PO20 9EJ
T: (01243) 606080 F: (01243) 606068 E: holidays@bunnleisure.co.uk
W: www.bunnleisure.co.uk

🏕 (20) £168.00-£1055.00

With its coveted award for its traditional atmosphere, White Horse Holiday Park is perfect for families. Offering a relaxed holiday, though never far from all the facilities and entertainment. **Directions:** From A27 Chichester bypass take B2145 to Selsey. White Horse is clearly signed on the right once you are in town. **Open:** March to January.

Site: Payment: Leisure: Property: Children: Catering:

For **key to symbols** see page 7

Don't Miss...

Buckingham Palace
London, SW1A 1AA
(020) 7766 7300
www.royalcollection.org.uk
Buckingham Palace is the office and London residence of Her Majesty The Queen. It is one of the few working royal palaces remaining in the world today. The State Rooms are used extensively by The Queen and Members of the Royal Family and during August and September, when The Queen makes her annual visit to Scotland, the Palace's nineteen state rooms are open to visitors.

Houses of Parliament
Westminster, London SW1A 0AA
020 7219 4565
www.parliament.uk/visiting
Tours of the Houses of Parliament offer a unique combination of one thousand years of history, modern day politics, and stunning art and architecture. Visit the Queen's Robing Room, the Royal Gallery and the Commons Chamber, scene of many lively debates.

National Gallery
Westminster WC2N 5DN
(020) 7747 2888
www.nationalgallery.org.uk
The National Gallery houses one of the greatest collections of Western European painting in the world. Discover inspiring art by Botticelli, Caravaggio, Leonardo da Vinci, Monet, Raphael, Rembrandt, Titian, Vermeer and Van Gogh.

Natural History Museum
Kensington and Chelsea SW7 5BD
(020) 7942 5000
www.nhm.ac.uk
The Natural History Museum reveals how the jigsaw of life fits together. Animal, vegetable or mineral, the best of our planet's most amazing treasures are here for you to see - for free.

Madame Tussauds
Marylebone Road, London, NW1 5LR
(0871) 894 3000
www.madametussauds.com/London/
Experience the legendary history, glitz and glamour of Madame Tussauds London. Visit the 14 exciting, interactive zones and the amazing Marvel Super Heroes 4D movie experience. Strike a pose with your favourite movie star, enjoy an audience with the Queen or plant a cheeky kiss on Prince Harry's cheek.

London

London

Grand landmarks, gorgeous gardens, spectacular shopping, exciting attractions, museums, galleries, theatres, sporting venues and all the buzz and history of the capital - London's treasures are beyond measure. A single trip is never enough and you'll find yourself returning time and again to take in the many unforgettable sights and experiences on offer.

Explore – London

In the Central/West End area the most visited sights are the now public rooms of Buckingham Palace, the National Gallery in Trafalgar Square, Tate Britain on Millbank, Westminster Abbey, Houses of Parliament and Cabinet War Rooms.

Hotspot: Watch the Changing the Guard ceremony at Buckingham Palace for an impressive display of British pomp and ceremony at 11.30am every day.

Westminster Abbey, nearly a thousand years old, has tombs of many English kings, queens, statesmen and writers. The British Museum in Bloomsbury houses one of the world's largest selections of antiquities, including the Magna Carta, the Elgin Marbles and the first edition of Alice in Wonderland. This entire area can be well viewed from The London Eye on the South Bank.

No visit to London is complete without a spot of shopping. Head for bustling Oxford Street and the stylish shops on Regent Street and Bond Street, or check out the trendy boutiques around Carnaby Street.

For entertainment, enjoy a wide range of theatre, bars, restaurants and culture in Covent Garden and don't forget to take in a musical or an off-beat play and the amazing nightime atmosphere around Leicester Square. Madame Tussauds features all your favourite celebrities and super heroes, or if you fancy an historical fright, visit the London Dungeon near Tower Bridge or explore the streets of old London on a Jack the Ripper tour.

London's parks are its lungs. St James, the oldest, was founded by Henry VIII in 1532. Hyde Park, bordering Kensington, Mayfair and Marylebone, is the largest at 630 acres and one of the greatest city parks in the world. You can enjoy any number of outdoor activities, visit the Serpentine Galleries for contemporary art or Speakers' Corner, the most famous location for free speech in the world. Regents Park, with its zoo, lies north of Oxford Circus and was given to the nation by the Prince Regent.

Heading East, St Pauls Cathedral in the city of London was redesigned by Sir Christopher Wren and the nearby the Tower of London, a medieval fortress dominated by the White Tower and dating from 1097, houses The Crown Jewels, guarded by the famous Beefeaters. Even further East, the Queen Elizabeth Olympic Park is the exciting legacy of the 2012 Olympic Games and is situated at the heart of a new, vibrant East London. The main stadium re-opens in October 2015 for the Rugby World Cup, before being permanently transformed into the national centre for athletics in the UK and the new home of West Ham United Football Club.

To the South East of the capital, Canary Wharf is one of Londons main financial centres and on the south bank, opposite Docklands, attractions include the National Maritime Museum incorporating the Royal Greenwich Observatory, the Cutty Sark and The O2, one of London's premier entertainment venues.

Hotspot: Come face to face with some of the hairiest, scariest, tallest and smallest animals on the planet - right in the heart of the capital at the ZSL London Zoo.
T: (020) 7722 3333
www.zsl.org/zsl-london-zoo

On Saturday 14th November 2015, the 800th Lord Mayors Show will feature a parade of over 6,000 people, military marching bands, acrobats, a procession of decorated floats, a gilded State Coach that the Lord Mayor travels and starts with an RAF flypast. After the procession London's City Guides will be on hand to lead free guided tours of the City's more strange and wonderful corners, and in the evening fireworks will light up the sky over the river. Visit their website for more information. www.lordmayorsshow.org.

In the North of the capital, trendy Camden is an eclectic mix of intriguing and unique experiences. Locals and visitors alike hunt for vintage treasures in the open air markets at Camden Lock and far-out attire in the alternative shops that line the high street, or spend time celebrity spotting or strolling along Regent's Canal. There's a different kind of food at every turn, from street vendors to swanky sushi restaurants, and Camden is also home to an extraordinary array of bars, live music and arts venues including the Roundhouse.

Hotspot: The Globe Theatre, Globe Exhibition & Tour and Globe Education seek to further the experience and international understanding of Shakespeare in performance. www.shakespearesglobe.com

Indulge – London

Relax and take in the breathtaking views of London while you enjoy a glass of chilled champagne on the **London Eye** with a Champagne Experience, perfect for couples and celebrations. www.londoneye.com

Head to the stunning open-air Vista bar on the rooftop of **The Trafalgar Hotel** for cheeky cocktails. Relax and enjoy the view as you sip on something delicious. 2 Spring Gardens, Trafalgar Square SW1A 2TS www.thetrafalgar.com.

For a well earned pampering, head to the opulent **St Pancras Spa** in the basement of the beautifully renovated St Pancras Renaissance hotel. This subterranean haven has a stunning pool area bedecked in Victorian tiles, steam room, sauna and luxurious treatment rooms offering exotic sounding treatments like Balinese massage and a Creme de Rassoul Moroccan body wrap. www.stpancrasspa.co.uk

Porters has served mouth watering food in the heart Covent Garden since 1979. World renowned for traditional dinners like Steak and Kidney Pudding and Fisherman's Pie, not to mention the heavenly steamed syrup sponge pudding and homemade ice creams, this is a treat not to be missed. www.porters.co.uk T: 020 7836 6466

Since its foundation in 1707, **Fortnum & Mason** has been supplying Londoners and visitors with the very finest goods and services. Enjoy a thoroughly delightful English tradition in elegant surroundings with afternoon tea in the Diamond Jubilee Tea Salon. www.fortnumandmason.com

Attractions with this sign participate in the Visitor Attraction Quality Assurance Scheme.

Apsley House
Westminster W1J 7NT
(020) 7499 5676
www.english-heritage.org.uk/daysout/properties/
apsley-house/
This great 18th century town house pays homage to the Duke's dazzling military career, which culminated in his victory at Waterloo in 1815.

Bateaux London Restaurant Cruisers
Westminster WC2N 6NU
(020) 7695 1800
www.bateauxlondon.com
Bateaux London offers lunch and dinner cruises, combining luxury dining, world-class live entertainment and five-star customer care.

The Boat Race
April, Putney Bridge
www.theboatrace.org
Boat crews from the universities of Oxford and Cambridge battle it out on the Thames.

British Museum
Camden WC1B 3DG
(020) 7323 8299
www.britishmuseum.org.uk
Founded in 1753, the British Museum's remarkable collections span over two million years of human history and culture, all under one roof.

Chessington World of Adventures
Kingston upon Thames KT9 2NE
0870 444 7777
www.chessington.com
Explore Chessington - it's a whole world of adventures! Soar on the Vampire rollercoaster, discover the mystery of Tomb Blaster or visit the park's own SEA LIFE Centre.

Chinese New Year
February, Various venues
www.visitlondon.com
London's Chinese New Year celebrations are the largest outside Asia, with parades, performances and fireworks.

Chiswick House

Hounslow W4 2RP
(020) 8995 0508
www.english-heritage.org.uk/daysout/properties/chiswick-house/
The celebrated villa of Lord Burlington with impressive grounds featuring Italianate garden with statues, temples, obelisks and urns.

Churchill Museum and Cabinet War Rooms

Westminster SW1A 2AQ
(020) 7930 6961
www.iwm.org.uk
Learn more about the man who inspired Britain's finest hour at the highly interactive and innovative Churchill Museum, the world's first major museum dedicated to life of the 'greatest Briton'. Step back in time and discover the secret.

City of London Festival

June-July, Various venues
www.visitlondon.com
The City of London Festival is an annual extravaganza of music, dance, art, film, poetry, family and participation events that takes place in the city's Square Mile.

Eltham Palace

Greenwich SE9 5QE
(020) 8294 2548
www.elthampalace.org.uk
A spectacular fusion of 1930s Art Deco villa and magnificent 15th century Great Hall. Surrounded by period gardens.

Greenwich Heritage Centre

Greenwich SE18 4DX
(020) 8854 2452
www.royalgreenwich.gov.uk
Local history museum with displays of archaeology, natural history and geology. Also temporary exhibitions, schools service, sales point and Saturday club.

Hampton Court Palace

Richmond upon Thames KT8 9AU
(0870) 752 7777
www.hrp.org.uk
This magnificent palace set in delightful gardens was famously one of Henry VIII's favourite palaces.

HMS Belfast

Southwark SE1 2JH
(020) 7940 6300
www.iwm.org.uk
HMS Belfast, launched 1938, served throughout WWII, playing a leading part in the destruction of the German battle cruiser Scharnhorst and in the Normandy Landings.

Imperial War Museum

Southwark SE1 6HZ
(020) 7416 5000
www.iwm.org.uk
This award-winning museum tells the story of conflict involving Britain and the Commonwealth since 1914. See thousands of imaginatively displayed exhibits, from art to aircraft, utility clothes to U-boats.

Kensington Palace State Apartments

Kensington and Chelsea W8 4PX
(0844) 482 7777
www.hrp.org.uk
Home to the Royal Ceremonial Dress Collection, which includes some of Queen Elizabeth II's dresses worn throughout her reign, as well as 14 of Diana, Princess of Wales' evening dresses.

Kenwood House

Camden NW3 7JR
(020) 8348 1286
www.english-heritage.org.uk/daysout/properties/kenwood-house/
Beautiful 18th century villa with fine interiors, and a world class collection of paintings. Also fabulous landscaped gardens and an award-winning restaurant.

Museums At Night
May, Various venues
www.visitlondon.com
Explore arts and heritage after dark at museums across London. Packed with special events, from treasure trails to pyjama parties, Museums at Night is a great opportunity to explore culture in a new light.

Museum of London
City of London EC2Y 5HN
(020) 7001 9844
www.museumoflondon.org.uk
Step inside Museum of London for an unforgettable journey through the capital's turbulent past.

London Eye River Cruise Experience
Lambeth E1 7PB
0870 500 0600
www.londoneye.com
See London from a different perspective and enjoy a unique 40 minute circular sightseeing cruise on the river Thames.

London Festival of Architecture
June - July
www.londonfestivalofarchitecture.org
See London's buildings in a new light during the Festival of Architecture.

London Film Festival
October, Various venues
www.bfi.org.uk/lff
A two-week showcase of the world's best new films, the BFI London Film Festival is one of the most anticipated events in London's cultural calendar.

London Transport Museum
Westminster WC2E 7BB
(020) 7379 6344
www.ltmuseum.co.uk
The history of transport for everyone, from spectacular vehicles, special exhibitions, actors and guided tours to film shows, gallery talks and children's craft workshops

London Wetland Centre
Richmond upon Thames SW13 9WT
(020) 8409 4400
www.wwt.org.uk
The London Wetland Centre is a unique wildlife visitor attraction just 25 minutes from central London. Run by the Wildfowl and Wetlands Trust (WWT), it is acclaimed as the best urban site in Europe to watch wildlife.

Lord's Tour
Westminster NW8 8QN
(020) 7616 8595
www.lords.org/history/tours-of-lords/
Guided tour of Lord's Cricket Ground including the Long Room, MCC Museum, Real Tennis Court, Mound Stand and Indoor School.

National Maritime Museum
Greenwich SE10 9NF
(020) 8858 4422
www.nmm.ac.uk
Britain's seafaring history housed in an impressive modern museum. Themes include exploration, Nelson, trade and empire, passenger shipping, luxury liners, maritime London, costume, art and the sea, the future and environmental issues.

National Portrait Gallery
Westminster WC2H 0HE
(020) 7306 0055
www.npg.org.uk
The National Portrait Gallery houses the world's largest collection of portraits. Visitors come to face with the people who have shaped British history from Elizabeth I to David Beckham. Entrance is free.

Notting Hill Carnival
August, Various venues
www.thenottinghillcarnival.com
The streets of West London come alive every August Bank Holiday weekend as London celebrates Europe's biggest street festival.

RHS Chelsea Flower Show
May, Royal Hospital Chelsea
www.rhs.org.uk/Chelsea-Flower-Show
Experience the greatest flower show in the world at London's Royal Hospital Chelsea.

Royal Air Force Museum Hendon
Barnet NW9 5LL
(020) 8205 2266
www.rafmuseum.org
Take off to the Royal Air Force Museum and flypast the history of aviation with an exciting display of suspended aircraft, touch screen technology, simulator rides, hands-on section, film shows, licensed restaurant.

Royal Observatory Greenwich
Greenwich SE10 9NF
(020) 8858 4422
www.rmg.co.uk
Stand on the Greenwich Meridian Line, Longitude Zero, which divides East and West. Watch the time-ball fall at 1 o'clock. Giant refracting telescope.

Science Museum
Kensington and Chelsea SW7 2DD
0870 870 4868
www.sciencemuseum.org.uk
The Science Museum is world-renowned for its historic collections, awe-inspiring galleries, family activities and exhibitions - and it's free!

Somerset House
Westminster WC2R 1LA
(020) 7845 4670
www.somersethouse.org.uk
This magnificent 18th century building houses the celebrated collections of the Courtauld Institute of Art Gallery, Gilbert Collection and Hermitage Rooms.

Southbank Centre
Lambeth SE1 8XX
(020) 7960 4200
www.southbankcentre.co.uk
A unique arts centre with 21 acres of creative space, including the Royal Festival Hall, Queen Elizabeth Hall and The Hayward.

Southwark Cathedral
Southwark SE1 9DA
(020) 7367 6700
http://cathedral.southwark.anglican.org
Oldest Gothic church in London (c.1220) with interesting memorials connected with the Elizabethan theatres of Bankside.

Tate Britain
Westminster SW1P 4RG
(020) 7887 8888
www.tate.org.uk
Tate Britain presents the world's greatest collection of British art in a dynamic series of new displays and exhibitions.

Tate Modern
Southwark SE1 9TG
(020) 7887 8888
www.tate.org.uk/modern
The national gallery of international modern art and is one of London's top free attractions. Packed with challenging modern art and housed within a disused power station on the south bank of the River Thames.

Tower Bridge Exhibition
Southwark SE1 2UP
(020) 7403 3761
www.towerbridge.org.uk
Inside Tower Bridge Exhibition you will travel up to the high-level walkways, located 140 feet above the Thames and witness stunning panoramic views of London before visiting the Victorian Engine Rooms.

Tower of London
Tower Hamlets EC3N 4AB
0844 482 7777
www.hrp.org.uk
The Tower of London spans over 900 years of British history. Fortress, palace, prison, arsenal and garrison, it is one of the most famous fortified buildings in the world, and houses the Crown Jewels, armouries, Yeoman Warders and ravens.

Victoria and Albert Museum
Kensington and Chelsea SW7 2RL
(020) 7942 2000
www.vam.ac.uk
The V&A is the world's greatest museum of art and design, with collections unrivalled in their scope and diversity.

Virgin London Marathon
April, Various venues
www.virginlondonmarathon.com
Whether you run, walk or cheer from the sidelines, this is a London sporting institution you won't want to miss.

Vodafone London Fashion Weekend
www.londonfashionweekend.co.uk
London's largest and most exclusive designer shopping event.

Wembley Stadium Tours

Brent HA9 0WS
0844 847 2478
www.wembleystadium.com
Until your dream comes true, there's only one way to experience what it's like winning at Wembley - take the tour.

William Morris Gallery
Lloyd Park, Forest Road, Walthamstow E17 4PP
(020) 8496 4390
www.wmgallery.org.uk
The William Morris Gallery is devoted to the life and legacy of one of Britain's most remarkable designers and is housed in the grade II listed Georgian house that was his family home in north-east London from 1848 to 1856.*

Wimbledon Lawn Tennis Championships
June - July, Wimbledon
www.wimbledon.com
The world of tennis descends on Wimbledon in South West London every summer for two weeks of tennis, strawberries and cream, and good-natured queuing.

Wimbledon Lawn Tennis Museum

Merton SW19 5AG
(020) 8944 1066
www.wimbledon.com
A fantastic collection of memorabilia dating from 1555, including Championship Trophies, Art Gallery, and special exhibitions, reflecting the game and championships of today.

Tourist Information Centres

When you arrive at your destination, visit a Tourist Information Centre for quality assured help with accommodation and information about local attractions and events, or email your request before you go.

City of London
St Paul's Churchyard
(020) 7606 3030
stpauls.informationcentre@cityoflondon.gov.uk

Greenwich
2 Cutty Sark Gardens
(0870) 608 2000
tic@greenwich.gov.uk

Harrow
Gayton Library
(0208) 427 6012
gayton.library@harrow.gov.uk

Regional Contacts and Information

For more information on accommodation, attractions, activities, events and holidays in London, contact Visit London.

Go to visitlondon.com for all you need to know about London. Look for inspirational itineraries with great ideas for weekends and short breaks.

Or call 0870 1 LONDON (0870 1 566 366) for:

• A London visitor information pack
• Visitor information on London
• Accommodation reservations

Speak to an expert for information and advice on museums, galleries, attractions, riverboat trips, sightseeing tours, theatre, shopping, eating out and much more!

Entries appear alphabetically by town name in each county. A key to symbols appears on page 7

Lee Valley Campsite - Sewardstone

Sewardstone Road, Chingford, London E4 7RA
T: (020) 8529 5689 **F:** (020) 8559 4070 **E:** sewardstonecampsite@leevalleypark.org.uk
W: www.visitleevalley.org.uk/wheretostay **£ BOOK ONLINE**

🚐	(65)	£13.50-£19.20
🚍	(65)	£13.50-£19.20
⛺	(35)	£13.50-£19.20
🏠	(17)	£25.00-£50.00

65 touring pitches

Lee Valley Campsite, Sewardstone is less than 40 minutes from central London and is close to the scenic Hertfordshire and Essex countryside. Come camping, caravanning or stay in one of our cosy cocoons or woodland cabins – it's perfect for families, couples or groups of friends looking for affordable accommodation in London.

Directions: The campsite is situated on the A112 between Chingford and Waltham Abbey to the South of the M25. Leave M25 at junction 26 and follow the signs.

Open: 1st March - 31st January.

Site: ⚠🅿 **Payment:** 💳 ☀ **Leisure:** ♿ 🎣 ∪ **Children:** 🛝 🎠 **Catering:** 🍴 **Park:** 🐕 📦 🏪 🏧
Touring: 🚿 🔌 💧 🔧

Take a trip into The Capital

Stay at **Abbey Wood Caravan Club Site** and you can take the short walk to the station of the same name – hop on the train and you can be in Central London within 35 mins! Alternatively take a leisurely river cruise to Kew or Hampton Court (to name but a few) they operate close to the site too. If you don't have a 'van don't worry we have cosy Camping Pods here too.

Abbey Wood Caravan Club Site

Book now: **01342 488 356**
www.caravanclub.co.uk/visitbritainsites
Lines are open Mon-Fri 8.45am-5.30pm. Calls may be recorded.

THE **CARAVAN CLUB**

LONDON N9, Inner London   *Map ref 2D2*   *SatNav N9 0AR*

Lee Valley Camping and Caravan Park - Edmonton

Meridian Way, Edmonton, London N9 0AR
T: (020) 8803 6900 **F:** (020) 8884 4975 **E:** edmontoncampsite@leevalleypark.org.uk
W: www.visitleevalley.org.uk/wheretostay **£ BOOK ONLINE**

⊕ (100)	£14.00-£22.00
🚐 (100)	£14.00-£22.00
Å (60)	£14.00-£22.00
🛖 (12)	£175.00-£350.00
100 touring pitches	

A peaceful site that puts you in easy each of both central London and the many attractions of Lee Valley Regional Park. With excellent facilities including an on-site shop and children's play area, plus a golf course, athletics centre, cinema and restaurant all located within the complex. Overnight holding area available.

Directions: Leave M25 at J25, follow signs for City. Turn left for Freezywater at traffic lights, follow signs for Lee Valley Leisure Complex.

Open: All year.

Site: Åⴗ Payment: 💷 ☀ Leisure: ♪ ⵑ ∪ Children: ⵚ ⵜ Catering: ⵐ Park: ⵗ ⵞ 🛢 🏪 🌲
Touring: 🚰 ⴕ ⴖ ♪

Looking for something else?

The official and most comprehensive guide to independently inspected, quality-assessed accommodation.

- **B&Bs and Hotels**
- **Self Catering**
- **Camping, Touring and Holiday Parks**

Now available in all good bookshops and online at

www.hudsons.co.uk/shop

Don't Miss

ZSL Whipsnade Zoo
Dunstable, Bedfordshire LU6 2LF
(020) 7449 6200
www.zsl.org/zsl-whipsnade-zoo
Set on 600 acres in the rolling Chiltern Hills, Whipsnade is home
to more than 2500 species and you can get close to some of the
world's hairiest, scariest, tallest and smallest animals here. Meet
the animals, take a steam train ride, visit the Hullabazoo Farm or
even be a keeper for the day.

The Fitzwilliam Museum
Trumpington Street, Cambridge CB2 1RB
(01223) 332900
http://www.fitzmuseum.cam.ac.uk/

A short walk away from the colleges and the River Cam in the
heart of Cambridge, the Fitzwilliam Museum with its imposing
neo-classical facade and columns is one of the city's most iconic
buildings. Founded in 1816 when the 7th Viscount Fitzwilliam
of Merrion left his vast collections of books, art and music to the
University of Cambridge, it now has over half a million artworks
and artefacts dating back as far as 2500BC in its collection.

Audley End House & Gardens
Saffron Walden, Essex CB11 4JF
www.english-heritage.org.uk

At Audley End near Saffron Walden, you can discover one of
England's grandest stately homes. Explore the impressive mansion
house, uncover the story behind the Braybrooke's unique natural
history collection, visit an exhibition where you can find out about
the workers who lived on the estate in the 1800s and even try
dressing the part with dressing up clothes provided.

The Broads
Norfolk
www.broads-authority.gov.uk

The Norfolk Broads with its scenic waterways, rare wildlife and rich
history has National Park status. This ancient mosaic of lakes, land
and rivers covering 303 square kilometres in the east of England, is
the UK's largest protected wetland and boasts a variety of habitats
including fen, carr woodland and grazing marshes, as well as
pretty villages and no less than 11,000 species of wildlife. Walking,
cycling, fishing, boating, wildlife spotting, the list of things to do
here is endless and there is something for all ages to enjoy.

Holkham Hall
Wells-next- the-Sea, Norfolk, NR23 1AB
(01328) 710227
www.holkham.co.uk
Steeped in history, magnificent Holkham Hall on the North Norfolk
Coast, is a stunning Palladian mansion with its own nature reserve.
It is home to many rare species of flora and fauna, a deer park and
one of the most beautiful, unspoilt beaches in the country. Step
back in time in the Bygones Museum or explore the 18th Century
walled gardens which are being restored, while the children have
fun in the woodland adventure play area.

East of England

Bedfordshire, Cambridgeshire, Essex, Hertfordshire, Norfolk, Suffolk

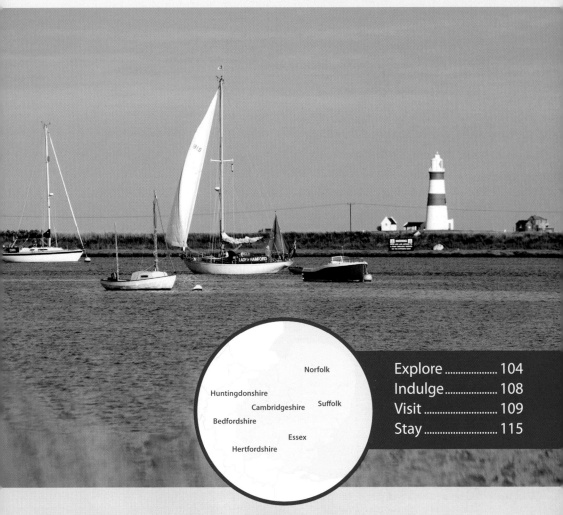

Norfolk

Huntingdonshire

Cambridgeshire   Suffolk

Bedfordshire

Essex

Hertfordshire

Loved for its unspoiled character, rural landscape, architecture and traditions, the East of England is full of beautiful countryside, idyllic seaside, historic cities and vibrant towns. The Norfolk Broads and Suffolk Coast have always been popular with yachtsmen and the North Norfolk Coast has become a fashionable getaway in recent years. Cambridge is steeped in history and oozes sophistication, while Bedfordshire, Hertfordshire and Essex each have their own charms, with pockets of beauty and fascinating heritage. This is a diverse region where you'll find plenty to keep you busy.

Bedfordshire & Hertfordshire

History, the arts, family entertainment and relaxing, unspoilt countryside - this area has it all. Bedfordshire has plenty of attractions, from exotic animals at Whipsnade Zoo to vintage aeroplanes at The Shuttleworth Collection and notable historic houses. Woburn Abbey, the still inhabited home of the Dukes of Bedford, stands in a 3000-acre park and is part of one of Europe's largest drive-through game reserves. The 18th century mansion's 14 state apartments are open to the public and contain an impressive art collection. Luton Hoo is a fine Robert Adam designed house in a 1200-acre Capability Brown designed park.

Hertfordshire also has its fair share of stately homes, with Hatfield House, built from 1707 by Robert Cecil, first Earl of Salisbury, leading the way. Nearby Knebworth House is the venue for popular summer concerts and events.

Roman walls, mosaic floors and part of an amphitheatre are still visible at Verulanium, St Albans and Much Hadham, where the Bishops of London used to have their country seat, is a showpiece village. Welwyn Garden City, one of Britain's first 20th century new towns retains a certain art deco charm.

Hotspot:
Dunstable Downs Kite Festival
July, Dunstable, Bedfordshire
www.dunstablekitefestival.co.uk
Kite enthusiasts from around the UK converge on Dunstable.

Cambridgeshire & Essex

Cambridge is a city of winding streets lined with old houses, world-famous colleges and churches, while the gently flowing Cam provides a serene backdrop to the architectural wonders. Kings College Chapel, started by Henry VI in 1446 should not be missed and the Fitzwilliam Museum is one of Europe's treasure houses, with antiquities from Greece and Rome. First-class shopping can be found in the quirky stores and exquisite boutiques tucked away along cobbled streets, and there's a vast choice of places to eat and drink.

Further afield, Cambridgeshire is a land of lazy waterways, rolling countryside, bustling market towns and quaint villages. Climb grand sweeping staircases in the stately homes of the aristocracy or relax as you chug along in a leisure boat, watching the wildlife in one of the wonderful nature reserves. Peterborough has a fine Norman cathedral with three soaring arches, whilst Ely has had an abbey on its cathedral site since AD 670.

Western Essex is dotted with pretty historic market towns and villages like Thaxted and Saffron Walden and plenty of historic sites. County town Colchester was founded by the Romans and its massive castle keep, built in 1067 on the site of the Roman Temple of Claudius, houses a collection of Roman antiquities. Explore the beautiful gardens and 110ft Norman Keep at Hedingham Castle, which also holds jousting and theatre performances.

Some of the region's loveliest countryside lies to the north, on the Suffolk Border around Dedham Vale where Constable and Turner painted, while further east you can find family seaside resorts such as Walton on the Naze and Clacton-on-Sea. Following the coast south, the Blackwater and Crouch estuaries provide havens for yachts and pleasure craft. Inland, Layer Marney Tower is a Tudor palace with buildings, gardens and parkland dating from 1520 in a beautiful, rural Essex setting. The county city of Chelmsford has a historic 15th century cathedral and Hylands House is a beautiful Grade II* listed neo-classical villa, set in over 500 acres of Hylands Park.

Hotspot: The Essex Way walking route weaves through rural Essex all the way from Epping to Harwich via picturesque Constable Country. Taking in open farmland, ancient woodlands, tranquil river valleys, charming villages and historic sites, it has plenty of country pubs worth a stop along the route.

The county town of Norfolk and unofficial capital of East Anglia is Norwich, a fine city whose cathedral walls are decorated with biblical scenes dating from 1046. There are 30 medieval churches in central Norwich and many other interesting historic sites, but modern Norwich is a stylish contemporary city with first rate shopping and cultural facilities. Sandringham, near Kings Lynn in the north west of the county, is the royal palace bought by Queen Victoria for the then Prince of Wales and where the present Queen spends many a family holiday.

The North Norfolk coast has become known as 'Chelsea-on-Sea' in recent years and many parts of the region have developed a reputation for fine dining. From Hunstanton in the west to Cromer in the east, this stretch of coastline is home to nature reserves, windswept beaches and quaint coastal villages. Wells-next-the-Sea, with its long sweeping beach bordered by pine woodland has a pretty harbour with small fishing boats where children fish for crabs.

Norfolk

Norfolk is not as flat as Noel Coward would have you believe, as any cyclist will tell you, but cycling or walking is still a great way to see the county. In the west Thetford Forest is said to be the oldest in England while in the east, the county is crisscrossed by waterways and lakes known as The Broads - apparently the remains of medieval man's peat diggings!

Hotspot: It's hard to beat Bressingham Steam and Gardens, where world renowned gardener and horticulturist Alan Bloom combined his passion for plants and gardens with his love of steam to create a truly unique experience for all the family. www.bressingham.co.uk

Suffolk

Suffolk is famous for its winding lanes and pastel painted, thatched cottages. The county town of Ipswich has undergone considerable regeneration in recent years, and now boasts a vibrant waterfront and growing arts scene. For history lovers, Framlingham Castle has stood intact since the 13th century and magnificent churches at Lavenham, Sudbury and Long Melford are well worth a visit.

The Suffolk Coast & Heaths Area of Outstanding Natural Beauty has 155 square miles of unspoilt wildlife-rich wetlands, ancient heaths, windswept shingle beaches and historic towns and villages for you to explore. Its inlets and estuaries are extremely popular with yachtsmen. Gems such as Southwold, with its brightly coloured beach huts, and Aldeburgh are home to some excellent restaurants. Snape Maltings near Aldeburgh offers an eclectic programme of events including the world famous Aldeburgh Festival of music.

Hotspot: The Anglo-Saxon burial site at Sutton Hoo is set on a stunning 255 acre estate with breathtaking views over the River Deben and is home to one of the greatest archaeological discoveries of all time. www.nationaltrust.org.uk

The historic market town of Woodbridge on the River Deben, has a working tide mill, a fabulous riverside walk with an impressive view across the river to Sutton Hoo and an abundance of delightful pubs and restaurants.

In the south of the county, the hills and valleys on the Suffolk-Essex border open up to stunning skies, captured in paintings by Constable, Turner and Gainsborough. At the heart of beautiful Constable Country, Nayland and Dedham Vale Area of Outstanding Natural Beauty are idyllic places for a stroll or leisurely picnic.

107

Indulge – East of England

Punting is quintessentially Cambridge and a great way to see The Backs of seven of the colleges and their beautiful bridges. Relax and enjoy a glass of Champagne on a leisurely chauffered punt tour or hire your own for an afternoon of delightful DIY sightseeing. (01223) 359750 or visit www.scudamores.com

Moored among the pleasure and fishing boats in the harbour at Wells-next-the-Sea, **The Albatros**, is a restored Dutch clipper built in 1899. It now serves up delicious sweet and savoury pancakes, real ale and live music, providing an interesting pit stop on the north Norfolk coast. www.albatroswells.co.uk

Pay a visit to **Adnams Brewery** in Southwold where you can explore behind the scenes of one of the most modern breweries in the UK, discover how their award-winning beers and spirits are made, or get creative and make your very own gin! www.adnams.co.uk

Aldeburgh Fish and Chip Shop has been serving up freshly caught, East coast fish since 1967. A tantalisingly tasty treat whether you are enjoying a day at the beach in the height of summer or a brisk walk on a stormy winter day, and especially when you eat them sitting on the sea wall. www.aldeburghfishandchips.co.uk

Indulge every little boy's fantasy with a trip to the **Shuttleworth Collection**, a vast collection of vintage aeroplanes, cars, motorcycles and bicycles at Old Warden Aerodrome, Nr. Biggleswade in Bedfordshire. www.shuttleworth.org

Visit – East of England

 Attractions with this sign participate in the Visitor Attraction Quality Assurance Scheme.

Bedfordshire

Bedfordshire County Show
July, Biggleswade, Bedfordshire
www.bedfordshirecountyshow.co.uk
Held in the beautiful grounds of Shuttleworth the Bedfordshire County Show is a showcase of town meets country.

Luton International Carnival
May, Luton, Bedfordshire
www.luton.gov.uk
The highlight is the spectacular carnival parade – an eye-catching, breathtaking procession through the town centre, superbly reflecting the diverse mix of cultures in Luton.

Woburn Safari Park
Bedfordshire MK17 9QN
(01525) 290407
www.woburnsafari.co.uk
Drive through the safari park with 30 species of animals in natural groups just a windscreen's width away, or even closer!

Wrest Park
Silsoe, Luton, Bedfordshire, MK45 4HR
0870 333 1181
www.english-heritage.org.uk
Enjoy a great day out exploring one of Britain's most spectacular French style mansions and 'secret' gardens. With hidden gems including a thatched-roof Bath house, ornate marble fountain, Chinese Temple and bridge and over 40 statues, as well as a kids audio trail and play area, it's popular with families and garden lovers alike.

Cambridgeshire

Cambridge Folk Festival
July/August, Cherry Hinton, Cambridgeshire
www.cambridgefolkfestival.co.uk
Top acts make this a must-visit event for folk fans.

Duxford Air Show
September, Duxford, nr Cambridge, Cambridgeshire
www.iwm.org.uk/duxford
Set within the spacious grounds of the famous former First and Second World War airfield, the Duxford Air Show features an amazing array of aerial displays.

Imperial War Museum Duxford
Cambridge CB22 4QR
(01223) 835000
www.iwm.org.uk/duxford
With its air shows, unique history and atmosphere, nowhere else combines the sights, sounds and power of aircraft quite like Duxford.

Kings College Chapel
Cambridge CB2 1ST
(01223) 331212
www.kings.cam.ac.uk
It's part of one of the oldest Cambridge colleges sharing a wonderful sense of history and tradition with the rest of the University.

The National Stud
Newmarket, Cambridgeshire CB8 0XE
(01638) 663464
www.nationalstud.co.uk
The beautiful grounds & facilities are a renowned tourist attraction in the eastern region.

Oliver Cromwell's House
Ely, Cambridgeshire CB7 4HF
(01353) 662062
www.olivercromwellshouse.co.uk
Visit the former Lord Protector's family's home and experience an exhibition on 17th Century life.

Peterborough Dragon Boat Festival
June, Peterborough Rowing Lake,
Thorpe Meadows, Cambridgeshire
www.peterboroughdragonboatfestival.com
Teams of up to 11 people, dragon boats and all equipment provided, no previous experience required. Family entertainment and catering stalls.

The Raptor Foundation
Huntingdon, Cambridgeshire PE28 3BT
(01487) 741140
www.raptorfoundation.org.uk
Bird of prey centre, offering 3 daily flying displays with audience participation, gift shop, Silent Wings tearoom, Raptor crafts shop.

Essex

Adventure Island
Southend-on-Sea, Essex SS1 1EE
(01702) 443400
www.adventureisland.co.uk
One of the best value 'theme parks' in the South East with over 60 great rides and attractions for all ages. No admission charge, you only 'pay if you play'.

Central Museum and Planetarium
Southend-on-Sea, Essex SS2 6ES
(01702) 434449
www.southendmuseums.co.uk
An Edwardian building housing displays of archaeology, natural history, social and local history.

Clacton Airshow
August, Clacton Seafront, Essex
www.clactonairshow.com
Impressive aerobatic displays take to the skies while a whole host of exhibition, trade stands, food court and on-site entertainment are available at ground level.

Colchester Medieval Festival
June, Lower Castle Park, Colchester, Essex
www.oysterfayre.co.uk
This medieval style fair remembers a time when folk from the countryside and neighbouring villages would travel to the 'Big Fair' in the town.

Colchester Zoo
Essex CO3 0SL
(01206) 331292
www.colchester-zoo.com
Enjoy daily displays, feed elephants and giraffes and see over 260 species in over 60 acres of parkland!

Maldon Mud Race
April, Maldon, Essex
www.maldonmudrace.com
The annual Maldon Mud Race is a wacky fun competition in which participants race to become the first to finish a 400m dash over the bed of the River Blackwater.

RHS Garden Hyde Hall
Chelmsford, Essex CM3 8AT
(01245) 400256
www.rhs.org.uk/hydehall
A garden of inspirational beauty with an eclectic range of horticultural styles from traditional to modern providing year round interest.

Royal Gunpowder Mills
Waltham Abbey, Essex EN9 1JY
(01992) 707370
www.royalgunpowdermills.com
A spectacular 170-acre location for a day of family fun. Special events including Spitfire flypast, award winning Secret History exhibition, tranquil wildlife walks, guided land train tours and rocket science gallery.

Sea-Life Adventure
Southend-on-Sea, Essex SS1 2ER
(01702) 442200
www.sealifeadventure.co.uk
With more than 30 display tanks and tunnels to explore, there are loads of fishy residents to discover at Sea-Life Adventure.

Southend Carnival
August, Southend-on-Sea, Essex
www.southend-on-seacarnival.org.uk
A wide range of events held over eight days.

Hertfordshire

Cathedral and Abbey Church of St Alban
St. Albans, Hertfordshire AL1 1BY
(01727) 860780
www.stalbanscathedral.org
St Alban is Britain's first Christian martyr and the Cathedral, with its shrine, is its oldest place of continuous worship.

Chilli Festival
August, Benington Lordship Gardens, Stevenage, Hertfordshire
www.beningtonlordship.co.uk
A popular family event attracting thousands of visitors over two days, offering a chance to buy Chilli plants, products and sample foods from around the world.

Hertfordshire County Show
May, Redbourn, Hertfordshire
www.hertsshow.com
County show with all the usual attractions.

Knebworth House
Hertfordshire SG1 2AX
(01438) 812661
www.knebworthhouse.com
Historic house, home to the Lytton family since 1490. Knebworth House offers a great day out for all the family with lots to do for all ages.

Norfolk

Banham Zoo

Norwich, Norfolk NR16 2HE
(01953) 887771
www.banhamzoo.co.uk
Wildlife spectacular which will take you on a journey to experience tigers, leopards and zebra plus some of the world's most exotic, rare and endangered animals.

Blickling Hall, Gardens and Park

Norwich, Norfolk NR11 6NF
(01263) 738030
www.nationaltrust.org.uk/blickling-estate
A Jacobean redbrick mansion with a garden, orangery, parkland and lake. Spectacular long gallery, plasterwork ceilings and fine collections of furniture, pictures and books. Walks.

Cromer Pier

Cromer, Norfolk NR27 9HE
www.cromer-pier.com
Cromer Pier is a Grade II listed seaside pier on the north coast of Norfolk. The pier is the home of the Cromer Lifeboat Station and the Pavilion Theatre

Fritton Lake Country World

Great Yarmouth, Norfolk NR31 9HA
(01493) 488288
A woodland and lakeside haven with a children's assault course, putting, an adventure playground, golf, fishing, boating, wildfowl, heavy horses, cart rides, falconry and flying displays.

Great Yarmouth Maritime Festival

September, Great Yarmouth, Norfolk
www.great-yarmouth.co.uk/maritime-festival
A mix of traditional and modern maritime vessels will be moored on South Quay for visitors to admire and go aboard.

King's Lynn May Garland Procession

May, King's Lynn, Norfolk
www.thekingsmorris.co.uk
The King's Morris dancers carry the May Garland around the town.

Norwich Castle Museum and Art Gallery

Norfolk NR1 3JU
(01603) 493649
www.museums.norfolk.gov.uk
Ancient Norman keep of Norwich Castle dominates the city and is one of the most important buildings of its kind in Europe.

Royal Norfolk Show

July, Norwich, Norfolk
www.royalnorfolkshow.co.uk
The Royal Norfolk Show celebrates everything that's Norfolk. It offers 10 hours of entertainment each day from spectacular grand ring displays, traditional livestock and equine classes, to a live music stage, celebrity guests and over 650 stands.

Sainsbury Centre for Visual Arts

UEA, Norwich, Norfolk NR4 7TJ
(01603) 593199
www.scva.ac.uk
Containing a collection of world art, it was one of the first major public buildings to be designed by the architect Norman Foster.

Sandringham

King's Lynn, Norfolk PE35 6EN
(01485) 545400
www.sandringhamestate.co.uk
H.M. The Queen. A fascinating house, an intriguing museum and the best of the Royal gardens.

Suffolk

Aldeburgh Music Festival
June, Snape Maltings, Suffolk IP17 1SP
www.aldeburgh.co.uk
The Aldeburgh Festival of Music and the Arts offers an eclectic mix of concerts, operas, masterclasses, films and open air performances at different venues in the Aldeburgh/Snape area in Suffolk.

Gainsborough's House
Sudbury, Suffolk CO10 2EU
(01787) 372958
www.gainsborough.org
Gainsborough's House is the only museum situated in the birthplace of a great British artist. The permanent collection is built around the works of Thomas Gainsborough.

Go Ape! High Wire Forest Adventure - Thetford, Suffolk
IP27 0AF (0845) 643 9215
www.goape.co.uk
Experience an exhilarating course of rope bridges, tarzan swings and zip slides... all set high in the trees above the forest floor.

Ickworth House, Park and Gardens
Bury St. Edmunds, Suffolk IP29 5QE
(01284) 735270
www.nationaltrust.org.uk/ickworth
Fine paintings, a beautiful collection of Georgian silver, an Italianate garden and stunning parkland.

Latitude Festival
July, Southwold, Suffolk
www.latitudefestival.com
Primarily a music festival but also has a full spectrum of art including film, comedy, theatre, cabaret, dance and poetry.

National Horseracing Museum and Tours
Newmarket, Suffolk CB8 8JH
(01638) 667333
www.nhrm.co.uk
Discover the stories of racing from its early origins at Newmarket to its modern-day heroes

RSPB Minsmere Nature Reserve
Saxmundham, Suffolk IP17 3BY
(01728) 648281
www.rspb.org.uk/minsmere
One of the UK's premier nature reserves, offering excellent facilities for people of all ages and abilities.

Somerleyton Hall and Gardens
Lowestoft, Suffolk NR32 5QQ
(01502) 734901
www.somerleyton.co.uk
12 acres of landscaped gardens to explore including our famous 1864 Yew hedge maze. Guided tours of the Hall.

Suffolk Show
May, Ipswich, Suffolk
www.suffolkshow.co.uk
Animals, food and drink, shopping…there's lots to see and do at this popular county show.

Tourist Information Centres

When you arrive at your destination, visit the Tourist Information Centre for quality assured help with accommodation and information about local attractions and events, or email your request before you go.

Aldeburgh	48 High Street	01728 453637	atic@suffolkcoastal.gov.uk
Aylsham	Bure Valley Railway Station	01263 733903	aylsham.tic@broadland.gov.uk
Beccles	The Quay	01502 713196	admin@beccles.info
Bedford	St Pauls Square	01234 718112	touristinfo@bedford.gov.uk
Bishop's Stortford	2 Market Square	01279 655831	tic@bishopsstortford.org
Brentwood	Town Hall	01277 312500	
Burnham Deepdale	Deepdale Information	01485 210256	info@deepdalefarm.co.uk
Bury St Edmunds	6 Angel Hill	01284 764667	tic@stedsbc.gov.uk
Cambridge	Peas Hill	0871 226 8006	info@visitcambridge.org
Clacton-On-Sea	Town Hall	01255 686633	clactontic@tendringdc.gov.uk
Colchester	1 Queen Street	01206 282920	vic@colchester.gov.uk
Cromer	Louden Road	0871 200 3071	cromerinfo@north-norfolk.gov.uk
Diss	Meres Mouth	01379 650523	dtic@s-norfolk.gov.uk
Dunstable	Priory House	01582 891420	tic@dunstable.gov.uk
Ely	Oliver Cromwell's House	01353 662062	tic@eastcambs.gov.uk
Felixstowe	91 Undercliff Road West	01394 276770	ftic@suffolkcoastal.gov.uk
Great Yarmouth	25 Marine Parade	01493 846346	gab@great-yarmouth.gov.uk
Hertford	10 Market Place	01992 584322	tic@hertford.gov.uk
Holt	3 Pound House	0871 200 3071/ 01263 713100	holtinfo@north-norfolk.gov.uk
Hoveton	Station Road	01603 782281	hovetontic@broads-authority.gov.uk
Hunstanton	Town Hall	01485 532610	info@visithunstanton.info
Ipswich	St Stephens Church	01473 258070	tourist@ipswich.gov.uk
King's Lynn	The Custom House	01553 763044	kings-lynn.tic@west-norfolk.gov.uk
Lavenham	Lady Street	01787 248207	lavenhamtic@babergh.gov.uk
Letchworth Garden City	33-35 Station Road	01462 487868	tic@letchworth.com
Lowestoft	East Point Pavilion	01502 533600	touristinfo@waveney.gov.uk
Luton	Luton Central Library	01582 401579	tourist.information@lutonculture.com
Maldon	Wenlock Way	01621 856503	tic@maldon.gov.uk
Newmarket	63 The Guineas	01638 719749	tic.newmarket@forest-heath.gov.uk
Norwich	The Forum	01603 213999	tourism@norwich.gov.uk
Peterborough	9 Bridge Street	01733 452336	tic@peterborough.gov.uk
Saffron Walden	1 Market Place	01799 524002	tourism@saffronwalden.gov.uk
Sandy	Rear of 10 Cambridge Road	01767 682 728	tourism@sandytowncouncil.gov.uk
Sheringham	Station Approach	01263 824329	sheringhaminfo@north-norfolk.gov.uk
Skegness	Embassy Theatre	0845 6740505	skegnessinfo@e-lindsey.gov.uk
Southend-On-Sea	Pier Entrance	01702 215620	vic@southend.gov.uk
Southwold	69 High Street	01502 724729	southwold.tic@waveney.gov.uk
St Albans	Old Town Hall	01727 864511	tic@stalbans.gov.uk
Stowmarket	The Museum of East Anglian Life	01449 676800	tic@midsuffolk.gov.uk
Sudbury	Sudbury Library	01787 881320/ 372331	sudburytic@sudburytowncouncil.co.uk
Swaffham	The Shambles	01760 722255	swaffham@eetb.info
Waltham Abbey	6 Highbridge Street	01992 660336	tic@walthamabbey-tc.gov.uk
Wells-Next-The-Sea	Staithe Street	0871 200 3071/ 01328 710885	wellsinfo@north-norfolk.gov.uk
Whitlingham	Whitlingham Country Park	01603 756094	whitlinghamtic@broads-authority.gov.uk
Wisbech	2-3 Bridge Street	01945 583263	tourism@fenland.gov.uk
Witham	61 Newland Street	01376 502674	tic@witham.gov.uk
Woodbridge	Woodbridge Library	01394 446510/ 276770	felixstowetic@suffolkcoastal.gov.uk
Wymondham	Market Cross	01953 604721	wymondhamtic@btconnect.com

Regional Contacts and Information

For more information on accommodation, attractions, activities, events and holidays in the East of England, contact the following regional tourism organisation. Their website has a wealth of information.

East of England Tourism (01284) 727470 info@eet.org.uk www.visiteastofengland.com

Entries appear alphabetically by town name in each county. A key to symbols appears on page 7

CAMBRIDGE, Cambridgeshire *Map ref 2D1* *SatNav CB23 7DG*

★★★★
TOURING &
CAMPING PARK

Highfield Farm Touring Park

Long Road, Comberton, Cambridge CB23 7DG
T: (01223) 262308 F: (01223) 262308 E: enquiries@highfieldfarmtouringpark.co.uk
W: www.highfieldfarmtouringpark.co.uk

🚐 (60) £14.50-£24.00
🚙 (60) £14.50-£24.00
🅰 (60) £13.00-£24.00
120 touring pitches

A popular, family-run park with excellent facilities close to the University City of Cambridge and Imperial War Museum, Duxford. Ideally situated for touring East Anglia and within easy access of the Cambridge park and rides. Prices for Caravans and motorvans are based on two people with electric included. Please view our website for further information.

Directions: From Cambridge take the A1303 to Bedford. After 3 miles, left at roundabout, follow sign to Comberton. From M11 jct 12, A603 to Sandy. Then B1046 to Comberton.

Open: April to October.

Site: A🄿 Payment: € ☀ Leisure: ♪ ⏵ ∪ Children: ⚒ 🅐 Catering: 🅑 Park: 🐕 🗑 🛢 🕋 Touring: 🚽 🖒 🔌 ♪

HUNTINGDON, Cambridgeshire *Map ref 3A2* *SatNav PE28 9AJ*

★★★★
HOLIDAY, TOURING
& CAMPING PARK

Quiet Waters Caravan Park

Hemingford Abbots, Huntingdon, Cambridgeshire PE28 9AJ
T: (01480) 463405 F: (01480) 463405 E: quietwaters.park@btopenworld.com
W: www.quietwaterscaravanpark.co.uk

🚐 (18) £17.00-£21.00
🚙 (18) £17.00-£21.00
🅰 (2)   £17.00-£21.00
🚍 (9)   £310.00-£440.00
18 touring pitches

A quiet, family owned riverside park in the centre of a picturesque village. Fishing, boating & excellent walking area. Luxury holiday static caravans and touring pitches, seasonal pitches also available. Disabled facilities available. **Directions:** Junction 25 off the A14, 13 miles from Cambridge, 5 miles from Huntingdon. **Open:** 1st April to 30th October.

Site: A🄿 Payment: 🄴 ☀ Leisure: ♪ ⏵ Children: ⚒ Park: 🐕 🗑 🛢 🕋 Touring: 🚽 🖒 🔌 ♪

HUNTINGDON, Cambridgeshire *Map ref 3A2* *SatNav PE28 3DE*

★★★★★
HOLIDAY, TOURING
& CAMPING PARK

Stroud Hill Park

Fen Road, Pidley, Huntingdon, Cambridgeshire PE28 3DE
T: (01487) 741333 E: info@stroudhillpark.co.uk
W: www.stroudhillpark.co.uk

🚐 £24.00-£26.00
🚙 £24.00-£26.00
🅰 £24.00-£26.00
60 touring pitches

Stroud Hill Park is a privately owned, exclusively adult, touring caravan site in Pidley, Cambridgeshire. The quiet, attractive, rural site provides a central Cambridgeshire location for touring caravans and campers. This premier site has been awarded many industry accolades in recognition of the high standard of the on-site facilities. **Open:** All Year.

Site: 🄰🄿 Payment: 🄴 ☀ Leisure: ♪ ⏵ ⚲ Catering: ✕ 🅑 Park: 🐕 🗑 🛢 🕋 Touring: 🚽 🖒 🔌 ♪

HUNTINGDON, Cambridgeshire   Map ref 3A2   SatNav PE28 2AA

Wyton Lakes Holiday Park

enjoyEngland.com ★★★★ HOLIDAY PARK

Banks End, Wyton, Huntingdon, Cambridgeshire PE28 2AA
T: (01480) 412715 / 07785 294419 **E:** loupeter@supanet.com
W: www.wytonlakes.com

⚲ (60)	£20.00
⚲ (60)	£20.00
Å (20)	£17.00
⚑ (1)	£400.00-£500.00

80 touring pitches

Adult-only park. Some pitches beside the on-site carp and coarse-fishing lakes. River frontage. Close to local amenities. Toilet and shower block, dishwashing, laundry. 2 Bedroomed chalet for weekly hire. Excellent local bus service. **Directions:** Exit 23 off A14. Follow signs A141 March. Go past 4 roundabouts. At 4th roundabout take A1123 to St Ives. Park approx 1 mile on right. **Open:** April to October.

Payment: 🖃 Leisure: ♪ Property: 🐕 🚐 🛢

COLCHESTER, Essex   Map ref 3B2   SatNav CO5 8FE

Fen Farm Camping and Caravan Site

enjoyEngland.com ★★★★ HOLIDAY PARK

Moore Lane, East Mersea, Colchester, Essex CO5 8FE
T: (01206) 383275 **F:** (01206) 386316 **E:** havefun@fenfarm.co.uk
W: www.fenfarm.co.uk

⚲ (30)	£18.00-£30.00
⚲ (30)	£18.00-£30.00
Å (30)	£18.00-£30.00

Celebrating 90 years of camping, peaceful family run caravan & camping park on the Essex Coast. Excellent for families. Modern facilities. No hire vans. We welcome tents, tourers and motorhomes of any size. Dogs welcome. **Directions:** Follow the B1025 to Mersea, take left fork onto Island. Follow road to 'Dog and Pheasant' pub, 1st turn on right leads to Fen Farm. **Open:** March - November.

Site: Å🅿 Payment: 🖃 ☼ Leisure: ♪ ▶ Children: 🛝 🎠 Catering: 🛒 Park: 🐕 🚐 🛢 🎣 Touring: 🚿 ♻ 🗑 🎣

COLCHESTER, Essex   Map ref 3B2   SatNav CO5 8SE

Waldegraves Holiday Park

enjoyEngland.com ★★★★ HOLIDAY, TOURING & CAMPING PARK

Waldegraves Lane, West Mersea, Colchester, Essex CO5 8SE
T: (01206) 382898 **F:** (01206) 385359 **E:** holidays@waldegraves.co.uk
W: www.waldegraves.co.uk

VisitEngland Awards for Excellence 2014 BRONZE WINNER

⚲ (60)	£18.00-£35.00
⚲ (60)	£18.00-£35.00
Å (60)	£18.00-£35.00
⚑ (26)	£120.00-£750.00

60 touring pitches

Ideal family park. Private Beach. Grassland sheltered with trees and four fishing lakes, boating lake, undercover golf driving range, heated swimming pool, pitch and putt and crazy golf. Family entertainment. Licensed bar and restaurant. **Directions:** Junction 26 off A12 join B1025 to Mersea Island cross the Strood, take left to East Mersea, 2nd right. **Open:** 1st March to 30th November.

f t(witter)

Site: 🏕 Å🅿 Payment: 🖃 ☼ Leisure: ♪ ▶ ⚲ 🎿 Children: 🛝 🎠 Catering: ✗ 🛒 Park: 🐕 🎵 🚐 🛢 🎣 Touring: 🚿 ♻ 🗑 🎣

ST. LAWRENCE, Essex   Map ref 3B3   SatNav CM0 7LY

St Lawrence Holiday Park
10 Main Road, St. Lawrence Bay, Southminster CM0 7LY
T: (01621) 779434 **F:** (01621) 778311 **E:** office@slcaravans.co.uk
W: www.slcaravans.co.uk

Over the last ten years there has been major reinvestment and redevelopment of the park with the installation of a new launderette, Wi-Fi, a launching ramp for the beach and expansion of the St Lawrence Inn to include a children's room and an Indian restaurant offering fine cuisine and take-away menu. This quality graded park was a finalist in the 2010 & 2013 Caravan Park Essex Tourism awards. Please contact for 2015 rates.

Directions: On the A130 turn exit at Rettendon turnpike, take A132 towards South Woodham Ferrers. Then take the B1012 to Latchingdon. At the Church turn left into Bradwell Road, follow our brown tourism signs, though Mayland and Steeple, turn left into Main Road. The park is 1km on the right hand side.

Open: March - November.

Site: 🏕 Leisure: ♪ ► ♣ Property: 🐕 🎵 🖥 📖 Catering: ✗

Looking for something else?

The official and most comprehensive guide to independently inspected, quality-assessed accommodation.

B&Bs and Hotels - B&Bs, Hotels, farmhouses, inns, campus and hostel accommodation in England.

Self Catering - Self-catering holiday homes, approved caravan holiday homes, serviced apartments, boat accommodation and holiday cottage agenciesin England.

Camping, Touring and Holiday Parks - Touring parks, camping holidays and holiday parks and villages in Britain.

Now available in all good bookshops and online at:

www.visitor-guides.co.uk

HODDESDON, Hertfordshire   Map ref 2D1   SatNav EN11 0AS

Lee Valley Caravan Park - Dobbs Weir

Charlton Meadows, Essex Road, Hoddesdon, Hertfordshire EN11 0AS
T: (08456) 770609 E: dobbsweircampsite@leevalleypark.org.uk
W: www.visitleevalley.org.uk/wheretostay £ BOOK ONLINE

🚐 (46) £14.00-£22.00
🚍 (46) £14.00-£22.00
⛺ (138) £14.00-£22.00

Lee Valley Caravan Park, Dobbs Weir is nestled in the picturesque countryside of Hertfordshire and Essex and is perfect for a relaxing stay whether in a tent, caravan, motorhome or a pre-pitched tent! Your site fee includes free car parking near the local train station, which means you can be exploring the sights of London or Cambridge within an hour. Holiday homes are also available to purchase.

Directions: From the A10 take the Hoddesdon turn off, then at the second roundabout, turn left signposted Dobbs Weir. Lee Valley Caravan Park is on the right within 1 mile.

Open: From 1st March - 31st January.

Site: 🅰🅿 Payment: 💷 ☼ Leisure: ♿ 🎣 Children: 🐴 ⛲ Catering: 🛍 Park: 🔦 🚮 🔋 🐾 Touring: ♿ ♿ 🚰 ⚡

GREAT YARMOUTH, Norfolk   Map ref 3C1   SatNav NR29 3BL

Clippesby Hall

Hall Lane, Clippesby, Norfolk NR29 3BL
T: (01493) 367800 F: (01493) 367809 E: holidays@clippesby.com
W: www.clippesby.com £ BOOK ONLINE

🚐 (104) £16.50-£39.00
🚍 (104) £16.50-£39.00
⛺ (126) £12.50-£39.00
🏠 (4) £525.00-£1095.00
🏡 (11) £320.00-£1499.00
125 touring pitches

Clippesby Hall is a 5 star touring & camping holiday park in the heart of the Norfolk Broads, with Gold awards from David Bellamy Conservation and the Green Tourism Business Scheme. Family-friendly, with loads to do on and off site. **Directions:** From the A47, between Norwich & Great Yarmouth, take the A1064 at Acle (Caister-on-sea road), turn left at Clippesby on the B1152, turn first left. **Open:** All year (Easter - October for catering).

Site: 🅰🅿 Payment: 💷 ☼ Leisure: ♿ 🏹 🎣 Children: 🐴 ⛲ Catering: ✕ 🛍 Park: 🔦 🚮 🔋 🐾 Touring: ♿ ♿ 🚰 ⚡

GREAT YARMOUTH, Norfolk   Map ref 3C1   SatNav NR29 3QG

The Grange Touring Park

Yarmouth Road, Ormesby St Margaret, Great Yarmouth, Norfolk NR29 3QG
T: (01493) 730306 E: info@grangetouring.co.uk
W: www.grangetouring.co.uk

🚐 £12.50-£25.50
🚍 £12.50-£25.00
⛺ £12.50-£25.50
70 touring pitches

In a sylvan setting three miles north of Great Yarmouth. 70 touring/tent/motorvan level grassy pitches with lighting, made-up roadways and high standard toilet/shower/disabled facilities. Graded four star/ticks with Quality in Tourism and the AA. **Directions:** We are just five minutes drive from Great Yarmouth at the junction of the A149 and B1159. **Open:** Mid March - End September.

Site: 🅰🅿 Payment: 💷 € Leisure: ▶ Children: 🐴 ⛲ Park: 🚮 🔋 🐾 Touring: ♿ 🚰 ⚡

GREAT YARMOUTH, *Norfolk* Map ref 3C1   *SatNav NR29 3NW*

enjoyEngland.com
★★★★
HOLIDAY PARK

(133) £184.00-£699.00
(28) £269.00-£477.00

Summerfields Holiday Park

Beach Road, Scratby, Great Yarmouth NR29 3NW
T: (01692) 582277 **E:** info@richardsonsgroup.net
W: www.richardsonsholidayparks.co.uk **£ BOOK ONLINE**

Featuring an indoor heated pool with sauna, spa bath and solarium. Amusements and entertainment for children and adults. Chalet and caravan accommodation. Eight hundred yards from the beach. Children's club with Ellie the Elephant and Richie the Monkey plus evening entertainment for all the family.

Directions: Please contact us.   **Open:** April-October.

Site: ❦ Payment: 🄴 Leisure: ♣ ᠀ Property: 🐾 ♫ 🖵 🏠 Children: ⛱ 🎢 Catering: ✗

GREAT YARMOUTH, *Norfolk* Map ref 3C1   *SatNav NR30 1TB*

enjoyEngland.com
★★★★★
HOLIDAY &
TOURING PARK

(213)
(213)
(213)
(5)
(48)
(389)

213 touring pitches

Vauxhall Holiday Park

Acle New Road, Great Yarmouth, Norfolk NR30 1TB
T: (01493) 857231 **F:** (01493) 331122 **E:** info@vauxhallholidays.co.uk
W: www.vauxhall-holiday-park.co.uk **£ BOOK ONLINE**

Five star Vauxhall Holiday Park in Great Yarmouth, Norfolk is a long established holiday park offering superb accommodation, camping mega pods and touring facilities. Offers family holidays, short breaks and music weekender events. **Directions:** Please contact us for directions. **Open:** All year.

Site: ❦ 🅰🄿 Payment: 🄴 Leisure: 🚲 ▶ ♣ ᠀ ✎ Children: ⛱ 🎢 Catering: ✗ 🍖 Park: ♫ 🖵 🄱 🏠 🌧 Touring: 🚰 🚻 🔌 ♬

Sign up for our newsletter

Visit our website to sign up for our e-newsletter and receive regular information on events, articles, exclusive competitions and new publications.

www.visitor-guides.co.uk

Hemsby Beach Holiday Park

Beach Road, Hemsby, Great Yarmouth NR29 4HT
T: (01692) 582277 **E:** info@richardsonsgroup.net
W: www.richardsonsholidayparks.co.uk **£ BOOK ONLINE**

(211) £192.00-£954.00

Family holiday park with on-site facilities, children's club with loads of activities & daily entertainment. Just minutes from the sandy beach, arcades & diners on Beach Road. Hemsby Beach has acres of green lawns providing open spaces for everyone to play and never feel crowded. The facilities at Hemsby Beach include a heated pool and play areas.

Directions: Please contact us for directions.   **Open:** April to October.

Site: Payment: Leisure: Property: Children:

Searles Leisure Resort

South Beach Road, Hunstanton PE36 5BB
T: (01485) 534211 **F:** (01485) 533815 **E:** bookings@searles.co.uk
W: www.searles.co.uk **£ BOOK ONLINE**

(157)
(50)
(125)
(156)
332 touring pitches

SPECIAL PROMOTIONS
Superb themed breaks every autumn. Beauty breaks, music weekends, Turkey and Tinsel breaks. Please check website for more details.

Creating happiness for all ages. Family-run, established for fifty years, Searles has something for everyone: superb range of accommodation, award winning touring park, bars, restaurants, entertainment, swimming pools, 27 hole golf, fishing lake and more - all 200yds from a sandy beach. The ideal base for exploring the Norfolk coast. Overnight holding area available. Please contact us for prices.

Directions: From King's Lynn take the A149 to Hunstanton. Upon entering Hunstanton follow B1161 to South Beach.

Open: Touring - All year. Holiday hire - Feb to Nov.

Site: Payment: Leisure: Children: Catering:
Park: Touring:

East of England - Norfolk

MUNDESLEY, Norfolk   Map ref 3C1   SatNav NR11 8DF

Sandy Gulls Caravan Park

Cromer Road, Mundesley, Norfolk NR11 8DF
T: (01263) 720513 / 07876 594699 **E:** info@sandygulls.co.uk
W: www.sandygulls.co.uk

🚐 (40) £15.00-£26.00
�caravan (40) £12.00-£25.00
🏠 (2) £250.00-£465.00
40 touring pitches

SPECIAL PROMOTIONS
New & used holiday
caravans for sale.
Luxury caravans to hire
with panoramic sea
views.

The area's only cliff-top touring park. Located just south of Cromer. All pitches have panoramic sea views, electric/TV hook-ups. Free access to superb shower facilities. Miles of clean, sandy beaches and rural footpaths. Managed by the owning family for thirty years. Gold David Bellamy Conservation Award. Adults only.

Directions: From Cromer drive south along coast road for 5 miles.

Open: 1st March - 30th November.

Payment: € ☼ Leisure: ♪ ► ∪ Catering: ⚲ Park: 🐕 ⬛ 🛒 📶 Touring: 🚰 🕒 🚐 ⚡

NORTH RUNCTON, Norfolk   Map ref 3B1   SatNav PE33 0RA

Kings Lynn Caravan & Camping Park

New Road, North Runcton, King's Lynn, Norfolk PE33 0RA
T: (01553) 840004 **E:** klcc@btconnect.com
W: www.kl-cc.co.uk **£ BOOK ONLINE**

🚐 (150) £18.00
�caravan (150) £18.00
⛺ (150) £11.00
🏠 (4) £350.00
150 touring pitches

Set in approximately ten acres of beautiful mature parkland, the site is situated on the edge of the village of North Runcton, one mile from the Hardwick roundabout where the A47, A10, A149 and A17 meet. Situated in a prime position for touring Norfolk and the Fens, which are both Areas of Outstanding Natural Beauty, it is also the nearest campsite to the historic port and market town of Kings Lynn. Fishing, golf, riding, bowling and clay pigeon shooting are a few of the sports available locally. **Open:** All year.

Site: ⛺📶 Payment: 💷 € ☼ Leisure: ♪ ► ∪ Children: 🧒 Catering: ⚲ Park: 🐕 ⬛ 🛒 📶 Touring: 🚰 🕒 🚐 ⚡

Need more information?

Visit our websites for detailed information, up-to-date availability and to book your accommodation online. Includes over 20,000 places to stay, all of them star rated.
www.visitor-guides.co.uk

122   The Official Tourist Board Guide to **Camping, Touring & Holiday Parks 2015**

NORWICH, Norfolk — Map ref 3C1 — SatNav NR12 0EW

Cable Gap Holiday Park

Coast Road, Bacton, Norfolk NR12 0EW
T: (01692) 650667 **E:** holiday@cablegap.co.uk
W: www.cablegap.co.uk **£ BOOK ONLINE**

(1) £425.00-£710.00
(17) £205.00-£700.00

Cable Gap Holiday Park is a family run 5 star park open mid March to mid November. Situated next to the beach with some caravans enjoying a sea view. The majority of our caravans offer double glazing and central heating. **Directions:** Follow B1150 from Norwich or B1159 from Cromer. **Open:** Mid March to Mid November.

Payment: Leisure: Property: Children:

BUNGAY, Suffolk — Map ref 3C1 — SatNav NR35 1HG

Outney Meadow Caravan Park

Outney Meadow, Bungay, Suffolk NR35 1HG
T: (01986) 892338 **E:** info@outneymeadow.co.uk
W: www.outneymeadow.co.uk

(45) £14.00-£21.00
(45) £14.00-£21.00
(45) £14.00-£21.00
45 touring pitches

Easy walking distance to Bungay market town. Situated between the River Waveney (canoe trail) and golf course, ideal base for exploring the beautiful countryside. Fishing, bikes and canoes available. Overnight holding area available. **Directions:** The park entrance is signposted from the roundabout, junction A143 and A144 . **Open:** March to October.

Payment: Leisure: Children: Park: Touring:

FELIXSTOWE, Suffolk — Map ref 3C2 — SatNav IP11 2HB

Peewit Caravan Park

Walton Avenue, Felixstowe, Suffolk IP11 2HB
T: (01394) 284511 **E:** peewitpark@aol.com
W: peewitcaravanpark.co.uk

(35) £15.00-£28.00
(35) £15.00-£28.00
(10) £15.00-£33.00
(209)
45 touring pitches

Family run and operated, Peewit Caravan Park is an oasis of peace and tranquility. Situated just 900 metres from Felixstowe's seafront, a short walk from the Edwardian town centre. **Directions:** A14 to Port of Felixstowe Dock Gate 1 roundabout. Entrance 100 yards on left. Site 500 yds up driveway. **Open:** Easter or April to October.

Site: Payment: Leisure: Children: Park: Touring:

LOWESTOFT, Suffolk — Map ref 3C1 — SatNav NR33 7BQ

Pakefield Caravan Park

Arbor Lane, Pakefield, Lowestoft NR33 7BQ
T: (01502) 561136 **F:** (01502) 539264 **E:** info@pakefieldcaravanpark.co.uk
W: www.pakefieldpark.co.uk

(12)
(12)
12 touring pitches

Set on the Sunrise coast, with fantastic sea views, this park is an ideal location to explore all that Suffolk and the Norfolk coast has to offer. Please contact us for prices. **Directions:** From the A12 take the Pakefield exit and pass the water tower on left. Turn right Grayson Drive, then right down Grayson Avenue. **Open:** March - October.

Site: Payment: Leisure: Property: Children: Catering:

Don't Miss...

Chatsworth

Bakewell, Derbyshire DE45 1PP
(01246) 565300
www.chatsworth.org
Chatsworth is a spectacular historic house set in
the heart of the Peak District in Derbyshire, on the
banks of the river Derwent. There are over 30 rooms
to explore, including the magnificent Painted Hall
and Sculpture Gallery. In the garden, discover water
features, giant sculptures and beautiful flowers set in
one of Britain's most well-known historic landscapes.

Twycross Zoo

Hinckley, Leicestershire CV9 3PX
(01827) 880250
http://twycrosszoo.org
Set in more than 80 acres and renowned as a World
Primate Centre, Twycross Zoo has around 500 animals
of almost 150 species, including many endangered
animals and native species in the Zoo's Nature
Reserve. Pay a visit to meet the famous orangutans,
gorillas and chimpanzees plus many other mammals,
birds and reptiles.

Burghley House

Stamford, Lincolnshire PE9 3JY
(01780) 752451
www.burghley.co.uk
Used in films Pride and Prejudice and The Da Vinci
Code, the house boasts eighteen magnificent
State Rooms and a huge collection of works and
art, including one of the most important private
collections of 17th century Italian paintings, the
earliest inventoried collection of Japanese ceramics in
the West and wood carvings by Grinling Gibbons and
his followers.

Sherwood Forest

Sherwood Forest Visitor Centre,
Edwinstowe, Nottinghamshire NG21 9HN
www.nottinghamshire.gov.uk
Once part of a royal hunting forest and legendary
home of Robin Hood, Sherwood Forest National
Nature Reserve covers 450 acres of ancient
woodlands where veteran oaks over 500 years old
grow, as well as being home to a wide variety of flora
and fauna.

Castle Ashby Gardens

Northamptonshire NN7 1LQ
(01604) 695200
www.castleashbygardens.co.uk
A haven of tranquility and beauty in the heart of
Northamptonshire. Take your time to explore these
beautiful gardens and enjoy fascinating attractions,
from the rare breed farmyard to the historic orangery.

East Midlands

Derbyshire, Leicestershire, Lincolnshire,
Northamptonshire, Nottinghamshire, Rutland

Lincolnshire

Derbyshire

Nottinghamshire

Rutland

Leicestershire

Northamptonshire

The East Midlands is a region of historic castles and cathedrals, lavish houses, underground caves, a rich industrial heritage and spectacular countryside including the Peak District and the Lincolnshire Wolds. Climb to enchanting hilltop castles for breathtaking views. Explore medieval ruins and battlefields. Discover hidden walks in ancient forests, cycle across hills and wolds, or visit one of the regions many events and attractions.

Explore – East Midlands

Derbyshire

'There is no finer county in England than Derbyshire. To sit in the shade on a fine day and look upon verdure is the most perfect refreshment' according to Jane Austen. Derbyshire is the home of the UK's first National Park, the Peak District, which has been popular with holidaymakers for centuries. It forms the beginning of the Pennine Chain and its reservoirs and hills are second to none in beauty. This is excellent walking, riding and cycling country and contains plenty of visitor attractions and historic sites such as Gullivers Theme Park at Matlock Bath and the 17th century Palladian Chatsworth, seat of the Duke of Devonshire.

Hotspot: Speedwell Cavern and Peak District Cavern offer the chance for amazing adventures in the heart of the Peak District, with unusual rock formations, the largest natural cave entrance in the British Isles and an incredible underground boat trip. www.speedwellcavern.co.uk

Hotspot: There's plenty to keep everyone entertained at Rutland Water, with a huge range of watersports, fantastic fishing, an outdoor adventure centre and nature reserves teeming with wildlife. www.rutlandwater.org.uk

Leicestershire & Rutland

Leicester is a cathedral city with a 2000-year history, now host to a modern university and the county's pastures fuel one of its main exports: cheese. Foxton Locks is the largest flight of staircase locks on the English canal system with two 'staircases' of five locks bustling with narrowboats. Belvoir Castle in the east dominates its vale. Rockingham Castle at Market Harborough was built by William the Conqueror and stands on the edge of an escarpment giving dramatic views over five counties and the Welland Valley below. Quietly nestling in the English countryside, England's smallest county of Rutland is an idyllic rural destination with an array of unspoilt villages and two charming market towns, packed with rich history and character.

Lincolnshire

Lincolnshire is said to produce one eighth of Britain's food and its wide open meadows are testament to this. Gothic triple-towered Lincoln Cathedral is visible from the Fens for miles around, while Burghley House hosts the famous annual Horse Trials and is a top tourist attraction. The Lincolnshire Wolds, a range of hills designated an Area of Outstanding Natural Beauty and the highest area of land in eastern England between Yorkshire and Kent, is idyllic walking and cycling country

Northamptonshire

County town Northampton is famous for its shoe making, celebrated in the Central Museum and Art Gallery, and the county also has its share of stately homes and historic battlefields. Silverstone in the south is home to the British Grand Prix. Althorp was the birthplace and is now the resting place of the late Diana Princess of Wales.

Nottinghamshire

Nottingham's castle dates from 1674 and its Lace Centre illustrates the source of much of the city's wealth, alongside other fine examples of Nottinghamshire's architectural heritage such as Papplewick Hall & Gardens. Legendary tales of Robin Hood, Sherwood Forest and historic battles may be what the county is best known for, but it also hosts world class sporting events, live performances and cutting edge art, and there's plenty of shopping and fine dining on offer too. To the north, the remains of Sherwood Forest provide a welcome breathing space and there are plenty of country parks and nature reserves, including the beautiful lakes and landscape of the National Trust's Clumber Park.

Hotspot: The Newark International Antiques and Collectors Fair at Newark & Nottingham Showground is the largest event of its kind in Europe. It is the ultimate treasure hunting ground with 2,500 stands attracting thousands of dealers and buyers from around the globe. www.iacf.co.uk/newark

Indulge – East Midlands

Dine in style with a four-course lunch aboard one of the **Great Central Railway**'s First Class Restaurant Cars as a steam locomotive takes you on a leisurely journey through the Charnwood's glorious countryside. A pause on Swithland viaduct takes in the magnificent view across the reservoir to Charnwood Forest. www.gcrailway.co.uk

Enjoy a Champagne Sunset hot air balloon flight over the Peak District and the Derbyshire Dales with **Ladybird Balloons**, based in the Vale of Belvoir near Belvoir Castle and Langar Hall. (01949) 877566 or visit www.ladybirdballoons.co.uk

Indulge in lunch or a sumptuous afternoon tea at **The Dining Room at 78 Derngate** in Northampton, the beautifully restored house remodelled by the world-famous designer and architect, Charles Rennie Mackintosh in his iconic Modernist style. www.78derngate.org.uk / www.thediningroom.org

Stamford Cheese Cellar has a mouth-watering range of artisan cheeses, chutneys, jams, crackers, pâtés and sundries to tantalise your taste buds. Treat yourself to a couple of chunks of something delicious for lunch, or even a luxury hamper and a nice bottle from their selection of specialist drinks upstairs at 17 St Mary's Street, Stamford. www.stamfordcheese.com

A stone's throw from Nottingham railway station, cool and quirky **Hopkinson** is three eclectic floors of art, antiques, vintage clothes, and collectibles with a café and tea bar offering a staggering twenty-one varieties of tea. A paradise for treasure seekers, vintage lovers and curators of beautiful home aesthetics, it is housed in a restored historic building that is also home to local artists, designers and makers. www.hopkinson21.co.uk

Visit – East Midlands

🏵 Attractions with this sign participate in the Visitor Attraction Quality Assurance Scheme.

Derbyshire

Buxton Festival
July, Buxton, Derbyshire
www.buxtonfestival.co.uk
A summer celebration of the best opera, music and literature, at the heart of the beautiful Peak District.

Creswell Crags 🏵
Chesterfield, Derbyshire S80 3LH
(01909) 720378
www.creswell-crags.org.uk
A world famous archaeological site, home to Britain's only known Ice Age cave art.

Derby Museum and Art Gallery 🏵
Derby DE1 1BS
(01332) 716659
www.derbymuseums.org
Derby Museum and Art Gallery holds collections and displays relating to the history, culture and natural environment of Derby and its region.

Derbyshire Food & Drink Festival
May, Derby, Derbyshire
www.derbyshirefoodfestival.co.uk
Over 150 stalls will showcase the best local produce from Derbyshire and the Peak District region, as well as unique and exotic foods from further afield.

Gulliver's Kingdom Theme Park
Matlock Bath, Derbyshire DE4 3PG
(01629) 580540
www.gulliversfun.co.uk
With more than 40 rides & attractions, Gulliver's provides the complete family entertainment experience. Fun & adventure with Gully Mouse, Dora the explorer, Diego and "The Lost World".

Haddon Hall 🏵
Bakewell, Derbyshire DE45 1LA
(01629) 812855
www.haddonhall.co.uk
Haddon Hall is a stunning English Tudor and country house on the River Wye at Bakewell in Derbyshire, Haddon Hall is one of England's finest examples of a medieval manor.

Hardwick Hall
Chesterfield, Derbyshire S44 5QJ
(01246) 850430
www.nationaltrust.org.uk/hardwick
Owned by the National Trust, Hardwick Hall is one of Britain's greatest Elizabethan houses. The water-powered Stainsby Mill is fully functioning and the Park has a fishing lake and circular walks.

Renishaw Hall and Gardens 🏵
Dronfield, Derbyshire S21 3WB
(01246) 432310
www.renishaw-hall.co.uk
The Gardens are Italian in design and were laid out over 100 years ago by Sir George Sitwell. The garden is divided into 'rooms' with yew hedges, flanked with classical statues.

Kedleston Hall
Derby DE22 5JH
(01332) 842191
www.nationaltrust.org.uk/main/w-kedlestonhall
A fine example of a neo-classical mansion built between 1759-65 by the architect Robert Adam and set in over 800 acres of parkland and landscaped pleasure grounds. Administered by The National Trust.

The Silk Mill - Museum of Industry and History
Derby DE1 3AF
(01332) 255308
www.derbymuseums.org
The Silk Mill was completed around 1723 and the re-built Mill now contains displays on local history and industry.

Sudbury Hall
Ashbourne, Derbyshire DE6 5HT
(01283) 585305
www.nationaltrust.org.uk/sudburyhall/
Explore the grand 17th Century hall with its richly decorated interior and see life below stairs.

Leicestershire & Rutland

Artisan Cheese Fair
May, Melton Mowbray, Leicestershire
www.artisancheesefair.co.uk
A chance to taste the huge range of cheeses that are made locally and further afield.

Ashby-de-la-Zouch Castle
Leicestershire LE65 1BR
(01530) 413343
www.english-heritage.org.uk/daysout/properties/
ashby-de-la-zouch-castle
Visit Ashby-de-la-Zouch Castle where you will see the ruins of this historical castle, the original setting for many of the scenes of Sir Walter Scott's classic tale 'Ivanhoe'.

Bosworth Battlefield Heritage Centre
Market Bosworth, Leicestershire CV13 0AD
(01455) 290429
www.bosworthbattlefield.com
Delve into Leicestershire's fascinating history at Bosworth Battlefield Country Park - the site of the 1485 Battle of Bosworth.

Conkers Discovery Centre
Ashby-de-la-Zouch, Leicestershire DE12 6GA
(01283) 216633
www.visitconkers.com/thingstodo/discoverycentre
Enjoy the great outdoors and explore over 120 acres of the award winning parkland.

Easter Vintage Festival
April, Great Central Railway, Leicestershire
www.gcrailway.co.uk
A real treat for all this Easter with traction engines, classic cars and buses, fairground rides, trade stands, a beer tent as well as lots of action on the double track.

Great Central Railway
Leicester LE11 1RW
(01509) 230726
www.gcrailway.co.uk
The Great Central Railway is Britain's only double track main line steam railway. Enjoy an exciting calendar of events, a footplate ride or dine in style on board one of the steam trains.

National Space Centre
Leicester LE4 5NS
(0845) 605 2001
www.spacecentre.co.uk
The award winning National Space Centre is the UK's largest attraction dedicated to space. From the moment you catch sight of the Space Centre's futuristic Rocket Tower, you'll be treated to hours of breathtaking discovery & interactive fun.

Twinlakes Theme Park
Melton Mowbray, Leicestershire LE14 4SB
(01664) 567777
www.twinlakespark.co.uk
Twinlakes Theme Park - packed with variety, fun and endless adventures for every member of your family.

Lincolnshire

Ayscoughfee Hall Museum and Gardens
Spalding, Lincolnshire PE11 2RA
(01775) 764555
www.ayscoughfee.org
Ayscoughfee Hall Museum is housed in a beautiful wool merchant's house built in 1451 on the banks of the River Welland.

Belton House
Belton, Lincolnshire NG32 2LS
(01476) 566116
www.nationaltrust.org.uk/main/w-beltonhouse
Belton, is a perfect example of an English Country House.

Burghley Horse Trials
September, Burghley House, Lincolnshire
www.burghley-horse.co.uk
One of the most popular events in the British equestrian calendar.

Doddington Hall
Lincoln LN6 4RU
(01522) 694308
www.doddingtonhall.com
A superb Elizabethan mansion by the renowned architect Robert Smythson. The hall stands today as it was completed in 1600 with walled courtyards, turrets and gatehouse.

Hardys Animal Farm
Ingoldmells, Lincolnshire PE25 1LZ
(01754) 872267
www.hardysanimalfarm.co.uk
An enjoyable way to learn about the countryside and how a farm works. There are animals for the children to enjoy as well as learning about the history and traditions of the countryside.

Lincolnshire Show
June, Lincolnshire Showground
www.lincolnshireshow.co.uk
Agriculture remains at the heart of the Lincolnshire Show with livestock and equine competitions, machinery displays and the opportunity to find out where your food comes from and to taste it too!

Lincolnshire Wolds Walking Festival
May, Louth, Lincolnshire
www.woldswalkingfestival.co.uk
Over 90 walks, taking place in an Area of Outstanding Natural Beauty and surrounding countryside.

Normanby Hall Museum and Country Park
Scunthorpe, Lincolnshire DN15 9HU
(01724) 720588
www.normanbyhall.co.uk
Normanby Hall is a classic English mansion set in 300 acres of gardens, parkland, deer park, woods, ornamental and wild birds, with a well-stocked gift shop.

RAF Waddington Air Show
July, Waddington, Lincoln, Lincolnshire
www.waddingtonairshow.co.uk
The largest of all RAF air shows, regularly attended by over 150,000 visitors.

Tattershall Castle
Lincolnshire LN4 4LR
(01526) 342543
www.nationaltrust.org.uk/tattershall-castle
Tattershall Castle was built in the 15th Century to impress and dominate by Ralph Cromwell, one of the most powerful men in England. The castle is a dramatic red brick tower.

Northamptonshire

Althorp
Northampton NN7 4HQ
(01604) 770107
www.althorp.com
Come and visit one of England's finest country houses, home of the Spencer family for over 500 years and ancestral home of Diana, Princess of Wales.

British Grand Prix
July, Silverstone, Northamptonshire
www.silverstone.co.uk
The only place in the UK to see the world's best Formula One drivers in action.

Lamport Hall and Gardens
Northamptonshire NN6 9HD
(01604) 686272
www.lamporthall.co.uk
Grade 1 listed building that was home to the Isham family and their collections for over four centuries.

National Waterways Museum - Stoke Bruerne
Towcester, Northamptonshire NN12 7SE
(01604) 862229
www.stokebruernecanalmuseum.org.uk
Stoke Bruerne is an ideal place to explore the story of our waterways.

Northampton Museum & Art Gallery
Northampton NN1 1DP
(01604) 838111
www.northampton.gov.uk/museums
Displays include footwear and related items, paintings, ceramics and glass and the history of Northampton.

Prebendal Manor Medieval Centre
Nassington, Northamptonshire PE8 6QG
(01780) 782575
www.prebendal-manor.co.uk
Visit a unique medieval manor and enjoy the largest recreated medieval gardens in Europe.

Rockingham Castle
Market Harborough, Northamptonshire LE16 8TH
(01536) 770240
www.rockinghamcastle.com
Rockingham Castle stands on the edge of an escarpment giving dramatic views over five counties and the Welland Valley below.

Salcey Forest
Hartwell, Northamptonshire NN17 3BB
(01780) 444920
www.forestry.gov.uk/salceyforest
Get a birds eye view of this wonderful woodland on the tremendous Tree Top Way.

Sulgrave Manor
Northamptonshire OX17 2SD
(01295) 760205
www.sulgravemanor.org.uk
A Tudor manor house and garden, the ancestral home of George Washington's family with authentic furniture shown by friendly guides

Wicksteed Park
Kettering, Northamptonshire NN15 6NJ
(01536) 512475
www.wicksteedpark.co.uk
Wicksteed Park remains Northamptonshire's most popular attraction and entertainment venue.

Nottinghamshire

Armed Forces Weekend
June, Wollaton Park, Nottingham, Nottinghamshire
www.experiencenottinghamshire.com
*Nottingham welcomes the annual national event
celebrating our Armed Forces past and present.*

Festival of Words
Nottingham, Nottinghamshire
www. nottwords.org.uk
*Celebrating Nottingham's love of words, this dazzling
line up of events and diverse range of host venues pay a
fitting tribute to Nottinghamshire's rich literary heritage.*

Galleries of Justice Museum

Nottingham NG1 1HN
(0115) 952 0555
www.galleriesofjustice.org.uk
*You will be delving in to the dark and disturbing past
of crime and punishment.*

GameCity
October, Nottingham,
Nottinghamshire
www.gamecity.org
*GameCity is the largest festival
dedicated to the videogame
culture in Europe.*

Holme Pierrepont Country Park
Newark, Nottinghamshire NG24 1BG
(01636) 655765
www.newark-sherwood.gov.uk
*Set in 270 acres of beautiful parkland and home to
the National Watersports Centre. With excellent water
sports facilities, Family Fun Park, Life Fitness Gym and
marvellous nature trails for cycling and walking,*

Newark Castle
Holme Pierrepont, Nottinghamshire NG12 2LU
(0115) 982 1212
www.nwscnotts.com
*At the heart of the town for many centuries the castle
has played an important role in historical events.*

Newark Air Museum

Nottinghamshire NG24 2NY
(01636) 707170
www.newarkairmuseum.org
*The museum is open to the public every day except
December 24th, 25th, 26th and January 1st.*

Nottingham Castle

Nottingham NG1 6EL
(0115) 915 3700
www.nottinghamcity.gov.uk/museums
*Situated on a high rock, Nottingham Castle commands
spectacular views over the city and once rivalled the
great castles of Windsor and the Tower of London.*

Nottinghamshire County Show
May, Newark Showground, Nottinghamshire
www.newarkshowground.com
*A fantastic traditional county show promoting
farming, food, rural life and heritage in
Nottinghamshire and beyond.*

Papplewick Hall & Gardens
Nottinghamshire NG15 8FE
(0115) 963 3491
www.papplewickhall.co.uk
*A fine Adam house, built in 1787 and Grade I listed
building with a park and woodland garden.*

Robin Hood Beer Festival
October, Nottingham Castle, Nottinghamshire
www.beerfestival.nottinghamcamra.org
*Set in the stunning grounds of Nottingham Castle,
the Robin Hood Beer Festival offers the world's
largest selection of real ales and ciders.*

Robin Hood Festival
August, Sherwood Forest, Nottinghamshire
www.nottinghamshire.gov.uk/robinhoodfestival
*Celebrate our most legendary outlaw in Sherwood
Forest's medieval village.*

Sherwood Forest Country Park
Nottinghamshire NG21 9HN
(01623) 823202
www.nottinghamshire.gov.uk/sherwoodforestcp
*Sherwood Forest Country Park covers 450 acres
and incorporates some truly ancient areas of
native woodland.*

Sherwood Forest Farm Park
Nottinghamshire NG21 9HL
(01623) 823558
www.sherwoodforestfarmpark.co.uk
*Meet over 30 different rare farm breeds, plus other
unusual species!*

Sherwood Pines Forest Park

Edwinstowe, Nottinghamshire NG21 9JL
(01623) 822447
www.forestry.gov.uk/sherwoodpines
*The largest forest open to the public in the
East Midlands and centre for a wide variety of
outdoor activities.*

Tourist Information Centres

When you arrive at your destination, visit the Tourist Information Centre for quality assured help with accommodation and information about local attractions and events, or email your request before you go.

Ashbourne	13 Market Place	01335 343666	ashbourneinfo@derbyshiredales.gov.uk
Ashby-de-la-Zouch	North Street	01530 411767	ashby.tic@nwleicestershire.gov.uk
Bakewell	Old Market Hall	01629 813227	bakewell@peakdistrict.gov.uk
Boston	Boston Guildhall	01205 356656/ 720006	ticboston@boston.gov.uk
Buxton	The Pavilion Gardens	01298 25106	tourism@highpeak.gov.uk
Castleton	Buxton Road	01433 620679	castleton@peakdistrict.gov.uk
Chesterfield	Rykneld Square	01246 345777	tourism@chesterfield.gov.uk
Derby	Assembly Rooms	01332 643411	tourism@derby.gov.uk
Glossop	Glossop One Stop Shop	0845 1297777	
Grantham	The Guildhall Centre, Council Offices	01476 406166	granthamtic@southkesteven.gov.uk
Horncastle	Wharf Road	01507 601111	horncastle.info@cpbs.com
Kettering	Municipal Offices	01536 315115	tic@kettering.gov.uk
Leicester	51 Gallowtree Gate	0844 888 5181	info@goleicestershire.com
Lincoln Castle Hill	9 Castle Hill	01522 545458	visitorinformation@lincolnbig.co.uk
Loughborough	Loughborough Town Hall	01509 231914	loughborough@goleicestershire.com
Louth	Cannon Street	01507 601111	louth.info@cpbs.com
Mablethorpe	Louth Hotel, Unit 5	01507 474939	mablethorpeinfo@e-lindsey.gov.uk
Melton Mowbray	The Library, Wilton Road	0116 305 3646	
Newark	Keepers Cottage, Riverside Park	01636 655765	newarktic@nsdc.info
Northampton	Sessions House, County Hall	01604 367997/8	tic@northamptonshire.gov.uk
Nottingham City	1-4 Smithy Row	08444 775 678	tourist.information@nottinghamcity.gov.uk
Retford	40 Grove Street	01777 860780	retford.tourist@bassetlaw.gov.uk
Rutland Water	Sykes Lane	01780 686800	tic@anglianwater.co.uk
Sherwood	Sherwood Heath	01623 824545	sherwoodtic@nsdc.info
Silverstone	Silverstone Circuit	0844 3728 200	Elicia.Bonamy@silverstone.co.uk
Spalding	South Holland Centre	01775 725468/ 764777	touristinformationcentre@sholland.gov.uk
Stamford	Stamford Tourist Information	01780 755611	stamfordtic@southkesteven.gov.uk
Swadlincote	Sharpe's Pottery Museum	01283 222848	gail.archer@sharpespotterymusuem.org.uk
Woodhall Spa	The Cottage Museum	01526 353775	woodhall.spainfo@cpbs.com

Regional Contacts and Information

For more information on accommodation, attractions, activities, events and holidays in the East Midlands, contact one of the following regional or local tourism organisations. Their websites have a wealth of information and many produce free publications to help you get the most out of your visit.

East Midlands Tourism
www.eastmidlandstourism.com

Experience Nottinghamshire
www.experiencenottinghamshire.com

Peak District and Derbyshire
www.visitpeakdistrict.com

Discover Rutland
(01572) 722577
www.discover-rutland.co.uk

Lincolnshire
(01522) 545458
www.visitlincolnshire.com

VisitNorthamptonshire
www.visitnorthamptonshire.co.uk

Leicestershire
0844 888 5181
www.goleicestershire.com

Entries appear alphabetically by town name in each county. A key to symbols appears on page 7

ALSOP-EN-LE-DALE, Derbyshire   Map ref 4B2   SatNav DE6 1QU

enjoyEngland.com
★★★★
HOLIDAY, TOURING & CAMPING PARK

Rivendale Caravan & Leisure Park
Buxton Road, Nr Alsop En Le Dale, Ashbourne DE6 1QU
T: (01335) 310311 F: (01335) 310100 E: enquiries@rivendalecaravanpark.co.uk
W: www.rivendalecaravanpark.co.uk £ BOOK ONLINE

🚐 (81)	£18.50-£26.00
🚏 (81)	£19.00-£27.00
🛆 (30)	£18.00-£26.00
🏠 (12)	£40.00-£90.00
🚏 (2)	£490.00-£910.00

111 touring pitches

SPECIAL PROMOTIONS
Stay Sunday - Thursday & get 5 nights for the price of 4.

Surrounded by spectacular Peak District scenery, convenient for Alton Towers, Chatsworth, Dove Dale and Carsington Water. Ideal for cyclists and ramblers with the Tissington Trail 100 metres away and footpaths running directly from site into Dove Dale. Choice of pitch surfaces. Yurts, Camping Pods, accessible Pine Lodges & bedroom suites. Fly fishing lake. Overnight holding area.

Directions: From A515, Rivendale is situated 6.5 miles north of Ashbourne, directly off the A515 Buxton road on the right-hand side, travelling north.

Open: All year except 3rd Jan - 28th Jan.

Site: 🅿 Payment: 💳 ☼ Leisure: ⛱ ♪ ∪ Children: ⛱ ⚠ Catering: ✗ 🛒 Park: 🐾 🚬 🗑 🎮 📷
Touring: 🚰 🕒 🔌 ♨

ASHBOURNE, Derbyshire   Map ref 4B2   SatNav DE6 2AQ

enjoyEngland.com
★★★★
HOLIDAY PARK

Sandybrook Country Park
Buxton Road, Ashbourne, Derbyshire DE6 2AQ
T: (01335) 300000 F: (01335) 342679 E: enquiries@sandybrook.co.uk
W: www.sandybrook.co.uk

🏠 (51) £365.00-£1589.00

Award winning Sandybrook Country Park has fantastic facilities including a swimming pool, restaurant and children's play area. Many of our luxury lodges include a private hot tub and the park is close to the picturesque market town of Ashbourne and Alton Towers. With its breathtaking views, Sandybrook is an ideal location for exploring the Peak District with an abundance of walks and cycle routes in the local area. **Open:** All year.

Site: 🅿 Payment: 💳 Leisure: ⛱ ▶ 🎣 ☂ ✎ Property: 🐾 🚬 🗑 🎮 Children: ⛱ ⚠ Catering: ✗ 🛒

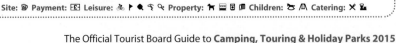

BUXTON, Derbyshire   Map ref 4B2

SatNav SK17 9TQ

Beech Croft Farm Caravan & Camping Park

Blackwell-in-the-Peak, Nr Buxton, Derbyshire SK17 9TQ
T: (01298) 85330 **E:** mail@beechcroftfarm.co.uk
W: www.beechcroftfarm.co.uk

🚐 (30)   £20.00-£22.50
🚍 (30)   £20.00-£22.50
⛺ (40)   £6.00-£16.00
30 touring pitches

SPECIAL PROMOTIONS
October - 'Reduced Season Rates for Tents' Please contact for details.

In the heart of the Peak District, Beech Croft is a small family run site, alongside their small sheep farm. Southerly facing with views towards the rolling Derbyshire hills. On the Pennine Bridleway with Monsal Trail & Limestone Way close by. All hardstandings have 16 amp EHU, water tap and TV aerial socket. Environmentally friendly underfloor heated toilet & shower block. Free Wi-Fi.

Directions: Midway between Buxton & Bakewell being 6 miles to each town. Signposted & easily accessible from the A6.   **Open:** All year.

Site: 🅰️🅿️ **Payment:** 💷 ☼ **Children:** 🧸 **Catering:** 🍴 **Park:** 🐕 🖥️ 🗑️ 🚿 **Touring:** 📶 🔌 🍽️

BUXTON, Derbyshire   Map ref 4B2

SatNav SK17 0DT

Newhaven Caravan and Camping Park

Newhaven, Buxton SK17 0DT
T: (01298) 84300 **F:** (01332) 726027 **E:** newhavencaravanpark@btconnect.com
W: www.newhavencaravanpark.co.uk

🚐 (73)   £15.25-£19.75
🚍 (14)   £15.25-£19.75
⛺ (30)   £11.50-£19.75
95 touring pitches

Halfway between Ashbourne and Buxton in the Peak District National Park. Well-established park with modern facilities, close to the Tissington and High Peak trails, local towns and villages, historic houses and Derbyshire Dales. **Directions:** Half way between Ashbourne and Buxton on the A515 at junction with A5012. **Open:** March to October.

Site: 🅰️🅿️ **Payment:** 💷 ☼ **Leisure:** ♪ **Children:** 🧸 ⚠️ **Catering:** 🍴 **Park:** 🐕 🗑️ 🚿 **Touring:** 📶 🔌 🍽️

MATLOCK, Derbyshire   Map ref 4B2

SatNav DE4 5LN

Darwin Forest Country Park

Darley Moor, Two Dales, Matlock, Derbyshire DE4 5LN
T: (01629) 732428 **F:** (01629) 735015 **E:** enquiries@darwinforest.co.uk
W: www.darwinforest.co.uk

🏠 (110) £402.00-£1899.00

Award winning Darwin Forest provides the perfect base for exploring the stunning Derbyshire Peak District. Many of our luxury lodges include a private hot tub and our fabulous on-site facilities include a swimming pool, spa, gym, indoor and outdoor play areas and an award winning restaurant. Our 5 star park is close to Chatsworth House and an abundance of spectacular walking and cycling routes. **Open:** All year.

Site: 🏠 **Payment:** 💷 **Leisure:** 🏊 ▶ 🎣 🎿 🎱 **Children:** 🧸 ⚠️ **Catering:** ✕ 🍴 **Park:** 🐕 🖥️ 🗑️ 📻

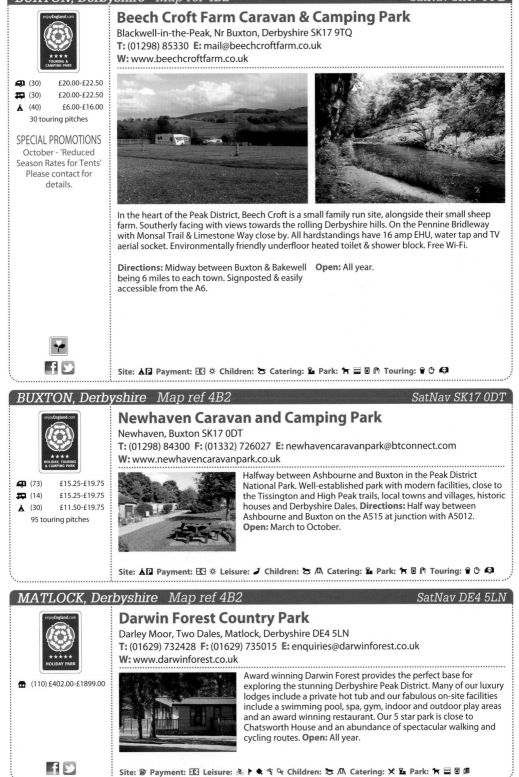

ANDERBY, Lincolnshire Map ref 4D2

SatNav PE24 5YB

TOURING & CAMPING PARK ★★★

Manor Farm Caravan Park

Sea Road, Anderby, Skegness PE24 5YB
T: (01507) 490372 **E:** manorfarmtina@aol.com
W: www.manorfarmcaravanpark.co.uk

🚐 (130)
🚏 (10)
▲ (50)
140 touring pitches

A peaceful and relaxed atmosphere await those who choose our park as their base to enjoy the East Coast and surrounding countryside. Overnight holding area available. Please contact us for prices. **Directions:** Turn right off A52 Skegness to Mablethorpe into Anderby 1.5 miles on the left. **Open:** March to November.

Site: ▲🅿 Payment: 💷 ☼ Leisure: ♪ ⏵ ∪ Children: 🛝 🎢 Park: 🐕 🔲 📷 Touring: 🚻 🔌 🎣

LINCOLN, Lincolnshire Map ref 4C2

SatNav LN6 0EY

TOURING PARK ★★★

Hartsholme Country Park

Skellingthorpe Road, Lincoln LN6 0EY
T: (01522) 873578 **E:** hartsholmecp@lincoln.gov.uk
W: www.lincoln.gov.uk/hartsholmecampsite

🚐 £15.60-£22.00
🚏 £15.60-£22.00
▲ (8) £8.60-£18.00
26 touring pitches

Our 3 star English Tourism rated site offers flat, level grassy pitches set in mature wooded parkland. Easy access to city centre and local attractions. **Directions:** Main entrance is on the B1378 (Skellingthorpe Road). It is signposted from the A46 (Lincoln Bypass) and from the B1003 (Tritton Road). **Open:** 1st March to 31st October.

Payment: 💷 ☼ Leisure: ♪ Children: 🛝 🎢 Catering: ✕ 🛒 Park: 🐕 📷 Touring: 🚻 🔌

SKEGNESS, Lincolnshire Map ref 4D2

SatNav PE24 4RE

TOURING PARK ★★★

Pine Trees Leisure Park

Croft Bank, Skegness, Lincolnshire PE24 4RE
T: (01754) 762949 **E:** enquiries@pinetreesholidays.co.uk
W: www.pinetreesholidays.co.uk

🚐 (170) £13.00-£29.00
🚏 (170) £13.00-£29.00
▲ (170) £13.00-£29.00
🏠 (8) £190.00-£400.00

Pine Trees is a quiet facility for tents, touring caravans, camper vans and self-catering cottages. Pine Trees has central heating, amenity blocks including social club with licensed bar and a 1.5 acre fishing lake. **Open:** 1st March - November 30th

[f]

Site: 📶 ▲🅿 Payment: 💷 ☼ Leisure: ♪ ⏵ 🔍 Children: 🛝 🎢 Catering: ✕ 🛒 Park: 🐕 🎵 🔲 📷 Touring: 🚻 🚰 🔌

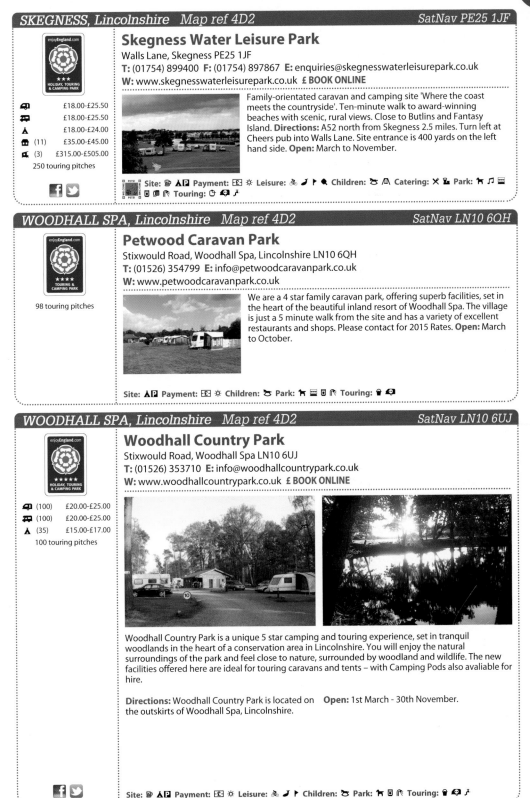

SKEGNESS, Lincolnshire   Map ref 4D2
SatNav PE25 1JF

enjoyEngland.com
★★★
HOLIDAY, TOURING
& CAMPING PARK

Skegness Water Leisure Park
Walls Lane, Skegness PE25 1JF
T: (01754) 899400 F: (01754) 897867 E: enquiries@skegnesswaterleisurepark.co.uk
W: www.skegnesswaterleisurepark.co.uk £ BOOK ONLINE

🚐		£18.00-£25.50
🚚		£18.00-£25.50
⛺		£18.00-£24.00
🏠	(11)	£35.00-£45.00
🛏	(3)	£315.00-£505.00

250 touring pitches

Family-orientated caravan and camping site 'Where the coast meets the countryside'. Ten-minute walk to award-winning beaches with scenic, rural views. Close to Butlins and Fantasy Island. **Directions:** A52 north from Skegness 2.5 miles. Turn left at Cheers pub into Walls Lane. Site entrance is 400 yards on the left hand side. **Open:** March to November.

Site: **Payment:** ☼ **Leisure:** **Children:** **Catering:** **Park:** **Touring:**

WOODHALL SPA, Lincolnshire   Map ref 4D2
SatNav LN10 6QH

enjoyEngland.com
★★★★
TOURING &
CAMPING PARK

Petwood Caravan Park
Stixwould Road, Woodhall Spa, Lincolnshire LN10 6QH
T: (01526) 354799 E: info@petwoodcaravanpark.co.uk
W: www.petwoodcaravanpark.co.uk

98 touring pitches

We are a 4 star family caravan park, offering superb facilities, set in the heart of the beautiful inland resort of Woodhall Spa. The village is just a 5 minute walk from the site and has a variety of excellent restaurants and shops. Please contact for 2015 Rates. **Open:** March to October.

Site: **Payment:** ☼ **Children:** **Park:** **Touring:**

WOODHALL SPA, Lincolnshire   Map ref 4D2
SatNav LN10 6UJ

enjoyEngland.com
★★★★★
HOLIDAY, TOURING
& CAMPING PARK

Woodhall Country Park
Stixwould Road, Woodhall Spa LN10 6UJ
T: (01526) 353710 E: info@woodhallcountrypark.co.uk
W: www.woodhallcountrypark.co.uk £ BOOK ONLINE

🚐	(100)	£20.00-£25.00
🚚	(100)	£20.00-£25.00
⛺	(35)	£15.00-£17.00

100 touring pitches

Woodhall Country Park is a unique 5 star camping and touring experience, set in tranquil woodlands in the heart of a conservation area in Lincolnshire. You will enjoy the natural surroundings of the park and feel close to nature, surrounded by woodland and wildlife. The new facilities offered here are ideal for touring caravans and tents – with Camping Pods also avaliable for hire.

Directions: Woodhall Country Park is located on the outskirts of Woodhall Spa, Lincolnshire.   **Open:** 1st March - 30th November.

Site: **Payment:** ☼ **Leisure:** **Children:** **Park:** **Touring:**

Don't Miss...

Alton Towers
Alton, Staffordshire, ST10 4DB
0871 222 3330
www.altontowers.com
Alton Towers Resort is an exciting destination, with tons of terrific rides, blockbusting attractions, amazing live shows, weird and wonderful costume characters and much more. There's something for the whole family to enjoy!

Dudley Zoological Gardens
Dudley, West Midlands DY1 4QB
(01384) 215313
www.dudleyzoo.org.uk
From lions and tigers to snakes and spiders there's something for all ages. Animal feeding, encounters, face painting, land train and fair rides.

Iron Bridge and Toll House
Telford, Shropshire TF8 7DG
(01952) 433424
www.ironbridge.org.uk
The Ironbridge Gorge is a remarkable and beautiful insight into the region's industrial heritage. Ten award-winning Museums spread along the valley beside the wild River Severn - still spanned by the world's first Iron Bridge, where you can peer through the railings and conjure a vision of sailing vessels heading towards Bristol and the trading markets of the world.

Shakespeare's Birthplace Trust
Stratford-upon-Avon, Warwickshire CV37 6QW
www.shakespeare.org.uk
A unique Shakespeare experience with outstanding archive and library collections, inspiring educational and literary event programmes and five wonderful houses all directly relating to Shakespeare. Shakespeare's Birthplace itself is a fascinating house that offers a tantalising glimpse into Shakespeare's early world.

Warwick Castle
Warwickshire CV34 4QU
0871 265 2000
www.warwick-castle.co.uk
Battlements, towers, turrets, History, magic, myth and adventure - Warwick Castle is a Scheduled Ancient Monument and Grade 1 listed building packed with things to do, inside and out.

Heart of England

Herefordshire, Shropshire, Staffordshire,
Warwickshire, West Midlands, Worcestershire

Staffordshire

Shropshire

West
Midlands

Warwick-   Worcestershire   shire

Herefordshire

The Heart of England: a name that defines this lovely part of the country so
much better than its geographical name: The Midlands. Like a heart it has
many arteries and compartments, from the March counties of Shropshire
and Herefordshire, through Birmingham and the West Midlands, birthplace
of the Industrial revolution. It is a region rich in history and character and
you'll find pretty villages, grand castles and plenty of canals and waterways
to explore.

Explore – Heart of England

Coventry & Warwickshire

From castles and cathedrals to art galleries, museums and exciting events, this region captivates visitors from all over the world.

A beautifully preserved Tudor town on the banks of the Avon and Warwickshire's most visited, Stratford-upon-Avon is the bard's birthplace with numerous theatres playing Shakespeare and other dramatists' work. The city of Warwick is dominated by its 14th century castle and its museums, and plenty of family activities are staged throughout the year. Historic Coventry has over 400 listed buildings and is most famous for its cathedrals, with the modern Church of St Michael sitting majestically next to the 'blitzed' ruins of its 14th century predecessor.

Herefordshire

Herefordshire's ruined castles in the border country and Iron Age and Roman hill-forts recall a turbulent battle-scarred past. Offa's Dyke, constructed by King Offa of Mercia in the 8th century marks the border with Wales but today the landscape is peaceful, with delightful small towns and villages and Hereford cattle grazing in pastures beside apple orchards and hop gardens.

Hereford has an 11th century cathedral and the Mappa Mundi while in the west, the Wye meanders through meadows and valleys. Hay-on-Wye is now best known for its annual Book Festival and plethora of second hand bookshops.

Staffordshire

Staffordshire, squeezed between the Black Country to the south and Manchester to the north, is home to the Potteries, a union of six towns made famous by Wedgwood, Spode and other ceramic designers. Lichfield has a magnificent three-spired 13th century cathedral and was birthplace of Samuel Johnson.

The unspoilt ancient heathland of Cannock Chase, leafy woodlands of the National Forest and secluded byways of South Staffordshire all offer the chance to enjoy the great outdoors.

Shropshire

Tucked away on the England/Wales border, Shropshire is another March county that saw much conflict between English and Welsh, hostilities between warring tribes and invading Romans.

The Wrekin and Stretton Hills were created by volcanoes and in the south the Long Mynd rises to 1700 ft with panoramic views of much of the Severn plain. Ironbridge, near the present day Telford, is said to be where the Industrial Revolution started in Britain. County town Shrewsbury was an historic fortress town built in a loop of the river Severn and these days joins Ludlow, with its 11th century castle, as one of the gastronomic high spots of Britain.

Hotspot: The British Ironwork Centre at Oswestry is a treasure trove of magnificent animal sculptures and decorations, including of a 13ft-high gorilla made from an incredible 40,000+ spoons donated by people from all over the world.
www.britishironworkcentre.co.uk

West Midlands

The Industrial revolution of the 19th century led to the growth of Birmingham into Britain's second city - the city of a thousand trades. Its prosperity was based on factories, hundreds of small workshops and a network of canals, all of which helped in the production of everything from needles and chocolate to steam engines and bridges. Nowadays the city has one of the best concert halls in Europe, excellent shopping and a regenerated waterside café culture.

The West Midlands is an urban area, criss-crossed by motorways, and still represents the powerhouse of Central Britain. Wolverhampton has been called Capital of the Black Country, made famous through its ironwork and Walsall, birthplace of Jerome K Jerome, has three museums.

Hotspot: Visit the 15 acres of ornamental gardens and glasshouses at Birmingham Botanical Gardens and Glasshouses in Edgbaston. www.birminghambotanicalgardens.org.uk

Affluent Sutton Coldfield and Solihull have proud civic traditions and a number of pretty parks including Sutton Park and Brueton Park. Many of Solihull's rural villages sit along the Stratford-upon-Avon canal and offer plenty of picturesque pubs along the tow path from which to watch the gentle meander of passing narrow boats.

Worcestershire

The beautiful county of Worcestershire has a fantastic selection of historic houses and gardens to discover and Worcester itself has a famous cathedral, cricket ground, and 15th century Commandery, now a Civil war museum.

Hotspot: Ride the Severn Valley Railway for a 16 mile long, steam powered journey through the breathtaking landscape of the Severn Valley from Kidderminister all the way to Bridgnorth in Shropshire. www.svr.co.uk

Great Malvern, still a Spa town, is famous as the birthplace of Sir Edward Elgar, who drew much of his inspiration from this countryside and who is celebrated at the annual Malvern Festival. The old riverside market town of Evesham is the centre of the Vale of Evesham fruit and vegetable growing area which, with the tranquil banks of the river Avon and the undulating hills and peaceful wooded slopes of the Cotswolds, offers some of the prettiest landscapes in the country.

Droitwich, known in Roman times as Salinae, still has briny water in its spa baths and can trace the origins of salt extraction in the area back to prehistoric times, it even holds an annual Salt Festival to celebrate this unique heritage.

Indulge – Heart of England

Enjoy a romantic cruise along the **River Avon** at Stratford-upon-Avon on a traditional Edwardian passenger launch. Cruise downstream from the Bancroft gardens past the Royal Shakespeare Theatre and Holy Trinity Church (the site of Shakespeare's tomb) before turning around and passing under the 15th Century Clopton Bridge to discover quiet river-banks and meadows. www.avon-boating.co.uk

Dine in style at **Harry's Restaurant** at The Chase Hotel, a magnificent georgian country house hotel set in 11 acres of award-winning parkland on the outskirts of Ross-on-Wye. (01989) 768330, www.chasehotel.co.uk

In the quaint, sleepy town of Church Stretton lies one of the best delicatessens in Britain. **Van Doesburg's** deli serves gourmet treats all made on the premises and the desserts are incredible. 3 High Street, Church Stretton, Shropshire. www.vandoesburgs.co.uk

Cadbury World, at the historic Bourneville village near Birmingham, tells the mouth-watering story of Cadbury's chocolate and includes chocolate-making demonstrations with free samples, attractions for all ages, free parking, shop and restaurant. Phone to check availability and book admission. 0845 450 3599 www.cadburyworld.co.uk

Arts and crafts lovers can indulge in a spot of shopping for unusual gifts and artworks at the delightful **Jinney Ring Craft Centre** in Hanbury near Redditch. A range of craftspeople work on site and there's a quirky gift shop and gallery, as well as a daytime restaurant in a rustic old barn, and all set in lovely gardens with duck ponds and stunning views across to the Malvern Hills. www.jinneyring.co.uk

Visit – Heart of England

Attractions with this sign participate in the Visitor Attraction Quality Assurance Scheme.

Coventry & Warwickshire

Coventry Cathedral - St Michael's
West Midlands CV1 5AB
(024) 7652 1257
www.coventrycathedral.org.uk
Glorious 20th century Cathedral, with stunning 1950's art & architecture, rising above the stark ruins of the medieval Cathedral destroyed by German air raids in 1940.

Compton Verney
Stratford-upon-Avon CV35 9HZ
(01926) 645500
www.comptonverney.org.uk
Award-winning art gallery housed in a grade I listed Robert Adam mansion.

Festival of Motoring
August, Stoneleigh, Warwickshire
www.festival-of-motoring.co.uk
This major event takes place at Stoneleigh Park in Warwickshire. In addition to hundreds of fantastic cars to look at, there will be the traditional historic vehicle 'run' through delightful Warwickshire countryside, car gymkhanas and auto tests.

Godiva Festival
July, Coventry, Warwickshire
www.godivafestival.com
The Godiva Festival is the UK's biggest free family festival held over a weekend in the War Memorial Park, Coventry. The event showcases some of the finest local, national and International artists, live comedy, family entertainment, Godiva Carnival, and lots more.

Heart Park
Fillongley, Warwickshire CV7 8DX
(01676) 540333
www.heartpark.co.uk
"We believe that the heart of our Park is the beach and lake. But for those of you who'd like to try out a few 'different' activities - we've got a great assortment for you to try."

Heritage Open Days
September, Coventry, Warwickshire
www.coventry.gov.uk/hod
Heritage Open Days celebrate England's architecture and culture by allowing visitors free access to interesting properties that are either not usually open or would normally charge an entrance fee. Heritage Open Days also include tours, events and activities that focus on local architecture and culture.

Kenilworth Castle and Elizabethan Garden
Warwickshire CV8 1NE
(01926) 852078
www.english-heritage.org.uk/kenilworth
One of the most spectacular castle ruins in England.

Packwood House
Solihull, Warwickshire B94 6AT
0844 800 1895
www.nationaltrust.org.uk/main/w-packwoodhouse
Restored tudor house, park and garden with notable topiary.

Ragley Hall
Stratford-upon-Avon, Warwickshire B49 5NJ
(01789) 762090
www.ragley.co.uk
Ragley Hall is set in 27 acres of beautiful formal gardens.

Ryton Pools Country Parks
Coventry, Warwickshire CV8 3BH
(024) 7630 5592
www.warwickshire.gov.uk/parks
The 100 acres of Ryton Pools Country Park are just waiting to be explored. The many different habitats are home to a wide range of birds and other wildlife.

Stratford River Festival
July, Stratford, Warwickshire
www.stratfordriverfestival.co.uk
The highly successful Stratford-upon-Avon River Festival brings the waterways of Stratford alive, with boatloads of family fun, on the first weekend of July.

Three Counties Show
June, Malvern, Warwickshire
www.threecounties.co.uk
Three jam-packed days of family entertainment and fun, all in celebration of the great British farming world and countryside.

Herefordshire

Eastnor Castle
Ledbury, Herefordshire HR8 1RL
(01531) 633160
www.eastnorcastle.com
Fairytale Georgian Castle dramatically situated in the Malvern Hills.

Goodrich Castle
Ross-on-Wye, Herefordshire HR9 6HY
(01600) 890538
www.english-heritage.org.uk/goodrich
Come and relive the turbulent history of Goodrich Castle with our free audio and then climb to the battlements for breathtaking views over the Wye Valley.

The Hay Festival
May, Hay-on-Wye, Herefordshire
www.hayfestival.com
Some five hundred events see writers, politicians, poets, scientists, comedians, philosophers and musicians come together on a greenfield site for a ten day fesitval of ideas and stories at the Hay Festival.

Hereford Cathedral
Herefordshire HR1 2NG
(01432) 374202
www.herefordcathedral.org
Some of the finest examples of architecture from Norman times to the present day.

Hereford Museum and Art Gallery
Herefordshire HR4 9AU
(01432) 260692
www.herefordshire.gov.uk/leisure/museums_galleries/2869.asp
In the museum, aspects of Herefordshire history and life - in the Gallery, regularly changing exhibitions of paintings, photography and crafts.

Hergest Croft Gardens
Kington, Herefordshire HR5 3EG
(01544) 230160
www.hergest.co.uk
The gardens extend over 50 acres, with more than 4000 rare shrubs and trees. With over 60 champion trees and shrubs it is one of the finest collections in the British Isles.

Ledbury Heritage Centre
Herefordshire, HR8 1DN
(01432) 260692
www.herefordshire.gov.uk/leisure
The story of Ledbury's past displayed in a timber-framed building in the picturesque lane leading to the church.

Shropshire

Darby Houses (Ironbridge)
Telford, Shropshire TF8 7EW
(01952) 433424
www.ironbridge.org.uk
In the Darby houses, Dale House and Rosehill House, you can delve in to the everyday life of Quaker families.

Enginuity
Telford, Shropshire TF8 7DG
(01952) 433424
www.ironbridge.org.uk
At Enginuity you can turn the wheels of your imagination, test your horse power and discover how good ideas are turned in to real things.

English Haydn Festival
June, Bridgnorth, Shropshire
www.englishhaydn.com
An array of the music of Joseph Haydn and his contemporaries, performed in St. Leonards Church, Bridgnorth.

Ludlow Food Festival
September, Ludlow, Shropshire
www.foodfestival.co.uk
More than 160 top quality independent food and drink producers inside Ludlow Castle.

Much Wenlock Priory
Shropshire TF13 6HS
(01952) 727466
www.english-heritage.org.uk/wenlockpriory
Wenlock Priory, with its stunning clipped topiary, has a pastoral setting on the edge of lovely Much Wenlock

RAF Cosford Air Show
June, Shifnal, Shropshire
www.cosfordairshow.co.uk
This RAF-organised show usually features all the airshow favourites, classic and current British and foreign aircraft, exhibits and trade stalls all on this classic RAF airbase.

Royal Air Force Museum Cosford
Shifnal, Shropshire TF11 8UP
(01902) 376200
www.rafmuseum.org
FREE Admission. The award winning museum houses one of the largest aviation collections in the United Kingdom.

Shrewsbury Folk Festival
August, Shrewsbury, Shropshire
www.shrewsburyfolkfestival.co.uk
Shrewsbury Folk Festival has a reputation for delivering the very finest acts from the UK and around the world.

Stokesay Castle
Craven Arms, Shropshire SY7 9AH
(01588) 672544
www.english-heritage.org.uk/stokesaycastle
Stokesay Castle, nestles in peaceful South Shropshire countryside near the Welsh Border. It is one of more than a dozen English Heritage properties in the county.

V Festival
August, Weston Park, Shropshire
www.vfestival.com
Legendary rock and pop festival.

Wenlock Olympian Games
July, Much Wenlock, Shropshire
www.wenlock-olympian-society.org.uk
The games that inspired the modern Olympic Movement.

Wroxeter Roman City
Shrewsbury, Shropshire SY5 6PH
(01743) 761330
www.english-heritage.org.uk/wroxeter
Wroxeter Roman City, or Viroconium, to give it its Roman title, is thought to have been one of the largest Roman cities in the UK with over 200 acres of land, 2 miles of walls and a population of approximately 5,000.

Staffordshire

Abbots Bromley Horn Dance
September, Abbots Bromley, Staffordshire
www.abbotsbromley.com
Ancient ritual dating back to 1226. Six deer-men, a fool, hobby horse, bowman and Maid Marian perform to music provided by a melodian player.

Aerial Extreme Trentham
Staffordshire ST4 8AX
0845 652 1736
www.aerialextreme.co.uk/index.php/courses/trentham-estate
Our tree based adventure ropes course, set within the tranquil grounds of Trentham Estate is a truly spectacular journey.

Etruria Industrial Museum
Staffordshire ST4 7AF
(07900) 267711
www.stokemuseums.org.uk
Discover how they put the 'bone' in bone china at the last working steam-powered potters mill in Britain. Includes a Bone and Flint Mill and family-friendly interactive exhibition.

Lichfield Cathedral
Staffordshire WS13 7LD
(01543) 306100
www.lichfield-cathedral.org
A medieval Cathedral with 3 spires in the heart of an historic City set in its own serene Close.

Midlands Grand National
March, Uttoxeter Racecourse, Staffordshire
www.uttoxeter-racecourse.co.uk
Biggest fixture in Uttoxeter's calendar.

National Memorial Arboretum
Lichfield, Staffordshire DE13 7AR
(01283) 792333
www.thenma.org.uk
150 acres of trees and memorials, planted as a living tribute to those who have served, died or suffered in the service of their Country.

The Roaches
Upper Hulme, Leek, Staffordshire ST13 8UB
www.staffsmoorlands.gov.uk
The Roaches (or Roches) is a wind-carved outcrop of gritstone rocks that rises above the waters or Tittesworth reservoir, between Leek in Staffordshire and Buxton in Derbyshire. It's impressive gritstone edges and craggy rocks are loved by walkers and climbers alike.

Stone Food & Drink Festival
October, Stone, Staffordshire
www.stonefooddrink.org.uk
Staffordshire's biggest celebration of all things gastronomic.

Tamworth Castle
Staffordshire B79 7NA
(01827) 709629
www.tamworthcastle.co.uk
The number one Heritage attraction located in the town. Explore over 900 years of history in the magnificent Motte and Bailey Castle.

Wedgwood Visitor Centre
Stoke-on-Trent, Staffordshire ST12 9ER
(01782) 282986
www.wedgwoodvisitorcentre.com
Enjoy the past, buy the present and treasure the experience. The Wedgwood Visitor Centre offers a unique chance to immerse yourself in the heritage of Britain's greatest ceramics company.

West Midlands

Artsfest
September, Birmingham, West Midlands
www.visitbirmingham.com
Artsfest is one of the UK's biggest free arts festival and showcases work across the performing arts, visual arts and digital arts genres to promote emerging and established talent.

Barber Institute of Fine Arts
Edgbaston, West Midlands B15 2TS
(0121) 414 7333
www.barber.org.uk
British and European paintings, drawings and sculpture from the 13th century to mid 20th century.

Birmingham Literature Festival
October, Birmingham, West Midlands
www.visitbirmingham.com
Celebrating the city's literature scene, the Birmingham Literature Festival takes places every year with its trademark mix of literature events, talks and workshops.

Birmingham International Jazz and Blues Festival
July, Birmingham, West Midlands
www.visitbirmingham.com
Musicians and fans come to the city from every corner of the UK as well as from further afield and significantly, almost all of the events are free to the public.

Black Country Living Museum
Dudley, West Midlands DY1 4SQ
(0121) 557 9643
www.bclm.co.uk
Britain's friendliest open-air museum - visit original shops and houses, ride on fair attractions, take a look down the underground coalmine.

Frankfurt Christmas Market & Craft Fair
November-December, Birmingham, West Midlands
www.visitbirmingham.com
The largest authentic German market outside Germany and Austria and the centrepiece of the city's festive event calendar.

Moseley Folk Festival
September, Birmingham, West Midlands
www.visitbirmingham.com
Offering an inner city Shangri-la bringing together people from all ages and backgrounds to witness folk legends playing alongside their contemporaries.

Thinktank-Birmingham Science Museum
West Midlands B4 7XG
(0121) 202 2222
www.thinktank.ac
Thinktank is Birmingham's science museum where the emphasis is firmly on hands on exhibits and interactive fun.

Worcestershire

The Almonry Museum & Heritage Centre
Evesham, Worcestershire WR11 4BG
(01386) 446944
www.almonryevesham.org
The 14th century house has 12 rooms of exhibits from 2000 years of Evesham history and pleasant gardens to the rear.

Hanbury Hall
Droitwich Spa, Worcestershire WR9 7EA
(01527) 821214
www.nationaltrust.org.uk/hanburyhall
Early 18th century house, garden & park owned by the Vernon family for nearly 300 years.

Worcester Cathedral
Worcestershire WR1 2LA
(01905) 732900
www.worcestercathedral.co.uk
Worcester Cathedral is one of England's most magnificent and inspiring buildings, a place of prayer and worship for 14 centuries.

West Midland Safari and Leisure Park Bewdley, Worcestershire DY12 1LF
(01299) 402114 www.wmsp.co.uk
Are you ready to SAFARI and come face to face with some of the fastest, tallest, largest and cutest animals around?

Worcester City Art Gallery & Museum
Worcestershire WR1 1DT
(01905) 25371
www.worcestercitymuseums.org.uk
The art gallery & museum runs a programme of exhibitions/events for all the family. Explore the fascinating displays, exhibitions, café, shop and Worcestershire Soldier Galleries.

Tourist Information Centres

When you arrive at your destination, visit the Tourist Information Centre for quality assured help with accommodation and information about local attractions and events, or email your request before you go.

Bewdley	Load Street	0845 6077819	bewdleytic@wyreforestdc.gov.uk
Birmingham Library	Centenary Square	0844 888 3883	visit@marketingbirmingham.com
Bridgnorth	The Library	01746 763257	bridgnorth.tourism@shropshire.gov.uk
Bromyard	The Bromyard Centre	01885 488133	enquiries@bromyard-live.org.uk
Church Stretton	Church Street	01694 723133	churchstretton.scf@shropshire.gov.uk
Droitwich Spa	St Richard's House	01905 774312	heritage@droitwichspa.gov.uk
Ellesmere, Shropshire	The Boathouse Visitor Centre	01691 622981	ellesmere.tourism@shropshire.gov.uk
Evesham	The Almonry	01386 446944	tic@almonry.ndo.co.uk
Hereford	1 King Street	01432 268430	reception@visitherefordshire.co.uk
Ironbridge	Museum of The Gorge	01952 433424/ 01952 435900	tic@ironbridge.org.uk
Kenilworth	Kenilworth Library	0300 5558171	kenilworthlibrary@warwickshire.gov.uk
Ledbury	38 The Homend	0844 5678650	info@vistledbury.info
Leek	1 Market Place	01538 483741	tourism.services@staffsmoorlands.gov.uk
Leominster	1 Corn Square	01568 616460	leominstertic@herefordshire.gov.uk
Lichfield	Lichfield Garrick	01543 412112	info@visitlichfield.com
Ludlow	Castle Street	01584 875053	ludlow.tourism@shropshire.gov.uk
Malvern	21 Church Street	01684 892289	info@visitthemalverns.org
Market Drayton	49 Cheshire Street	01630 653114	marketdrayton.scf@shropshire-cc.gov.uk
Much Wenlock	The Museum - VIC	01952 727679/ 01743 258891	muchwenlock.tourism@shropshire.gov.uk
Newcastle-Under-Lyme	Newcastle Library	01782 297313	tic.newcastle@staffordshire.gov.uk
Nuneaton	Nuneaton Library	0300 5558171	nuneatonlibrary@warwickshire.gov.uk
Oswestry (Mile End)	Mile End	01691 662488	oswestrytourism@shropshire.gov.uk
Oswestry Town	The Heritage Centre	01691 662753	ot@oswestry-welshborders.org.uk
Redditch	Palace Theatre	01527 60806	info.centre@bromsgroveandredditch.gov.uk
Ross-On-Wye	Market House	01989 562768/ 01432 260675	visitorcentreross@herefordshire.gov.uk
Royal leamington spa	Royal Pump Rooms	01926 742762	vic@warwickdc.gov.uk
Rugby	Rugby Art Gallery Museum	01788 533217	visitor.centre@rugby.gov.uk
Shrewsbury	Barker Street	01743 281200	visitorinformation@shropshire.gov.uk
Solihull	Central Library	0121 704 6130	artscomplex@solihull.gov.uk
Stafford	Stafford Gatehouse Theatre	01785 619619	tic@staffordbc.gov.uk
Stoke-On-Trent	Victoria Hall, Bagnall Street	01782 236000	stoke.tic@stoke.gov.uk
Stratford-Upon-Avon	Bridge Foot	01789 264293	tic@discover-stratford.com
Tamworth	Philip Dix Centre	01827 709581	tic@tamworth.gov.uk
Telford	The Telford Shopping Centre	01952 238008	tourist-info@telfordshopping.co.uk
Upton Upon Severn	The Heritage Centre	01684 594200	upton.tic@malvernhills.gov.uk
Warwick	Visit Warwick	01926 492212	info@visitwarwick.co.uk
Whitchurch (Shropshire)	Whitchurch Heritage Centre	01948 664577	heritage@whitchurch-shropshire-tc.gov.uk
Worcester	The Guildhall	01905 726311/ 722561	touristinfo@visitworcester.com
Coventry	St Michael's Tower, Coventry Cathedral Ruins	024 7622 5616	tic@coventry.gov.uk

Regional Contacts and Information

For more information on accommodation, attractions, activities, events and holidays in the Heart of England, contact one of the following regional or local tourism organisations. Their websites have a wealth of information and many produce free publications to help you get the most out of your visit.

Marketing Birmingham
(0844) 888 3883
www.visitbirmingham.com

Visit Coventy & Warwickshire
(024) 7622 5616
www.visitcoventryandwarwickshire.co.uk

Visit Herefordshire
(01432) 268430
www.visitherefordshire.co.uk

Shakespeare Country
(0871) 978 0800
www.shakespeare-country.co.uk

Shropshire Tourism
(01743) 261919
www.shropshiretourism.co.uk

Destination Staffordshire
(01785) 277397
www.enjoystaffordshire.com

Stoke-on-Trent
(01782) 236000
www.visitstoke.co.uk

Destination Worcestershire
(0845) 641 1540
www.visitworcestershire.org

Stay – Heart of England

Entries appear alphabetically by town name in each county. A key to symbols appears on page 7

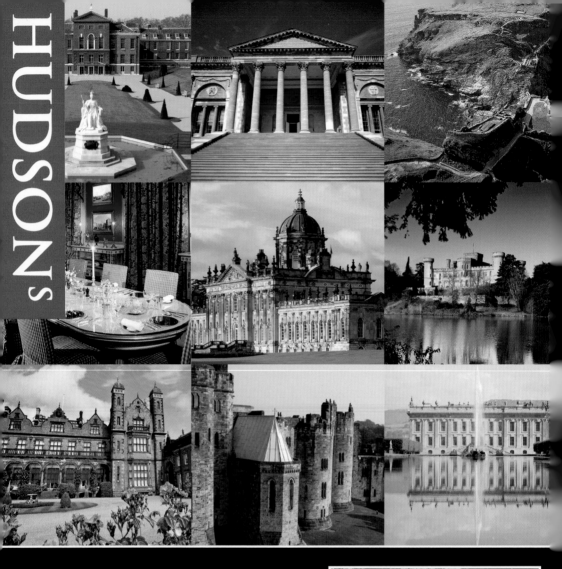

CRAVEN ARMS, Shropshire   Map ref 4A3 — SatNav SY7 9LU

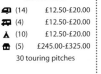

ALTERNATIVE ACCOMMODATION

Greenway Touring & Glamping Park

Greenway, Shawbank, Nr Craven Arms, Shropshire SY7 9LU
T: (01584) 861431 E: enquiries@shropshirehillstouringandglamping.co.uk
W: www.shropshirehillstouringandglamping.co.uk

🚐 (14)	£12.50-£20.00
🚏 (4)	£12.50-£20.00
🏕 (10)	£12.50-£20.00
🛖 (5)	£245.00-£325.00

30 touring pitches

A scenic retreat for adults in the beautiful Corvedale Hills, an Area of Outstanding Natural Beauty in South Shropshire. The touring and glamping park is an ideal base for walkers, cyclists and sightseeing, near to Ludlow and Welsh Border. Pods are £35-60 Per Night. **Directions:** From the A49, Craven Arms - travel East along B4368 for 1.8 miles. Site entrance on left, at centre of wide grass splay. Do not turn up narrow lane. **Open:** All year inc Christmas and New Year.

WALKERS   CYCLISTS   PETS!   **Payment:** 💳 **Property:** 🐕 🚽

STRATFORD-UPON-AVON, Warwickshire   Map ref 2B1 — SatNav CV37 9SR

TOURING & CAMPING PARK

Dodwell Park

Evesham Road (B439), Dodwell, Stratford-upon-Avon CV37 9SR
T: (01789) 204957 E: enquiries@dodwellpark.co.uk
W: www.dodwellpark.co.uk

🚐 (50)	£18.00-£27.00
🚏 (50)	£18.00-£27.00
🏕 (50)	£17.00-£25.00

50 touring pitches

Small, family-run touring park 2 miles SW of Stratford-upon-Avon. Country walks to River Avon and Luddington village. Ideal for visiting Warwick Castle, Shakespeare properties and Cotswolds. Brochure on request. Rallies welcome. Over 50 years as a family business! **Directions:** Leaving Stratford-Upon-Avon take the B439 signposted 'B349 Bidford' (also signposted Racecourse) for 2 miles, we are on left (after going over a large hill). **Open:** All year.

Site: A P **Payment:** 💳 ☼ **Leisure:** 🎣 🎵 ▶ **Children:** 🧒 **Catering:** 🍴 **Park:** 🐕 🌳 **Touring:** 🚽 🚿 🔌

Don't Miss...

Castle Howard

Malton, North Yorkshire YO60 7DA
(01653) 648444
www.castlehoward.co.uk
A magnificent 18th century house situated in breathtaking parkland, dotted with temples, lakes statues and fountains; plus formal gardens, woodland garden and ornamental vegetable garden. Inside the House guides share stories of the house, family and collections, while outdoor-guided tours reveal the secrets of the architecture and landscape.

National Media Museum

Bradford, West Yorkshire BD1 1NQ
0870 701 0200
www.nationalmediamuseum.org.uk
The Museum is home to over 3.5 million items of historical significance including the National Photography, National Cinematography, National Television and National New Media Collections. Admission to the National Media Museum is free (charges apply for cinemas/IMAX).

National Railway Museum

York, North Yorkshire YO26 4XJ
0844 815 3139
www.nrm.org.uk
Awesome trains, interactive fun – and the world's largest railway museum make for a great day out.

The Deep

Hull, East Riding of Yorkshire HU1 4DP
(01482) 381000
www.thedeep.co.uk
Full with over 3500 fish and more than 40 sharks, The Deep tells the amazing story of the world's oceans through stunning marine life, interactives and audio-visual presentations making it a fun-filled family day out for all ages.

Yorkshire Wildlife Park

Doncaster, South Yorkshire DN3 3NH
(01302) 535057
www.yorkshirewildlifepark.co.uk2
A fabulous fun day and animal experience. Walk through 'Lemur Woods' and meet these mischievous primates, or come face to face with the wallabies in Wallaby Walk.

Yorkshire

Yorkshire

Yorkshire, the largest county in England, is one of the most popular and boasts award-winning culture, heritage and scenery. There's cosmopolitan Leeds, stylish Harrogate and rural market towns full of charm and character. The wild moors and deserted dales of the Yorkshire Dales and North York Moors National Parks are majestic in their beauty and the county has a spectacular coastline of rugged cliffs and sandy beaches. The region also has a wealth of historic houses, ruined castles, abbeys and fortresses for visitors to discover.

Explore – Yorkshire

North Yorkshire

Steeped in history, North Yorkshire boasts some of the country's most splendid scenery. Wherever you go in The Dales, you'll be faced with breathtaking views and constant reminders of a historic and changing past. In medieval days, solid fortresses like Richmond and Middleham were built to protect the area from marauding Scots. Ripley and Skipton also had their massive strongholds, while Bolton Castle in Wensleydale once imprisoned Mary, Queen of Scots. The pattern of history continues with the great abbeys, like Jervaulx Abbey, near Masham, where the monks first made Wensleydale cheese and the majestic ruins of Fountains Abbey in the grounds of Studley Royal. Between the Dales and the North York Moors, Herriot Country is named for one of the world's best loved writers, James Herriot, who made the area his home for more than 50 years and whose books have enthralled readers with tales of Yorkshire life.

Hotspot: Take a classic steam train from Pickering to Grosmont on the famous North Yorkshire Moors Railway for breathaking scenery. www.nymr.co.uk

Escape to the wild, deserted North York Moors National Park with its 500 square miles of hills, dales, forests and open moorland, neatly edged by a spectacular coastline. Walking, cycling and pony trekking are ideal ways to savour the scenery and there are plenty of greystone towns and villages dotted throughout the Moors that provide ideal bases from which to explore. From Helmsley, visit the ruins of Rievaulx Abbey, founded by Cistercian monks in the 12th century or discover moorland life in the Ryedale Folk Museum at Hutton-le-Hole. The Beck Isle Museum in Pickering provides an insight into the life of a country market town and just a few miles down the road you'll find Malton, once a Roman fortress, and nearby Castle Howard, the setting for Brideshead Revisited.

Hotspot: The Forbidden Corner is a unique labyrinth of tunnels, chambers, follies and surprises in the heart of the beautiful Yorkshire Dales. www.theforbiddencorner.co.uk

Leeds & West Yorkshire

For centuries cloth has been spun from the wool of the sheep grazing in the Pennine uplands and the fascinating story of this industrial heritage can be seen in the numerous craft centres and folk museums throughout West Yorkshire. To enjoy the countryside, take a trip on the steam hauled Keighley and Worth Valley Railway. Not far from Haworth is Bingley, where the Leeds & Liverpool canal makes its famous uphill journey, a route for the coal barges in days gone by, nowadays replaced by holidaymakers in gaily painted boats. Leeds itself is a vibrant city with its Victorian shopping arcades, Royal Armories Museum and lively arts scene.

Hotspot: Stop off at **Haworth**, home of the Bronte sisters, to visit The Bronte Parsonage museum and experience the rugged atmosphere of Wuthering Heights. www.bronte.org.uk

York

Wherever you turn within the city's medieval walls, you will find glimpses of the past. The splendours of the 600-year old Minster, the grim stronghold of Clifford's Tower, the National Railway Museum, the medieval timbers of the Merchant Adventurers' Hall and the fascinating Jorvik Viking Centre all offer an insight into the history of this charming city. Throughout the city, statues and monuments remind the visitor that this was where Constantine was proclaimed Holy Roman Emperor, Guy Fawkes was born and Dick Turpin met his end.

Modern York is has excellent shopping, a relaxed cafe culture, first class restaurants and bars, museums, tours and attractions. Whether you visit for a romantic weekend or a fun-filled family holiday, there really is something for everyone.

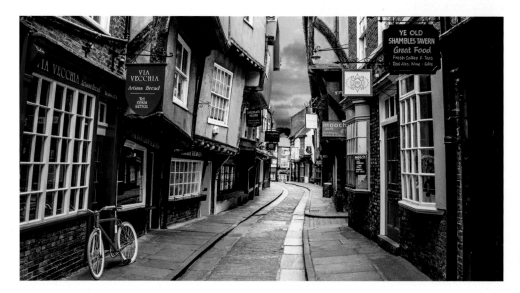

Yorkshire Coastline

The Yorkshire coastline is one of the UK's most naturally beautiful and rugged, where pretty fishing villages cling to rocky cliffs, in turn towering over spectacular beaches and family-friendly seaside destinations.

At the northern end of the coastline, Saltburn is a sand and shingle beach popular with surfers and visitors can ride the Victorian tram from the cliff to the promenade during the summer. Whitby is full of quaint streets and bestowed with a certain Gothic charm. At Scarborough, one of Britain's oldest seaside resorts, the award-winning North Bay and South Bay sand beaches are broken by the rocky headland, home to the historic Scarborough Castle. Filey, with its endless sands, has spectacular views and a 40-mile stretch of perfect sandy beach sweeps south from the dramatic 400 ft high cliffs at Flamborough Head. Along this coastline you can find the boisterous holiday destination of Bridlington, or a gentler pace at pretty Hornsea and Withernsea.

Hotspot: With its 3,000 year history, stunning location and panoramic views over the dramatic Yorkshire coastline, Scarborough Castle is one of the finest tourist attractions in Yorkshire.
www.english-heritage.org.uk

East Yorkshire

From cosmopolitan Hull to the hills and valleys of the Yorkshire Wolds, East Yorkshire is wonderfully diverse. A landscape of swirling grasslands, medieval towns, manor houses and Bronze Age ruins contrasting with the vibrant energy and heritage of the Humber. The Wolds are only a stones throw from some great seaside resorts and Beverley, with its magnificent 13th century minster and lattice of medieval streets, is just one of the many jewels of architectural heritage to be found here. Hull is a modern city rebuilt since the war, linked to Lincolnshire via the impressive 1452 yd Humber Bridge.

Hotspot: The St Leger at Doncaster Racecourse is the oldest classic horse race in the world, and the town celebrates in style with a whole festival of events. www.visitdoncaster.co.uk

South Yorkshire

The historic market town of Doncaster was founded by the Romans and has a rich horseracing and railway heritage. The area around Sheffield - the steel city - was once dominated by the iron and steel industries and was the first city in England to pioneer free public transport. The Industrial Museum and City Museum display a wide range of Sheffield cutlery and oplate. Today, Meadowhall shopping centre, with 270 stores under one roof, is a must-visit for shopaholics.

Indulge in a spot of retail therapy with a trip to **Leeds**. The Grand Arcade is one of the oldest shopping arcades in Leeds City Centre and is well worth a visit for its independent retailers. The stunning architecture of the Victoria Quarter's Grade II* arcades are a spectacular setting for a shopping spree, while VQ is home to over 75 of the world's leading fashion and lifestyle brands, including Vivienne Westwood, Paul Smith, Louis Vuitton, Mulberry and Illamasqua.

Tantalise your taste buds with traditional fish & chips from **The Quayside**, the UK's Fish and Chip Shop of the year 2014. Find them at 7 Pier Road, Whitby. (01947) 825346 or visit www.whitbyfishandchips.com

The bustling **Lewis & Cooper** store in Northallerton has been a multi award-winning independent gourmet food store since 1899 and is packed with flavoursome foodie treats, fine wines, delicious gift baskets and sumptuous food hampers. Treat yourself to a mouth watering picnic spread and head out into the surrounding countryside. www.lewisandcooper.co.uk

Enjoy an elegant afternoon tea at the famous **Bettys Cafe Tea Rooms**, Harrogate. Speciality teas, dainty sandwiches, handmade cakes and scones, and splendid surroundings make this a truly indulgent occasion and you can even buy your favourites from the bakery to take home. (01423) 814070 or visit www.bettys.co.uk

Feel relaxed, exhilarated and cleansed after an indulgent visit to the **Turkish Baths** in Harrogate. The unique Royal Baths building first opened in 1896 and today you can enjoy a contemporary spa experience in magnificent surroundings. Treatments, refreshments and a spot of lunch are all available. (01423) 556746 or visit www.turkishbathsharrogate.co.uk

Visit – Yorkshire

North Yorkshire

Flamingo Land Theme Park and Zoo
Malton, North Yorkshire YO17 6UX
0871 911 8000
www.flamingoland.co.uk
One-price family funpark with over 100 attractions, 5 shows and Europe's largest privately-owned zoo.

Grassington Festival
June, Grassington, North Yorkshire
www.grassington-festival.org.uk
15 days of music and arts in the Yorkshire Dales.

Malton Food Lovers Festival
May, Malton, North Yorkshire
www.maltonyorkshire.co.uk
Fill up on glorious food and discover why Malton is considered 'Yorkshire's Food Town' with mountains of fresh produce.

Ripon International Festival
September, Ripon, North Yorkshire
www.riponinternationalfestival.com
A festival packed with music events, solo dramas, intriguing theatre, magic, fantastic puppetry, literary celebrities, historical walks - and more!

Scarborough Jazz Festival
September, Scarborough, North Yorkshire
www.jazz.scarboroughspa.co.uk
Offering a variety and range of jazz acts with a balanced programme of predominantly British musicians, with the addition of a few international stars.

Scarborough Seafest
July, Scarborough, North Yorkshire
www.discoveryorkshirecoast.com
Seafest celebrates Scarborough's maritime heritage and brings together seafood kitchen cooking demonstrations, exhibitor displays and musical performances.

Swaledale Festival
May - June, Various locations, North Yorkshire
www.swaledale-festival.org.uk
Varied programme of top-quality events, individually ticketed, realistically priced, and spread over two glorious weeks.

The Walled Garden at Scampston
Malton, North Yorkshire YO17 8NG
(01944) 759111
www.scampston.co.uk
An exciting 4 acre contemporary garden, created by Piet Oudolf, with striking perennial meadow planting as well as traditional spring/autumn borders.

York

York Early Music Festival
July, York, North Yorkshire
www.ncem.co.uk
The 2015 festival takes as its starting point the 600th anniversary of the Battle of Agincourt and features cross-currents between France and England from the Middle Ages through to the Baroque.

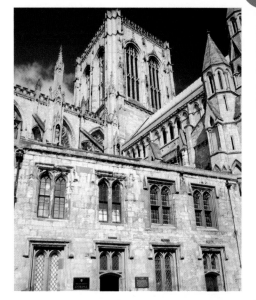

JORVIK Viking Centre
York, North Yorkshire YO1 9WT
(01904) 615505
www.jorvik-viking-centre.co.uk
Travel back 1000 years on board your time machine through the backyards and houses to the bustling streets of Jorvik.

York Boat Guided River Trips
North Yorkshire YO1 7DP
(01904) 628324
www.yorkboat.co.uk
Sit back, relax and enjoy a drink from the bar as the sights of York city and country sail by onboard a 1 hour Guided River Trip with entertaining live commentary.

York Minster
York, North Yorkshire YO1 7JN
(0)1904 557200
www.yorkminster.org
Regularly voted one of the most popular things to do in York, the Minster is not only an architecturally stunning building but is a place to discover the history of York over the centuries, its artefacts and treasures.

Yorkshire Air Museum
York, North Yorkshire YO41 4AU
(01904) 608595
www.yorkshireairmuseum.org
The Yorkshire Air Museum is based on a unique WWII Bomber Command Station with fascinating exhibits and attractive award-winning Memorial Gardens.

Leeds & West Yorkshire

Eureka! The National Children's Museum
Halifax, West Yorkshire HX1 2NE
(01422) 330069
www.eureka.org.uk
Eureka! The National Children's Museum is a magical place where children play to learn and grown-ups learn to play.

Harewood House
Leeds, West Yorkshire LS17 9LG
(0113) 218 1010
www.harewood.org
Harewood House, Bird Garden, Grounds and Adventure Playground - The Ideal day out for all the family.

Haworth 1940's Weekend
May, Haworth, West Yorkshire
www.haworth1940sweekend.co.uk
A fabulous weekend celebrating and comemorating the 1940s.

Leeds Festival
August, Wetherby, Leeds
www.leedsfestival.com
From punk and metal, through rock, alternative and indie to dance, Leeds offers music fans a chance to see hot new acts, local bands, huge stars and exclusive performances.

Lotherton Hall & Gardens
Leeds, West Yorkshire LS25 3EB
(0113) 264 5535
www.leeds.gov.uk/lothertonhall
Lotherton is an Edwardian country house set in beautiful grounds with a bird garden, red deer park and formal gardens.

National Coal Mining Museum for England
Wakefield, West Yorkshire WF4 4RH
(01924) 848806
www.ncm.org.uk
The National Coal Mining Museum offers an exciting and enjoyable insight into the working lives of miners through the ages.

Pontefract Liquorice Festival
July, Wakefield, West Yorkshire
www.yorkshire.com
The festival celebrates this unusual plant, the many wonderful products created from it and its historic association with the town.

Royal Armouries Museum
Leeds, West Yorkshire LS10 1LT
0870 034 4344
www.royalarmouries.org
Over 8,000 objects displayed in five galleries - War, Tournament, Oriental, Self Defence and Hunting. Among the treasures are Henry VIII's tournament armour and the world record breaking elephant armour. Regular jousting and horse shows.

Xscape Castleford
Castleford, West Yorkshire WF10 4TA
(01977) 5230 2324
www.xscape.co.uk
The ultimate family entertainment awaits! Dine, bowl, snow, skate, climb, movies, shop, dance on ice.

Yorkshire Sculpture Park
West Bretton,
West Yorkshire WF4 4LG
(01924) 832631
www.ysp.co.uk
YSP is an extraordinary place that sets out to challenge, inspire, inform and delight.

East Yorkshire

East Riding Rural Life Museum
Beverley, East Yorkshire HU16 5TF
(01482) 392777
www.museums.eastriding.gov.uk
Working early 19th century four-sailed Skidby Windmill,
plus Museum of East Riding Rural Life.

Ferens Art Gallery
Hull, East Riding of Yorkshire HU1 3RA
(01482) 613902
www.hullcc.gov.uk/museums
Combines internationally renowned permanent
collections with a thriving programme of
temporary exhibitions.

RSPB Bempton Cliffs Reserve
Bridlington, East Riding of Yorkshire YO15 1JF
(01262) 851179
www.rspb.org.uk
A family favourite, and easily the best place in
England to see, hear and smell seabirds! More
than 200,000 birds (from April to August) make the
towering chalk cliffs seem alive.

Skipsea Castle
Hornsea, East Riding of Yorkshire
0870 333 1181
www.english-heritage.org.uk/daysout/properties/
skipsea-castle/
The remaining earthworks of a motte-and-bailey
castle dating from the Norman era.

Treasure House and Art Gallery
Beverley, East Riding of Yorkshire HU17 8HE
(01482) 392790
www.museums.eastriding.gov.uk/treasure-house-
and-beverley-art-gallery
Enthusiasts for East Riding history can access archive,
library, art gallery and museum material. Exhibitions.

Wilberforce House
Hull, East Riding of Yorkshire HU11NQ
(01482) 300300
www.hullcc.gov.uk/museums
Slavery exhibits, period rooms and furniture, Hull
silver, costume, Wilberforce and abolition.

South Yorkshire

RSPB Old Moor Nature Reserve
Barnsley, South Yorkshire S73 0YF
(01226) 751593
www.rspb.org.uk
Whether you're feeling
energetic or just fancy some
time out visit Old Moor to get
closer to the wildlife.

Brodsworth Hall and Gardens
Doncaster, South Yorkshire DN5 7XJ
(01302) 722598
www.english-heritage.org.uk/daysout/properties/
brodsworth-hall-and-gardens
One of England's most complete surviving Victorian
houses. Inside many of the original fixtures & fittings
are still in place, although faded with time. Outside
the 15 acres of woodland & gardens have been
restored to their 1860's heyday.

Magna Science Adventure Centre
Rotherham, South Yorkshire S60 1DX
(01709) 720002
www.visitmagna.co.uk
Magna is the UK's 1st Science Adventure Centre set in
the vast Templeborough steelworks in Rotherham. Fun
is unavoidable here with giant interactives.

Sheffield Botanical Gardens
South Yorkshire S10 2LN
(0114) 268 6001
www.sbg.org.uk
Extensive gardens with over 5,500 species of plants,
Grade II Listed garden pavillion.

Sheffield: Millennium Gallery
South Yorkshire S1 2PP
(0114) 278 2600
www.museums-sheffield.org.uk
One of modern Sheffield's landmark public spaces.
Whether you're in town or just passing through, the
Gallery always has something new to offer.

Tourist Information Centres

When you arrive at your destination, visit the Tourist Information Centre for quality assured help with accommodation and information about local attractions and events, or email your request before you go.

Aysgarth Falls	Aysgarth Falls National Park Centre	01969 662910	aysgarth@yorkshiredales.org.uk
Beverley	34 Butcher Row	01482 391672	beverley.tic@eastriding.gov.uk
Bradford	Brittainia House	01274 433678	bradford.vic@bradford.gov.uk
Bridlington	25 Prince Street	01262 673474/ 01482 391634	bridlington.tic@eastriding.gov.uk
Brigg	The Buttercross	01652 657053	brigg.tic@northlincs.gov.uk
Danby	The Moors National Park Centre	01439 772737	moorscentre@northyorkmoors.org.uk
Doncaster	Blue Building	01302 734309	tourist.information@doncaster.gov.uk
Filey	The Evron Centre	01723 383637	fileytic2@scarborough.gov.uk
Grassington	National Park Centre	01756 751690	grassington@yorkshiredales.gov.uk
Halifax	The Piece Hall	01422 368725	halifax@ytbtic.co.uk
Harrogate	Royal Baths	01423 537300	tic@harrogate.gov.uk
Hawes	Dales Countryside Museum	01969 666210	hawes@yorkshiredales.org.uk
Haworth	2/4 West Lane	01535 642329	haworth.vic@bradford.gov.uk
Hebden Bridge	New Road	01422 843831	hebdenbridge@ytbtic.co.uk
Holmfirth	49-51 Huddersfield Road	01484 222444	holmfirth.tic@kirklees.gov.uk
Hornsea	Hornsea Museum	01964 536404	hornsea.tic@eastriding.gov.uk

Horton-In-Ribblesdale	Pen-y-ghent Cafe	01729 860333	mail@pen-y-ghentcafe.co.uk
Huddersfield	Huddersfield Library	01484 223200	huddersfield.information@kirklees.gov.uk
Hull	1 Paragon Street	01482 223559	tourist.information@hullcc.gov.uk
Humber Bridge	North Bank Viewing Area	01482 640852	humberbridge.tic@eastriding.gov.uk
Ilkley	Town Hall	01943 602319	ilkley.vic@bradford.gov.uk
Ingleton	The Community Centre Car Park	015242 41049	ingleton@ytbtic.co.uk
Knaresborough	9 Castle Courtyard	01423 866886	kntic@harrogate.gov.uk
Leeds	The Arcade	0113 242 5242	tourinfo@leedsandpartners.com
Leeming Bar	The Yorkshire Maid, 88 Bedale Road	01677 424262	thelodgeatleemingbar@btconnect.com
Leyburn	The Dales Haven	01969 622317	
Malham	National Park Centre	01969 652380	malham@ytbtic.co.uk
Otley	Otley Library & Tourist Information	01943 462485	otleytic@leedslearning.net
Pateley Bridge	18 High Street	0845 389 0177	pbtic@harrogate.gov.uk
Pickering	Ropery House	01751 473791	pickeringtic@btconnect.com
Reeth	Hudson House, The Green	01748 884059	reeth@ytbtic.co.uk
Richmond	Friary Gardens	01748 828742	hilda@richmondtouristinformation.co.uk
Ripon	Minster Road	01765 604625	ripontic@harrogate.gov.uk
Rotherham	40 Bridgegate	01709 835904	tic@rotherham.gov.uk
Scarborough	Brunswick Shopping Centre	01723 383636	scarborough2@scarborough.gov.uk
Scarborough (Harbourside)	Harbourside TIC	01723 383636	scarborough2@scarborough.gov.uk
Selby	Selby Library	0845 034 9540	selby@ytbtic.co.uk
Settle	Town Hall	01729 825192	settle@ytbtic.co.uk
Sheffield	Unit 1 Winter Gardens	0114 2211900	visitor@marketingsheffield.org
Skipton	Town Hall	01756 792809	skipton@ytbtic.co.uk
Sutton Bank	Sutton Bank Visitor Centre	01845 597426	suttonbank@northyorkmoors.org.uk
Todmorden	15 Burnley Road	01706 818181	todmorden@ytbtic.co.uk
Wakefield	9 The Bull Ring	0845 601 8353	tic@wakefield.gov.uk
Wetherby	Wetherby Library & Tourist Centre	01937 582151	wetherbytic@leedslearning.net
Whitby	Langborne Road	01723 383637	whitbytic@scarborough.gov.uk
Withernsea	Withernsea Lighthouse Museum	01964 615683/ 01482 486566	withernsea.tic@eastriding.gov.uk
York	1 Museum Street	01904 550099	info@visityork.org

167

Regional Contacts and Information

For more information on accommodation, attractions, activities, events and holidays in Yorkshire, contact one of the following regional or local tourism organisations.

Welcome to Yorkshire
www.yorkshire.com
(0113) 322 3500

Entries appear alphabetically by town name in each county. A key to symbols appears on page 7

HORNSEA, East Yorkshire Map ref 4D1   SatNav YO25 8SY

Skirlington Leisure Park

Hornsea Road, Skipsea, Driffield, East Yorkshire YO25 8SY
T: (01262) 468213 **F:** (01262) 468105 **E:** enquiries@skirlington.com
W: www.skirlington.com

(250) £11.00-£26.00
(250) £11.00-£26.00
(20) £239.00-£595.00
250 touring pitches

Skirlington Leisure Park is a five star holiday destination set in over 70 acres of superb parkland with open views across breathtaking countryside and the beautiful East Yorkshire coast, what better place to unwind and relax?

We cater for tourers, motorhomes, owner occupied holiday homes, and people wishing to hire a static holiday home. Our adjacent park at Atwick also accept tents. We are also 5 AA pennant rated and are a Gold Bellamy Award Winner for 2014/15.

Directions: 1.5 miles South of Skipsea on the B1242, 2 miles North of Hornsea.

Open: 1st March - 30th November.

Site: 🌸 **Payment:** 💳 ☼ **Leisure:** ♪ ► ♦ **Children:** ⛏ 🎠 **Catering:** ✗ 🛒 **Park:** 🐕 🎵 ▤ 🗐 📖 🏧 **Touring:** 🚿 🔄 🔌 🎣

TUNSTALL, East Yorkshire Map ref 4D1   SatNav HU12 0JF

Sand le Mere Holiday Village

Southfield Lane, Tunstall, East Yorkshire HU12 0JF
T: (01964) 670403 **E:** info@sand-le-mere.co.uk
W: www.sand-le-mere.co.uk

(59)
(50)
(6)
(50)
59 touring pitches

£4 million recently spent on new park facilities, including new leisure complex with indoor heated pool, splashzone, waterslide and indoor & outdoor adventure play areas. Family entertainment available throughout the season. Fantastic park setting overlooking Tunstall beach, fresh water & beach fishing available. Close to Hull, historic York and the pretty town of Beverley. Please contact for 2015 rates.

Directions: From Hull to Hedon take the B1362 at Withernsea, B1242 to Roos. Look for brown signs marked SLM.

Open: 20th March - 6th November.

Site: 🌸 **Payment:** 💳 ☼ **Leisure:** ♪ ► ♦ ♦ **Children:** ⛏ 🎠 **Catering:** ✗ 🛒 **Park:** 🐕 🎵 ▤ 🗐 📖 🏧 **Touring:** 🚿 🔄 🔌 🎣

FILEY, North Yorkshire Map ref 5D3 · SatNav YO14 9PS

★★★★ HOLIDAY PARK

Crows Nest Caravan Park

Crows Nest Caravan Park, Gristhorpe, Filey, North Yorkshire YO14 9PS
T: (01723) 582206 E: enquiries@crowsnestcaravanpark.com
W: www.crowsnestcaravanpark.com **£ BOOK ONLINE**

🚐 (50)	£15.00-£35.00
🚏 (50)	£15.00-£35.00
🏕 (200)	£15.00-£35.00
🏠 (40)	£250.00-£590.00

Crows Nest Caravan Park is located on the beautiful Yorkshire coast between Scarborough and Filey, it is the ideal park to enjoy these two great seaside towns and their glorious sandy beaches.

Privately owned and operated by the Palmer family, this award winning park is the perfect base for families and couples wishing to explore one of England´s finest holiday destinations.

Directions: 2 miles north of Filey, 5 miles south of Scarborough. Just off A165 main road, turn off at roundabout with Jet petrol station.

Open: March 1st - October 31st.

Site: 🏕 🅿 Payment: 💳 ☀ Leisure: ► ♦ ☕ Children: 🛝 🎠 Catering: ✗ 🍴 Park: 🐕 🎵 🏧 🗑 🚿 🎣 Touring: 🚿 🚾 ⚡

FILEY, North Yorkshire Map ref 5D3 · SatNav YO14 9ET

★★★ TOURING & CAMPING PARK

Filey Brigg Caravan and Camping Park

Church Cliff Drive, North Cliff, Arndale, Filey, North Yorkshire YO14 9ET
T: (01723) 513852 E: fileybrigg@scarborough.gov.uk
W: www.discoveryorkshirecoast.com

🚐 (155)	
🚏 (155)	
🏕 (20)	

Filey Brigg is a grassy 9 acre site set in a country park with splendid views of Filey Bay and Filey Brigg. The site has 2 heated amenity blocks, children's play area and site shop. The beach is just a short walk away as is the seaside town of Filey. The site is also ideal for touring the Yorkshire Coast. Please contact for 2015 Rates.
Directions: Please contact us. **Open:** 28th February - 2nd January.

Site: 🅿 Payment: 💳 ☀ Leisure: 🎵 ► ∪ Children: 🛝 🎠 Catering: 🍴 Park: 🐕 🗑 🚿 🎣 Touring: 🚿 🚾 ⚡

Yorkshire - North Yorkshire

SatNav YO14 0PU

Orchard Farm Holiday Village
Stonegate, Hunmanby, Filey YO14 0PU
T: (01723) 891582 F: (01723) 891582 E: info@orchardfarmholidayvillage.co.uk
W: www.orchardfarmholidayvillage.co.uk

£14.00-£22.00
£14.00-£22.00
(25) £14.00-£22.00
(7) £355.00-£889.00
60 touring pitches

Family park in edge-of-village location with easy access to resorts of Filey, Scarborough and Bridlington. Amenities include children's play area, fishing lake and entertainment during peak season. **Directions:** From A165 from Scarborough take 1st right to Hunmanby under railway bridge 1st right. **Open:** March to October.

Site: Payment: Leisure: Children: Catering: Park: Touring:

SatNav HG3 1JH

Rudding Holiday Park
Follifoot, Harrogate, North Yorkshire HG3 1JH
T: (01423) 870439 E: holiday-park@ruddingpark.com
W: www.ruddingholidaypark.co.uk £ BOOK ONLINE

£18.00-£44.00
£18.00-£44.00
£18.00-£44.00
141 touring pitches

Award winning park for touring and camping with extensive facilities; outdoor pool, family pub, adventure playground and golf courses. Minutes from Harrogate and the motorway. Self-catering timber lodges also available. **Directions:** Situated 3 miles south of Harrogate, Rudding Park lies just off the A658 linking the A61 from Leeds to the A59 York Road. **Open:** March - January.

Site: Payment: Leisure: Children: Catering: Park: Touring:

SatNav YO62 5YQ

Golden Square Caravan and Camping Park
Oswaldkirk, Helmsley, York YO62 5YQ
T: (01439) 788269 F: (01439) 788236 E: reception@goldensquarecaravanpark.com
W: www.goldensquarecaravanpark.com £ BOOK ONLINE

£17.00-£26.00
£17.00-£26.00
£15.00-£26.00
(21)
129 touring pitches

Award winning secluded family park. Panoramic views across the North York Moors. Heated shower block, bathrooms, shop, indoor/outdoor playarea. Tents, touring, seasonal/pitches. Storage compound. Holiday Homes for sale. Sports Centre nearby. **Directions:** From South Leave A1 junction 49 onto A168 to Thirsk A170 and A19 to York. Follow Caravan Route to Coxwold Ampleforth 1 mile signposted Helmsley. **Open:** March-October.

Site: Payment: Leisure: Children: Catering: Park: Touring:

Need more information?
Visit our websites for detailed information, up-to-date availability and to book your accommodation online. Includes over 20,000 places to stay, all of them star rated.
www.visitor-guides.co.uk

HELMSLEY, North Yorkshire   Map ref 5C3   SatNav YO62 7RY

TOURING & CAMPING PARK (enjoyEngland.com ★★★★★)

Wombleton Caravan Park
Moorfield Lane, Wombleton, Helmsley YO62 7RY
T: (01751) 431684 **E:** info@wombletoncaravanpark.co.uk
W: www.wombletoncaravanpark.co.uk **£ BOOK ONLINE**

🚐 (100)   £20.00-£24.00
🚏 (6)   £20.00-£24.00
⛺ (10)   £8.00-£24.00
100 touring pitches

A quiet park halfway between Helmsley and Kirkbymoorside, a flat level site with electric hook-ups, modern shower block/disabled facilities and a small shop. Touring and seasonal pitches, tents welcome. Wi-Fi Available. **Directions:** Off the A170 through Wombleton village, drive through the village turn left at the war memorial and left down the lane towards the airfield. **Open:** March to October.

Payment: 💳 ☼ **Leisure:** ∪ **Children:** ⌁ **Catering:** 🛒 **Park:** 🐕 🚮 🖥 🛢 🕍 ☔ **Touring:** 🔌 🚰 🐕 🎣

SCARBOROUGH, North Yorkshire   Map ref 5D3   SatNav YO11 3NN

TOURING & CAMPING PARK (enjoyEngland.com ★★★★)

Cayton Village Caravan Park Ltd
Mill Lane, Cayton Bay, Scarborough YO11 3NN
T: (01723) 583171 **E:** info@caytontouring.co.uk
W: www.caytontouring.co.uk

🚐 (235)   £13.00-£35.00
🚏 (20)   £15.00-£35.00
⛺ (55)   £13.00-£28.00
310 touring pitches

Playground, recreation field, dog walk, shop and bus service from park entrance. Seasonal pitches, winter storage, caravan sales. Super sites, Hardstanding and grass pitches. Beach 0.5m, Scarborough 3m. Adjoining village with fish shop & pub. **Directions:** From A64 take B1261 to Filey. In Cayton turn left onto Mill Lane. From A165 turn inland at Cayton Bay roundabout onto Mill Lane. 0.5m on RHS. **Open:** 1st March to 1st November.

Site: ⛺🅿 **Payment:** 💳 ☼ **Leisure:** 🎣 ▶ **Children:** ⌁ ⛰ **Catering:** 🛒 **Park:** 🐕 🚮 🖥 🛢 ☔ **Touring:** 🔌 🚰 🐕 🎣

SCARBOROUGH, North Yorkshire   Map ref 5D3   SatNav YO11 3NU

HOLIDAY, TOURING & CAMPING PARK (enjoyEngland.com ★★★★★)

Flower of May Holiday Park
Flower of May Holiday Park, Lebberston, Scarborough, North Yorkshire YO11 3NU
T: (01723) 584311 **F:** (01723) 585716 **E:** info@flowerofmay.com
W: www.flowerofmay.com **£ BOOK ONLINE**

🚐 (300)   £22.00-£28.00
🚏 (20)   £22.00-£28.00
⛺ (60)   £22.00-£28.00
🛖 (20)   £380.00-£690.00

SPECIAL PROMOTIONS
Early booking offer and other offers available. Please refer to website.

Excellent family-run park. Luxury indoor pool, adventure playground, bar complex, mini-market, fish & chip shop, cafe and 9 hole golf course. Ideal for coast and country. Prices per pitch, per night includes four people and one car.

Luxury caravans for hire. Seasonal serviced pitches. Brand new Glamping Pods available for a unique experience (please check our website for prices).

Directions: From A64 take the A165 Scarborough/Filey coast road. Well signposted at Lebberston.

Open: Easter to October.

Site: 🏠 ⛺🅿 **Payment:** 💳 ☼ **Leisure:** 🎣 ▶ 🎱 ♨ **Children:** ⌁ ⛰ **Catering:** ✕ 🛒 **Park:** 🐕 🎠 🎵 🚮 🖥 🛢 🕍 ☔ **Touring:** 🚰 🐕 🎣

Jasmine Park

Cross Lane, Snainton, Scarborough YO13 9BE
T: (01723) 859240 E: enquiries@jasminepark.co.uk
W: www.jasminepark.co.uk £ BOOK ONLINE

(74)   £17.00-£37.00
(74)   £17.00-£37.00
(20)   £17.00-£37.00
(1)   £300.00-£580.00
94 touring pitches

Family-owned, tranquil park in picturesque countryside setting between Scarborough (8 miles) and Pickering. Superbly maintained facilities including our fantastic children's play area. Yorkshire Coast Caravan Park of the Year 2010. Tents and tourers welcome. Seasonal pitches and storage available. Luxury caravans for hire.

Directions: Turn south off the A170 in Snainton opposite the junior school at traffic lights. Signposted.   **Open:** March to October.

Payment: ▨ ☼ Leisure: ♨ ♪ ↑ ∪ Children: ☠ ⌂ Catering: ☎ Park: ♞ ▥ ▦ ◫ ☗ Touring: ♀ ☊ ⊕ ♣ ♪

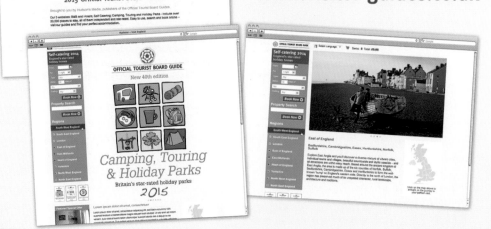

Bowland Fell Park

Tosside, Skipton, North Yorkshire BD23 4SD
T: (01729) 840278 **E:** info@bowlandfellpark.co.uk
W: www.bowlandfellpark.co.uk **£ BOOK ONLINE**

(163) £249.00-£649.00

SPECIAL PROMOTIONS
Please contact us for
special offers.

Luxury holiday homes to buy or hire ideally located between the Forest of Bowland and Yorkshire Dales with views spanning from Pen-Y-Ghent to Pendle Hill. An ideal location for families and couples to explore the unspoilt countryside. 12 month holiday season, pet friendly and excellent facilities including a heated swimming pool, on-site pub, shop, and indoor games room. Camping Pods coming soon!

Directions: Please contact us for directions.   **Open:** All year.

Site: 🏕 Payment: 💳 Leisure: ♿ ♪ ⮑ ∪ ♨ ♛ Property: 🐕 🎵 🖥 🗑 Children: 🛝 ⛷ Catering: ✕ 🍴

Robin Hood Caravan Park

Slingsby, York YO62 4AP
T: (01653) 628391 **F:** (01653) 628392 **E:** info@robinhoodcaravanpark.co.uk
W: www.robinhoodcaravanpark.co.uk **£ BOOK ONLINE**

🚐 (38)   £20.00-£28.00
🚎 (38)   £20.00-£28.00
⛺ (38)   £15.00-£25.00
🏠 (15)   £195.00-£515.00
      38 touring pitches

SPECIAL PROMOTIONS
Loyalty card available
for campers.

An award winning, privately owned park set in the heart of picturesque Ryedale. Peaceful and tranquil, a perfect base for families and couples wishing to explore the stunning countryside of North Yorkshire. Within easy reach of York, Castle Howard, Flamingoland and the coastal resorts of Scarborough, Whitby and Filey. Overnight holding area available.

Directions: Situated on the edge of Slingsby   **Open:** March to October.
with access off the B1257 Malton to Helmsley
road.

Payment: 💳 ☀ Leisure: ♪ ∪ Children: 🛝 ⛷ Catering: 🍴 Park: 🐕 🖥 🗑 📖 Touring: 🚾 🚻 🚐

SOUTH OTTERINGTON, North Yorkshire Map ref 5C3   SatNav DL7 9JB

Otterington Park

Station Road, South Otterington, Northallerton, North Yorkshire DL7 9JB
T: (01609) 780656 **E:** info@otteringtonpark.com
W: www.otteringtonpark.com **£ BOOK ONLINE**

(66)
(66)
66 touring pitches

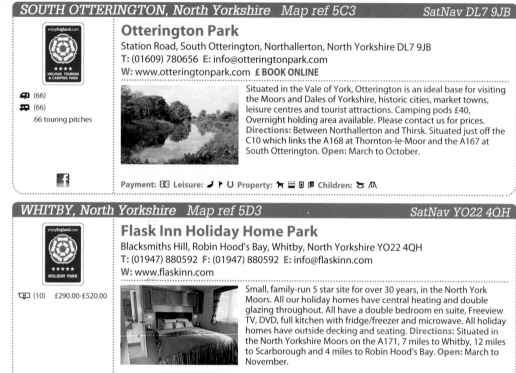

Situated in the Vale of York, Otterington is an ideal base for visiting the Moors and Dales of Yorkshire, historic cities, market towns, leisure centres and tourist attractions. Camping pods £40, Overnight holding area available. Please contact us for prices.
Directions: Between Northallerton and Thirsk. Situated just off the C10 which links the A168 at Thornton-le-Moor and the A167 at South Otterington. **Open:** March to October.

Payment: ☒ Leisure: ♪ ▶ ♨ Property: ☂ ▦ ▢ ▦ Children: ☍ ⛰

WHITBY, North Yorkshire Map ref 5D3   SatNav YO22 4QH

Flask Inn Holiday Home Park

Blacksmiths Hill, Robin Hood's Bay, Whitby, North Yorkshire YO22 4QH
T: (01947) 880592 **F:** (01947) 880592 **E:** info@flaskinn.com
W: www.flaskinn.com

(10) £290.00-£520.00

Small, family-run 5 star site for over 30 years, in the North York Moors. All our holiday homes have central heating and double glazing throughout. All have a double bedroom en suite, Freeview TV, DVD, full kitchen with fridge/freezer and microwave. All holiday homes have outside decking and seating. **Directions:** Situated in the North Yorkshire Moors on the A171, 7 miles to Whitby, 12 miles to Scarborough and 4 miles to Robin Hood's Bay. **Open:** March to November.

Site: ☎ Payment: ☒ Leisure: ♿ ♪ ♨ Property: ▦ ▢ ▦ Children: ☍ ⛰ Catering: ✗ ☕

Middlewood Farm Holiday Park

Middlewood Lane, Fylingthorpe, North Yorkshire YO22 4UF
T: (01947) 880414 **F:** (01947) 880871 **E:** info@middlewoodfarm.com
W: www.middlewoodfarm.com

🚐 (21)   £16.00-£28.00
🚎 (24)   £16.00-£28.00
⛺ (100)   £14.00-£27.00
🚐 (30)   £195.00-£619.00

SPECIAL PROMOTIONS

Holiday Hire: Short breaks available early & late season - from £135.00.

Gypsy Cabins: Available All Year.

Tourers & Motorhomes: 11 month season (closed 7th Jan - 7th Feb).

Tents: March till October.

Peaceful, 5 Star Award-Winning family park. A walkers paradise with magnificent panoramic coastal and moorland views! Level, sheltered hardstandings, electric hook ups, luxury facilities (heated early & late season), private wash-cubicles, bath, Wi-Fi and children's play area. 10 minutes walk to pub, shop, beach and Robin Hood's Bay. Superb Holiday Homes & Gypsy Cabins for hire. A friendly welcome awaits!

Directions: Follow A171 Scarborough/Whitby road, signposted from Fylingthorpe/Robin Hood's Bay junction. In Fylingthorpe turn onto Middlewood Lane. Park is 500yards. Follow brown tourist signs.

Open: Holiday Hire: All year.
Touring: 11 Months (Closed 7th Jan - 7th Feb).

Site: 🅰🅿 Payment: 💷 Children: 🐎 ⚠ Catering: 🐾 Park: 🐕 🚮 🚻 📷 Touring: 🚰 🚽 🔌

Northcliffe & Seaview Holiday Parks

Bottoms Lane, High Hawsker, Whitby, North Yorkshire YO22 4LL
T: (01947) 880477 **F:** (01947) 880972 **E:** enquiries@northcliffe-seaview.com
W: www.northcliffe-seaview.com **£ BOOK ONLINE**

🚐 (62) £1500.00-£1950.00
🚐 (3)   £285.00-£665.00

SPECIAL PROMOTIONS

Visit our website to view our new caravans for sale, check availability & book your holiday.

Register your email address to receive our 'special offers' by email.

These award winning parks are situated on the beautiful Heritage Coast twixt Whitby and RHB. Both Gold Award Conservation parks have fabulous countryside and coastal views with access to superb walks and a cycle track.

We sell and hire luxury caravans, have a 4 Star Gold Award cottage and an exclusive seasonal only touring park. Facilities include the Coast Café Bar, play parks, football pitches and lots more.

Directions: Located 3 miles south of Whitby on A171. Turn left onto the B1447 through Hawsker Village, turn left at the top of the hill onto the private road Bottoms Lane.

Open: March 1st until November 7th.

Site: 🏕 Payment: 💷 Leisure: ♿ 🎵 🏌 ↻ 🎣 Property: 🖥 🔌 Children: 🐎 ⚠ Catering: ✖ 🐾

WHITBY, North Yorkshire   Map ref 5D3   SatNav YO22 4JX

Whitby Holiday Park - Touring Park

Whitby Holiday Park, Saltwick Bay, North Yorkshire YO22 4JX
T: (01947) 602664 **F:** (01947) 602979 **E:** info@whitbyholidaypark.co.uk
W: www.whitbypark.co.uk **£ BOOK ONLINE**

Ideal base for touring the beautiful North Yorkshire Moors. Whitby Holiday Park is a touring site (No Tent pitches available) located in Saltwick Bay. It is a small friendly holiday park for all the family. Please contact us for 2015 rates. **Directions:** Please contact for directions. **Open:** March - October.

Site: **Payment:** **Leisure:** **Children:** **Catering:** **Park:** **Touring:**

YORK, North Yorkshire   Map ref 4C1   SatNav YO61 1RY

Alders Caravan Park

Home Farm, Monk Green, Alne nr Easingwold, York YO61 1RY
T: (01347) 838722 **F:** (01347) 838722 **E:** enquiries@homefarmalne.co.uk
W: www.alderscaravanpark.co.uk

(87)	£20.00-£22.00	
	£20.00-£22.00	
	£20.00	
(2)	£38.00	

87 touring pitches

A working farm in historic parkland where visitors may enjoy peace and tranquillity. York (on bus route), Moors, Dales and coast nearby. Tastefully landscaped, adjoins village cricket ground. Woodland walk. **Directions:** From A19 exit at Alne sign, in 1.5 miles turn left at T-junction, 0.5 miles park on left in village centre. **Open:** March to October.

Site: **Payment:** **Leisure:** **Children:** **Catering:** **Park:** **Touring:**

YORK, North Yorkshire   Map ref 4C1   SatNav YO61 1ET

Goosewood Holiday Park

Sutton on the Forest, York, North Yorkshire YO61 1ET
T: (01347) 810829 **F:** (01347) 811498 **E:** info@flowerofmay.com
W: www.flowerofmay.com **£ BOOK ONLINE**

(90)	£22.00-£28.00	
(10)	£22.00-£28.00	
(19)	£340.00-£1248.00	
(5)	£340.00-£610.00	

SPECIAL PROMOTIONS
Early booking offer and other offers available. Please refer to website.

A quiet, peaceful park with fishing lake, children's adventure play area and leisure complex with indoor pool, bar and games room. Luxury holiday lodges and caravans, many with hot tubs available to hire. A perfect place to relax and amble through wooded walks. Ideal for visiting the historic city of York and surrounding beauty spots of Yorkshire. A warm welcome. For accommodation call 01723 584311, for touring please book online.

Directions: North of York. Follow route to Strensall.   **Open:** March - 2nd January.

Site: **Payment:** **Leisure:** **Children:** **Catering:** **Park:** **Touring:**

YORK, North Yorkshire   Map ref 4C1 — SatNav YO60 6QP

AA
▶▶▶▶

75 touring pitches

York Meadows Caravan Park
York Road, Sheriff Hutton, York YO60 6QP
T: (01347) 878508 **E:** reception@yorkmeadowscaravanpark.com
W: www.yorkmeadowscaravanpark.com **£ BOOK ONLINE**

York Meadows Caravan Park at Sheriff Hutton is set in an idyllic location surrounded by rolling farmland, nestled in the stunning and tranquil splendour of the Howardian Hills and Vale of York. Situated in a perfect area to explore the hustle and bustle of the Historic City of York, or perhaps one of the greatest private residences in Britain, Castle Howard Stately Home just 5 miles from the park. Please contact for 2015 rates. **Directions:** Please see website. **Open:** 1st March 31st October.

Site: A🅿 Payment: 💷 Children: ⛺ 🛝 Park: 🐕 🚐 🚽 🕻 Touring: 🚻 🚾 🚰 🎣

HOLMFIRTH, West Yorkshire   Map ref 4B1 — SatNav HD9 7TD

enjoyEngland.com
★★★
TOURING & CAMPING PARK

🚐 (62)   £17.00-£21.00
🚎 (62)   £13.50-£19.50
⛺ (62)   £7.50-£21.50
62 touring pitches

Holme Valley Camping and Caravan Park
Thongsbridge, Holmfirth, West Yorkshire HD9 7TD
T: (01484) 665819 **E:** enquiries@holmevalleycamping.com
W: www.holmevalleycamping.com

Picturesque setting in 'Summer Wine' country. Grass, concrete and gravel pitches. 16-amp hook-ups. Well-stocked food shop. Off-licence. Fishing in small lake and river. Children's play area. Five minutes walk from village. David Bellamy Gold Award. **Directions:** Turn into our lane off A6024, 1 mile north of Holmfirth, by bottle banks. Use either entrance. Follow lane to valley bottom, without turning left. **Open:** All year.

Site: A🅿 Payment: 💷 € ☼ Leisure: 🚴 🏃 Children: ⛺ 🛝 Catering: 🛒 Park: 🐕 🚽 🕻 Touring: 🚻 🚾 🚰

Don't Miss...

Chester Zoo
Cheshire CH2 1EU
(01244) 380280
www.chesterzoo.org
The UK's number one zoo with over 11000 animals and 400 different species, including some of the most exotic and endangered species on the planet.

Jodrell Bank Discovery Centre
Macclesfield, Cheshire SK11 9DL
(01477) 571766
www.jodrellbank.net
A great day out for all the family, explore the wonders of the universe and learn about the workings of the giant Lovell Telescope.

Muncaster Castle
Ravenglass, Cumbria CA18 1RQ
(01229) 717614
www.muncaster.co.uk
Medieval Muncaster Castle is a treasure trove of paintings, silver, embroideries and more. With acres of Grade 2 woodland gardens, famous for rhododendrons and breathtaking views of the Lake District.

Blackpool Illuminations
Sept-Nov, Blackpool
www.blackpool-illuminations.net
This world famous display lights up Blackpool's promenade with over 1 million glittering lights that will make you oooh and aaah in wonder. Head for the big switch on or buy tickets for the Festival Weekend.

Tate Liverpool
Merseyside L3 4BB
(0151) 702 7400
www.tate.org.uk/liverpool
Tate Liverpool presents displays and international exhibitions of modern and contemporary art in beautiful light filled galleries and is free to visit except for special exhibitions.

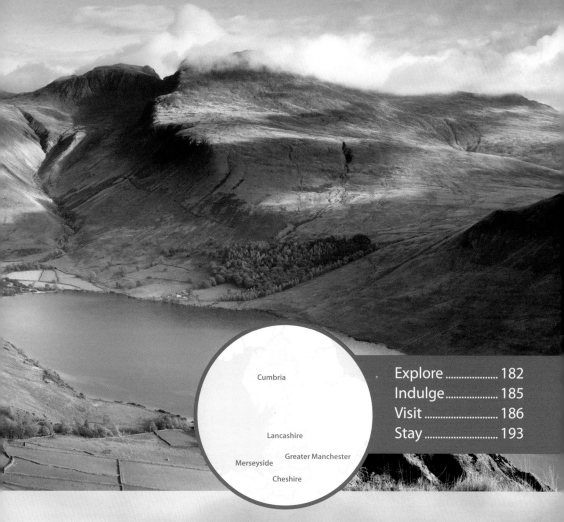

North West

Cheshire, Cumbria, Lancashire,
Greater Manchester, Merseyside

Cumbria

Lancashire

Greater Manchester

Merseyside

Cheshire

The breathtaking scenery of the Lake District dominates the North West, but urban attractions such as cosmopolitan Manchester and Liverpool, with its grand architecture and cultural credentials, have much to recommend them. Further afield, you can explore the Roman and Medieval heritage of Chester, discover Lancashire's wealth of historic houses and gardens, or make a date for one of the huge variety of events that take place in this region throughout the year.

Explore – North West

Cheshire

The charms of the old walled city of Chester and the picturesque villages that dot Cheshire's countryside contrast sharply with the industrial towns of Runcorn and Warrington. Iron age forts, Roman ruins, Medieval churches, Tudor cottages and elegant Georgian and Victorian stately homes are among the many attractive sights of the county. South Cheshire, like Cumbria to the north, has long been the home of the wealthy from Manchester and Liverpool and boasts a huge selection of of excellent eateries. It also has peaceful, pretty countryside, and is within easy reach of the wilder terrain of the Peak District and North Wales.

Hotspot: Walk the city walls, step inside the magnificent gothic Cathedral, take a cruise along the River Dee or browse the picturesque medieval shopping streets of Eastgate and Watergate - Chester has over 2000 years of Roman and Medieval history to show you, as well as some seriously good shopping and eating on offer too!

Hotspot: Explore the breathtaking beauty of England's largest lake with a cruise on Lake Windermere for the most scenic views of the Lakeland fells.

Cumbria

In this lovely corner of England, there is beauty in breathtaking variety. The area is loved by many who come back time and again to its inspirational magic, brilliant blue lakes and craggy mountain tops. The central Lake District with its mountains, lakes and woods is so well known that there is a tendency to forget that the rest of Cumbria contains some of the most varied and attractive landscape in Britain. In the east of the county, the peaceful Eden Valley is sheltered by the towering hills of the Pennines, with charming little red sandstone villages and reminders of the Roman occupation everywhere. Alston, with its cobbled streets is the highest town in England, and has been used for numerous TV location sets.

Cumbria's long coastline is full of variety with rocky cliffs, sea birds, sandy estuaries, miles of sun-trap sand dunes and friendly harbours. In Autumn the deciduous woodlands and bracken coloured hillsides glow with colour. In Winter, the snow covered mountain tops dazzle magnificently against blue skies. In Spring, you can discover the delights of the magical, constantly changing light and the joy of finding carpets of wild flowers.

The Lake District is an outdoor enthusiasts paradise offering everything from walking and climbing to orienteering, potholing, cycling, riding, golf, sailing, sailboarding, canoeing, fishing and waterskiing. A great way to take in the beauty of this unique area is to plan your own personal route on foot, or cycle one of the many formal trails such as the Cumbria Cycle Way. The Cumbrian climate is ideal for gardens and the area is famous for the rhododendrons and azaleas which grow here in abundance. If you fancy a break from the great outdoors there is a wealth of historic houses, from small cottages where famous writers have lived to stately homes, that have seen centuries of gracious living and architectural importance.

Hotspot: Cholmondeley Castle Garden in Cheshire is among the most romantically beautiful gardens in the country. Visitors can enjoy the tranquil Temple Water Garden, Ruin Water Garden, memorial mosaic, Rose garden & many mixed borders. www.cholmondeleycastle.com

Lancashire

Lancashire's Forest of Bowland is an area of outstanding natural beauty with wild crags, superb walks, streams, valleys and fells. Blackpool on the coast has been the playground of the North West for many years and still draws millions of holiday makers every year, attracted to its seven miles of beach, illuminations, Pleasure Beach Amusement Park and golf. Morecambe, Southport, Lytham St Annes and Fleetwood also offer wide beaches, golf and bracing walks. Lancaster, a city since Roman times, has fine museums, a castle and an imitation of the Taj Mahal, the Ashton Memorial.

Manchester

Manchester's prosperity can be traced back to the 14th century when Flemish weavers arrived to transform a market town into a thriving boom city at the forefront of the Industrial Revolution. Now known as The Capital of the North, the city is rich in culture with plenty of galleries, museums, libraries and theatres. The City Art Gallery displays its famous pre-Raphaelite collection while the Halle Orchestra regularly fills the Bridgewater Hall. At Granada Studios you can still tour the set of Coronation Street and you can find quality shopping locations and sporting (particularly football) traditions. Cosmopolitan Manchester makes a great place to stay for a spot of retail therapy too!

Hotspot: Set in a stunning waterside location at the heart of the redeveloped Salford Quays in Greater Manchester, The Lowry is an architectural gem that brings together a wide variety of performing and visual arts, including the works of LS Lowry and contemporary exhibitions. www.thelowry.com

Merseyside

Liverpool was an important city long before The Beatles emerged from their Cavern in the Swinging Sixties. It grew from a village into a prosperous port, where emigrants sailed for the New World and immigrants arrived from Ireland. Today the ocean going liners are fewer, but the revitalised dock complex ensures that the city is as vibrant as ever. Liverpool's waterfront regeneration flagship is the Albert Dock Village, which includes the Maritime Museum and Tate Gallery Liverpool. The city has two modern cathedrals, a symphony orchestra, plenty of museums and Britain's oldest repertory theatre The Playhouse. In recent years, Liverpool has seen the opening of an extensive range of cafés, restaurants and accommodation to suit all tastes and budgets.

Hotspot: Discover objects rescued from the Titanic among the treasures at the Merseyside Maritime Museum, one of the venues that make up the National Museums Liverpool, an eclectic group of free museums and galleries. www.liverpoolmuseums.org.uk

Treat yourself to delicious sandwiches, scones, cakes, a nice chilled glass of Champagne and breathtaking views at the **White Star Grand Hall**, 30 James Street, Liverpool. Formerly the White Star Line's first-class lounge, the superb architecture recreates the splendour of a more glamorous era.
www.rmstitanichotel.co.uk

One for the boys? Experience the world's greatest sport at the **National Football Museum** in Manchester. Whether you're a diehard football fan, planning a visit with your family or on a weekend break to the great city of Manchester, visit the world's biggest and best football museum.
www.nationalfootballmuseum.com

Indulge in some seriously foodie fun at the 10th Anniversary of the **World's Original Marmalade Awards & Festival** at historic Dalemain Mansion & Gardens, in the Lake District. With a range of events including of course, delicious marmalade tasting. Saturday 28th Feb-Sun 1st Mar 2015.
www.dalemainmarmaladeawards.co.uk

Enjoy a sophisticated feast at Simon Radley's chic, award-winning **Restaurant at the Chester Grosvenor** which has retained its Michelin star since 1990 and holds 4 AA Rosettes. (01244) 324024
www.chestergrosvenor.com

Take a trip on a steam-hauled dining train with the **East Lancashire Railway** and step into a world of vintage glamour and sophistication. Excellent food and a relaxed and friendly atmosphere in plush surroundings capture the essence of bygone days.
www.eastlancsrailway.org.uk

Visit – North West

 Attractions with this sign participate in the Visitor Attraction Quality Assurance Scheme.

Cheshire

Arley Hall & Gardens

Northwich, Cheshire CW9 6NA
(01565) 777353
www.arleyhallandgardens.com
Arley Hall's gardens are a wonderful example of the idea that the best gardens are living works of art.

Catalyst Science Discovery Centre
Widnes, Cheshire WA8 0DF
(0151) 420 1121
www.catalyst.org.uk
Interactive science centre whose aim is to make science exciting and accessible to people of all ages and abilities.

©Val Corbett

Chester Cathedral
Cheshire CH1 2HU
(01244) 324756
www.chestercathedral.com
A must-see for Chester, a beautiful cathedral with a fascinating history.

Go Ape! Hire Wire Forest Adventure - Delamere
Northwich, Cheshire CW8 2JD
(0845) 643 9215
www.goape.co.uk
Take to the trees and experience an exhilarating course of rope bridges, tarzan swings and zip slides, all set high above the forest floor.

Grosvenor Park Open Air Theatre
July-August, Grosvenor Park, Chester, Cheshire
www.grosvenorparkopenairtheatre.co.uk
The greatest open air theatre outside of London returns for a summer of exciting performances.

Hare Hill Gardens
Macclesfield, Cheshire SK10 4QB
(01625) 584412
www.nationaltrust.org.uk/harehill
A small but perfectly formed and tranquil woodland garden.

National Waterways Museum
Ellesmere Port, Cheshire CH65 4FW
(0151) 335 5017
www.canalrivertrust.org.uk
Unlock the wonders of our waterways.

RHS Flower Show Tatton Park
July, Tatton Park, Knutsford, Cheshire
www.rhs.org.uk
A fantastic display of flora and fauna and all things garden related in stunning Cheshire countryside.

Cumbria

Coniston Water Festival
July, Coniston Water, Lake District, Cumbria
www.conistonwaterfestival.org.uk
*Features fun activities and events focused on the
Coniston lake and the unique aspects of water-
related culture and sport.*

Grizedale Forest Visitor Centre
Hawkshead, Cumbria LA22 0QJ
(01229) 860010
www.forestry.gov.uk/northwestengland
*Grizedale Forest offers a range of activities for all
ages through the year, from mountain biking to
relaxing walks, Go-Ape to the sculpture trails.*

Holker Hall & Gardens
Grange-over-Sands, Cumbria LA11 7PL
(01539) 558328
www.holker.co.uk
*Home to Lord and Lady Cavendish, Victorian wing,
glorious gardens, parkland and woodlands.*

Museum of Lakeland Life
Kendal, Cumbria LA9 5AL
(01539) 722464
www.lakelandmuseum.org.uk
*This award-winning museum takes you and your
family back through time to tell the story of the Lake
District and its inhabitants.*

Penrith Castle
Cumbria CA11 7HX
(01912) 691200
www.english-heritage.org.uk/daysout/properties/
penrith-castle/
*The mainly 15th Century remains of a castle begun
by Bishop Strickland of Carlisle and developed by the
Nevilles and Richard III.*

Ravenglass & Eskdale Railway
Cumbria CA18 1SW
(01229) 717171
www.ravenglass-railway.co.uk
*Heritage steam engines haul open-top and cosy
covered carriages from the Lake District coastal
village of Ravenglass to the foot of England's highest
mountains.*

South Lakes Safari Zoo
Dalton-in-Furness, Cumbria LA15 8JR
(01229) 466086
www.southlakessafarizoo.com
*The ultimate interactive animal experience. Get close
to wildlife at Cumbria's top tourist attraction.*

Ullswater Steamers
Cumbria CA11 0US
(01768) 482229
www.ullswater-steamers.co.uk
*The 'Steamers' create the perfect opportunity to
combine a cruise with some of the most famous and
spectacular walks in the lake District.*

Windermere Lake Cruises, Lakeside
Newby Bridge, Cumbria LA12 8AS
(01539) 443360
www.windermere-lakecruises.co.uk
*Steamers and launches sail daily between Ambleside,
Bowness and Lakeside.*

Great North Swim
June, Windermere, Cumbria
www.greatswim.org
*Europe's biggest open water
swim series comes to the
Lake District.*

The World of Beatrix Potter
Bowness, Cumbria LA23 3BX
(01539) 488444
www.hop-skip-jump.com
*A magical indoor attraction that brings to life all 23
Beatrix Potter's Peter Rabbit tales.*

Lancashire

Blackpool Dance Festival
May, Blackpool, Lancashire
www.blackpooldancefestival.com
The world's first and foremost festival of dancing.

Blackpool Pleasure Beach
Blackpool, Lancashire FY4 1EZ
(0871) 222 1234
www.blackpoolpleasurebeach.com
The UK's most ride intensive theme park and home to the legendary Big One and Valhalla.

Clitheroe Food Festival
August, Clitheroe, Lancashire
www.clitheroefoodfestival.com
Celebrating the very finest Lancashire food and drink produces. Includes chef demos, tastings and cookery workshops.

Farmer Ted's Farm Park
Ormskirk, Lancashire L39 7HW
(0151) 526 0002
www.farmerteds.com
An interactive children's activity park, sited on a working farm within the beautiful Lancashire countryside.

Garstang Walking Festival
May, Garstang, Lancashire
www.visitlancashire.com
A celebration of springtime in the stunning countryside of Garstang and the surrounding area. Guided walks and activities for all the family.

Lytham Proms Festival
August, Lytham & St Annes, Lancashire
www.visitlancashire.com
Summer proms spectacular with shows from leading performers.

Sandcastle Waterpark
Blackpool, Lancashire FY4 1BB
(01253) 343602
www.sandcastle-waterpark.co.uk
The UK's Largest Indoor Waterpark and with 18 slides and attractions.

Ribchester Roman Museum
Preston, Lancashire PR3 3XS
(01254) 878261
www.ribchesterromanmuseum.org
Lancashire's only specialist Roman museum, located on the North bank of the beautiful River Ribble.

Wyre Estuary Country Park
Thornton Lancashire FY5 5LR
(01253) 857890
www.wyre.gov.uk
The award winning Wyre Estuary Country Park offers year-round activities and events for all the family including ranger-led walks, environmentally themed activities and annual events like the Family Sculpture Day.

Manchester

East Lancashire Railway

Bury, Greater Manchester BL9 0EY
(0161) 764 7790
www.eastlancsrailway.org.uk
The beautifully restored East Lancashire Railway takes you on a captivating journey to discover the region's rich transport heritage.

Greater Manchester Marathon in Trafford

April, Trafford, Manchester
www.greatermanchestermarathon.com
The UK's flattest, fastest and friendliest Marathon with a superfast course, great entertainment, outstanding crowd support and glorious finish at Manchester United Football Club.

Manchester Art Gallery

Greater Manchester M2 3JL
(0161) 235 8888
www.manchestergalleries.org
Houses one of the country's finest art collections in spectacular Victorian and Contemporary surroundings. Also changing exhibitions and a programme of events and a host of free family friendly resources.

Manchester Histories Festival

March, Various city centre locations
www.manchesterhistoriesfestival.org.uk
The ten-day MHF celebrates the heritage and history of Manchester across numerous city centre venues. The festival offers a fantastic opportunity to explore and learn this great city and is a great event for old and young alike.

Whitworth Art Gallery

Manchester M15 6ER
(0161) 275 7450
www.manchester.ac.uk/whitworth
The Whitworth Art Gallery is home to an internationally-famous collection of British watercolours, textiles and wallpapers.

Manchester Museum

Greater Manchester M13 9PL
(0161) 275 2648
www.manchester.ac.uk/museum
Found on Oxford Road, on The University of Manchester campus (in a very impressive gothic-style building). Highlights include Stan the T.rex, mummies, live animals such as frogs and snakes, object handling and a varied programme of events.

Manchester United Museum & Tour Centre

Greater Manchester M16 0RA
(0161) 868 8000
www.manutd.com
The official museum and tour offers every football fan a unique insight into Manchester United Football Club and a fantastic day out.

People's History Museum

Greater Manchester M3 3ER
(0161) 838 9190
www.phm.org.uk
National centre for the collection, conservation, interpretation and study of material relating to the history of working people in Britain.

Ramsbottom Chocolate Festival

April, Ramsbottom, Greater Manchester
www. ramsbottomchocolatefestival.com
Alongside the two-day chocolate market expect interactive workshops and activities for adults/ children, alfresco dining, chocolate real ale tour, music, competitions, Giant Easter Egg display, and much more.

Saddleworth and District Whit Friday Brass Band Contest

June, Oldham, Greater Manchester
www.whitfriday.brassbands.saddleworth.org
Well over a hundred brass bands compete in contests at venues scattered around the moorland villages and towns on the western edge of the Pennines. All of the contests are open-air, many in delightful surroundings.

Merseyside

Beatles Story

Liverpool, Merseyside L3 4AD
(0151) 709 1963
www.beatlesstory.com
Located within Liverpool's historic Albert Dock, the Beatles Story is a unique visitor attraction that transports you on an enlightening and atmospheric journey into the life, times, culture and music of the Beatles.

Birkenhead Festival of Transport
September, Birkenhead, Merseyside
www.bheadtransportfest.com
Featuring classic cars, steam engines and other modes of vintage transport.

Croxteth Hall & Country Park
Liverpool, Merseyside L12 0HB
(0151) 233 6910
www.liverpoolcityhalls.co.uk/croxteth-hall/
Stately home with 500 acres estate including visitor farm, Victorian walled garden and seasonal events.

The Gallery Liverpool
Merseyside L8 5RE
(0151) 709 2442
www.thegalleryliverpool.co.uk
Set in the heart of Liverpool's Independent Cultural District, the gallery occupies the entire upper floor of the industrial premises of John O'Keeffe and Son Ltd.

Grand National
April, Aintree, Merseyside
www.aintree.co.uk
The most famous horse race over jumps takes place over the challenging Aintree fences.

Knowsley Safari Park

Merseyside L34 4AN
(0151) 430 9009
www. knowsleysafariexperience.co.uk
Enjoy a 5 mile safari through 450 acres of historic parkland.

Liverpool Football Club
Merseyside L4 0TH
(0151) 260 6677
www.liverpoolfc.com
Meet an LFC Legend; get your photograph with one of our many trophies or indulge yourself in one of our award winning Experience Days.

Liverpool Sound City
May, Bramley Moore Dock, Liverpool
www.liverpoolsoundcity.co.uk
An unrivalled 3-day festival of incredible live music and arts that includes a groundbreaking 2-day music and digital industry conference.

Speke Hall, Gardens & Estate
Liverpool, Merseyside L24 1XD
(0151) 427 7231
www.nationaltrust.org.uk/main/w-spekehall
One of the most famous half timbered houses in Britain, dating from the 15th century.

Walker Art Gallery
Liverpool, Merseyside L3 8EL
(0151) 478 4199
www.walkerartgallery.org.uk
Home to outstanding works by Rubens, Rembrandt, Poussin, Gainsborough and Hogarth, the Walker Art Gallery is one of the finest art galleries in Europe

Wirral Folk on the Coast Festival
June, Wirral, Merseyside
www.wirralfolkonthecoast.com
All-on-one-site friendly festival at Whitby Sports & Social Club, with fine music real ale and good food being served plus many more visitor attractions.

World Museum Liverpool
Merseyside L3 8EN
(0151) 478 4393
www.liverpoolmuseums.org.uk/wml
One of Britain's finest museums, with extensive collections from the Amazonian Rain Forest to the mysteries of outer space.

Tourist Information Centres

When you arrive at your destination, visit the Tourist Information Centre for quality assured help with accommodation and information about local attractions and events, or email your request before you go.

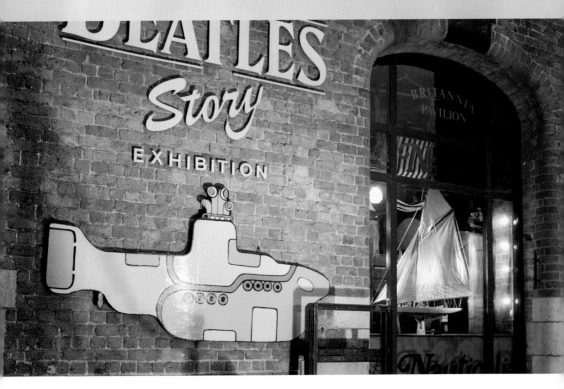

Accrington	Town Hall	01254 380293	information@leisureinhyndburn.co.uk
Alston Moor	Town Hall	01434 382244	alston.tic@eden.gov.uk
Altrincham	20 Stamford New Road	0161 912 5931	tourist.information@trafford.gov.uk
Ambleside	Central Buildings	015394 32582	tic@thehubofambleside.com
Appleby-In-Westmorland	Moot Hall	017683 51177	tic@applebytown.org.uk
Barnoldswick	Post Office Buildings	01282 666704 / 661661	tourist.info@pendle.gov.uk
Barrow-In-Furness	Forum 28	01229 876543	touristinfo@barrowbc.gov.uk
Blackburn	Blackburn Market	01254 688040	visit@blackburn.gov.uk
Blackpool	Festival House, The People's Promenade	01253 478222	tic@blackpool.gov.uk
Bolton	Central Library Foyer	01204 334321 / 334271	tourist.info@bolton.gov.uk
Bowness	Glebe Road	015394 42895	bownesstic@lakedistrict.gov.uk
Brampton	Moot Hall	016977 3433/ 01228 625600	bramptontic@gmail.co.uk
Broughton-In-Furness	Town Hall	01229 716115	broughtontic@btconnect.com
Burnley	Regeneration and Planning Policy	01282 477210	tic@burnley.gov.uk
Bury	The Fusilier Museum	0161 253 5111	touristinformation@bury.gov.uk
Carlisle	Old Town Hall	01228 625600	tourism@carlisle.gov.uk
Chester (Town Hall)	Town Hall	0845 647 7868	welcome@chestervic.co.uk
Cleethorpes	Victoria Square	01253 853378	cleveleystic@wyrebc.gov.uk
Clitheroe	Platform Gallery & VIC	01200 425566	tourism@ribblevalley.gov.uk
Cockermouth	4 Old Kings Arms Lane	01900 822634	cockermouthtouristinformationcentre@btconnect.com

Congleton	Town Hall	01260 271095	congletontic@cheshireeast.gov.uk
Coniston	Ruskin Avenue	015394 41533	mail@conistontic.org
Discover Pendle	Boundary Mill Stores	01282 856186	discoverpendle@pendle.gov.uk
Egremont	12 Main Street	01946 820693	lowescourt@btconnect.com
Ellesmere Port	McArthur Glen Outlet Village	0151 356 5562	enquiries@cheshiredesigneroutlet.com
Garstang	1 Cherestanc Square	01995 602125	garstangtic@wyrebc.gov.uk
Glennridding Ullswater	Bekside Car Park	017684 82414	ullswatertic@lakedistrict.gov.uk
Grange-Over-Sands	Victoria Hall	015395 34026	council@grangeoversands.net
Kendal	25 Stramongate	01539 735891	info@kendaltic.co.uk
Keswick	Moot Hall	017687 72645	keswicktic@lakedistrict.gov.uk
Kirkby Stephen	Market Square	017683 71199	visit@uecp.org.uk
Lancaster	The Storey	01524 582394	lancastervic@lancaster.gov.uk
Liverpool Albert Dock	Anchor Courtyard	0151 233 2008	jackie.crawford@liverpool.gov.uk
Liverpool John Lennon Airport	Information Desk	0151 907 1058	information@liverpoolairport.com
Lytham St Annes	c/o Town Hall	01253 725610	touristinformation@fylde.gov.uk
Macclesfield	Town Hall	01625 378123 / 378062	karen.connon@cheshireeast.gov.uk
Manchester	45-50 Piccadilly Plaza	0871 222 8223	touristinformation@visitmanchester.com
Maryport	The Wave Centre	01900 811450	info@thewavemaryport.co.uk
Millom	Millom Council Centre	01946 598914	millomtic@copelandbc.gov.uk
Morecambe	Old Station Buildings	01524 582808	morecambevic@lancaster.gov.uk
Nantwich	Civic Hall	01270 537359	nantwichtic@cheshireeast.gov.uk
Northwich	Information Centre	01606 288828	infocentrenorthwich@cheshirewestandchester.gov.uk
Oldham	Oldham Library	0161 770 3064	tourist@oldham.gov.uk
Pendle Heritage Centre	Park Hill	01282 677150	pendleheritagecentre@htnw.co.uk
Penrith	Middlegate	01768 867466	pen.tic@eden.gov.uk
Preston	The Guildhall	01772 253731	tourism@preston.gov.uk
Rheged	Redhills	01768 860015	tic@rheged.com
Rochdale	Touchstones	01706 924928	tic@link4life.org
Rossendale	Rawtenstall Queens Square	01706 227911	rawtenstall.library@lancashire.gov.uk
Saddleworth	Saddleworth Museum	01457 870336	saddleworthtic@oldham.gov.uk
Salford	The Lowry, Pier 8	0161 848 8601	tic@salford.gov.uk
Sedbergh	72 Main Street	015396 20125	tic@sedbergh.org.uk
Silloth-On-Solway	Solway Coast Discovery Centre	016973 31944	sillothtic@allerdale.gov.uk
Southport	112 Lord Street	01704 533333	info@visitsouthport.com
Stockport	Staircase House	0161 474 4444	tourist.information@stockport.gov.uk
Ulverston	Coronation Hall	01229 587120 / 587140	ulverstontic@southlakeland.gov.uk
Windermere	Victoria Street	015394 46499	info@ticwindermere.co.uk

Regional Contacts and Information

For more information on accommodation, attractions, activities, events and holidays in North West England, contact one of the following regional or local tourism organisations. Their websites have a wealth of information and many produce free publications to help you get the most out of your visit.

Visit Chester
www.visitchester.com

Cumbria Tourism
T (01539) 822 222
E info@cumbriatourism.org
www.golakes.co.uk

Visit Lancashire
T (01257) 226600 (Brochure request)
E info@visitlancashire.com
www.visitlancashire.com

Visit Manchester
T 0871 222 8223
E touristinformation@visitmanchester.com
www.visitmanchester.com

Visit Liverpool
T (0151) 233 2008 (information enquiries)
T 0844 870 0123 (accommodation booking)
E info@visitliverpool.com (accommodation enquiries)
E liverpoolvisitorcentre@liverpool.gov.uk (information enquiries)
www.visitliverpool.com

Entries appear alphabetically by town name in each county. A key to symbols appears on page 7

APPLEBY-IN-WESTMORLAND, Cumbria Map ref 5B3   SatNav CA16 6EJ

Wild Rose Park

Ormside, Appleby-in-Westmorland CA16 6EJ
T: (017683) 51077 **F:** (017683) 52551 **E:** reception@wildrose.co.uk
W: www.harrisonholidays.com **£ BOOK ONLINE**

🚐	£20.00-£40.00
🚏	£16.00-£33.50
🛖 (25)	£265.00-£619.00
250 touring pitches	

Friendly, family park in the lovely, unspoilt Eden Valley with mountain views. Within easy reach of the Lakes and the Dales. Spotless, super loos and private wash cubicles. Overnight holding area available. Wild Rose Park offers a five star treatment for your touring holidays, along with luxury holiday homes to rent for short and week long stays. We also have Wigwams & electric bike hire for the ultimate Eden camping experience. **Directions:** Please contact us for Directions. **Open:** All year.

Site: 🏤 ▲🅿 **Payment:** 💷 ☼ **Leisure:** 🎣 ♪ ⏩ ♺ 🎾 ♿ **Children:** 🧸 🛝 **Catering:** ✗ 🛒 **Park:** 🐕 🎵 🔲 🛁 🌳 **Touring:** 🔌 🚿 ⚡ 🎣

BASSENTHWAITE, Cumbria Map ref 5A2   SatNav CA12 4QZ

Bassenthwaite Lakeside Lodges

Scarness, Bassenthwaite, Keswick, Cumbria CA12 4QZ
T: (017687) 76641 **E:** enquiries@blll.co.uk
W: www.blll.co.uk

🏠 (17) £255.00-£1385.00

Bassenthwaite Lakeside Lodges is an exclusive privately-owned holiday park offering exceptional self-catering accommodation on the edge of Bassenthwaite Lake at the foot of Skiddaw in the Lake District National Park. Pets accepted by prior arrangement. Hot Tubs available. Please see website for the full range of lodges and amenities available. **Directions:** Please see website for directions. **Open:** All year.

Payment: 💷 **Leisure:** ♪ ⏩ **Property:** 🐕 🖥 🔲 🛁 **Children:** 🧸 🛝

GRANGE-OVER-SANDS, Cumbria Map ref 5A3   SatNav LA11 6HR

Greaves Farm Caravan Park

c/o Nether Edge, Field Broughton, Grange-over-Sands, Cumbria LA11 6HR
T: (01539) 536587 **E:** info@greavesfarmcaravanpark.co.uk
W: www.greavesfarmcaravanpark.co.uk

🚐 (20)	£16.00-£20.00
🚏 (5)	£16.00-£18.00
⛺ (10)	£14.00-£18.00
🛖 (2)	£250.00-£450.00
20 touring pitches	

Small, quiet park in rural location 2 miles north of Cartmel. Family owned and supervised. Convenient base for South Lakes, within easy reach of Windermere, Kendal and Furness Peninsula. 30 minutes from M6. Two luxury holiday caravans for hire on small static park, Spacious touring and camping park, hard-standings available, level grass pitches around 4 acre meadow.

Directions: Exit 36 off M6. Follow A590 signed Barrow. 1 mile before Newby Bridge just after end of dual carriageway, take left hand road signed Cartmel Holker. Continue 1.5m, Site is signed.

Open: Early March to End October.

Payment: ☼ **Leisure:** ♪ ⏩ ♺ **Children:** 🧸 **Park:** 🐕 🔲 🛁 **Touring:** 🔌 🚿 ⚡

GRANGE-OVER-SANDS, Cumbria Map ref 5A3 — SatNav LA11 7LT

Lakeland Leisure Park

Moor Lane, Flookburgh, Grange-over-Sands, Cumbria LA11 7LT
T: (01442) 203079 **E:** enquiries@haven.com
W: www.haven.com/parks/lake-district/lakeland/

🚐 (185)
🚏 (185)
▲ (185)

If you're looking for a gateway into the poetic beauty of the Lake District, our park is the place for you. We're around 30 minutes from Windermere, a stunningly beautiful setting full of the peace and calm of this special part of the UK. We also offer Holiday Home ownership if you love the Lake District and want to pitch up for longer.

Tent, Electric and Euro pitches are available, with Electric and Euro having an awning space and a car parking space next to them. There's also a refurbished and extended heated shower block, a family room and 2 dishwashing areas. Being just five minutes' walk from the park facilities, everything's in place for a great touring holiday. Please contact for 2015 rates.

Directions: Please contact for directions. **Open:** 21st March - 2nd November.

Site: 🏕 **Payment:** 💷 **Leisure:** 🚵 🏹 🔍 🎣 🪝 **Property:** 🐴 🎵 🖥 📱 🕹 **Children:** 🐥 🎠 **Catering:** ✖ 🥘

KENDAL, Cumbria Map ref 5B3 — SatNav LA7 7NN

Waters Edge Caravan Park

Crooklands, Kendal, Cumbria LA7 7NN
T: (01539) 567708 **E:** info@watersedgecaravanpark.co.uk
W: www.watersedgecaravanpark.co.uk

🚐 (26)	£17.35-£24.90
🚏 (26)	£17.35-£24.90
▲ (6)	£10.00-£27.50
26 touring pitches	

Friendly site in open countryside. Lake District, Morecambe and Yorkshire Dales nearby. All hardstanding pitches. Lounge, bar, pool room and patio area. Shower block with laundry. Local pub/restaurant within 300yds. Overnight holding area available. **Directions:** Leave M6 at jct 36, take A65 toward Kirkby Lonsdale for approx 100 yds, then left on A65 toward Crooklands. Site approx 1 mile on the right. **Open:** 1st March to 14th November.

Site: 🏕 🅰🅿 **Payment:** 💷 ☀ **Leisure:** 🎣 🏹 ⛵ 🪝 **Children:** 🐥 **Catering:** 🥘 **Park:** 🐴 🖥 📱 🕹 **Touring:** 🚽 💧 🚰

KESWICK, Cumbria Map ref 5A3 — SatNav CA12 4TE

Castlerigg Hall Caravan & Camping Park

Castlerigg Hall, Keswick, Cumbria CA12 4TE
T: (01768) 774499 **E:** info@castlerigg.co.uk
W: www.castlerigg.co.uk / www.foodatjiggers.co.uk

🚐 (65)	£19.75-£33.00
🚏 (65)	£19.75-£33.00
▲ (120)	£16.40-£23.40
🏠 (12)	£295.00-£550.00

Our elevated position commands wonderful panoramic views of the surrounding fells. Formerly a Lakeland hill farm, Castlerigg Hall has been sympathetically developed into a quality touring park. Facilities include Campers store, Food at Jiggers and Castlerigg Gallery. **Directions:** Head out of Keswick on the A591 direction Windermere. At the top of the hill turn right at the brown tourist sign indicating Castlerigg Hall. **Open:** 11th March - 9th November.

Payment: 💷 **Leisure:** 🎣 🏹 **Property:** 🐴 🖥 📱 🕹 **Children:** 🐥 **Catering:** ✖

KIRKBY LONSDALE, Cumbria *Map ref 5B3* *SatNav LA6 2SE*

Woodclose Park

Chapel House Lane, High Casterton, Kirkby Lonsdale LA6 2SE
T: (01524) 271597 **F:** (01524) 272301 **E:** info@woodclosepark.com
W: www.woodclosepark.com **£ BOOK ONLINE**

(17)	£15.00-£27.00
(14)	£15.00-£27.00
(5)	£14.50-£18.00

52 touring pitches

Enjoy England award winning park, set in the beautiful Lune valley between the Yorkshire Dales and the Lake District National Park, walking distance to Kirkby Lonsdale Town. Tourers, camping, self catering Wigwams and holiday homes and lodges for sale. Holiday Home extended season until January. **Directions:** M6 jct 36, follow A65 for approx 6 miles. The park entrance can be found just past Kirkby Lonsdale on the left-hand side, up the hill. **Open:** 1st March - 31st October. Holiday Homes until 1st January.

Payment: **Leisure:** **Children:** **Catering:** **Park:** **Touring:**

PENRITH, Cumbria *Map ref 5B2* *SatNav CA11 0JB*

Flusco Wood

Flusco, Penrith CA11 0JB
T: (01768) 480020 **E:** info@fluscowood.co.uk
W: www.fluscowood.co.uk

(26)	£21.00-£24.00
(10)	£21.00-£24.00

36 touring pitches

A high-standard, quiet woodland touring caravan park with fully serviced pitches and centrally heated amenity building. Short drive to many attractions and places of interest in the Lake District. Overnight holding area available. **Directions:** M6 jct 40, travel west on A66 towards Keswick. After about 4 miles turn right (signposted Flusco). Entrance along lane on the left. **Open:** Easter to November.

Payment: **Leisure:** **Children:** **Catering:** **Park:** **Touring:**

SILLOTH, Cumbria *Map ref 5A2* *SatNav CA7 4HH*

Stanwix Park Holiday Centre

Greenrow, Silloth, Wigton, Cumbria CA7 4HH
T: (016973) 32666 **F:** (016973) 32555 **E:** enquiries@stanwix.com
W: www.stanwix.com

(127)	£93.00-£118.00
(127)	£93.00-£118.00
(4)	£30.00-£50.00

Caravan holiday homes for hire. Large leisure centre. Swimming pools, ten-pin bowling and amusement arcade, family entertainment, disco and adult cabaret. Situated on the Solway Coast, popular destination to explore the Lake District. Tents & touring prices are per week. Camping Pod prices are per night. **Directions:** Please contact for directions. **Open:** All year.

Site: **Payment:** **Leisure:** **Children:** **Catering:** **Park:** **Touring:**

ULLSWATER, Cumbria *Map ref 5A3* *SatNav CA10 2LT*

Hillcroft Holiday Park

Roe Head Lane, Pooley Bridge, Penrith, Cumbria CA10 2LT
T: (017684) 86363 **E:** info@hillcroftpark.co.uk
W: www.hillcroftpark.co.uk

(14)	£18.00-£30.00
(14)	£18.00-£30.00
(50)	£15.00-£30.00
(16)	£35.00-£55.00
(13)	£410.00-£980.00
(5)	£345.00-£680.00

A warm and friendly welcome awaits you when you visit Hillcroft Park, Ullswater in the northern part of the Lake District. Hillcroft Park is the perfect holiday retreat, especially for those who love the outdoor life. Various pitches, lodges & caravans available, Some with Hot Tubs! Please see website for further details.
Directions: Please see website.
Open: Camping & Pods: 1st March – 15th November.
Static Caravans & lodges: 1st March to 6th January.

Site: **Payment:** **Leisure:** **Children:** **Catering:** **Park:** **Touring:**

Pitch perfect in Penrith

Nestled near a babbling brook, enjoy a great value break at **Troutbeck Head Caravan Club Site** and explore the beautiful North Lakeland countryside.

Best of all the whole family can enjoy a holiday because kids stay for just one penny a night.

Kids for a penny*

Troutbeck Head Caravan Club Site

Book now: **01342 488 356**
www.caravanclub.co.uk/visitbritainsites

*A supplement for non-members (where admitted) is applicable at an additional £10 per night. Date restrictions apply.
Lines are open Mon-Fri 8.45am-5.30pm. Calls may be recorded.

THE CARAVAN CLUB

ULLSWATER, Cumbria Map ref 5A3 — SatNav CA11 0JF

Waterfoot Caravan Park
Pooley Bridge, Penrith, Ullswater CA11 0JF
T: (017684) 86302 **F:** (017684) 86728 **E:** info@waterfootpark.co.uk
W: www.waterfootpark.co.uk **£ BOOK ONLINE**

🚐 (34)   £15.50-£28.00
🚏 (34)   £15.50-£28.00
34 touring pitches

Set in the grounds of a Georgian mansion overlooking Ullswater. Waterfoot Park is a 5 star holiday park with excellent facilities for touring and self catering wigwam holidays. David Bellamy Conservation Gold Award. Holiday Homes for sale. **Directions:** M6 jct40, follow signs marked Ullswater Steamers. West on A66 1 mile. Left at roundabout A592 (Ullswater). Park located on right. Satnav not compatable. **Open:** 1st March to 14th November.

Site: 🏕 ⚓🅿 Payment: 💷 ☼ Leisure: ♿ ♪ ⏃ ♺ Children: ⛵ ⚠ Catering: ⚓ Park: ⻗ 🚮 🗑 🏚 🎋 Touring: ☂ ♗ 🎇

WINDERMERE, Cumbria Map ref 5A3 — SatNav LA12 8NR

Hill of Oaks Park
Tower Wood, Windermere LA12 8NR
T: (015395) 31578 **F:** (015395) 30431 **E:** enquiries@hillofoaks.co.uk
W: www.hillofoaks.co.uk **£ BOOK ONLINE**

🚐 (43)   £21.00-£41.00
🚏 (43)   £21.00-£41.00
🏠 (3)   £325.00-£595.00
43 touring pitches

Hill of Oaks is a 5 star award-winning park, located on the shores of Windermere. Excellent facilities include boat launching slipway and jetties, electric car hire and woodland walks. Self catering properties on weekly let and Holiday Homes & Lodges. **Directions:** M6 jct 36, west on A590 towards Barrow and Newby Bridge. At roundabout turn right, onto A592. Park is approx 3 miles on left-hand side. **Open:** 1st March to Mid November.

Site: ⚓🅿 Payment: 💷 ☼ Leisure: ♪ Children: ⛵ ⚠ Catering: ⚓ Park: ⻗ 🚮 🗑 🏚 🎋 Touring: ☂ ♗ 🎇 🎇

WINDERMERE, Cumbria Map ref 5A3 — SatNav LA23 3PG

Park Cliffe Camping & Caravan Estate
Birks Road, Windermere LA23 3PG
T: (015395) 31344 **F:** (015395) 31971 **E:** info@parkcliffe.co.uk
W: www.parkcliffe.co.uk **£ BOOK ONLINE**

🚐 (60)   £26.00-£32.00
🚏 (60)   £26.00-£32.00
⛺ (80)   £20.00-£35.00
🏠 (3)   £168.00-£630.00
60 touring pitches

The winner of many top-quality awards, Park Cliffe is set in 25 acres of picture-postcard countryside above the eastern shores of Windermere with sweeping views across the lake. Tourer & camping pitches, caravans & camping pods for hire. **Directions:** Do not follow SatNav - M6 jct 36, follow A590 towards Barrow. At Newby Bridge take A592 towards Windermere. After 3.6 miles turn right into Birks Road. **Open:** 1st March to 8th November.

Site: 🏕 ⚓🅿 Payment: 💷 ☼ Leisure: ♪ Children: ⛵ ⚠ Catering: ✗ ⚓ Park: ⻗ 🚮 🗑 🏚 🎋 Touring: ☂ ♗ 🎇 🎇

OLDHAM, Greater Manchester Map ref 4B1 SatNav OL3 5UN

Moorlands Caravan Park

Ripponden Road, Denshaw, Oldham OL3 5UN
T: (01457) 874348 **E:** moorlandscp@aol.com
W: www.moorlandscp.co.uk

🚐 (40)   £18.00-£21.00
🚃 (40)   £18.00-£21.00
⛺ (20)   £6.00
40 touring pitches

Newly refurbished, 4 star park on the moors of Saddleworth. Ideal for walkers, horse riders, or just a family stay. Half a mile from the Pennine Way and Pennine Bridal Way. Short walk to pub and stunning views for tents, caravans and camping pods. Limited winter availability. **Directions:** Junction 22 of the M62, 2 miles in the direction of Saddleworth. **Open:** All year.

Site: ⛺🅿 Payment: 💷 ☼ Leisure: ♪ ► ∪ Children: 🐎 Park: 🐕 🗑 🚿 Touring: 💡 🚰 🍽 ♪

ROCHDALE, Greater Manchester Map ref 4B1 SatNav OL15 0AS

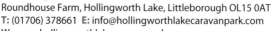

Hollingworth Lake Caravan Park

Roundhouse Farm, Hollingworth Lake, Littleborough OL15 0AT
T: (01706) 378661 **E:** info@hollingworthlakecaravanpark.com
W: www.hollingworthlakecaravanpark.com

🚐 (30)
🚃 (10)
⛺ (10)
50 touring pitches

A popular, five-acre park adjacent to Hollingworth Lake. At the foot of the Pennines, within easy reach of many local attractions. Backpackers walking the Pennine Way are welcome at this family-run park. Hardstanding and grass areas. Excellent train service into Manchester Victoria. 20 minutes from Littleborough/Smithybridge. Overnight holding area available. Restaurant/cafe within 1m of site. Please contact for 2015 rates. **Directions:** From M62. Jct 21 Milnrow. Follow Hollingworth signs to Fishermans Inn/The Wine Press. Take Rakewood Road then 2nd on right. **Open:** All year.

Payment: ☼ Leisure: ♪ ∪ Catering: 🍽 Park: 🗑 🛒 🚿 Touring: 💡 🚰 🍽 ♪

CARNFORTH, Lancashire   Map ref 5B3   SatNav LA5 8TN

Bay View Holiday Park
A6 Main Road, Bolton Le Sands, Carnforth, Lancashire LA5 8ES
T: (01524) 701508 **F:** (01524) 701580 **E:** info@holgates.co.uk
W: www.holgates.co.uk

🚐 (190)	£22.00-£27.00
🚐 (190)	£22.00-£27.00
⛺	£17.00-£27.00
🏠	£199.00-£599.00
199 touring pitches	

With fields that run down to the shore, there is plenty of room for touring caravans and tents - you can even book your pitch for the whole season. We also have four luxurious holiday homes available to hire. **Directions:** Exit the M6 at J35. Take the A601 for Carnforth. At traffic lights continue ahead. 500m after mini roundabout turn right into Bay View Holiday Park. **Open:** All year.

Site: ⊕ ⅋🅿 Payment: 💷 Leisure: ♦ Catering: ✕ 🛒 Park: 🐕 🗑 📻 🏠 Touring: ♺ 🔌

CARNFORTH, Lancashire   Map ref 5B3   SatNav LA5 0SH

Holgates Caravan Park
Cove Road, Silverdale, Carnforth, Lancashire LA5 0SH
T: (01524) 701508 **F:** (01524) 701580 **E:** reception@holgates.co.uk
W: www.holgates.co.uk **£ BOOK ONLINE**

🚐 (90)	£34.50
🚐 (90)	£34.50
⛺ (6)	£34.50
🏠 (13)	£284.00-£820.00

Join us for a relaxing get-away-from-it-all break, or a fun-filled family adventure. We take touring caravans, motor homes and tents with camping pods for hire. An idyllic 100 acre country setting, close to the sea and lovely villages. **Directions:** Exit the M6 at Junction 35 and take the A601 for Carnforth. Follow signs for Silverdale, then 'Holgates' at Cove Road. **Open:** All year.

Site: ⊕ ⅋🅿 Payment: 💷 ☼ Leisure: ▶ ♦ ⌇ Children: 🐎 ⚑ Catering: ✕ 🛒 Park: 🐕 🗑 📻 🏠 Touring: ☎ ♺ 🔌 ♪

CARNFORTH, Lancashire   Map ref 5B3   SatNav LA5 0SL

Hollins Farm Caravan Park
Hollins Farm - Far Arnside, Silverdale, Carnforth, Lancashire LA5 0SL
T: (01524) 701508 **F:** (01524) 701508 **E:** reception@holgates.co.uk
W: www.hollinsfarm.co.uk **£ BOOK ONLINE**

🚐 (50)	£32.00
🚐 (50)	£32.00
⛺ (25)	£32.00
50 touring pitches	

A friendly site, Hollins Farm lies in an Area of Outstanding Natural Beauty between two of North Lancashire's most picturesque coastal villages, Silverdale and Arnside. Loo of the Year Platinum 2014. Access to leisure facilities on main site. **Directions:** Jcn 35 of M6, follow signs for Carnforth, then Silverdale. Follow brown signs for Holgates, drive past main gate and take 2nd left road for Hollins. **Open:** March - November.

Site: ⅋🅿 Payment: 💷 ☼ Leisure: ▶ Children: 🐎 Park: 🐕 🏠 Touring: ☎ ♺ ♪

LANCASTER, Lancashire   Map ref 5A3   SatNav LA2 9HH

New Parkside Farm Caravan Park, Lancaster
Denny Beck, Caton Road, Lancaster LA2 9HH
T: (01524) 770723 **E:** enquiries@newparksidefarm.co.uk
W: www.newparksidefarm.co.uk

🚐 (36)	£15.00-£18.00
🚐 (4)	£15.00-£18.00
⛺ (8)	£8.00-£15.00
40 touring pitches	

Peaceful, family-run park on a working farm on the edge of the Forest of Bowland. Extensive views of the Lune Valley and Ingleborough. Excellent base for exploring the Lakes, Dales and unspoilt coast and countryside of North Lancashire. **Directions:** Leave M6 at junction 34, A683 east towards Caton/Kirkby Lonsdale, caravan park entrance 1 mile from motorway junction on the right (signposted). **Open:** 1st March to 31st October.

Site: ⅋🅿 Payment: ☼ Leisure: ♪ Children: 🐎 Park: 🐕 🏠 Touring: ☎ ♺ 🔌

Eastham Hall Caravan Park

Saltcotes Road, Lytham St Annes, Lancashire FY8 4LS
T: (01253) 737907 E: info@easthamhall.co.uk
W: www.easthamhall.co.uk

🚐 (140)   £25.00
🏕 (150)   £2282.00

SPECIAL PROMOTIONS
Please see website for discounts throughout the year.

Eastham Hall Caravan Park has been owned and managed by the Kirkham family for 50 years. Whether you buy a holiday home on the park or visit with your touring caravan, you can share our lovely rural retreat in a highly sought after location. The park has an on-site shop which is open seven days a week selling essential items including bread, milk, ice cream and newspapers (a newspaper ordering service is provided).

We have a children's adventure playground, extensive playing fields and a dedicated dog exercise area and a dog walk. Touring Pitches: 100 Seasonal, 40 nightly.

Directions: Please see website.

Open: Touring: 1st March - 1st December
Holiday Homes: 20th February - 3rd January.

Site: Payment: Children: Catering: Park: Touring:

Need more information?

Visit our websites for detailed information, up-to-date availability and to book your accommodation online. Includes over 20,000 places to stay, all of them star rated.

www.visitor-guides.co.uk

PRESTON, Lancashire Map ref 4A1 SatNav PR4 3HA

Mowbreck Holiday and Residential Park

Mowbreck Lane, Wesham, Preston, Lancashire PR4 3HA
T: (01772) 682494 E: info@mowbreckpark.co.uk
W: www.mowbreckpark.co.uk

enjoyEngland.com ★★★★★ HOLIDAY PARK

(4) £230.00-£495.00

Enjoy the peace & quiet at Mowbreck, set in a delightful woodland location. Mowbreck is family owned and run to the highest standard. Luxury holiday home for hire, central heating, double-glazed, TV, Microwave, 2 and 3 bedrooms. **Directions:** Turn off the M55 at Jct 3, follow the signs for Kirkham and Wesham. Turn left at St Joseph's Church into Mowbreck Lane. We are situated 1/2 mile down. **Open:** 1st February to 16th January.

Payment: **Leisure:** **Property:** **Children:**

AINSDALE, Merseyside Map ref 4A1 SatNav PR8 3ST

Willowbank Holiday Home and Touring Park

Coastal Road, Ainsdale, Southport PR8 3ST
T: (01704) 571566 E: info@willowbankcp.co.uk
W: www.willowbankcp.co.uk

enjoyEngland.com ★★★★★ HOLIDAY & TOURING PARK

(87) £15.20-£20.25
(87) £15.20-£20.25
(228)
87 touring pitches

SPECIAL PROMOTIONS
Please see our web site for offers.

Willowbank Holiday Home & Touring Park offers an easily accessible location, convenient for Southport & Liverpool with well maintained modern facilities in a quiet and relaxed atmosphere. The park is open from 14th Feb to 31st January for holiday homes, touring caravans, motor homes and trailer tents. Last check in 9.00pm. Check out 12.00pm. No Commercial vehicles. Please note we do not let out holiday homes.

Directions: From M6 jct 26 for M58, from the M62 jct for M57. A5036 & A5207 leading to A565 towards Southport, RAF Woodvale, Coastal Rd.

Open: 14th February to 31st January.

Payment: **Leisure:** **Children:** **Park:** **Touring:**

SOUTHPORT, Merseyside Map ref 4A1 SatNav PR9 8DF

Riverside Holiday Park

Southport New Road, Banks, Southport, Merseyside PR9 8DF
T: (01704) 228886 F: (01704) 505886 E: reception@harrisonleisureuk.com
W: www.harrisonholidays.com £ BOOK ONLINE

enjoyEngland.com ★★★ HOLIDAY, TOURING & CAMPING PARK

(150) £17.00-£40.00
(150) £17.00-£40.00
(60) £295.00-£635.00
150 touring pitches

Riverside Holiday Park, located in Banks, Southport is an award winning Holiday Park. A warm welcome awaits you, with luxury self catering holiday homes and touring areas with standard and fully serviced pitches. **Open:** All year.

Site: **Payment:** **Leisure:** **Children:** **Catering:** **Park:**
Touring:

Don't Miss...

Alnwick Castle

Northumberland NE66 1NQ
(01665) 511100
www.alnwickcastle.com

Alnwick Castle's remarkable past is filled with drama, intrigue, tragedy and romance, as well as a host of fascinating people including gunpowder plotters, kingmakers and England's most famous medieval knight: Harry Hotspur. Today, it is a significant visitor attraction with lavish State Rooms and superb art collections, as well as engaging activities and events for all ages, and all set in beautiful landscape by Northumberland-born 'Capability' Brown. Potter fans will recognise Alnwick as Hogwarts from the Harry Potter films - don't miss Potter-inspired magic shows and broomstick training!

BALTIC Centre for Contemporary Art ⊚

Gateshead, Tyne and Wear NE8 3BA
(01914) 781810
www.balticmill.com

Housed in a landmark industrial building on the south bank of the River Tyne in Gateshead, BALTIC is a major international centre for contemporary art and is the biggest gallery of its kind in the world. It presents a dynamic, diverse and international programme of contemporary visual art, ranging from blockbuster exhibitions to innovative new work and projects created by artists working within the local community.

Beamish Museum ⊚

County Durham DH9 0RG
(01913) 704000
www.beamish.org.uk

Beamish - The Living Museum of the North, is a world-famous open air museum vividly recreating life in the North East in the early 1800's and 1900's. It tells the story of the people of North East England during the Georgian, Victorian, and Edwardian periods through a costumed cast, engaging exhibits and an exciting programme of events including The Great North Festival of Transport, a Georgian Fair, The Great North Festival of Agriculture.

Durham Cathedral

County Durham DH1 3EH
(0191) 3864266
www.durhamcathedral.co.uk

Durham Cathedral is perhaps the finest example of Norman church architecture in England or even Europe. It is a World Heritage Site and houses the tombs of St Cuthbert and The Venerable Bede.

Lindisfarne Priory

Holy Island
Northumberland TD15 2RX
(01289) 389200
www.english-heritage.org.uk/lindisfarnepriory

Lying just a few miles off the beautiful Northumberland coast, Holy Island contains a wealth of history and is home to one of the region's most revered treasures, Lindisfarne Priory. The epicentre of Christianity in Anglo Saxon times and once the home of St Oswald, it was the birthplace of the Lindisfarne Gospels, one of the world's most precious books and remains a place of pilgrimage today. Take in panoramic views of the Northumbrian coast, unpack a picnic in the priory grounds, and take a break from the hustle and bustle of life. NB: watch the tides as the causeway is only open at low tide.

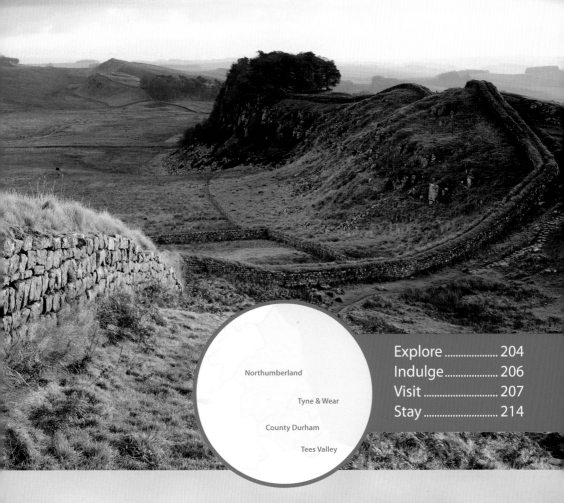

North East

County Durham, Northumberland,
Tees Valley, Tyne & Wear

Northumberland

Tyne & Wear

County Durham

Tees Valley

The North East contains two Areas of Outstanding Natural Beauty, a National Park, Hadrian's Wall, the dynamic city of Newcastle, and County Durham, with its fine cathedral and castle. This region is awash with dramatic hills, sweeping valleys, vast expanses of dune-fringed beaches and ragged cliffs with spectacular views. Littered with dramatic castles, ruins and historic houses, there are plenty of exciting family attractions and walking routes galore.

County Durham & Tees Valley

Durham Cathedral, the greatest Norman building in England, was once a prison and soars grandly above the Medieval city and surrounding plain. Famed for its location as much as for its architecture, it is the burial place of both St Cuthbert, a great northern saint, and the Venerable Bede, author of the first English history.

The Vale of Durham is packed full of award-winning attractions including Locomotion: The National Railway Museum at Shildon and Beamish – The Living Museum of the North, the country's largest open air museum. Auckland Castle was the palace of Durham's unique Prince Bishops for more than 900 years. Part of the North Pennines Area of Outstanding Natural Beauty, the Durham Dales including Teesdale and Weardale, is a beautiful landscape of hills, moors, valleys and rivers, with numerous picturesque villages and market towns.

Comprising miles of stunning coastline and acres of ancient woodland, Tees Valley covers the lower, flatter area of the valley of the River Tees. This unique part of the UK, split between County Durham and Yorkshire, has nearly a hundred visitor attractions, including Preston Hall and Saltholme Nature Reserve, which can both be found in Stockton-on-Tees.

The Durham Heritage Coast, from Sunderland to Hartlepool, is one of the finest in England. The coastal path that runs along much of its length takes you on a spectacular journey of natural, historical and geological interest, with dramatic views along the shore and out over the North Sea. The historic port city of Hartlepool has award-winning attractions, a fantastic marina, beaches and countryside.

Hotspot: Durham University is home to The Oriental Museum, housing a unique collection of Chinese, Indian & Egyptian Art, and the Botanic Garden is also well worth a visit while you are there.

Step back in time 2,000 years along Hadrian's Wall, explore the hills, forests and waterfalls of the National Parks, and discover historic castles, splendid churches and quaint towns. Visitors can trace man's occupation of the region from prehistoric times through rock carvings, ancient hill forts, Saxon churches, Norman priories, medieval castles, and a wealth of industrial archaeology.

Newcastle & Tyne And Wear

Newcastle-upon-Tyne, once a shipbuilding centre, is a rejuvenated city of proud civic tradition with fine restaurants, theatres, and one of the liveliest arts scenes outside London. As well as the landmark Baltic, there's the Laing Art Gallery, the Great North Museum and The Sage concert venue. The Theatre Royal is the third home of the Royal Shakespeare Company and a venue for major touring companies. The Metro Centre in neighbouring Gateshead attracts shoppers from all over the country with more than 300 outlets and 11 cinema screens.

Northumberland

Northumbria, to use its ancient name, is an undiscovered holiday paradise where the scenery is wild and beautiful, the beaches golden and unspoiled, and the natives friendly. The region is edged by the North Sea, four national parks and the vast Border Forest Park. Its eastern sea boundary makes a stunning coastline, stretching 100 miles from Staithes on the Cleveland boundary, to Berwick-on-Tweed, England's most northerly town, frequently fought over and with the finest preserved example of Elizabethan town walls in the country. In between you'll find as many holiday opportunities as changes of scenery.

Housesteads Roman Fort at Haydon Bridge is the most complete example of a British Roman fort. It features magnificent ruins and stunning views of the countryside surrounding Hadrian's Wall.

The region has a rich maritime heritage too. Ruined coastal fortifications such as Dunstanburgh and fairy-tale Lindisfarne are relics of a turbulent era. Agriculture is also one of the region's most important industries. Take a trip on the Heatherslaw Light Railway, a narrow gauge line operating from Etal Village to Heatherslaw Mill, a restored waterdriven corn mill and agricultural museum near the delightful model village of Ford.

Indulge in a leisurely sightseeing trip along the **River Wear at Durham**. A one hour cruise includes sepctacular views of historic Durham City, Cathedral, Castle and bridges with full commentary including history, natural history and geography. www.princebishoprc.co.uk or call (0191) 386 9525 for sailing times and prices.

Don't miss **The Rugby World Cup 2015** which will see three matches played at **St James' Park** in Newcastle. South Africa vs Scotland, New Zealand vs Tonga and Samoa vs Scotland all take place in early October and are sure to be spectacular sporting events. www.rugbyworldcup.com

Enjoy an elegant lunch or tempting tea at the fabulous **Earl Grey Tearooms**, Howick – home of Earl Grey for whom the tea was invented. Situated in the old ballroom of the hall, it serves a variety of teas, home made and local produce, snacks and light lunches exclusively for visitors to the garden and makes a great place for a rest while exploring the arboretum and stunning gardens. See www.howickhallgardens.org for opening times.

It's hard not to get caught up in the quirky atmosphere of **Barter Books** at the Victorian Alnwick Railway Station. This rambling, atmospheric secondhand bookshop has open fires, armchairs, a simple cafe and best of all, model trains, and is noted for its use of a barter system, whereby customers can exchange their books for credit against future purchases. It is one of the largest second-hand bookstores in Europe and an unmissable diversion if you're in this neck of the woods. www.barterbooks.co.uk or call (01665) 604888 for opening times.

For a romantic dinner for two or a great night out with friends, dine in style at **Alnwick Garden's Treehouse Restaurant**, one of the most magical and unique restaurants to be found anywhere. Set high up in the treetops, with a roaring fire in the centre of the room and trees growing through the floor, this stunning restaurant serves local fish and seafood, meats from Northumberland's farmlands and other mouthwatering local and regional specialities. Call (01665) 511852 to for reservations.

Attractions with this sign participate in the Visitor Attraction Quality Assurance Scheme.

County Durham & Tees Valley

Adventure Valley
Durham, County Durham DH1 5SG
(01913) 868291
www.adventurevalley.co.uk
Adventure Valley, split into six Play Zones (with three under cover), you'll find the very best in family fun come rain or shine.

Billingham International Folklore Festival
August, Billingham, County Durham
www.billinghamfestival.co.uk
A festival of traditional and contemporary world dance, music and arts.

Bishop Auckland Food Festival
April, Bishop Auckland, County Durham
www.bishopaucklandfoodfestival.co.uk
Be inspired by cookery demonstrations and entertained by performers.

The Bowes Museum
Barnard Castle, County Durham DL12 8NP
(01833) 690606
www.thebowesmuseum.org.uk
The Bowes Museum houses a collection of outstanding European fine and decorative arts and offers an acclaimed exhibition programme, alongside special events and children's activities.

DLI Museum and Durham Art Gallery
Durham, County Durham DH1 5TU
(01913) 842214
www.dlidurham.org.uk
Telling the 200-year story of Durham's famous regiment. Art Gallery has changing exhibition programme.

Durham Book Festival
October/November, Durham, County Durham
www.durhambookfestival.com
With writers covering everything from politics to poetry, and fiction to feminism, there's something for everyone at the Durham Book Festival. See website for dates and full programme.

Durham Castle

County Durham DH1 3RW
(01913) 343800
www.durhamcastle.com
Durham Castle is part of the Durham City World Heritage Site and has enjoyed a long history of continuous use. Along with Durham Cathedral, it is among the greatest monuments of the Norman Conquest of Britain and is now home to students of University College, Durham. Entrance is by guided tour only, please telephone opening and tour times.

Durham Folk Party

July, Durham, County Durham
www.communigate.co.uk/ne/durhamfolkparty
It is a celebration of folk song, music and dance which began in 1990 after the demise of the excellent Durham City Folk Festival and has developed into an important part of the music year of the city.

Hall Hill Farm

Durham, County Durham DH7 0TA
(01388) 731333
www.hallhillfarm.co.uk
Award-winning farm attraction set in attractive countryside, see and touch the animals at close quarters.

Hamsterley Forest

Bishop Auckland, County Durham DL13 3NL
(01388) 488312
www.forestry.gov.uk/northeastengland
A 5,000 acre mixed woodland open to the public all year.

Hartlepool Art Gallery

Hartlepool, Tees Valley TS24 7EQ
(01429) 869706
www.hartlepool.gov.uk/info/100009/leisure_and_
culture/1506/hartlepool_art_gallery/1/3
Former church building also includes the TIC and a bell tower viewing platform looking over Hartlepool.

Hartlepool's Maritime Experience

Tees Valley TS24 0XZ
(01429) 860077
www.hartlepoolsmaritimeexperience.com
An authentic reconstruction of an 18th century seaport.

Head of Steam

Tees Valley DL3 6ST
(01325) 460532
www.darlington.gov.uk/Culture/headofsteam/
welcome.htm
Restored 1842 station housing a collection of exhibits relating to railways in the North East of England, including Stephenson's Locomotion, call for details of events.

High Force Waterfall

Middleton-in-Teesdale, County Durham DL12 0XH
(01833) 640209
www.rabycastle.com/high_force.htm
The most majestic of the waterfalls on the River Tees.

HMS Trincomalee

Hartlepool, Tees Valley TS24 0XZ
(01429) 223193
www.hms-trincomalee.co.uk
HMS Trincomalee, built in 1817, is one of the oldest ship afloat in Europe. Come aboard for a unique experience of Navy life two centuries ago.

Killhope, The North of England
Lead Mining Museum
Bishop Auckland, County Durham DL13 1AR
(01388) 537505
www.killhope.org.uk
Fully restored Victorian lead mine and the most complete lead mining site in Great Britain.

Locomotion: The National Railway Museum at Shildon
Shildon, County Durham DL4 1PQ
(01388) 777999
www.nrm.org.uk/locomotion
The first National Museum in the North East. Free admission. View over 60 vehicles, children's play area and interactive displays.

mima
Middlesbrough, Tees Valley TS1 2AZ
(01642) 726720
www.visitmima.com
mima, Middlesbrough Institute of Modern Art, is a £14.2m landmark gallery in the heart of Middlesbrough. mima showcases an international programme of fine art and applied art from the 1900s to the present day.

Preston Hall Museum and Park
Stockton-on-Tees, Tees Valley TS18 3RH
(01642) 527375
www.prestonparkmuseum.co.uk
A Georgian country house set in beautiful parkland overlooking the River Tees. A Museum of social history with a recreated Victorian street and working craftsmen.

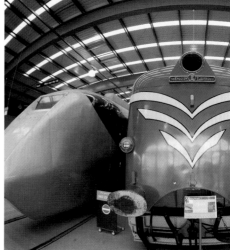

Hotspot: *Hartlepool Museum, situated beside Hartlepool Historic Quay, includes local historical exhibits, PSS Wingfield Castle and the original lighthouse light. (01429) 860077 www.hartlepoolsmaritimeexperience.com*

Raby Castle
Staindrop, County Durham DL2 3AH
(01833) 660202
www.rabycastle.com
Home of Lord Barnard's family since 1626, includes a 200 acre deer park, gardens, carriage collection, adventure playground, shop and tearoom.

Saltburn Smugglers Heritage Centre
Saltburn-by-the-Sea, Tees Valley TS12 1HF
(01287) 625252
www.redcar-cleveland.gov.uk/museums
Step back into Saltburn's past and experience the authentic sights, sounds and smells.

Saltholme Wildlife Reserve
Middlesbrough, Tees Valley TS2 1TU
(01642) 546625
www.rspb.org.uk/reserves/guide/s/saltholme
An amazing wildlife experience in the Tees Valley.

Newcastle & Tyne And Wear

Arbeia Roman Fort and Museum
South Shields, Tyne and Wear NE33 2BB
(01914) 561369
www.twmuseums.org.uk/arbeia
Arbeia is the best reconstruction of a Roman fort in Britain and offers visitors a unique insight into the every day life of the Roman army, from the soldier in his barrack room to the commander in his luxurious house.

Centre for Life
Newcastle-upon-Tyne, Tyne and Wear NE1 4EP
(01912) 438210
www.life.org.uk
The Centre for Life is an award-winning science centre where imaginative exhibitions, interactive displays and special events promote greater understanding of science and provoke curiosity in the world around us.

Discovery Museum
Newcastle-upon-Tyne, Tyne and Wear NE1 4JA
(01912) 326789
www.twmuseums.org.uk/discovery
A wide variety of experiences for all the family to enjoy.

Evolution Festival
May, Newcastle, Tyne and Wear
www.evolutionfestival.co.uk
The North East's premier music event, taking place over a Bank Holiday.

Great North Museum: Hancock
Newcastle-upon-Tyne, Tyne and Wear NE2 4PT
(01912) 226765
www.twmuseums.org.uk/great-north-museum
See major new displays showing the wonder of the animal and plant kingdoms, spectacular objects from the Ancient Greeks and a planetarium and a life-size T-Rex.

Hatton Gallery
Newcastle-upon-Tyne, Tyne and Wear NE1 7RU
(01912) 226059
www.twmuseums.org.uk/hatton
Temporary exhibitions of contemporary and historical art. Permanent display of Kurt Schwitters' Merzbarn.

Hotspot: *Enjoy an ever-changing programme of exhibitions, live glass blowing, and banqueting and a stunning restaurant at the National Glass Museum, overlooking the River Wear.*
(01915) 155555
www.nationalglasscentre.com

Laing Art Gallery
Newcastle-upon-Tyne, Tyne and Wear NE1 8AG
(01912) 327734
www.twmuseums.org.uk/laing
The Laing Art Gallery is home to an important collection of 18th and 19th century painting, which is shown alongside temporary exhibitions of historic and contemporary art.

Newcastle Theatre Royal
Newcastle upon Tyne NE1 6BR
(0844) 811 2121
www.theatreroyal.co.uk
The Theatre Royal is a Grade I listed building situated on historic Grey Street in Newcastle-upon-Tyne. It hosts a variety of shows, including ballet, contemporary dance, drama, musicals and opera in a restored 1901 Frank Matcham Edwardian interior.

Segedunum Roman Fort, Baths & Museum
Wallsend, Tyne and Wear NE28 6HR
(01912) 369347
www.twmuseums.org.uk/segedunum
Segedunum Roman Fort is the gateway to Hadrian's Wall. Explore the excavated fort site, visit reconstructions of a Roman bath house, learn about the history of the area in the museum and enjoy the view from the 35 metre viewing tower.

Tyneside Cinema
Newcastle upon Tyne, Tyne and Wear NE1 6QG
(0845) 217 9909
www.tynesidecinema.co.uk
Showing the best films in beautiful art deco surroundings, Tyneside Cinema's programme ranges from mainstream to arthouse and world cinema. As the last surviving Newsreel theatre still operating full-time in the UK, this Grade II-listed building is a must-visit piece of lovingly restored heritage.

WWT Washington Wetland Centre
Washington, Tyne and Wear NE38 8LE
(01914) 165454
www.wwt.org.uk/visit/washington
45 hectares of wetland, woodland and wildlife reserve. Home to wildfowl, insects and flora with lake-side hides, wild bird feeding station, waterside cafe, picnic areas, sustainable garden, playground and events calendar.

Northumberland

Alnwick Beer Festival
September, Alnwick, Northumberland
www.alnwickbeerfestival.co.uk
If you enjoy real ale, or simply want to enjoy a fantastic social event, then make sure you pay this festival a visit.

The Alnwick Garden
Alnwick, Northumberland NE66 1YU
01665 511350
www.alnwickgarden.com
An exciting, contemporary design with beautiful and unique gardens, features and structures, brought to life with water and including the intriguing Poison Garden which holds dangerous plants and their stories. Fantastic eating, drinking, shopping and a range of events throughout the year.

Bailiffgate Museum
Alnwick, Northumberland NE66 1LX
(01665) 605847
www.bailiffgatemuseum.co.uk
Bailiffgate Museum brings to life the people and places of North Northumberland in exciting interactive style.

Bamburgh Castle
Northumberland NE69 7DF
(01668) 214515
www.bamburghcastle.com
A spectacular castle with fantastic coastal views. The stunning Kings Hall and Keep house collections of armour, artwork, porcelain and furniture.

Chillingham Castle
Northumberland, NE66 5NJ
01668 215359
www.chillingham-castle.com
A remarkable Medieval fortress with Tudor additions, torture chamber, shop, dungeon, tearoom, woodland walks, furnished rooms and topiary garden.

Cragside House, Gardens & Estate
Morpeth, Northumberland NE65 7PX
01669 620333
www.nationaltrust.org.uk/cragside/
Built on a rocky crag high above Debdon Burn, the house is crammed with ingenious gadgets and was the first in the world to be lit electrically. The gardens are breathtaking with 5 lakes, one of Europe's largest rock gardens, and over 7 million trees and shrubs.

Haydon Bridge Beer Festival
July, Haydon Bridge, Northumberland
www.haydonbeerfestival.co.uk
Annual celebration of the finest real ales and wines.

Hexham Abbey Festival
September-October, Hexham, Northumberland
www.hexhamabbey.org.uk
An exciting array of events to capture the imagination, bringing the very best world-class musicians and artists to Hexham.

Hexham Old Gaol
Northumberland NE46 3NH
(01434) 652349
www.hexhamoldgaol.org.uk
Tour the Old Gaol, 1330AD, by glass lift. Meet the gaoler, see a Reiver raid and try on costumes.

Kielder Castle Forest Park Centre
Northumberland NE48 1ER
(01434) 250209
www.forestry.gov.uk/northeastengland
Features include forest shop, information centre, tearoom and exhibitions. Bike hire available.

Lindisfarne Castle
(01289) 389244
www.nationaltrust.org.uk/lindisfarne-castle/
A picture perfect castle that rises from the sheer rock face at the tip of Holy Island off the Northumberland coast. It was built to defend a harbour sheltering English ships during skirmishes with Scotland and revamped by celebrated architect Edward Lutyens in 1901, today it remains relatively unchanged. Lindisfarne Castle.

RNLI Grace Darling Museum
Bamburgh, Northumberland NE69 7AE
(01668) 214910
www.rnli.org.uk/gracedarling
A museum dedicated to Grace Darling and her family, as well as all those who Save Lives at Sea.

Warkworth Castle
Warkworth, Northumberland NE65 0UJ
(01665) 711423
www.english-heritage.org.uk/warkworthcastle
Set in a quaint Northumberland town, this hill-top fortress and hermitage offers a fantastic family day out.

Tourist Information Centres

When you arrive at your destination, visit the Tourist Information Centre for quality assured help with accommodation and information about local attractions and events, or email your request before you go.

Alnwick	2 The Shambles	01670 622152/ 01670 622151	alnwick.tic@northumberland.gov.uk
Amble	Queen Street Car Park	01665 712313	amble.tic@northumberland.gov.uk
Bellingham	Station Yard	01434 220616	bellinghamtic@btconnect.com
Berwick-upon-Tweed	106 Marygate	01670 622155/ 625568	berwick.tic@northumberland.gov.uk
Bishop Auckland	Town Hall	03000 269524	bishopauckland.touristinfo@durham.gov.uk
Corbridge	Hill Street	01434 632815	corbridge.tic@northumberland.gov.uk
Craster	Craster Car Park	01665 576007	craster.tic@northumberland.gov.uk
Darlington	Central Library	01325 462034	crown.street.library@darlington.gov.uk
Durham Visitor Contact Centre	1st Floor	03000 262626	visitor@thisisdurham.com
Gateshead	Central Library	0191 433 8420	libraries@gateshead.gov.uk
Guisborough	Priory Grounds	01287 633801	guisborough_tic@redcar-cleveland.gov.uk
Haltwhistle	Westgate	01434 322002	haltwhistle.tic@northumberland.gov.uk
Hartlepool	Hartlepool Art Gallery	01429 869706	hpooltic@hartlepool.gov.uk
Hexham	Wentworth Car Park	01434 652220	hexham.tic@northumberland.gov.uk
Middlesbrough	Middlesbrough Info.	01642 729900	tic@middlesbrough.gov.uk
Middleton-in-Teesdale	10 Market Place	01833 641001	tic@middletonplus.myzen.co.uk
Morpeth	The Chantry	01670 623455	morpeth.tic@northumberland.gov.uk
Newcastle-upon-Tyne	Newcastle Gateshead	0191 277 8000	visitorinfo@ngi.org.uk
North Shields	Unit 18	0191 2005895	ticns@northtyneside.gov.uk
Once Brewed	National Park Centre	01434 344396	tic.oncebrewed@nnpa.org.uk
Otterburn	Otterburn Mill	01830 521002	tic@otterburnmill.co.uk
Saltburn by Sea	Saltburn Library	01287 622422/ 623584	saltburn_library@redcar-cleveland.gov.uk
Seahouses	Seafield Car Park	01665 720884/ 01670 625593	seahouses.tic@northumberland.gov.uk
South shields	Haven Point	0191 424 7788	tourism@southtyneside.gov.uk
Stockton-on-Tees	High Street	01642 528130	visitorinformation@stockton.gov.uk
Whitley Bay	York Road	0191 6435395	susan.clark@northtyneside.gov.uk
Wooler	The Cheviot Centre	01668 282123	wooler.tic@northumberland.gov.uk

Regional Contacts and Information

For more information on accommodation, attractions, activities, events and holidays in North East England, contact one of the regional or local tourism organisations. Their websites have a wealth of information and many produce free publications to help you get the most out of your visit.

www.visitnortheastengland.com

www.thisisdurham.com
www.newcastlegateshead.com
www.visitnorthumberland.com
www.visitadrianswall.co.uk
www.visitnorthtyneside.com
www.visitsouthtyneside.co.uk
www.seeitdoitsunderland.co.uk

Entries appear alphabetically by town name in each county. A key to symbols appears on page 7

Discover delightful Durham

Book your pitch at **Durham Grange Caravan Club Site** and explore one of the most picturesque cities in the UK. Panoramic views from every vantage point make Durham a must-see destination.

Take advantage of a 50% reduction on pitch fees for standard pitches on stays on selected midweek dates.

50% off pitch fees*

Durham Grange Caravan Club Site

Book now: **01342 488 356**
www.caravanclub.co.uk/visitbritainsites

*A supplement for non-members (where admitted) is applicable at an additional £10 per night. Lines are open Mon-Fri 8.45am-5.30pm. Calls may be recorded.

THE **CARAVAN CLUB**

HAMSTERLEY COLLIERY, Co Durham Map ref 5C2   *SatNav NE17 7RT*

★★★★
TOURING & CAMPING PARK

🚐 (31)   £15.00-£19.00
🚙 (6)   £15.00-£19.00
31 touring pitches

Byreside Caravan Site

Hamsterley Colliery, Newcastle upon Tyne NE17 7RT
T: (01207) 560280 **F:** (01207) 560280 **E:** byresidecaravansite@hotmail.co.uk
W: www.byresidecaravansite.co.uk

A small, secluded family-run site on a working farm. Ideally situated for visiting Durham, Newcastle and Northumberland. Adjacent to Derwent Walk, ideal for walkers and cyclists. **Directions:** From A1 at Swalwell follow A694 towards Consett. Turn left onto B6310 towards Medomsley. Turn right towards High Westwood. 0.5 miles on right hand side. **Open:** All year.

Payment: 💳 ☼ **Children:** 🛝 **Catering:** 🍴 **Park:** 🐕 🚻 **Touring:** 🚿 🚽 🚐

BAMBURGH, Northumberland Map ref 5C1   *SatNav NE70 7EE*

★★★★
HOLIDAY, TOURING & CAMPING PARK

🚐 (144)   £18.50-£25.00
🚙 (144)   £18.50-£25.00
⛺ (30)   £9.75-£22.00
🏠 (27)   £260.00-£640.00
144 touring pitches

SPECIAL PROMOTIONS
Please see website for special offers and details of our wigwams too!

Waren Caravan and Camping Park

Waren Mill, Bamburgh, Northumberland NE70 7EE
T: (01668) 214366 **F:** (01668) 214224 **E:** waren@meadowhead.co.uk
W: www.meadowhead.co.uk **£ BOOK ONLINE**

Waren Caravan and Camping Park is nestled in coastal countryside with spectacular views to Holy Island and Bamburgh Castle. On site facilities include restaurant and bar, splash-pool, shop and children's play area. Our welcoming environment means you have all you need if you wish to stay on-site but we also make a great base from which to explore Northumberland's coast and castles.

Directions: Follow B1342 from A1 to Waren Mill towards Bamburgh. By Budle turn right, follow Meadowhead's Waren Caravan and Camping Park signs.

Open: 7th March to 1st November.

Site: 🏠 **Payment:** 💳 € ☼ **Leisure:** 🎣 🏊 🎯 **Children:** 🛝 🎪 **Catering:** ✕ 🍴 **Park:** 🐕 🚻 🛒 🏧 🚿 **Touring:** 🚿 🚽 🚐 🎵

HEXHAM, Northumberland   Map ref 5B2   SatNav NE48 2JY

Bellingham Camping and Caravanning Club

Brown Rigg, Bellingham, Hexham, Northumberland NE48 2JY
T: (01434) 220175 F: (01434) 220175 E: bellingham.site@thefriendlyclub.co.uk
W: www.campingandcaravanningclub.co.uk/bellingham £ BOOK ONLINE

🚐 (50)	£12.00-£45.00
🚛 (43)	£12.00-£45.00
🅰 (25)	£7.00-£45.00
🛏 (4)	£40.00

70 touring pitches

Set in the glorious Northumberland National Park, Bellingham is a perfect base for exploring this undiscovered part of England. Visitors can enjoy beautiful walks or cycle rides from the site and explore some of the major attractions in the vicinity, for example, Kielder Water, Hadrian's Wall and Cragside. The North Tyne, one of England's best salmon rivers, is a short walk away, while the campsite is within the largest Dark Skies Park in Europe and is perfect for stargazing. **Open:** 1st March - 4th January.

Site: 🅰🅿 Payment: 💳 ☀ Leisure: 🎵 ▶ 🎣 Children: 🛝 ⚠ Catering: 🍴 Park: 🚲 🔲 📱 🛒 Touring: 🚿 🔄 🍴

HEXHAM, Northumberland   Map ref 5B2   SatNav NE46 2JP

Hexham Racecourse Caravan Site

High Yarridge, Yarridge Road, Hexham NE46 2JP
T: (01434) 606847 F: (01434) 605814 E: hexrace.caravan@btconnect.com
W: www.hexham-racecourse.co.uk

🚐 (50)	£14.00-£17.00
🚛 (30)	£14.00-£17.00
🅰 (10)	£10.00

50 touring pitches

Grass area, sloping in parts. Most pitches with electrical hook-up points. Separate area for tents. **Directions:** From Hexham take the B6305 Allendale Road for 3 miles turn left at T Junction, site 1.5 miles on the right. **Open:** May to September.

Site: 🅰🅿 Payment: 💳 ☀ Leisure: ▶ 🎣 Children: 🛝 ⚠ Park: 🐾 🔲 📱 🛒 Touring: 🚿 🔄 🍴

SEAHOUSES, Northumberland   Map ref 5C1   SatNav NE68 7SP

Seafield Caravan Park

Seafield Road, Seahouses NE68 7SP
T: (01665) 720628 F: (01665) 720088 E: info@seafieldpark.co.uk
W: www.seafieldpark.co.uk £ BOOK ONLINE

🚐 (18)	£25.00-£48.00
🚛 (18)	£25.00-£48.00
🏠 (44)	£245.00-£1035.00

18 touring pitches

Luxurious holiday homes and lodges for hire on Northumberland's 5* premier park. Fully serviced touring 'Super Pitches', booking recommended. Prices include use of Ocean Club facilities. Visit England Award for Excellence Gold Winner 2014. **Directions:** Take the B1340 from Alnwick for 14 miles, east towards the coast. **Open:** 9th Feb to 9th Jan.

Payment: 💳 ☀ Leisure: ♿ 🎵 ▶ ♻ 🎣 Children: 🛝 ⚠ Park: 🐾 🔲 📱 🛒 Touring: 🚿 🍴

Sign up for our newsletter

Visit our website to sign up for our e-newsletter and receive regular information on events, articles, exclusive competitions and new publications.

www.visitor-guides.co.uk

Don't Miss...

Edinburgh Castle
Edinburgh EH1 2NG
(0131) 225 9846
www.edinburghcastle.gov.uk

Edinburgh Castle, built on an extinct volcano, dominates the skyline of Scotland's capital city and houses a wealth of attractions including The Honours of Scotland - the nation's crown jewels; The Stone of Destiny - coronation stone of Scotland's ancient kings; The Great Hall, Laich Hall and St Margaret's Chapel - remarkable medieval rooms and buildings where royalty and nobles dined and worshipped. The famous One O'clock Gun is fired daily, except Sundays.

Edinburgh Festival Fringe
August, Edinburgh
www.edfringe.com

The Edinburgh Festival Fringe (The Fringe), the world's largest arts festival, takes place over three weeks in August. Originally established in 1947 as an alternative to the Edinburgh International Festival, these days thousands of performers take to hundreds of stages all over Edinburgh to present shows for every taste. From big names in the world of entertainment to unknown artists looking to build their careers, the festival caters for everyone. It includes theatre, comedy, dance, physical theatre, circus, cabaret, children's shows, musicals, opera, music, spoken word, exhibitions and events.

Isle of Skye
Scottish Highlands
www.visitscotland.com

The Isle of Skye is the largest and best known of the Inner Hebrides and one of the most popular tourist destinations in Scotland. Situated off the west coast of mainland Scotland and renowned for its natural beauty, Skye's landscape is distinctly Highland with its lochs, heather-clad moors and towering peaks. Visit romantic Dunvegan Castle, sample fine island whiskies, enjoy a great day's walking or take a fabulous cruise into the heart of the Cuillin Mountains, whose peaks are visible from all over the islands. The capital, Portree, has a picturesque, pastel cottage-lined harbour.

Loch Ness
Scottish Highlands
www.visitlochness.com

No holiday in Scotland is complete without a visit to Loch Ness, just 8 miles from Inverness. Over 20 miles long, a mile wide and 700 feet at its deepest, it is the largest lake in Scotland by volume. The surrounding area is filled with historic attractions, natural wonders, cosy places to stay and superb eateries. The central location of Loch Ness makes it the perfect destination for holidays in the Highlands and The Loch Ness Monster is just one of the many myths and legends to be discovered in this particularly beautiful part of Scotland.

New Lanark
New Lanark Visitor Centre, South Lanarkshire ML11 9DB
(01555) 661345
www.newlanark.org

Close to the famous Falls of Clyde, this cotton mill village was founded in 1785 and became famous as the site of Robert Owen's radical reforms. Now beautifully restored as both a living community and attraction, the fascinating history of the village has been interpreted in New Lanark Visitor Centre.

Scotland

Scotland

Scotland is a proud nation with much to be proud of, from famous inventors, writers, politicians and a resplendent history, to dramatic mountains, stunningly beautiful countryside, a breathtaking coastline and islands of every character. Golf was invented at St Andrews four centuries ago and the whole of Scotland is a playground for walkers, golfers, sailors, fishermen, skiers and other outdoor enthusiasts. If heritage is your thing, there's nowhere quite like this land of majestic castles, historic houses, grand gardens and atmospheric ruins. Alive with wildlife, heritage, culture, food and much more - a trip to Scotland is unforgettable.

Explore – Scotland

Aberdeen City & Shire

Discover a place where majestic landscapes meet the sea and the flourishing Granite City boasts beautiful architecture and cultural gems. Aberdeen City and Shire is adored by the Royal Family, and is a region with a rich maritime heritage, lively events and a selection of thrilling activities. There are too many castles in this region to list and many fine houses too, including Cairness House near Fraserburgh, one of the great houses of Scotland, and the magnificent Duff House in Banff, a grand example of Georgian architecture.

This is one of Scotland's most captivating regions with rolling countryside, lush forests and woodlands, sandy beaches, stunning coastline and magnificent mountains to explore. The excellent Coastal Trail covers the breathtaking north east coastline while The Victorian Heritage Trail is the perfect way to explore Royal Deeside and uncover the many royal connections in the area.

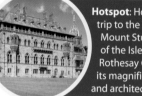

Hotspot: Hop aboard a ferry for a trip to the beautiful mansion of Mount Stuart on the East coast of the Isle of Bute, or head to Rothesay Castle to marvel at its magnificent circular design and architecture.

Argyll & The Isles

In Argyll & The Isles you can find the best of all worlds, from stunning coastal and Highland scenery to wildlife and watersports. Historic monuments, fascinating museums and lush gardens are just waiting to be discovered. Spend a day in Inveraray, where you can visit the imposing Inveraray Castle, a Clan Campbell stronghold since the time of King Robert the Bruce. Enjoy enchanting gardens steeped in history and surrounded by dramatic scenery at Benmore Botanic Garden, in its magnificent mountainside setting on the Cowal Peninsula.

Hotspot: The breathtakingly beautiful Cairngorms National Park are within easy reach of the city and there are plenty of charming towns and villages, together with a wealth of outdoor activities and remarkable wildlife.

Bustling Oban overlooks Oban Bay and is well known as the Gateway to the Outer and Inner Hebrides. The range of inter-island ferries is a great way to explore. On Mull, across the water from Oban, the picture-postcard town of Tobermory is famous for its colourful waterfront houses, used in the popular children's television series Balamory.

Ayrshire & Arran

With its bustling market towns and picturesque coastal fishing villages, this region is idyllic. The vivid greens of Ayrshire's rich pastures contrast strikingly with the steep mountainous profile of Arran as a backdrop. Discover ancient history and heritage, tantalise your tastebuds with fine food and whiskies, or enjoy some of the many outdoor pursuits and exciting events that take place here. The 18th century Dumfries House and the splendid Dean Castle and Country Park in Kilmarnock are must-visit attractions. For something a bit different, enjoy a day out with the animals at Heads of Ayr Farm Park, a wonderful family friendly attraction that lets you see, touch and feed exotic creatures from monkeys to meerkats.

Hotspot: With so many connections to Burns, Ayrshire & Arran boasts a wide range of related attractions including the Robert Burns Birthplace Museum and the Burns Cottage, historic landmarks where he set his greatest work, and the elegant Burns Monument and gardens that were created in his honour.

Arran's heritage dates back as far as the Stone Age and evidence of this can still be seen around the island with sites such as the stone circles at Machrie Moor. Brodick Castle, previously a seat of the Dukes of Hamilton, is set dramatically against the backdrop of Goat Fell Mountain, with stunning views over Brodick Bay to the Firth of Clyde.

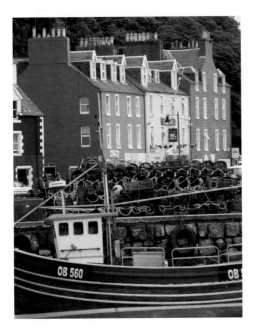

Dumfries & Galloway

From sparkling streams and spectacular summits to lush forests and sandy shores, the landscape here is naturally inspiring. The region's history, culture and beautiful scenery has filled artists and writers with the passion to create great works and it is the perfect setting for exciting activities and rare wildlife. With so much inspiration around, it's not surprising that the region boasts a thriving arts and culture scene. Once the home of Robert Burns, today Dumfries & Galloway continues to inspire modern artists and craftsmen.

Hotspot: In rural Angus, the stylish Pictavia visitor centre in the grounds of Brechin Castle Centre and Country Park provides the chance to uncover the lives of some of Scotland's ancient people, the Picts, as well as a children's adventure playground, farm animals and nature trail.

Dundee & Angus

Enjoy the best of both worlds in Dundee & Angus where cosmoplitan city attractions rub shoulders with majestic glens, pristine beaches and ancient forests perfect for walking. Uncover a captivating history, fantastic golf courses and a wide range of events and festivals. Visitor attractions include RRS Discovery, the ship which took Captain Scott on his remarkable voyage to Antarctica, and HMS Frigate Unicorn, a preserved warship which was first launched in 1824 and is the sixth oldest ship in the world. At Discovery Point you can experience the polar climate and the challenges that faced Captain Scott in his trip to the Antarctic a hundred years ago. Sensation is the city's science centre which has unusual exhibits to interact with, and at Mills Observatory you can see incredible images of the moon and stars at the UK's only full-time observatory.

Edinburgh & The Lothians

Edinburgh is the jewel in Scotland's crown with many facets: fortified hilltop architecture, sweeping Georgian crescents, tree-filled valleys, medieval cobbled crescents, graceful bridges soaring across chasms and green parks. Its centrepiece is the ancient Castle which dominates the city from its perch on an extinct volcano overlooking the city. Inside you will find treasures such as the Scottish Crown Jewels, housed in the Old Royal Palace, and the fascinating Scottish National War Museum is also within the castle walls. At the other end of Royal Mile is Holyroodhouse, Her Majesty the Queen's official residence when in Edinburgh, where portraits of 89 Scottish kings hang in the picture gallery.

Hotspot: Housing over 10,000 of Scotland's most precious artefacts, The National Museum of Scotland is just one Edinburgh's many public museums and galleries.

Some of Edinburgh's best scenery can be found in Holyrood Park, an extensive area of open countryside dominated by Arthur's Seat, the largest and most impressive of the volcanoes. The 18th century New Town, north of Princes Street, is officially recognised as the largest single area of Georgian architecture in Europe. One of the most unique ways to learn about the history of Edinburgh is on a visit to Camera Obscura and World of Illusions, a Victorian observatory on the Royal Mile. The National Gallery of Scotland and the Scottish National Gallery of Modern Art house two of Britain's finest collections of paintings.

Today the highlight of Edinburgh's cultural year is the Edinburgh Festival, the largest pan-arts festival in the world, and many of today's leading actors, comedians and writers cut their teeth at its 500+ 'fringe' events. Leith is the city's medieval port, now home to the former royal yacht Britannia. Edinburgh's

wider rural surroundings, the Lothians, are made up of gently rolling countryside, pretty towns and villages and an impressive collection of historic ruins. Sir Walter Scott lived in the Lammermuirs of East Lothian, where bitter battles once raged and the coast of East Lothian is dotted with castle remains.

Glasgow & The Clyde Valley

Glasgow, Scotland's 'Second Capital' and largest city, is one of the liveliest and most cosmopolitan destinations in Europe. It has been reborn as a vibrant centre of style, set against a backdrop of exceptional Victorian architecture. First-class events, world famous art collections, free attractions and beautiful parks and gardens are all here.

Glasgow Cathedral is built near the church site said to have been constructed in the 6th century by the city's founder, St Mungo. The Riverside Museum has a showroom of Scottish-built cars and the Clyde Room of ship models, and the revitalised riverside area offers numerous options for leisure and entertainment. The Glasgow Science Centre is an attractive titanium-clad complex which includes an IMAX cinema and a science mall.

Kelvingrove Park is one of the city's best-loved parks and contains Kelvingrove Art Gallery and Museum, a unique collection of European art and a famous array of European arms and armour. Take a walk around the Botanic Gardens to see the amazing A-listed Kibble Palace, an ornate Victorian glasshouse full of tropical plants from around the world. Glasgow Green is home to the social history museum, the People's Palace, and the Winter Gardens, and plays host to a variety of exciting events including the World Pipe Band Championships.

Beyond the city, the 42-mile long Clyde Valley driving route follows the River Clyde towards Lanark, passing through some spectacular countryside. Attractions include the World Heritage Site of New Lanark, a model industrial community founded in the 18th century, and the scenic Falls of Clyde. Further afield, Dams to Darnley covers over 1,350 acres of water, wetland, woodland and grassland including the striking Barrhead dams. Scotland's largest regional park, Clyde Muirshiel, sits to the west and the RSPB Nature Reserve at Lochwinnoch is a great place to enjoy the region's wildlife.

Hotspot: The Art Nouveau splendour of Scotland's best known architect Charles Rennie Mackintosh adorns attractions such as The Lighthouse, Glasgow School of Art, House for an Art Lover and the Hunterian Museum & Art Gallery.

The Highlands & Skye

Inverness is great for a relaxing city break. Make sure you see Inverness Castle and St Andrew's Cathedral, or take a stroll along the banks of the River Ness, crossing the suspension bridge for some peace and relaxation on the Ness Islands. Visit the Botanic Gardens for stunning flower displays and the indoor waterfall. Shoppers can pick up unique gifts at the Victorian Market or pay a visit to Leakey's, one of Scotland's largest second-hand bookshops.

Hotspot: The Highlands plays host to a number of events including the legendary summer games at Dornoch Highland Gathering and the Forres Highland Games.

The Highlands are famed for magnificent mountains, glens and lochs - think Ben Nevis and Loch Ness. Add in sandy beaches, stunning islands and and fascinating history to make a beautiful and inspiring region. Follow one of VisitScotland's many established tourist trails such as the Moray Coast trail or the Highland Pictish trail, or spend a few days visiting the region's historic castles, majestic monuments and famous battlefields. Learn all about the infamous massacre of 1692 at the Glencoe Visitor Centre and Glencoe Folk Museum. The Glenfinnan Monument, at the head of Loch Shiel, is a tribute to the Jacobite clansmen and the history of the Jacobite Rebellion led by Bonnie Prince Charlie. Culloden was the last battle fought on British soil - walk the battlefield and get vivid details of the Jacobites' 1746 defeat by government troops in the visitor centre. Nearby Fort George was built by the government in the wake of Culloden and is one of the finest feats of 18th century military engineering, taking 20 years to complete.

On Skye, the stark peaks of the famous Cuillin range attract climbers from around the globe and you'll also find astonishing geological marvels such as of the Trotternish peninsula's fantastical rock formations and pinnacles. Marvel at the Old Man of Storr, Mealt Falls, Duntulm Castle ruins, Kilt Rock and the extraordinary Quiraing.

The Kingdom of Fife

Compact Fife boasts a wonderful mix of stunning scenery and 300 miles of dedicated cycle routes. Walk or cycle through the lanes and past the sandy dunes to uncover a region that is filled with outdoor pursuits and activities. Try the Kingdom of Fife Millenium Cycle Ways or walk the superb Fife Coastal Path, a waymarked route that stretches 117 miles (188 km) from the Forth Estuary in the south to the Tay Estuary in north, taking in wildlife, historic sites and spectacular views along the way. Fife is also home to all three of Scotland's Blue Flag beaches: Elie Ruby Bay, Aberdour Silver Sands and Burntisland, as well as several other award-winning beaches.

Ancient castles, palaces, abbeys and tales of saints and monarchs can be found at almost every turn. Falkland Palace is a former royal palace of the Scottish Kings and was the favorite retreat of the Stuart dynasty, especially Mary Queen of Scots. Culross Palace, constructed by Sir George Bruce, is adorned with painted ceilings, pine panelling, antique furniture and ornaments. Fife has a wide range of visitor attractions from unique and interesting museums to aquariums, a secret war bunker and animal parks. Visit one of the many arts festivals, sample the excellent local food or stretch your legs with a round of golf. Head to the Lomond Hills Regional Park and take in geological marvels such as the bizarrely shaped Bonnet Stane and Carlin Maggie's Stane.

Loch Lomond, The Trossachs, Stirling & The Forth Valley

Visit a famous castle, an exciting safari park, an exhilarating adventure course and more in this diverse region. Doune Castle near Stirling is a magnificent 14th century courtyard castle with an intriguing movie connection. Callendar House in Falkirk is one of Scotland's finest baronial mansions where Mary Queen of Scots spent much of her early life - watch costumed interpreters recreate daily routines from the past and sample authentic dishes in the Georgian Kitchen. Tour Stirling Old Town Jail, meet the prison warden, the hangman and the convict determined to escape.

Hotspot: The Falkirk Wheel is the world's only rotating boatlift, a state of the art mechanical marvel that connects the Forth & Clyde and Union canals in central Scotland, and a fitting landmark worthy of Scotland's engineering tradition.

Orkney

Approximately seventy islands and skerries make up Orkney, with its incredible scenery, rugged coastline, abundant wildlife and mind-boggling wealth of archaeological sites. Orkney's history is a rich tapestry – before being annexed by the Scottish Crown in 1472, it was a Norse Earldom and was an important seat of power in the Viking Empire, a heritage reflected by the magnificent 12th century catherdral of St Magnus in Kirkwall and through the islands' distinctly Scandinavian place names. Further back, Orkney contains some of the oldest and best-preserved Neolithic sites in Europe. The Ness of Brodgar is an archaeological site covering 2.5 hectares, between the Ring of Brodgar and the Standing Stones of Stenness, in the Heart of Neolithic Orkney World Heritage Site. These days, with craft jewellers and artists drawing inspiration from the landscape and history, Orkney has a thriving arts and crafts scene. The islands are also heaven for food lovers, famed for salmon and shellfish, as well as the prized meat that comes from the legendary seaweed fed sheep of North Ronaldsay.

Outer Hebrides

The Outer Hebrides, also known as the Western Isles and the Long Island, is a paradise of powder white beaches, Atlantic waves, dark moorland, rugged mountains and amazing wildlife. This idyllic chain of 200 inter-linked islands in a 130 mile archipelago sits 30 miles off the north west coast of Scotland and is the perfect destination for walking, cycling, golfing, fishing, sightseeing and soaking up a rich and vibrant history and culture. From the magnificent Calanais Standing Stones on Lewis to Bosta Iron Age House on Great Bernera and the Barpa Langass on North Uist, the islands offer unique archaeology and boast 55 Sites of Special Scientific Interest and three National Nature Reserves. This unspoilt wilderness is an incredible natural playground for outdoor lovers. The contrasting terrain of low lying Lewis and mountainous Harris offer great adventures, from cycling, walking and fishing to climbing and watersports. Visit St Kilda for some amazing birdwatching or sample Hebridean delicacies such as Stornoway black pudding, fabulous seafood and unique whisky.

Perthshire

Perthshire is a place where you can explore majestic glens, championship golf courses and ancient forests. You can find centuries of history alongside adrenaline-packed adventure, delicious food and drink, incredible wildlife, some of the most exciting events and festivals in the country and much more.

Filled with tales of Jacobite uprisings, captive queens and ancient civilisations, Perthshire has a vast array of castles, historic buildings and museums that bring the region's fascinating past to life. Visit the original home of the legendary Stone of Destiny at Scone Palace, or see the ruined tower house where Mary Queen of Scots was incarcerated on Castle Island at Loch Leven in 1567. Uncover the 300-year-old history of the Black Watch, one of the world's most famous elite military regiments at Balhousie Castle. Step inside a fantastically recreated Iron-Age dwelling at the Scottish Crannog Centre on Loch Tay.

Hotspot: Explore the region's Jacobite past at Blair Castle where Bonnie Prince Charlie stayed during the Jacobite rising of 1745.

In the city, visit Perth Museum and Art Gallery where you can see everything from Pictish stones to works by the Old Masters. The Fergusson Gallery, a converted waterworks building, displays works by John Duncan Fergusson and other celebrated Scottish Colourists. On the banks of the River Tay, against the picturesque backdrop of the rolling countryside of Highland Perthshire, The Pitlochry Festival Theatre is one of Scotland's finest theatrical institutions where you can enjoy classic works and new, cutting-edge productions.

Scottish Borders

The real Scotland starts right at the border and it's easy to lose yourself amongst the spectacular scenery. The Tweed meanders from the coast along the border to rise in the Pentland Hills and the hazy blue peaks of the Elidon Hills have lifted the hearts of many a traveller crossing Carter Bar on the A68. En route from Carlisle towards Edinburgh, you will pass Bruce's Cave and numerous castle remains where he fought the English. The A7 scenic route passes through the gentle hills of Eskdale and the Moorfoots and you can take in the dramatic history and culture of the land of Sir Walter Scott at ruined castles and exciting festivals. Uncover a wonderful arts and crafts scene, enjoy delicious local produce and explore miles of rolling hills, leafy valleys and the beautiful coast. Wherever you travel here, you can be sure of a real Scottish welcome.

Shetland

The Shetland Islands, a cluster of over 100 wild, awe-inspiring islands each with its own heritage, history and character, were carved and shaped by ice over thousands of years. Classified as a global Geopark for its fascinating geology, the landscapes and seascapes provide endless inspiration for artists and photographers. Inhabited for over 6,000 years, Shetland has a unique culture. Archaeology, dialect (based on old Scots and Norse), place names, food and world-renowned traditional music all help to tell the story of its history. Some of the finest archaeological sites in Europe can be found here, including the best preserved broch in the world on the now uninhabited island of Mousa. The famous Jarlshof is a record of human occupation going back 5,000 years. The influence of Scandinavia can be seen everywhere and during the Second World War, Shetland was a base for the Norwegian resistance.

Hotspot: The cliffs and lighthouse at Eshaness are must-visits for walks with spectacular volcanic scenery and birdwatching.

There is a wealth of things to see and do all across Shetland, so be sure to visit more than just the mainland. Unst, Yell, Fetlar and the more outlying islands are equally impressive and offer very different experiences. The wildlife here is truly wild, with otters and seals at play in plain sight, whale-watching off the coast and a bird watchers paradise along the rugged, monumental cliffs. Anglers, golfers, sailors, cyclists, scuba-divers, surfers, kayakers and beachcombers will all find plenty to do here.

Indulge – Scotland

Experience a romantic cruise across the peaceful waters of Loch Katrine in the scenic Trossachs of Scotland, aboard the aptly-named classic steamship, SS Sir Walter Scott. www.lochkatrine.com or call (01877) 376315.

Enjoy an elegant afternoon tea with unrivalled views across the Irish Sea towards the Ailsa Craig and the Isle of Arran in **The Grand Tea Lounge** at Trump Turnberry Resort, on the Ayrshire Coast. Visit www.turnberryresort.co.uk/grand-tea-lounge or call (01655) 331000.

Indulge in a 'wee dram' with a visit to **The Glenmorangie Distillery** near Tain in the Highlands of Scotland. Tour the distillery and experience all stages of the whisky making process from mashing and fermenting to distilling and maturing - all culminating in a dram or two of your choice! To book visit www.glenmorangie.com or call (0)1862 882 477.

Scotland is the spiritual home of golf with more courses per head of population than anywhere else in the world. Whether it's a visit to the oldest, most iconic course in the world at St Andrews, or to Speyside to experience golfing in Malt Whisky country, you're certain to find your perfect place to tee off. See www.visitscotland.com for a list of courses.

Dine in style on delicious local oysters washed down with fine wine at the original **Loch Fyne Restaurant & Oyster Bar**, near the waters of Loch Fyne at Cairndow on the Kintyre peninsula. Visit www.lochfyne.com or call 01499 600 264.

Visit – Scotland

Attractions with this sign participate in the Visitor Attraction Quality Assurance Scheme (see page 7) which recognises high standards in all aspects of the visitor experience.

Aberdeen City & Shire

Aberdeen Winter Festival
November-December, Aberdeen
www.aberdeencity.gov.uk
Comedy, musicals, pantomime concerts and much more, taking place in several of Aberdeen's fantastic venues, such as the much-loved Lemon Tree.

Balmoral Castle
Aberdeenshire AB35 5TB
(01339) 742534
www.balmoralcastle.com
The Scottish holiday home of the Royal Family.

Delgatie Castle
Turriff, Aberdeenshire AB53 5TD
(01888) 563479
www.delgatiecastle.com
Dating from 1030 the Castle is steeped in Scottish history yet still has the atmosphere of a lived in home. It has some of the finest painted ceilings in Scotland, Mary Queen of Scots' bed-chamber. Clan Hay Centre.

Gordon Highlanders Museum
Aberdeen AB15 7XH
(01224) 311200
www.gordonhighlanders.com
Regimental collection of the Gordon Highlanders housed in St Lukes, former home of artist Sir George Reid.

Ayrshire & Arran

Culzean Castle & Country Park
Maybole, South Ayrshire KA19 8LE
(0844) 493 2149
www.nts.org.uk
An 18th century castle perched on a rocky promontory with superb panoramic views over the Firth of Clyde.

Isle of Arran Distillery Visitor Centre
North Ayrshire KA27 8HJ
(01770) 830264
www.arranwhisky.com
Isle of Arran Distillers produce a unique single malt whisky to rank with Scotland's greatest.

Banffshire

Drummuir Castle
Drummuir, By Keith, Banffshire, AB55 5JE
(01542) 810332
www.drummuircastle.com
Castellated Victorian Gothic-style castle built in 1847 by Admiral Duff. 60ft high lantern tower with fine plasterwork. Family portraits, interesting artefacts and other paintings.

Dumfries & Galloway

Caerlaverock Castle
Dumfries And Galloway DG1 4RU
(01387) 770244
www.historic-scotland.gov.uk
Caerlaverock is an awe inspiring ruin with a long history of lordly residence and wartime siege.

Logan Botanic Garden
Tranrae, Dumfries And Galloway DG9 9ND
(01776) 860231
www.rbge.org.uk
One of the National Botanic Gardens of Scotland, where many rare and exotic plants from temperate regions flourish outdoors. A plantsman's paradise.

Edinburgh & The Lothians

Edinburgh International Festival
August, Edinburgh
www.eif.co.uk
Three spellbinding weeks of international opera, dance, music, theatre and the visual arts.

Edinburgh Riding of the Marches
September, Edinburgh
www.edinburghridingthemarches.co.uk
The Edinburgh Riding of the Marches – men and women on horseback – set off on the edge of Edinburgh before heading into the city centre to be greeted by the Lord Provost.

National Museum of Scotland
Edinburgh EH1 1JF
(0131) 225 7534
www.nms.ac.uk
See treasures from the edges of history and trace Scotland's story from fascinating fossils to popular culture. For generations we've collected key exhibits from all over Scotland and beyond.

Royal Edinburgh Military Tattoo
August, Edinburgh
www.edintattoo.co.uk
Staged every year as part of the world-famous Edinburgh Festival, the Edinburgh Military Tattoo is a unique and memorable celebration of music, dance and military pageantry.

Our Dynamic Earth
Edinburgh EH8 8AS
(0131) 550 7800
www.dynamicearth.co.uk
Explore our planet's past present and future. Be shaken by volcanoes, fly over glaciers and feel the chill of polar ice.

The Royal Yacht Britannia
Ocean Terminal, Leith, Edinburgh EH6 6JJ
(0131) 555 5566
www.royalyachtbritannia.co.uk
The Royal Yacht Britannia was home to Her Majesty The Queen and the Royal Family for over 40 years, sailing over 1,000,000 miles. Follow in their footsteps to explore this most special of Royal residences.

Scottish National Portrait Gallery
Edinburgh EH2 1JD
(0131) 624 6200
www.nationalgalleries.org/portraitgallery
The Scottish National Portrait Gallery is one of Edinburgh's most remarkable buildings – a great red sandstone neo-gothic palace which explores the story of Scotland and her people, from famous historical figures such as Mary, Queen of Scots to recent pioneers in science, sport and the arts.

The Scotch Whisky Experience
Edinburgh EH1 2NE
(0131) 220 0441
www.scotchwhiskyexperience.co.uk
The mystery of whisky making revealed! Take a barrel ride through whisky history.

Glasgow & The Clyde Valley

The Burrell Collection
Pollok Country Park, Glasgow G43 1AT
(0141) 287 2550
www.glasgowlife.org.uk
In the heart of Pollok Country Park, this award-winning building houses a unique collection in a beautiful woodland setting. The collection is one of the greatest ever created by one person, comprising over 8000 objects.

Celtic Connections
January-February, Glasgow
www.celticconnections.com
Glasgow's annual folk, roots and world music festival, Celtic Connections celebrates Celtic music and its connections to cultures across the globe.

Clydebuilt
(Scottish Maritime Museum Braehead)
Glasgow, Renfrewshire G51 4BN
(0141) 886 1013
www.scottishmaritimemuseum.org
The story of the River Clyde and the contribution it made to the development of West Central Scotland is brought vividly to life at Clydebuilt, the Scottish Maritime Museum at Braehead.

Glasgow Film Festival
February, Glasgow
www.glasgowfilm.org
The festival has carved a reputation for staging thought-provoking film features.

Glasgow Merchant City Festival
July, Glasgow
www.merchantcityfestival.com
Annual event featuring theatre, music, visual arts, comedy, dance, film, literature and fashion.

Perthshire

Crieff Highland Games
August, Crieff
www.crieffhighlandgathering.com
*The first Crieff Highland Gathering was in 1870
and has occurred every year since with the two
exceptions of 1914-18 and 1939-49 when no
gatherings took place.*

Perth Festival of Arts
May, Perth
www.perthfestival.co.uk
*The 2015 Perth International Arts Festival is going
to be both epic and intimate, jam-packed with big
ideas, big-name artists and big opportunities for
you to get involved.*

Pitlochry Highland Games
September, Pitlochry
www.pitlochryhighlandgames.co.uk
*Pitlochry Highland Games has been hosting
competitors and enthralling spectators since 1852.*

Scottish Borders

Common Ridings
June-July, various venues
www.visitscotland.com
*Towns across the Scottish Borders are filled with
pageantry for the annual Common Riding festivals,
marking the turbulent times when settlement
boundaries were protected from raids on horseback.*

Paxton House and Country Park
Berwick-upon-Tweed, Scottish Borders TD15 1SZ
(01289) 386291
www.paxtonhouse.com
*An 18th century neo-palladian country house with
Adam plasterwork, Chippendale and Trotter furniture.*

Shetland

Up Helly Aa 2015
Lerwick, Shetland ZE1 0HL
www.uphellyaa.org
*Shetland's biggest fire festival is an incredible spectacle.
In mid-winter, the Up Helly Aa guizers of Lerwick burn
their Viking galley and then party all night long in a
triumphant celebration of Shetland history.*

Lanimer Day
June, Lanark, Clyde Valley
www.lanarklanimers.co.uk
*The Lanimer celebrations consist of nearly a week
of events including massed bands, a parade, lots
of ceremony and plenty of horses &
riders as well as the crowning of the
Lanimer Queen.*

Riverside Museum
Glasgow G3 8DP
(0141) 287 2720
www.glasgowlife.org.uk
*A unique collection of transport
and technology.*

The Highlands & Skye

Loch Ness Film Festival
May, Highlands
www.lochnessfilmfestival.co.uk
*The Highlands host an intimate yet expansive range
of movies during the Loch Ness Film Festival.
Airing everything from documentaries, amateur
shorts and features, the grassroots event is a non-
profit organisation, with all funds raised going to
charitable causes.*

The Official Loch Ness Monster Exhibition
Drumnadrochit, Highland IV63 6TU
(01456) 450573
www.lochness.com
*An exhibition incorporating the latest in technology for
visitor centres. Six room walkthrough is fully automated.*

Talisker Distillery
Isle of Skye, Highland IV47 8SR
(01478) 614306
www.whisky.com/distilleries/talisker_distillery.html
*The only distillery on the Isle of Skye, set in an
Area of Outstanding Natural Beauty. Guided tours,
exhibition, shop.*

The Kingdom of Fife

British Golf Museum
St. Andrews, Fife KY16 9AB
(01334) 460046
www.britishgolfmuseum.co.uk
*Tracing the history of golf, in both Britain and abroad,
from the middle ages through to the present day.*

Deep Sea World
North Queensferry, Fife KY11 1JR
(01383) 411 880
www.deepseaworld.com
*Travel through the UK's longest underwater viewing
tunnel, dive with sand tiger sharks, explore the seal
sanctuary and witness the beautiful coral reefs at
Deep Sea World, Scotland's national aquarium.*

Tourist Information Centres

When you arrive at your destination, visit the Tourist Information Centre for quality assured help with accommodation and information about local attractions and events, or email your request before you go.

Aberdeen	23 Union Street	01224 288828	aberdeen@visitscotland.com
Aberfeldy	The Square	01887 820276	aberfeldy@visitscotland.com
Aberfoyle	Main Street	01887 382352	aberfoyle@visitscotland.com
Alford	Railway Museum, Old Station Yard	019755 62052	alford@visitscotland.com
Anstruther	Scottish Fisheries Museum	01333 311073	anstruther@visitscotland.com
Arbroath	Fishmarket Quay	01241 872609	arbroath@visitscotland.com
Aviemore	Unit 7, Grampian Road	01479 810930	aviemore@visitscotland.com
Ayr	22 Sandgate	01292 290300	ayr@visitscotland.com
Ballater	Old Royal Station	013397 55306	ballater@visitscotland.com
Balloch	Balloch Road	01389 753533	balloch@visitscotland.com
Balloch (Park)	National Park Gateway Centre	01389 722600	info@lochlomond.visitscotland.com
Banchory	Bridge Street	01330 822000	banchory@visitscotland.com
Banff	Collie Lodge	01261 812419	banff@visitscotland.com
Blairgowrie	26 Wellmeadow	01250 876825	blairgowrie@visitscotland.com
Bo'ness	Bo'ness & Kinneil Railway Station	01506 826626	boness@visitscotland.com
Bowmore	The Square	01496 810254	islay@visitscotland.com
Braemar	The Mews	01339 741600	braemar@visitscotland.com
Brechin	Pictavia Visitor Centre	01356 623050	brechin@visitscotland.com
Brodick	The Pier	01770 303776	brodick@visitscotland.com
Callander	10 Ancaster Square	01877 330342	callander@visitscotland.com
Campbelltown	MacKinnon House	01586 552056	campbelltown@visitscotland.com
Castle Douglas	Market Hill	01556 502611	castledouglas@visitscotland.com
Castlebay	Pier Road	01871 810336	castlebay@visitscotland.com
Craignure	The Pier	01680 812377	mull@visitscotland.com
Crieff	Town Hall	01764 652578	crieff@visitscotland.com
Daviot Wood	Picnic Area	01463 791575	daviotwoods@visitscotland.com
Drumnadrochit	The Car Park	01456 459086	drumnadrochit@visitscotland.com
Dufftown	2 The Square	01340 820501	dufftown@visitscotand.com
Dumfries	64 Whitesands	01387 253862	dumfries@visitscotland.com
Dundee	Discovery Quay	01382 527527	dundee@visitscotland.com

Dunfermline	1 High Street	01383 720999	dumfermline@visitscotland.com
Dunkeld	The Cross	01350 727688	dunkeld@visitscotland.com
Dunoon	7 Alexandra Parade	01369 703785	dunoon@visitscotland.com
Durness	Durine	01971 511368	durnesstic@visitscotland.com
Edinburgh	3 Princes Street	0131 473 3898	info@visitscotland.com
Edinburgh Airport	Airport Tourist Information Desk	0131 344 3120	edinburgh.airport@visitscotland.com
Eyemouth	Auld Kirk	01890 750678	info@visitscotland.com
Falkirk	Lime Road	01324 620244	falkirk@visitscotland.com
Fort Augustus	Car Park	01320 366779	info@visitscotland.com
Fort William	15 High Street	01397 701801	info@visitscotland.com
Fraserburgh	3 Saltoun Square	01346 518315	fraserburgh@visitscotland.com
Glasgow	11 George Square	0141 204 4400	glasgow@visitscotland.com
Glasgow Airport	International Arrivals	0141 848 4440	glasgowairport@visitscotland.com
Grantown on Spey	54 High Street	01479 872773	grantown@visitscotland.com
Gretna Green	Unit 38, Gretna Gateway Outlet Village	01461 337834	gretnatic@visitscotland.com
Hawick	1 Tower Mill	01450 373993	info@visitscotland.com
Helensburgh	Clock Tower	01436 672642	helensburgh@visitscotland.com
Huntly	9a The Square	01466 792255	huntly@visitscotland.com
Inverary	Front Street	01499 302063	inverary@visitscotland.com
Inverness	Castle Wynd	01463 252401	inverness@visitscotland.com
Inverurie	18a High Street	01467 625800	inverurie@visitscotland.com
Jedburgh	Murray's Green	01835 863170	jedburgh@visitscotland.com
Kelso	Town House	01573 228055	kelso@visitscotland.com
Kirkaldy	The Merchant's House	01592 267775	kirkcaldy@visitscotland.com
Kirkcudbright	Harbour Square	01557 330494	kirkcudbright@visitscotland.com
Kirkwall	West Castle Street	01856 872856	kirkwall@visitorkney.com
Lanark	Horsemarket	01555 661661	lanark@visitscotland.com
Lerwick	Market Cross	01595 693434	info@visitshetland.com
Lochboisdale	Pier Road	01878 700286	lochboisdale@visitthebrides.com
Lochinver	Main Street	01571 844194	lochinver@visitscotland.com
Lochmaddy	Pier Road	01876 500321	lochmaddy@visitscotland.com
Melrose	Abbey House	01896 822283	melrose@visitscotland.com
Newton Stewart	Dashwood Square	01671 402431	newtownstewart@visitscotland.com
Newtongrange	Scottish Mining Museum	0131 663 4262	newtongrange@visitscotland.com
North Berwick	Quality Street	01620 892197	info@visitscotland.com
North Kessock	Picnic Site	01463 731836	northkessock@visitscotland.com
Oban	Argyll Square	01631 563122	oban@visitscotland.com
Peebles	23 High Street	01721 723159	peebles@visitscotland.com
Perth	Lower City Mills	01738 450600	perth@visitscotland.com
Pitlochry	22 Atholl Road	01796 472215	pitlochry@visitscotland.com
Portree	Bayfield House	01478 614906	portree@visitscotland.com
Rothesay	Isle of Bute Discovery Centre	01700 502151	rothesay@visitscotland.com
St Andrews	70 Market Street	01334 472021	standrews@visitscotland.com
Stirling	Old Town Jail	01786 475019	stirling@visitscotland.com
Stonehaven	66 Allardice Street	01569 762806	stonehaven@visitscotland.com
Stornoway	26 Cromwell Street	01851 703088	stornoway@visitscotland.com
Stranraer	28 Harbour Street	01776 702595	stranraer@visitscotland.com
Stromness	Ferry Terminal Building	01856 850716	stromness@visitscotland.com
Strontian	Strontian	01967 402382	strontian@visitscotland.com
Sumburgh Airport	Sumburgh Airport	01595 693434	info@visitshetland.com
Tarbert (Loch Fyne)	Harbour Street	01880 820132	tarbert@visitscotland.com
Tarbet (Loch Lomond)	Tarbet	01301 702260	tarbet@visitscotland.com
Thurso	Riverside	01847 893155	thurso@visitcotland.com
Tomintoul	The Square	01807 580285	tomintoul@visitscotland.com
Tyndrum	Main Street	01838 400246	tyndrum@visitscotland.com
Ullapool	20 Argyle Street	01854 612486	ullapool@visitscotland.com
Wick	McAllan's	01955 602547	info@visitscotland.com

Regional Contacts and Information

For more information on accommodation, attractions, activities, events and holidays in Scotland, contact VisitScotland or visit their website which has a wealth of information and publications to help you get the most out of your visit.

www.visitscotland.com

Entries appear alphabetically by town name in each county. A key to symbols appears on page 7

DUNBAR, *East Lothian* Map ref 6D2

Belhaven Bay Caravan and Camping Park

Edinburgh Road, West Barns, Dunbar EH42 1TU
T: (01368) 865956 **F:** (01368) 865022 **E:** belhavenbay@meadowhead.co.uk
W: www.meadowhead.co.uk £ **BOOK ONLINE**

Scottish
TOURIST BOARD
★★★
SMALL
HOLIDAY
PARK

🚐 (43)   £15.95-£28.75
🚙 (43)   £15.95-£28.75
⛺ (32)   £10.00-£30.00
🏠 (6)   £290.00-£645.00
59 touring pitches

Belhaven Bay is situated on the stunning East Lothian Coastline and adjoins the John Muir Country Park: a haven for wildlife and an area of natural beauty. Visitors can also enjoy direct access to the beach. Facilities include free showers, laundry and kitchen facilities. Enjoy a relaxing break in one of our Thistle Award holiday homes for hire. There are also holiday homes for sale, so you can appreciate the beauty of Belhaven Bay all season long.

Directions: The Park is located in the small village of Belhaven, just 2 minutes off the A1 dual carriageway North of Dunbar.

Open: 7th March to 30th November.

Site: 🅰🅿 Payment: 🖃 Leisure: ▶ Children: 🐶 🎠 Park: 🐾 🚽 🗑 📦 🏧 Touring: 🚽 🔌 🐕 🎵

Book your accommodation online

Visit our websites for detailed information, up-to-date availability and to book your accommodation online. Includes over 20,000 places to stay, all of them star rated.

www.visitor-guides.co.uk

NORTH BERWICK, East Lothian   Map ref 6D2   SatNav EH39 5NJ

Tantallon Caravan and Camping Park

Tantallon Road, North Berwick EH39 5NJ
T: (01368) 865956 **E:** tantallon@meadowhead.co.uk
W: www.meadowhead.co.uk £ **BOOK ONLINE**

Scottish TOURIST BOARD ★★★★ HOLIDAY PARK

Thistle

🚐 (108)	£18.95-£30.25
🚎 (108)	£18.95-£30.25
⛺ (65)	£9.50-£26.75
🏠 (10)	£310.00-£705.00
108 touring pitches	

SPECIAL PROMOTIONS
Please see our website
for up to date details
and to book online.

Tantallon Caravan and Camping Park is situated in an idyllic location which offers spectacular views to the Bass Rock and Firth of Forth. Whether touring or staying in one of our Thistle Award holiday homes, you will be holidaying in an area of natural beauty which also offers plenty to do for all the family. North Berwick is a bustling seaside town with fine beaches and boutique shopping. East Lothian is a paradise for golfers. Facilities include free showers and fully equipped laundry and kitchen.

Directions: From North Berwick, A198 towards Dunbar. From the South, turn of at A1 north of Dunbar and follow signs for North Berwick and Tantallon Park.

Open: 7th March - 30th November.

Payment: ☼ **Leisure:** ♪ ▶ ♦ **Children:** ⚠ **Park:** 🐾 🚮 🚻 🛗 🚿 **Touring:** 🚽 🚰 🚗 ♪

EDINBURGH, Edinburgh   Map ref 6C2   SatNav EH53 0HT

Linwater Caravan Park

West Clifton, East Calder, West Lothian, West Clifton EH53 0HT
T: (0131) 333 3326 **F:** (0131) 333 1952 **E:** queries@linwater.co.uk
W: www.linwater.co.uk

Scottish TOURIST BOARD ★★★★ TOURING PARK

🚐 (50)	£19.00-£23.00
🚎 (50)	£19.00-£23.00
⛺ (10)	£17.00-£20.00
🏠 (4)	
🛏	£900.00
60 touring pitches	

A peaceful family-run park, west of Edinburgh. Excellent facilities and lovely walks. Ideal for visiting Edinburgh from park and ride or touring. Also timbertents, as an alternative to camping, and a new self catering luxury lodge. **Directions:** Signposted from M9, junction 1 - Newbridge, or from Wilkieston on A71, along B7030. **Open:** Mid-March to end of October.

Payment: 🏧 € ☼ **Leisure:** ♪ **Children:** 🛝 **Park:** 🐾 🚮 🚻 🛗 🚿 **Touring:** 🚽 🚰 🚗

Looking for something else?

The official and most comprehensive guide to independently inspected, quality-assessed accommodation.

- **B&Bs and Hotels**
- **Self Catering**
- **Camping, Touring and Holiday Parks**

Now available in all good bookshops and online at

www.hudsons.co.uk/shop

Mortonhall Caravan and Camping Park

38 Mortonhall Gate, Frogston Road East, Edinburgh EH16 6TJ
T: (0131) 664 1533 **E:** mortonhall@meadowhead.co.uk
W: www.meadowhead.co.uk **£ BOOK ONLINE**

Scottish TOURIST BOARD ★★★★ HOLIDAY PARK

Thistle

🚐	(250)	£14.50-£34.50
🚉	(250)	£14.50-£34.50
🅰	(250)	£13.00-£29.75
🏠	(20)	£270.00-£885.00

250 touring pitches

SPECIAL PROMOTIONS
Please see our website for all our current special offers and details of our wigwams! You can also book online!

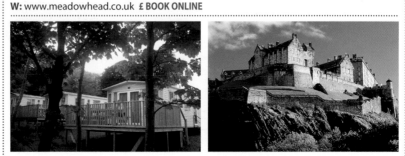

Situated in a 200 acre country estate and only 4 miles from Edinburgh's city centre. Mortonhall has beautifully maintained and landscaped parkland, with views to the Pentland Hills.

Only a short bus trip or drive, the capital's shopping, walking, arts, history and other leisure activities are all on our doorstep. Overnight holding area available.

Directions: From the north or south, exit the city bypass (A720) at Straiton or Lothianburn Junctions and follow the signs to Mortonhall.   **Open:** All year.

Site: 🅿 **Payment:** 🎫 € ☼ **Leisure:** 🎣 🏊 🏌 ⛳ 🎯 **Children:** 🛝 🎠 **Catering:** ✕ 🍴
Park: 🐕 🚮 🏧 📷 **Touring:** 🚽 ♿ 🔌 ♪

Black Rock Caravan Park

Balconie Street, Evanton IV16 9UN
T: (01349) 830917 **E:** enquiries@blackrockscotland.co.uk
W: www.blackrockscotland.co.uk

Scottish TOURIST BOARD ★★★★ HOLIDAY PARK

🅰	(18)
🚉	(1)
🏠	(46)

43 touring pitches

We are a small, family run park located in the shelter of beautiful, wooded Glenglass with views of an impressive local landmark, the Fyrish Monument. Please contact us for 2015 rates.

Directions: 1 mile off the A9, 15 miles North East of Inverness.   **Open:** 1st April - 31st October.

Payment: ☼ **Leisure:** 🏊 ⛳ 🎯 **Children:** 🛝 🎠 **Park:** 🐕 🚮 🏧 📷 **Touring:** 🚽 ♿ 🔌 ♪

Discover stunning Stirling

Maragowan Caravan Club Site is the perfect place for a family holiday with a wealth of outdoor activities within easy reach of the site. From Kayaking and mountaineering to hill walking and golf there's so much to enjoy.

The site is perfectly placed on the banks of the beautiful River Lochay, so if you'd rather, you can just sit and enjoy the view.

Maragowan Caravan Club Site

Book now: **01342 488 356**
www.caravanclub.co.uk/visitbritainsites
Lines are open Mon-Fri 8.45am-5.30pm. Calls may be recorded.

THE CARAVAN CLUB

CALLANDER, Stirling   Map ref 6B1   SatNav FK17 8LE

Scottish TOURIST BOARD
★★★★★
HOLIDAY PARK

Gart Caravan Park
Stirling Road, Callander FK17 8LE
T: (01877) 330002 **E:** enquiries@theholidaypark.co.uk
W: www.theholidaypark.co.uk

🚐 (128)   £24.00-£28.00
🚍 (128)   £24.00-£28.00
128 touring pitches

A peaceful and spacious park maintained to a very high standard with modern, heated shower block facilities. The ideal centre for cycling, walking and fishing or simply relaxing. Park wide Wi-Fi and hard standing pitches available. **Directions:** Leave jct 10 of the M9, West to Callander. **Open:** 1st April to 15th October.

Site: ▲🅿 Payment: 💷 ☼ Leisure: ♪ ► Children: 🧸 ⚠ Park: 🐕 🚰 🗑 🍴 🛈 Touring: 🚿 🕑 🛒 🎣

LINLITHGOW, West Lothian   Map ref 6C2   SatNav EH49 6PL

Scottish TOURIST BOARD
★★★★
TOURING PARK

Beecraigs Caravan and Camping Site
Beecraigs Country Park, Nr Linlithgow, West Lothian EH49 6PL
T: (01506) 844516 (option 1) **F:** (01506) 846256 **E:** mail@beecraigs.com
W: www.beecraigs.com

🚐 (28)   £18.50-£23.00
🚍 (28)   £18.50-£23.00
▲ (12)   £15.50-£23.00
40 touring pitches

Situated near historic Linlithgow town and within the Beecraigs Country Park. On-site facilities include electric hookups, modern toilet facilities with privacy cubicles, babychange and launderette. MHD point. Pets are welcome. **Directions:** From M9, follow A803, then Beecraigs Country Park & Caravan Site signs. Park is 2 miles South of Linlithgow. From M8, follow B792 & Country Park signs. **Open:** All year.

Payment: 💷 ☼ Leisure: 🚲 ♪ ► ∪ Children: 🧸 ⚠ Park: 🐕 🗑 🍴 🛈 Touring: 🚿 🕑 🛒

Need more information?

Visit our websites for detailed information, up-to-date availability and to book your accommodation online. Includes over 20,000 places to stay, all of them star rated.

www.visitor-guides.co.uk

Don't Miss...

Cardiff Castle

Cardiff CF10 3RB
(029) 2087 8100
www.cardiffcastle.com
Cardiff Castle is situated in the heart of the
capital and its enchanting fairytale towers
conceal an elaborate and splendid interior.
Climb up to the top of the 12th century
Norman keep for great views over the city.

National Botanic Garden of Wales

Carmarthen, Carmarthenshire SA32 8HG
(01558) 668768
www.gardenofwales.org.uk
A world-class botanic garden in 568 acres of
beautiful Carmarthenshire countryside.
A visitor attraction and centre for botanical
research and conservation, featuring the
world's largest single-span glasshouse.

National Eisteddfod of Wales 2015

August 1-8, Meifod, Montgomeryshire
www.eisteddfod.org.uk
One of the great festivals of the world,
attracting over 160,000 visitors every year. An
eclectic mixture of culture, music, visual arts
and all kinds of activities.

Snowdonia

North Wales
www.visitwales.com
www.visitsnowdonia.info
Nowhere else in Britain will you find such
variety, in such a compact area, as you will in
Snowdonia - or Eryri as it is known in Welsh.
With 823 square miles of National Park and 37
miles (60 km) of sublime coastline, the area is
best known for its impressive peaks. Mount
Snowdon is the highest mountain in Wales at
3,560 ft and Cadair Idris, near Dolgeallau, is one
of the most popular in Wales.

Wales Millennium Centre

Cardiff CF10 5AL
(029) 2063 6464
www.wmc.org.uk
The iconic Wales Millennium Centre, with
its amazing exterior, is an internationally
renowned cultural landmark and centre for the
performing arts. Home to The Welsh National
Opera, the spectacular building is all glass
and slate and looks very much like a Welsh
armadillo.

Wales

Wales

Wales is a land of beautiful coastline, lakes and forests, hidden valleys and high mountains. It has three National Parks in Snowdonia, the Pembrokeshire Coast and the Brecon Beacons, several official Areas of Outstanding Natural Beauty and long stretches of protected Heritage Coast, not to mention its own language, traditions, music and culture. From the fine beaches and seaside towns of the north, through mid wales with its rich, scenic landscape, coastal walks and castles, to the cultural capital and heritage trails of the south, every corner of Wales has something new to discover. Croeso means Welcome and you will hear it often.

Explore – Wales

North Wales

North Wales has been attracting holiday visitors for over two hundred years. Llandudno is a beautiful Victorian seaside resort at the foot of the Great Orme and has quite a mix of things to do – you can have an award-winning Victorian tea, visit 4,000-year-old mines, ride Britain's longest cable car, go to the mountain zoo, stroll along the beach and take a trip to the Victorian pier.

Within six miles of Llandudno you can find the peace of the Carneddau, one hundred square miles of beautiful mountain moorland, dotted with Neolithic tracks, standing stones, Bronze Age sites and beautiful lakes, without a single main road crossing it. The history of man can be traced from the Neolithic tombs of 6000 years ago to the Iron Age hill forts that were inhabited when the Roman legions arrived, then through the abbeys of the early Celtic church to the nonconformist chapels of the 19th century.

This is very much a place for rural pleasures. The Hiraethog Mountains in the north east, The Berwyns south of Llangollen and the beautiful river valleys of the Conwy, Clwyd, Dee and Glaslyn have a magic all of their own. When you stand on top of Moel Famau, the highest peak in the Clwydian Range, the views from the broken remains of the Jubilee Tower are stunning, with Merseyside, Snowdonia and the Dee Valley all laid out before you. Wrexham is the region's biggest town, superb for shopping, and a good base from which to explore nearby attractions including the splendid Erddig country house, and several museums dedicated to the area's lead, coal and iron heritage.

The pretty market town of Llangollen is another great holiday base, with the Llangollen Canal, Horseshoe Falls, Valle Crucis Abbey and Dinas Bran Castle all within walking distance of the town, and excellent white water rafting on the River Dee. Discover the wildlife of the Dee Estuary on the Alwen Trail, enjoy quiet riversides in Flintshire or forests and lakes of the Conwy Valley – there's more than enough space for a good ramble.

The 12th century Welsh castles and 13th century castles of Edward 1st reflect a more turbulent time, but what masterpieces of military architecture they left us. Conwy, Caernarvon, Beaumaris and Rhuddlan are breathtaking in their size and splendour, while the Welsh keeps of Dolwyddelan and Dolbadarn will appeal to more romantic souls. Chirk Castle is one of Edward I's 'ring of steel' fortresses and has the area's best formal gardens.

Hotspot: Pontcysyllte Aqueduct is just one of many water features in the North Wales Borderlands. Also known as 'the stream in the sky', it's a 300 metre long World Heritage Site and the world's tallest canal boat crossing, carrying the canal 40 metres over the valley below.

Medieval towns such as Ruthin, tiny cottages, splendid Jacobean farmhouses and Elizabethan houses such as Plas Mawr in Conwy show the different sides of life in the 16th-18th centuries. The Industrial Revolution brought changes to North Wales. Slate was the major industry and the slate caverns of Blaenau Ffestiniog, Glyn Ceiriog and The National Slate Museum at Llanberis can be explored today. Most of The Great Little Trains of Wales were first used to carry slate from the mines to the harbours, the one notable exception being the Snowdon Mountain Railway.

Hotspot: The fairytale Portmeirion Village and Gardens on the shores of Snowdonia makes a magical day out for all the family shops, cafes, beaches and woodland walks.

North Wales has some of the best scenery in the world, and is an exciting destination with a wide choice that includes the Snowdonia National Park, Llŷn Peninsula and Cambrian Coastline, castles, narrow-gauge railways, golf, cycling, walking, award winning beaches, country parks, World Heritage Site and Areas of Outstanding Natural Beauty. Snowdonia is justly famous for its magnificent mountains, lakes and forests. Some of the most spectacular roads in the British Isles are in this area. The road from Dolgellau to Tal-y-Lynn has heartstopping views or try Trawsfynydd via Llyn Celyn Lake to Bala. Swallow Falls, or Rhaeadr Ewynnol to give it its proper welsh name, is a spectacular waterfall on the A5 between Betws-y-Coed and Capel Curig and a must see for its sheer beauty.

Mid Wales

If you like the unusual then you'll love Mid Wales, a land of dramatic contrasts where the pleasures of coast and countryside can be equally enjoyed. It is a region of immense natural beauty with much of the Snowdonia National Park lying in this area and a coastline dotted with small fishing villages and popular seaside resorts. The western districts are strongholds of Welsh culture, where the language is in everyday use. Sandy beaches, rugged cliffs, secluded coves and campsites are firm family favourites and there are plenty of fun things to see and do for all ages.

Hotspot: The Centre for Alternative Technology (Cat) at Machynlleth has spent over 40 years pioneering new energy technologies to tackle climate change and diversify energy supplies. The centre's amazing water-balanced cliff railway is one of the steepest in the world, with a gradient of 35 degrees.

Rural life is centred around a series of strategic small towns, linked by splendid mountain roads or old drovers' ways. Pretty Llanidoes, with its 16th century market hall, stands almost at the centre of Wales at the confluence of the Severn and Clywedog rivers. Historic Machynlleth is where the Welsh rebel leader Owain Glyndwr set up his Welsh Parliament in 1404. Today it has a number of visitor attractions including MOMA Wales (Museum Of Modern Art, Wales) in four beautiful galleries alongside The Tabernacle, a former Wesleyan chapel which opened as a centre for the performing arts in 1986 - don't miss the ginger & pear cake from Café Glas! A ride on one of the Great Little Trains of Wales is a must for all steam enthusiasts.

and is also as impressive below ground as above, with one of Europe's longest cave networks. A world of weird and wonderful outdoor activities awaits in and around Llanwrtyd Wells, the smallest town in Britain. Have a go at the World Bog Snorkelling Championships, the Real Ale Ramble or the Man v Horse Marathon. Don't miss the awe-inspiring architecture of Brecon Cathedral or the annual summer Brecon Jazz festival, both of which draw visitors from far and wide.

Hotspot: Cardigan Bay is home to seals and one of only two resident groups of Bottlenose Dolphins in the UK.

To the east, the Welsh Marches with their traditional half-timbered black and white buildings were once governed by the Marcher Lords on behalf of the King. Further back in time, Offa, an 8th century Saxon king, built a massive dyke to keep marauding Welsh forces out of his kingdom. Significant traces of these earthworks remain along the border, forming the basis of Offa's Dyke Trail, a long distance walkway of 168 miles north to south. At Knighton a special Heritage Centre illustrates the significance of the Dyke.

Hotspot: At the National Showcaves of Wales, wonder at the enormous Cathedral Cave carved out millions of years ago, walk behind the 40 feet high waterfalls that cascade around you in the 'Dome of St Paul's', and learn how our ancestors used caves all those years ago in Bone Cave.

Ceredigion and Cardigan Bay is a diverse area with a wide range of attractions for visitors, both indoor and out. The award winning Aberystwyth Arts Centre is Wales' largest arts centre, with a wide-ranging artistic programme of drama, dance, music, visual arts, applied arts, film and new media. The Cambrian Mountains, Wales' backbone, is an upland region where hamlets and farms nestle in the folds of endless hills. One of the most beautiful sights is Devil's Bridge spanning the Mynach River - legend says it was built by the Devil in return for the soul of the first to cross it and apparently the townspeople tricked him by sending a dog over.

Mid Wales has always had a seafaring tradition - schooners used to set out from the little ports of Aberaeron, Aberdovey, Aberystwyth and New Quay, which today bustle with pleasure craft. The coastline here is stunningly beatiful and made for walking. The Wales Coast Path, ideal for novice and expert hikers alike, traces the entire shoreline of this region all the way down to Cardigan, the gateway to the picturesque Teifi Valley.

In the charming, lively market towns that jostle for attention in this area, outdoorsy types mingle with artists and writers. For adventure, hire a canoe at Glasbury on the River Wye to drift past meadows and bounce over gentle rapids, before stopping for lunch and book shopping in Hay-on-Wye, regarded as the second-hand book capital of the world. A year-round programme of festivals and cultural events is on offer including the Hay Festival and HowTheLightGetsIn.

The Brecon Beacons National Park includes majestic reservoirs, waterfalls and caves and is perfect for walking and horseriding, particularly around the Black Mountains, where both novice and experienced riders will find fabulous pony trekking. The Beacons Way is a 152km (95mile) magical walk across the Park – take the high-ground by day then dip down to towns each night. From gentle cycling between pretty villages to extreme mountain biking, the Beacons has something for every pedalling style

West Wales

In Pembrokeshire you'll find award-winning beaches, national parks and breathtaking views - heaven for swimmers, beachcombers, wildlife-watchers, walkers and outdoor adventures. At 186 miles long and guarded on its western rim by Britain's smallest city, St David's, the rugged Pembrokeshire Coastal Path offers sweeping cliff tops, secret coves, estuaries and wide sandy beaches. The Pembrokeshire Coast National Park has moorlands rising gently to the Preseli Hills, while Stone Age forts and Norman castles reflect the area's ancient history. St David's Cathedral was founded by the eponymous saint in the 8th century and is still in use today.

Hotspot: The Pembrokeshire coastline is popular with surfers and there are a number of great locations to catch a wave - try the magical Blue Flag Freshwater West beach.

Camarthenshire brings stories to life, from the intriguing mythology of Merlin to the gritty wildboy poetry of Dylan Thomas. Stretching from Carmarthen Bay in the south to the western Brecon Beacons in the north, think lush rural landscapes, crystalline coastlines and the rugged foothills of the Brecon Beacons National Park. You'll find chic places to stay, stylish eateries, great local produce and welcoming country pubs.

There's plenty of history here too. Near Carmarthen is Dylan Thomas' village of Laugharne, in whose churchyard he is buried. Up country the Dolaucothi gold mines, started by the Romans and re-opened from 1870 to 1938, are now a museum. Kidwelly Castle is on a par with the other great castles of Wales and the National Wool Museum tells the story of an important industry. Carmarthenshire is also home to the National Botanic Gardens of Wales and to some of Wales' longest beaches.

Sitting on the 5 mile sweep of Swansea Bay, Wales' second city enjoys a location that is hard to beat with most city centre attractions and shops only a short walk from the sea. At the National Waterfront Museum take in the sights and sounds of more than 300 years of Welsh industry and innovation. The Dylan Thomas Centre celebrates Swansea's famous son with a permanent exhibition on Dylan and his life, housed in a splendid listed building.

Hotspot: The Afan Forest Park is a 48-square-mile forest park near Neath and is well known for its mountain biking, hiking and hillwalking trails.

If you follow the coast you'll reach the UK's first Area of Outstanding Natural Beauty, the Gower Peninsula. A secluded world of its own, with limestone cliffs, remote bays and miles of golden sands, the Peninsula is Wales' very own the 'Riviera'. Historic sites not to be missed include 13th century Weobley Castle, the ruins of Threecliff Bay and Gower Farm Museum with its 100 year old farm memorabilia.

Outside Port Talbot, the 850 acre Margam Country Park includes an Iron Age hill fort, a restored abbey church with windows by William Morris, Margam Stones Museum with stones and crosses dating form the 5th-11th centuries and the main house with its 327ft orangery. En route to Cardiff are the late 19th century Castell Coch (Red Castle), a mixture of Victorian Gothic and fairytale styles and the well preserved 13th century Caerphilly Castle, with its famous leaning tower.

243

South Wales

Home to the most southerly point in Wales, the Vale of Glamorgan is perfect for those who love the outdoor life and discovering towns and villages packed full of traditional charm and character. Porthcawl and Barry Island are cheerful beach holiday resorts fringed by the striking Heritage Coast and lovely green countryside. The remains of the Norman Ogmore Castle can be found beside the river Ewenny, the joining point of two major Welsh counties of Bridgend and the Vale of Glamorgan. A few miles west of Cardiff, in the heart of the Vale of Glamorgan countryside, Dyffryn Gardens has over 55 acres of exceptional Edwardian garden design and is easily one of the most beautiful Gardens in Wales.

Cardiff is Wales' capital city and at its heart, the spectacular castle walls conceal a fascinating history. There's an array of events on throughout the year including midsummer evenings with Shakespeare, a Medieval Mêlée and Victorian Christmas, as well as musical performances and lectures on art and architecture. Modern Cardiff offers spectacular shopping, museums, dining and entertainment - be sure to visit the free National Museum Cardiff. Top class entertainment is also on offer at Cardiff Bay with its restaurants and waterside views.

Hotspot: Tour the Millennium Stadium in Cardiff, the national stadium of Wales. It is the home of the Wales national rugby union team and has also staged games of the Wales national football team.

Think of green valleys, warm welcomes, castles, myths and magic. Think of a unique industrial heritage, male voice choirs and stunning scenery. If you want a real Welsh experience then you must visit the South Wales Valleys.

Cyfarthfa Castle built in 1824, is an impressive homage to the Industrial Revolution and a great day out. Take a ride on a vintage steam locomotive through beautiful scenery along the length of the Taf Fechan Reservoir to Torpantau, high in the Brecon Beacons, on one of the most popular railways in Wales. Blaenavon is one of the best preserved 18th century ironworks in Europe, complete with furnaces, cast houses, a magnificent water balance tower, calcining kilns and ironworkers cottages. High on the bracken-covered moors of north Gwent near Blaenavon, Big Pit was a working coalmine until it closed in 1980. Part of the Blaenavon World Heritage Site, it is now the National Mining Museum of Wales and tells the history of Wales most well known industry.

Once upon a time in the borderlands of the Wye Valley and Vale of Usk, King Arthur ruled, the Romans bathed, the Normans settled and pilgrims worshipped. Today the area offers a wealth of heritage, dramatic landscapes, nature trails, walking, mountain biking and canoeing, as well as great food. Wales' boundary with England is marked by the Black Mountains, north of Abergavenny, rising to 2660 feet at Waun Fach. Hay Bluff, near Llanthony Priory affords amazing views westwards. Great castles are the legacy of Llywelyn the Great's resistance to the English, and ancient monastic settlements embody the solitude sought by the Augustinian and Cistercian orders.

Usk's charm lies in its riverside walks, hanging baskets, Rural Life Museum and annual agricultural show, as well as in its small independent shops, tearooms and pubs. The town hosts a fantastic Winter Festival, with music, markets, reindeer and, of course, Father Christmas. Further south, near Newport, the remains of Caerleaon Roman Fortress and Baths paint a vivid picture of life in second-century Roman Britain.

Hotspot: Chepstow Castle, with its Norman walls, stands guard on its rock above the swirling waters of the River Wye.

Tintern Abbey is one of the finest relics of Britain's monastic age, founded in the 12th century by Cistercian monks, rebuilt in the 13th and sacked by Henry VIII during the Dissolution of the Monasteries. Standing open to the skies, an outstanding example of the elaborate decorated style of Gothic architecture, it is easy to see why it inspired JMW Turner and William Wordsworth. Offa's Dyke was part of an 168-mile rampart built by King Offa of Mercia to keep the Welsh out, and the Offa's Dyke National Trail is just one of many long distance footpaths that criss-cross the Wye Valley & Vale of Usk. In the Welsh section of The Wye Valley Area of Outstanding Natural Beauty, the A466 is a beautiful valley road that winds along the gorge from Chepstow to Monmouth, perfect for a leisurely drive.

Indulge – Wales

Pamper yourself with a relaxing visit to **Lake Vyrnwy Hotel & Spa** at Llanwddyn in North Wales, for a luxurious spa experience with breathtaking views from the spa pool out over spectacular Lake Vyrnwy. www.lakevyrnwy.com (01691) 870692.

Tantalise your tastebuds at Glynhynod Farm, in Ceredigion, where **Caws Teifi Cheese** are part of Teifi Valley Cheese Producers, a group of artisan cheese makers of the highest quality. Located in the picturesque Teifi Valley, which has become known as the 'Loire of Welsh cheese making', a visit to this family-friendly farm, dairy and distillery will make your mouth water. Visit www.teificheese.co.uk or Tel: (01239) 851528.

Sample delicious Welsh cider and perry at the **Welsh Perry & Cider Festival** which takes place at historic Caldicot Castle, on the north side of the Severn estuary in South East Wales. With 80 brews, live music, food, craft stalls, camping and a 'Medieval Monday' family fancy dress day, 22-25 May 2015 are definitely dates for your diary! www.welshciderfestival.wordpress.com/

An elegant home-made afternoon tea in the drawing room of the 10th century **Miskin Manor** at Pontyclun, near Cardiff, is a feast ideal for special celebrations or just a lovely indulgent treat during your trip to the Vale of Glamorgan. www.miskin-manor.co.uk or Tel: (01443) 224 204.

Indulge in a seaside treat at **Fish Tram Chips**, an award-winning traditional fish and chip shop opposite one of the best known landmarks in Llandudno, The Great Orme Tramway. Ride the one mile journey to the summit, with its picturesque views of the Great Orme Country Park, Llandudno's sweeping bays and on a clear day the Isle of Man, then stop for mouth watering fish and chips on the way back down! 22 – 24 Old Road, Llandudno. Tel: (01492) 872673.

Visit – Wales

North Wales

Great Orme Tramway
Llandudno, Conwy LL30 2NB
(01492) 879306
www.greatormetramway.com
Take a ride on the 'San Francisco style' tramway - one of only three still in existence in the world today.

Harlech Castle
Harlech, Gwynedd LL46 2YH
(01766) 780552
www.cadw.wales.gov.uk/default
The castle's spectacular location atop a rocky crag assures you of a stunning photo opportunity.

Bodnant Gardens
Colwyn Bay, Conwy LL28 5RE
(01492) 650460
www.bodnantgarden.co.uk
Situated above the River Conwy with stunning views across Snowdonia, Bodnant Gardens is most well known for its laburnum arch, a 55m tunnel of golden blooms, most impressive in mid May-early June.

Bangor New Music Festival
March, Bangor
www.bnmf.co.uk
BNMF is an annual celebration of new and contemporary music.

Kaya Festival
May, Vaynol Estate, Gwynedd
www.kayafestival.co.uk
Overlooking the Snowdonia National Park in North Wales, Kaya is a festival of music, youth, diversity and culture.

All Wales Boat Show
June, Conwy
www.northwalesboatshow.com
The All Wales Boat Show is the country's only major boat show and a celebratory festival of all types of water-based activities.

Gweldd Conwy Feast
October, Conwy, various venues
www.gwleddconwyfeast.co.uk
160 food stalls, farming for food marquee, cookery demonstrations, bands and the blinc digital festival.

Gottwood Electonic Music & Arts Festival
June, Carreglwyd Forest , Anglesey
www.gottwood.co.uk
A free spirited, independent and very intimate underground electronic music festival with live music and a wide variety of soulful, world and tropical beats throughout the day and a focus on the dance floor into the night.

Harlech Castle
Harlech, Gwynedd LL46 2YH
(01766) 780552
www.cadw.wales.gov.uk/default
The castle's spectacular location atop a rocky crag assures you of a stunning photo opportunity.

Kaya Festival
May, Vaynol Estate, Gwynedd
www.kayafestival.co.uk
Overlooking the Snowdonia National Park in North Wales, Kaya is a festival of music, youth, diversity and culture.

Llandudno Victorian Extravanganza
May, Llandudno, Conwy
www.victorian-extravaganza.com
Llandudno is bustling with Victorian buildings and structures and every May Day Bank Holiday weekend, it plays host to a Victorian Extravaganza. There's a Victorian street fair, old time fair rides, fun stalls, steam engines, people dressed in Victorian costume, street parades at 12 midday each day and street entertainment the whole family will enjoy.

Sci-fi Weekender 6
March, Pwllheli, Gwynedd
www.scifiweekender.com
The Sci-fi Weekender at Hafan y Môr Holiday Park is the ultimate Sci-Fi experience. It's a festival of fun and activities for people who love science fiction and fantasy, packed with big-name guests, interviews, Q&A sessions, movie screenings, comic workshops, gaming, music, book readings and more.

Gigrin Farm
Rhayader, Powys LD6 5BL
(01597) 810243
www.gigrin.co.uk
Get up close and personal with the wild Red Kites - you'll be just 30 metres from the feeding ground. Feeding is every day at 3pm and 2pm in winter.

Mid Wales

Abertoir Film Festival
November, Aberystwyth
www.abertoir.co.uk
The national horror film festival which includes cult screenings and classics from around the world, as well as special guests, talks, masterclasses, live music and theatre events.

Brecon Jazz Festival
August, Brecon Beacons
www.breconjazz.com/en/
Held in the heart of the Brecon Beacons National park in mid-Wales, it plays host to a range of jazz musicians who travel from across the world.

Ceredigion Coast Path
Cardigan Bay, Ceredigion
(01545) 572105
www.ceredigioncoastpath.org.uk
A 96km route between the Teifi and Dyfi estuaries, offers walkers the opportunity to discover towns and villages, and take in the spectacular coastal scenery. You might even spot dolphins, seals and porpoises.

Green Man Festival
August, Crickhowell, Powys
www.greenman.net
A unique boutique festival which features three days of music as well as a full programme including art, literature, film, comedy, healing zones, ceilidhs, and Welsh language poetry.

Hay Festival
May - June, Hay-on-Wye
www.hayfestival.com
A literary festival with an international reputation. During the festival around 100,000 visitors will enjoy literature in all its forms and lots of music as well as plenty of celebrities.

HowTheLightGetsIn
May - June, Hay-on-Wye
www.howthelightgetsin.org
Hay-on-Wye is the internationally famous 'town of books', situated in a magical location on the edge of the Black Mountains. It's also the home of HowTheLightGetsIn, the world's first philosophy and music festival, now in its third year.

International Ceramics Festival

June, Aberystwyth

www.internationalceramicsfestival.org

This ever growing festival offers the chance to meet and study the work of distinguished, internationally known potters and ceramicists from Wales, the UK and around the world.

Man v Horse Marathon

June, Llanwrtyd Wells, Powys

www.green-events.co.uk

Possibly the world's most eccentic race where runners compete against riders on horseback over 22 miles (35 km) in the Welsh town of Llanwrtyd Wells every June. A first-rate cross-country course, combined with Welsh eccentricity and hospitality, and the added excitement of occasionally having to hurl yourself out of the way of a horse!

Powis Castle & Garden

Welshpool, Powys SY21 8RF

(01938) 551929

www.nationaltrust.org.uk/main/w-powiscastle_garden

A mecca for garden lovers. The impressive red medieval castle is framed by enormous clipped yew trees, and 18th century Italianate terraces with original lead statues, lush herbaceous borders and exotic plants cascading from the walls.

Vale of Rheidol Railway

Aberystwyth, Ceredigion SY23 1PG

(01970) 625819

www.rheidolrailway.co.uk

A narrow-gauge heritage railway that runs for just over 11 miles between Aberystwyth and Devil's Bridge.

Wonderwool Wales

April, Builth Wells, Powys

www.wonderwoolwales.co.uk

Wonderwool Wales at the Royal Welsh Showground is the premier Wool & Natural Fibre Festival in Wales, promoting wool and natural fibre production and its use in Wales. Exhibitors and trade stands cover all aspects of Felting, Knitting, Weaving, Spinning & Crochet along with Textile Art, raw materials, equipment, books and finished product.

West Wales

Dolaucothi Gold Mines

Llanwrda, Carmarthenshire SA19 8US

(01588) 650177

www.nationaltrust.org.uk/dolaucothi-gold-mines/

Try your hand at panning for gold, or take a guided tour through the Roman and underground workings and learn all about the history of the mine at the on-site exhibition and Interpretation Centre.

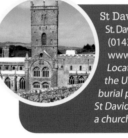

St Davids Cathedral

St. David's, Pembrokeshire SA62 6QW

(01437) 720691

www.stdavidscathedral.org.uk

Located in the smallest city in the UK, St Davids Cathedral is the burial place of Wales' patron saint St David (Dewi Sant) and has been a church since the 6th century.

The Dylan Thomas Centre

Swansea SA1 1RR

(01792) 463980

www.dylanthomas.com

Dylan Thomas is perhaps one of greatest poets of the 20th century, and the most famous literary figure to come from Wales.

Gower Folk Festival

June, Llanrhidian, Swansea

www.gowerfolkfestival.co.uk

The 22nd Gower Folk Festival will take place at The Greyhound Inn in Llanrhidian, an award-winning micro-brewery and home to a regular weekly folk club. With on-site camping, fabulous food and drink and a variety of excellent music.

Mumbles Festival

May, Swansea

www.mumblesfestival.co.uk

A brilliant family-friendly festival weekend at Oystermouth Castle where the music goes on all weekend, inbetween performances from authors, poets and artists, largely inspired by the works of Dylan Thomas. Stalls and medieval-themed picnics add to an easy weekend of lively entertainment, good hearty food and a full-on 'Welsh' experience.

Mumbles Triathlon

June, Swansea

www.mumblestri.com

The Mumbles Triathlon course is simply in one of the best locations in the UK. With a calm, safe and spectator friendly swim, picturesque ride for the short and long (with some tough climbs thrown in) bike and finally a fast and flat run, this event will take some beating!

South Wales

Abergavenny Food Festival
September, Abergavenny, Monmouthshire
www.abergavennyfoodfestival.com
Celebrate the sociability that surrounds eating and drinking, whether with friends or strangers, and enjoy real Welsh hospitality with Abergavenny's own burgeoning food community.

Big Pit
National Coal Museum
Blaenavon, Torfaen NP4 9XP
(01495) 790311
www.museumwales.ac.uk
Don a miners lamp and go 92m underground with a real miner and learn what life was like for the thousands of men who worked at the coal face.

Cardiff Museum
Cathays Park, Cardiff CF10 3NP
(029) 2057 3000
www.museumwales.ac.uk/cardiff/
Discover art, natural history and geology. With a busy programme of exhibitions and events, cardiff Museum has something to amaze everyone, whatever your interest.

Great British Cheese Festival
September, Cardiff Castle
www.greatbritishcheesefestival.co.uk
Sniff and nibble on more than 450 different cheeses of all shapes, sizes and flavours at Britain's biggest cheese market.

Green Gathering
July - August, Chepstow
www.greengathering.org.uk
Promoting sustainable lifestyles by combining education with entertainment. With an eclectic range of music as well as many talks and discussions, crafts and activities for all the family.

Millennium Stadium
Cardiff CF10 1NS
(029) 2082 2228
www.millenniumstadium.com/tours/index.php
Take a tour. Run down the player's tunnel, and imagine yourself being greeted by 74,500 people eagerly awaiting the pain and the glory of rugby at its best.

Penderyn Distillery
Aberdare Rhondda, Cynon, Taff CF44 0SX
(01685) 810651
www.welsh-whisky.co.uk
It's the only distillery in Wales and one of the smallest in the world. Take a tour of the visitor centre and distillery.

Rugby World Cup
September – October, Cardiff
www.rugbyworldcup.com
The Rugby World Cup 2015 will be a truly nationwide tournament with 13 venues hosting a total of 48 matches. At the Millennium Stadium, fans can look forward to seeing 8 matches, including two Quarter Finals when the tournament comes to town and the city is set for a spectacular 6 week celebration of rugby.

Velothon Wales
June, Cardiff
www.velothon-wales.co.uk
Velothon Wales is the latest event in the UCI Velothon Majors, a global series of cycling events and promises to be an exciting event for both spectators and participants in the Welsh capital. On the 14th June 2015, up to 15,000 riders will make history as they roll across the start line in the heart of Cardiff and embark on a completley closed road cycling sportive that takes in some of Wales' most breathtaking scenery.

Tourist Information Centres

When you arrive at your destination, visit the Tourist Information Centre for quality assured help with accommodation and information about local attractions and events, or email your request before you go.

Aberaeron	The Quay	01545 570602	aberaerontic@ceredigion.gov.uk
Aberdyfi *	The Wharf Gardens	01654 767321	tic.aberdyfi@eryri-npa.gov.uk
Abergavenny	The Tithe Barn	01873 853254	abergavenny.ic@breconbeacons.org
Aberystwyth	Terrace Road	01970 612125	aberystwythtic@ceredigion.gov.uk
Anglesey	Station Site	01248 713177	anglesey@nwtic.com
Barmouth	The Station	01341 280787	barmouth.tic@gwynedd.gov.uk
Beddgelert *	Canolfan Hebog	01766 890615	tic.beddgelert@eryri-npa.gov.uk
Betws y Coed	Royal Oak Stables	01690 710426	tic.byc@eryri-npa.gov.uk
Blaenavon	Blaenavon World Heritage Centre	01495 742333	Blaenavon.tic@torfaen.gov.uk
Brecon	Cattle Market Car park	01874 622485	brectic@powys.gov.uk
Caernarfon	Oriel Pendeitsh	01286 672232	caernarfon.tic@gwynedd.gov.uk
Caerphilly	The Twyn	029 2088 0011	tourism@caerphilly.gov.uk
Cardiff	The Old Library	029 20 873 573	visitor@cardiff.gov.uk
Cardiff Bay	Unit 1	029 2087 7927	visitorcentrecardiffbay@cardiff.gov.uk
Cardigan	Theatr Mwldan	01239 613230	cardigantic@ceredigion.gov.uk
Carmarthen	Castle House	01267 231557	carmarthentic@carmarthenshire.gov.uk
Chepstow	Castle Car Park	01291 623772	chepstow.tic@monmouthshire.gov.uk
Conwy	Castle Buildings	01492 577566	conwytic@conwy.gov.uk
Crickhowell	Crickhowell Resource & Information Centre (CRiC)	01873 812105	tic@visitcrickhowell.co.uk
Dolgellau	Ty Meirion	01341 422888	tic.dolgellau@eryri-npa.gov.uk
Elan Valley	Visitor Centre	01597 810898	elanrangers@dwrcymru.com
Fishguard	Town Hall	01437 776636	fishguard.tic@pembrokeshire.gov.uk
Harlech *	Llys y Graig	01766 780658	tic.harlech@eryri-npa.gov.uk
Knighton	Offa's Dyke Centre	01547 528753	oda@offasdyke.demon.co.uk
Llanberis *	Electric Mountain Visitor Centre	01286 870765	llanberis.tic@gwynedd.gov.uk
Llandovery*	Heritage Centre	01550 720693	llandovery.ic@breconbeacons.org
Llandudno	Library Building	01492 577577	llandudnotic@conwy.gov.uk
Llangollen	Y Capel	01978 860828	llangollen@nwtic.com
Merthyr Tydfil	14a Glebeland Street	01685 727474	tic@merthyr.gov.uk
Mold	Library & Museum	01352 759331	mold@nwtic.com
New Quay *	Church Street	01545 560865	newquaytic@ceredigion.gov.uk
Newport (pembs) *	2 Bank Cottages	01239 820912	NewportTIC@Pembrokeshirecoast.org.uk
Oswestry Mile End	Mile End Services	01691 662488	oswestrytourism@shropshire.gov.uk
Porthmadog	High Street	01766 512981	porthmadog.tic@gwynedd.gov.uk
Pwllheli*	Neuadd Dwyfor	01758 613000	pwllheli.tic@gwynedd.gov.uk
Rhyl	The Village	01745 355068	rhyl.tic@denbighshire.gov.uk
St Davids	Visitor Centre	01437 720392	info@orielyparc.co.uk
Swansea	Plymouth Street	01792 468321	tourism@swansea.gov.uk
Tenby	Unit 2	01834 842402	tenby.tic@pembrokeshire.gov.uk
Welshpool	Vicarage Gardens	01938 552043	ticwelshpool@btconnect.com
Wrexham	Lambpit Street	01978 292015	tic@wrexham.gov.uk

* Seasonal/Limited opening

Regional Contacts and Information

For more information on accommodation, attractions, activities, events and holidays in Wales, contact VisitWales.

t: 08708 300306
www.visitwales.com and www.visitwales.co.uk

Entries appear alphabetically by town name in each county. A key to symbols appears on page 7

PORTHMADOG, Gwynedd   Map ref 8A1

★★★
Cymru Wales
Parc Gwyliau
Holiday Park

Garreg Goch Caravan Park
Black Rock Sands, Morfa Bychan, Porthmadog LL49 9YD
T: (01766) 512210 **F:** (01766) 515820 **E:** info@garreggochcaravanpark.co.uk
W: www.garreggochpark.co.uk

🚐 (13)   £16.00-£22.00
🚛 (13)   £16.00-£22.00
🏠 (10)   £255.00-£615.00
13 touring pitches

Near to famous Black Rock Sands and ideal for touring Snowdonia. **Directions:** In Porthmadog town centre, take the turning between the Post Office and Factory Outlet. Then take the third left after the Spar shop. **Open:** 1st March - 10th January.

Payment: 💳 **Leisure:** ⛳ 🎣 ► ʊ **Property:** 🐕 🛁 📶 ℹ **Children:** 🛝 🎠 **Catering:** 🍴

FISHGUARD, Pembrokeshire   Map ref 8A2

★★★★
Cymru Wales
Parc Gwyliau, Teithio a Gwersylla
Holiday Touring & Camping Park

Fishguard Bay Caravan & Camping Park
Garn Gelli, Fishguard, Pembrokeshire SA65 9ET
T: (01348) 811415 **F:** (01348) 811425 **E:** enquiries@fishguardbay.com
W: www.fishguardbay.com **£ BOOK ONLINE**

🚐 (20)   £19.50-£23.50
🚛 (20)   £19.50-£23.50
⛺ (30)   £11.00-£25.50
🏠 (12)   £280.00-£650.00
20 touring pitches

Enjoy your stay on this beautiful stretch of Pembrokeshire National Park coastline. Ideal centre for walking and touring. Quiet, family-run park. Beautiful location, and superb views towards Fishguard harbour. **Open:** 1st March to 10th January.

Site: ⛺🅿 **Payment:** 💳 ☼ **Leisure:** 🎣 ► ʊ 🔍 **Children:** 🛝 🎠 **Catering:** 🍴 **Park:** 🐕 🛁 📶 📶 📡 **Touring:** 🔌 🚰 🚿

MANORBIER, Pembrokeshire   Map ref 8A3

★★★★★
Cymru Wales
Parc Teithio a Gwyliau
Touring & Holiday Park

Manorbier Country Park
Station Road, Manorbier, Tenby SA70 7SN
T: (01834) 871952 **F:** (01834) 871203 **E:** enquiries@countrypark.co.uk
W: www.countrypark.co.uk **£ BOOK ONLINE**

🚐 (45)   £18.00-£42.00
🚛 (5)   £18.00-£42.00
⛺ (4)   £16.00-£37.00
🏠 (25)   £137.00-£1130.00
50 touring pitches

SPECIAL PROMOTIONS
Short break bookings from £107.00 3-4 nights for 4 people.

The small park with the big heart. Indoor heated pool, tennis court, fully licensed bar & club, restaurant, live family entertainment, children's play areas, family entertainment centre, gym & solarium, sauna & steam room, big screen SKY Sports, laundrette and shop. What more could you want from your holiday? Overnight holding area available.

Directions: From Tenby follow A4139 to Pembroke, after Lydstep turn right for Manorbier Newton & Train Station, park located on left.

Open: March - November.

Site: 🏕 **Payment:** 💳 **Leisure:** ⛳ 🎣 ► ʊ 🔍 🎣 🔍 **Property:** 🐕 🎵 🛁 📶 ℹ 📶 **Children:** 🛝 🎠
Catering: ✗ 🍴

ST DAVIDS, Pembrokeshire *Map ref 8A3*   SatNav SA62 6QT

Cymru Wales
Parc Gwyliau, Teithio a Gwersylla
Holiday, Touring & Camping Park
★★★★

Caerfai Bay Caravan & Tent Park

St. Davids, Haverfordwest, Pembrokeshire SA62 6QT
T: (01437) 720274 **F:** (01437) 720577 **E:** info@caerfaibay.co.uk
W: www.caerfaibay.co.uk

🚐 (26)	£19.00-£24.00
🚙 (14)	£13.00-£24.00
⛺ (72)	£13.00-£17.50
🏠 (1)	£465.00-£770.00
🏕 (8)	£265.00-£505.00
40 touring pitches	

A quiet family-run park, situated within the Pembrokeshire Coast National Park. Caerfai Bay sandy bathing beach within 200 metres and St Davids within easy walking distance. Park situated at end of Caerfai road on the right. No dogs in tent fields during school summer holidays. **Directions:** Haverfordwest to St Davids: A487. Turn left at Oriel Y Parc (OYP)/Visitor Centre, Caerfai signposted. From Fishguard: A487 to St Davids. Turn right at OYP. **Open:** March to mid-November.

Payment: 💷 ☼ **Leisure:** 🐾 ♪ ▶ **Children:** 🛝 **Park:** 🖥 📶 🛁 📵 **Touring:** 🚰 🔌 🔥 ♪

BRECON, Powys *Map ref 8B3*   SatNav LD3 0LD

Cymru Wales
Parc Gwyliau, Teithio a Gwersylla
Holiday, Touring & Camping Park
★★★★

Anchorage Caravan Park

Bronllys, Brecon, Powys LD3 0LD
T: (01874) 711246 **F:** (01874) 711711
W: www.anchoragecp.co.uk

🚐 (60)	
🚙 (10)	
⛺ (40)	
110 touring pitches	

High standard, family-run park. Panoramic views of the Brecon Beacons National Park. Ideal for touring and walking mid and south Wales. Please contact us for 2015 rates. **Directions:** Midway between Brecon and Hay-On-Wye. In centre of Bronllys village. **Open:** All year.

Payment: ☼ **Leisure:** ♪ ∪ **Children:** 🛝 ⛰ **Catering:** 🛒 **Park:** 🔔 🖥 🛁 📵 **Touring:** 🚰 🔌 🔥

For **key to symbols** see page 7

Map 1

Location
Maps

Every place name featured in the regional accommodation sections of this guide has a map reference to help you locate it on the maps which follow. For example, to find Colchester, Essex, which has 'Map ref 3B2', turn to Map 3 and refer to grid square B2.

All place names appearing in the regional sections are shown with orange circles on the maps. This enables you to find other places in your chosen area which may have suitable accommodation – the place index (at the back of this guide) gives page numbers.

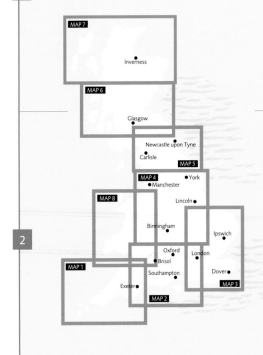

Key to regions: South West England

Map 1

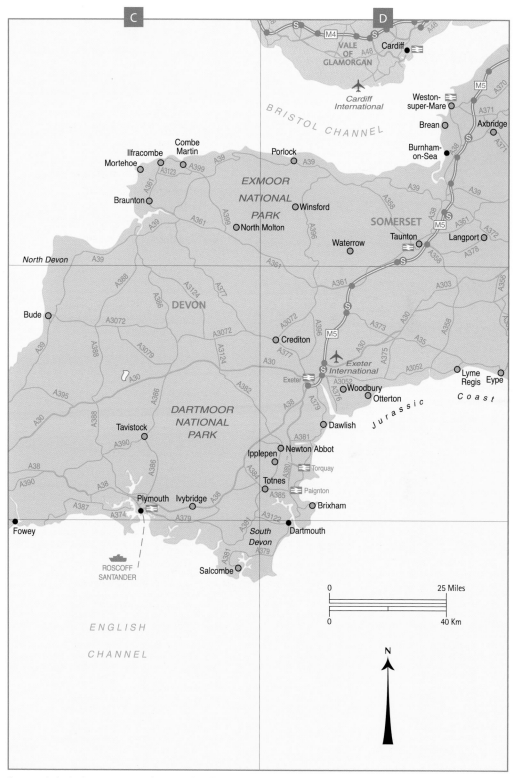

Orange circles indicate accommodation within the regional sections of this guide

Map 2

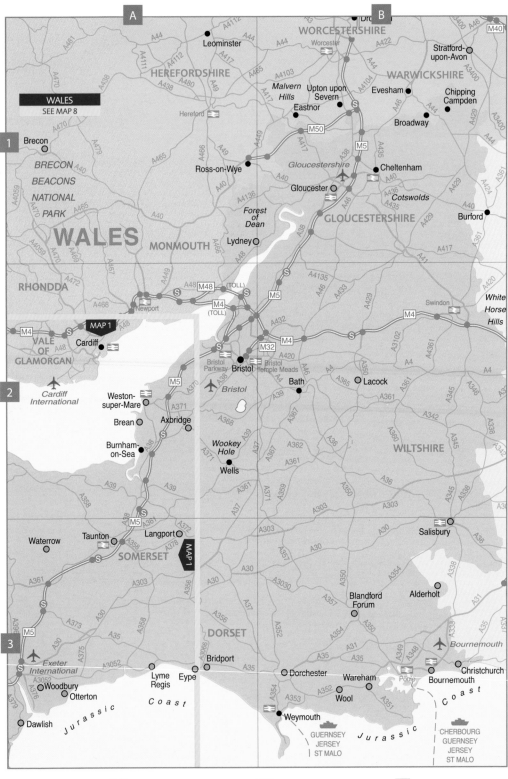

A

B

A4112 · A44 · Leominster · A44 · A44 · WORCESTERSHIRE · Dro... · M40

A461 · A4112 · A417 · A465 · A4103 · Worcester · A422 · Stratford-upon-Avon · A3400 · A46

A470 · A4111 · HEREFORDSHIRE · A480 · A49 · Malvern Hills · Upton upon Severn · A44 · A4104 · Evesham · WARWICKSHIRE · A3400 · Chipping Campden

A438 · A465 · A449 · Eastnor · S · A46 · A441 · Broadway · A44

WALES SEE MAP 8 · Hereford · A417 · M50 · A438 · M5 · A435 · Cheltenham · A429 · A40 · Burford

1 · Brecon · A470 · A479 · A466 · A49 · Ross-on-Wye · Gloucestershire · A40 · Gloucester · A436 · Cotswolds · A435 · A429

BRECON BEACONS NATIONAL PARK · A40 · A465 · A4136 · Forest of Dean · A38 · GLOUCESTERSHIRE · A41

A4059 · A470 · A465 · A40 · Lydney · A48 · A417

WALES · MONMOUTH · A466 · S · A4135 · A46 · A433 · A429 · Swindon · White Horse Hills

RHONDDA · A449 · A48 · M48 (TOLL) · S · M5 · A432 · A420 · M4 · A4361 · A4 · A4 · A420

A472 · A468 · Newport · S · M4 (TOLL) · S · M32 · M4 · S · A3102 · A4361 · A345

MAP 1 · M4 · A48 · S · Cardiff · Bristol Parkway · Bristol · Bristol Temple Meads · A4 · A46 · A365 · Lacock · A4 · A365 · A338

2 · VALE OF GLAMORGAN · Cardiff International · M5 · A370 · A38 · Bristol · A39 · A368 · A367 · A36 · WILTSHIRE · A342 · A345

Weston-super-Mare · Brean · Axbridge · A371 · Wookey Hole · A37 · A362 · A360 · A36 · A345 · A338

Burnham-on-Sea · A38 · A371 · Wells · A361 · A359 · A350 · A36 · A303

A358 · A39 · A39 · A371 · A303 · A357 · A30 · Salisbury · A36

3 · Waterrow · Taunton · M5 · Langport · MAP 1 · SOMERSET · A303 · A3030 · A350 · Blandford Forum · Alderholt · A31

A361 · A303 · A356 · A37 · DORSET · A354 · A350 · Bournemouth

M5 · Exeter International · Bridport · A35 · A31 · Poole · Christchurch · Bournemouth

Woodbury · Otterton · Lyme Regis · Eype · Dorchester · Wareham · A348 · A349

Dawlish · Jurassic Coast · A354 · A353 · A352 · Wool · A351 · Jurassic Coast

Weymouth · GUERNSEY JERSEY ST MALO · CHERBOURG GUERNSEY JERSEY ST MALO

Key to regions: South West England   South East England   London

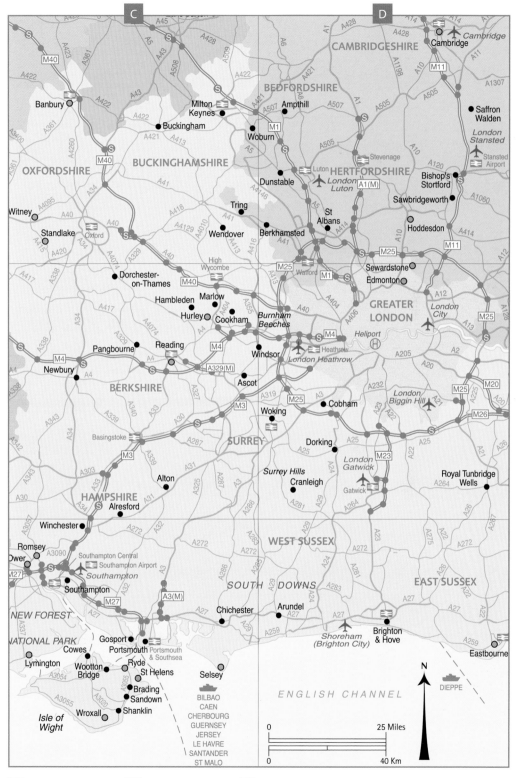

Map 2

East of England   East Midlands   Heart of England
Orange circles indicate accommodation within the regional sections of this guide

Map 3

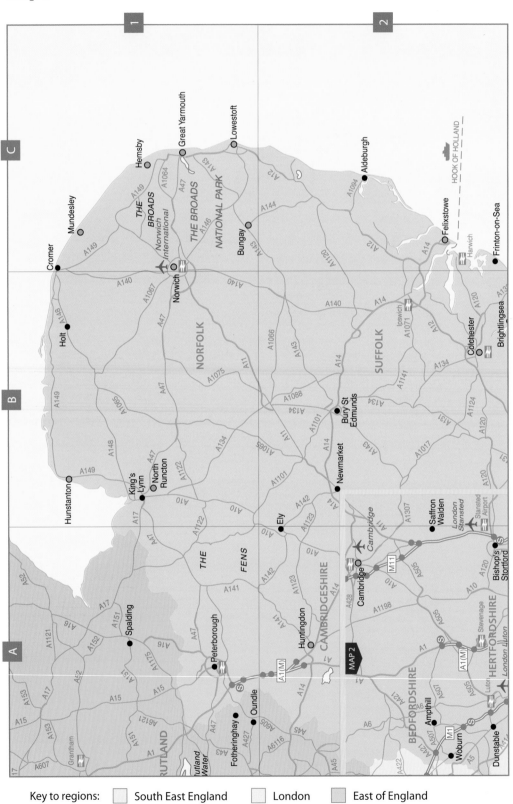

Key to regions: ☐ South East England ☐ London ☐ East of England

Map 3

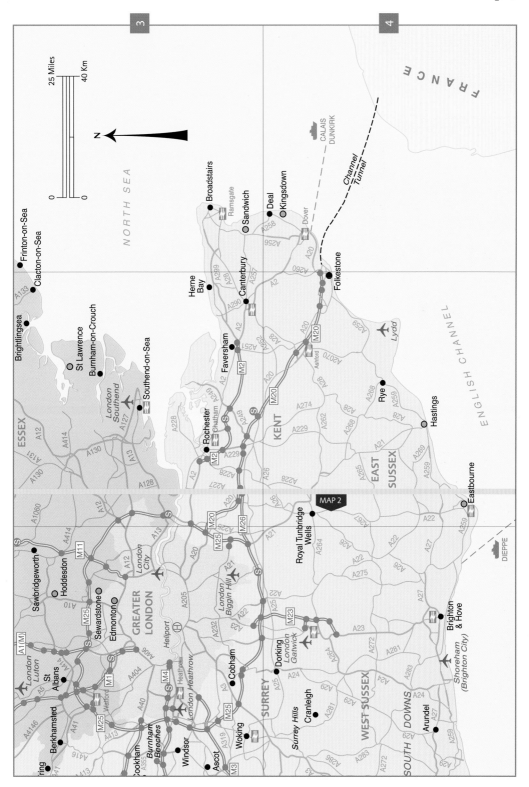

East Midlands

Orange circles indicate accommodation within the regional sections of this guide

Map 4

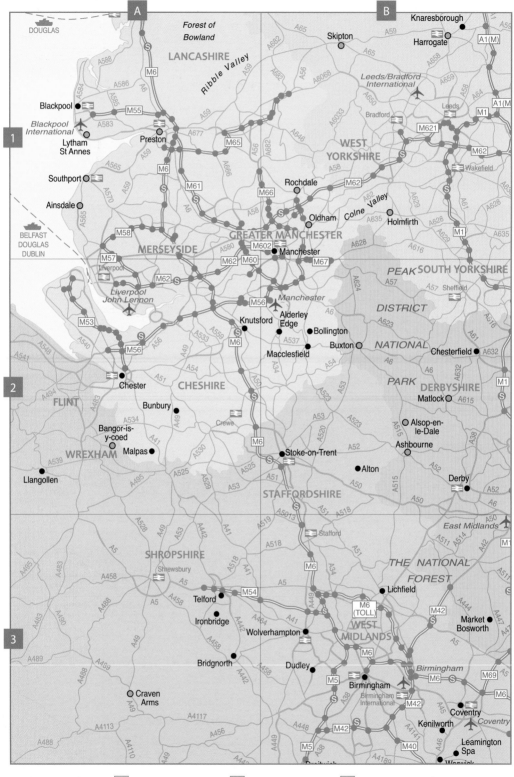

Key to regions: ▢ East of England ▢ East Midlands ▢ Heart of England

Map 4

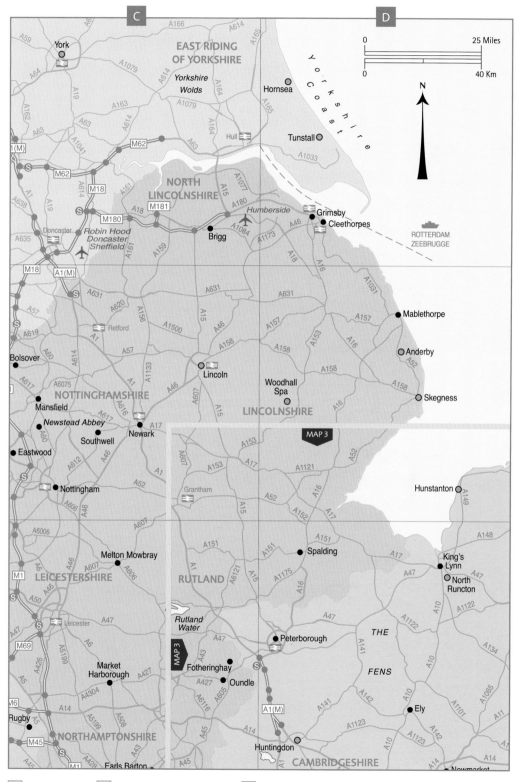

C   D

0 _____ 25 Miles
0 _____ 40 Km

N

York

EAST RIDING
OF YORKSHIRE

Yorkshire
Wolds

Hornsea

Y o r k s h i r e   C o a s t

Tunstall

Hull

M62

NORTH
LINCOLNSHIRE

M18

M180   M181

Humberside

Grimsby
Cleethorpes

ROTTERDAM
ZEEBRUGGE

Doncaster
Robin Hood
Doncaster
Sheffield

Brigg

Retford

Bolsover

Mansfield

Newstead Abbey

Southwell

Eastwood

NOTTINGHAMSHIRE

Newark

Nottingham

Lincoln

Woodhall
Spa

LINCOLNSHIRE

Mablethorpe

Anderby

Skegness

MAP 3

Grantham

Hunstanton

LEICESTERSHIRE

Melton Mowbray

RUTLAND

Spalding

King's
Lynn
North
Runcton

Leicester

Rutland
Water

MAP 3

Fotheringhay

Market
Harborough

Oundle

Peterborough

THE

FENS

Ely

Rugby

NORTHAMPTONSHIRE

Huntingdon

CAMBRIDGESHIRE

Earls Barton

Newmarket

☐ Yorkshire   ☐ North West England   ☐ North East England

Orange circles indicate accommodation within the regional sections of this guide

261

Map 5

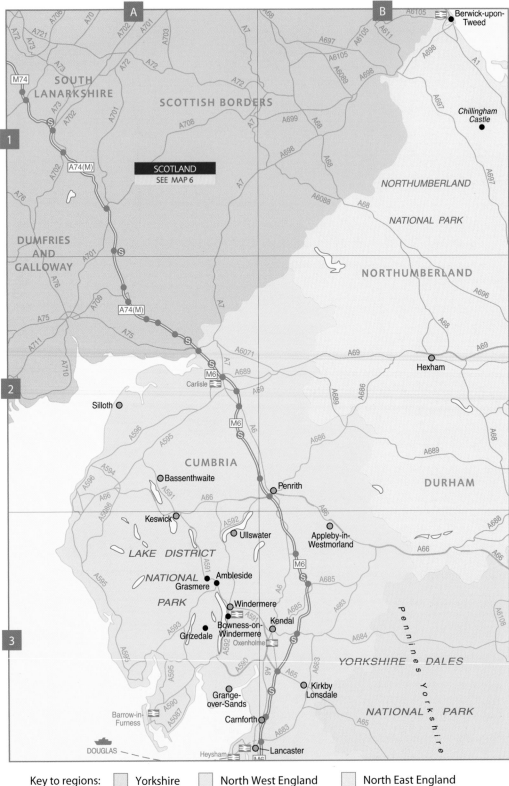

Key to regions: ☐ Yorkshire   ☐ North West England   ☐ North East England

Map 5

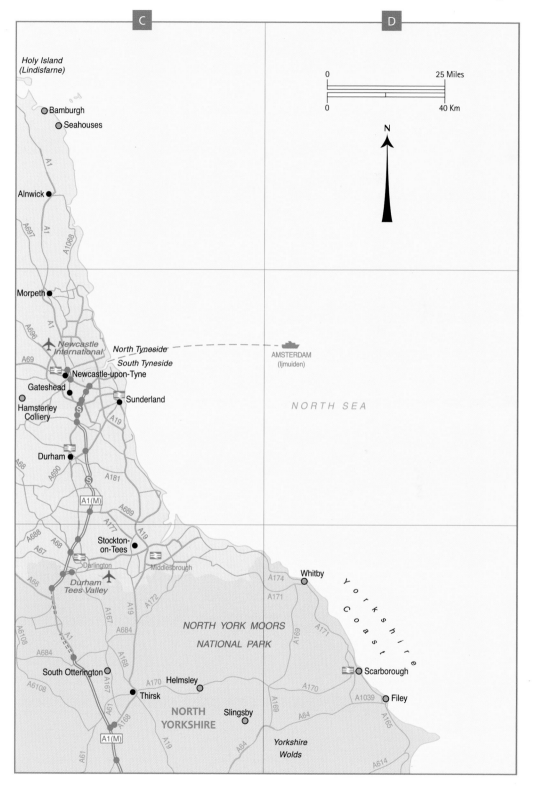

Holy Island
(Lindisfarne)

Bamburgh

Seahouses

Alnwick

Morpeth

Newcastle
International

North Tyneside

South Tyneside

Newcastle-upon-Tyne

Gateshead

Sunderland

Hamsterley
Colliery

Durham

A1(M)

Stockton-
on-Tees

Darlington

Middlesbrough

Durham
Tees Valley

South Otterington

Helmsley

Thirsk

NORTH
YORKSHIRE

Slingsby

A1(M)

NORTH YORK MOORS

NATIONAL PARK

Yorkshire
Wolds

Whitby

Y o r k s h i r e   C o a s t

Scarborough

Filey

AMSTERDAM
(Ijmuiden)

NORTH SEA

0   25 Miles

0   40 Km

N

Orange circles indicate accommodation within the regional sections of this guide

Map 6

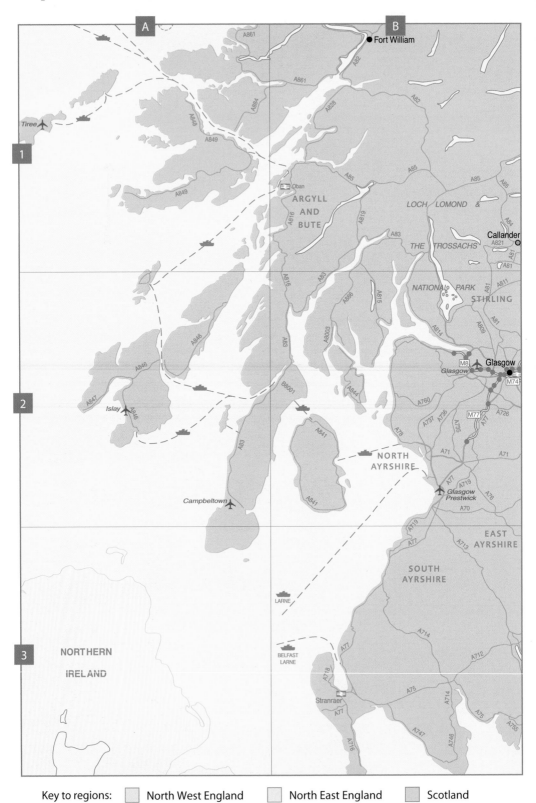

Key to regions: ☐ North West England ☐ North East England ☐ Scotland

Map 6

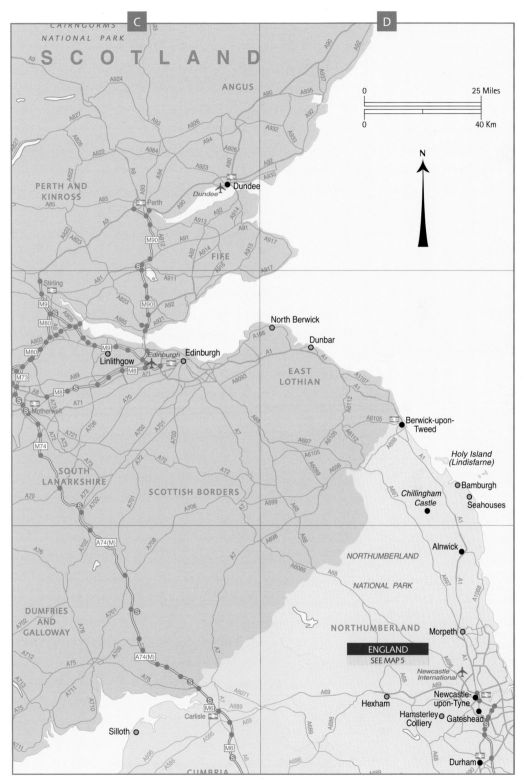

Orange circles indicate accommodation within the regional sections of this guide

Map 7

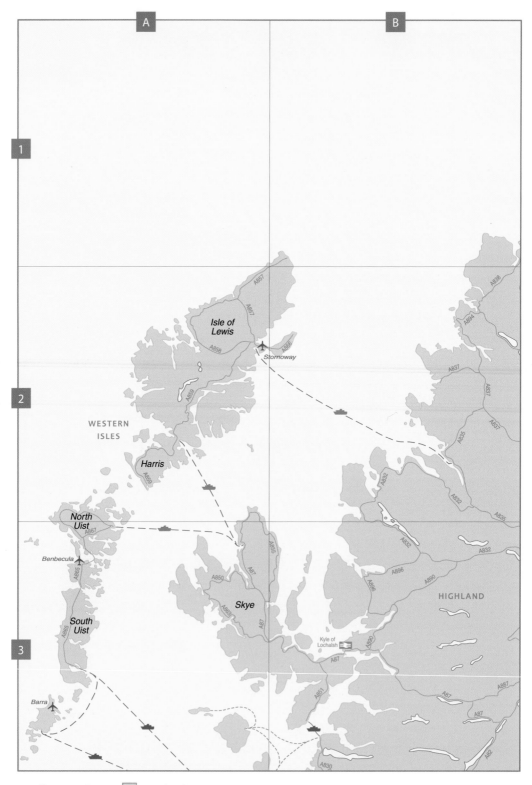

Key to regions: ☐ Scotland

Map 7

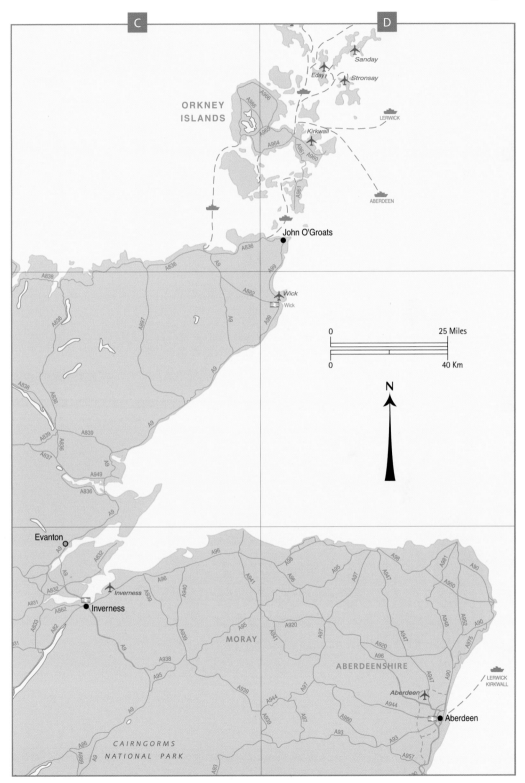

C   D

ORKNEY
ISLANDS

Sanday

Eday
Stronsay

LERWICK

Kirkwall

A966
A986
A960
A964
A961 A960
A961

ABERDEEN

John O'Groats
A836

A838
A9
A99

A836

A862
Wick
Wick

0   25 Miles

0   40 Km

A836

A897

N

A838
A836

A839

A859 A836
A837
A9

A949

A836

A9

Evanton

A96
A98
A95
A98
A90

A9
A832
A96
A97
A947
A960
A9
Inverness
A96
A939
A941
A92
A90
A832
A862
A939
A95
A948
A9
A853
Inverness
A920
A97
MORAY
A941
A92
A90
A92
A832
A938
A820
A96
A975
31
A9
ABERDEENSHIRE
A947
A95
A939
A944
A90
LERWICK
KIRKWALL
A9
Aberdeen
A944
A97
A886
CAIRNGORMS
A980
A957
NATIONAL PARK
A889
A93
A93
A93

● Aberdeen

Orange circles indicate accommodation within the regional sections of this guide

Map 8

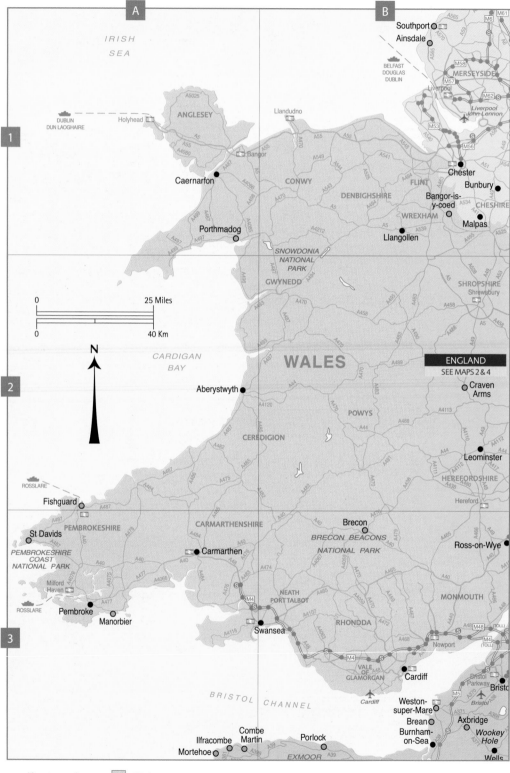

Key to regions: ▨ Wales

Orange circles indicate accommodation within the regional sections of this guide

Map 9
London

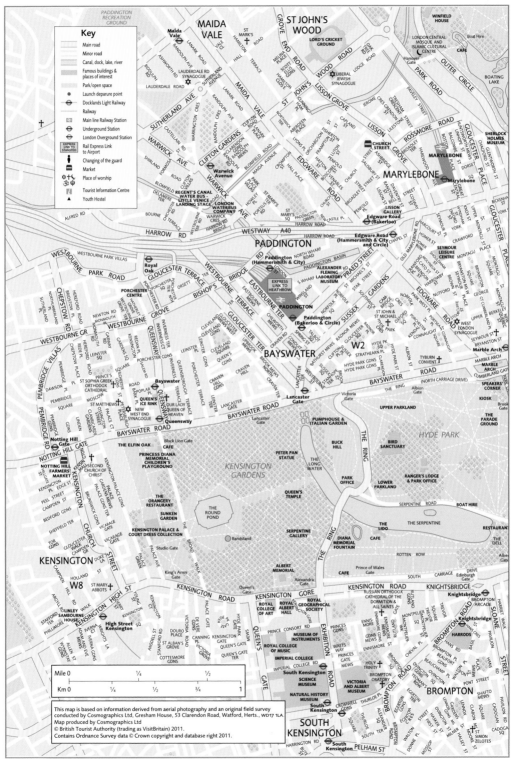

Map 10
London

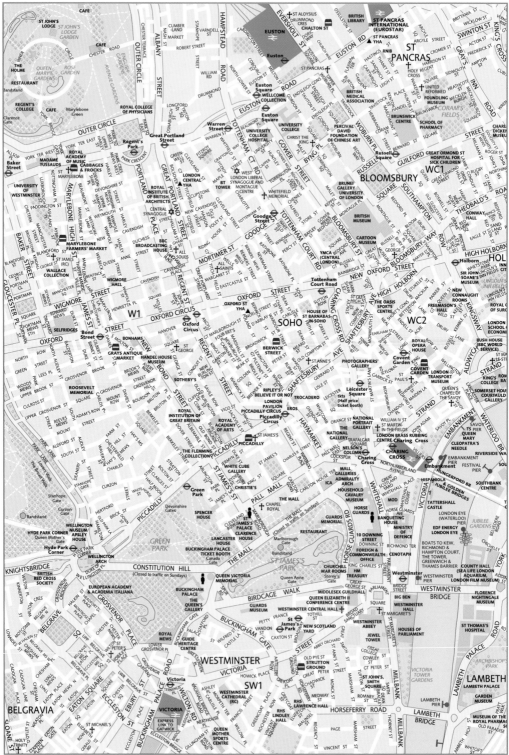

Map 11
London

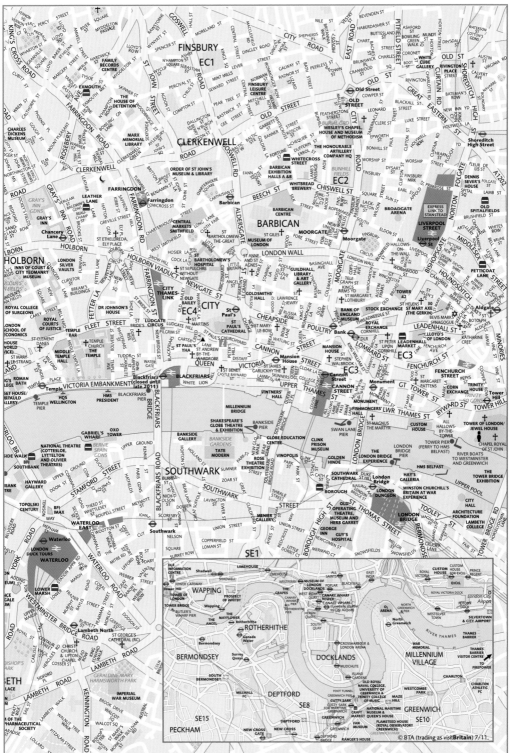

© BTA (trading as visitBritain) 7/11.

Motorway Service Area Assessment Scheme

Something we all use and take for granted, but how good are they?

The star ratings cover a wide range of aspects of each operation, including cleanliness, the quality and range of catering and also the quality of the physical aspects, as well as the service. It does not cover prices or value for money.

OPERATOR: EXTRA

Baldock	★★★★
Beaconsfield	★★★★
Blackburn	★★★★
Cambridge	★★★★
Cobham	★★★★
Cullompton	★★★
Peterborough	★★★★

OPERATOR: MOTO

Birch E	★★★
Birch W	★★★
Bridgwater	★★★
Burton in Kendal	★★★
Cherwell Valley	★★★★
Chieveley	★★★
Doncaster N	★★★★
Donington Park	★★★★
Exeter	★★★
Ferrybridge	★★★★
Frankley N	★★★
Frankley S	★★★
Heston E	★★★
Heston W	★★★
Hilton Park N	★★★
Hilton Park S	★★★
Knutsford N	★★★
Knutsford S	★★★
Lancaster N	★★★
Lancaster S	★★★
Leigh Delamere E	★★★★
Leigh Delamere W	★★★
Medway	★★★
Pease Pottage	★★★
Reading E	★★★★
Reading W	★★★
Severn View	★★
Southwaite N	★★★
Southwaite S	★★★★

Stafford N	★★★★
Tamworth	★★★
Thurrock	★★★★
Toddington N	★★★★
Toddington S	★★★
Trowell N	★★★
Trowell S	★★★
Washington N	★★★
Washington S	★★★
Wetherby	★★★★
Winchester N	★★★★
Winchester S	★★★
Woolley Edge N	★★★★
Woolley Edge S	★★★★

OPERATOR: ROADCHEF

Chester	★★★
Clacket Lane E	★★★
Clacket Lane W	★★★
Durham	★★★
Killington Lake	★★★
Maidstone	★★★
Northampton N	★★★
Northampton S	★★★
Norton Canes	★★★
Rownhams N	★★
Rownhams S	★★★
Sandbach N	★★★
Sandbach S	★★★
Sedgemoor S	★★★
Stafford S	★★★★
Strensham N	★★★
Strensham S	★★★
Taunton Deane N	★★
Taunton Deane S	★★★
Tibshelf N	★★★
Tibshelf S	★★★
Watford Gap N	★★★
Watford Gap S	★★

OPERATOR: WELCOME BREAK

Birchanger Green	★★★★
Burtonwood	★★★
Charnock Richard W	★★★
Charnock Richard E	★★★
Corley E	★★★
Corley W	★★★
Fleet N	★★★★
Fleet S	★★★★
Gordano	★★★★
Hartshead Moor E	★★★
Hartshead Moor W	★★★
Hopwood Park	★★★★
Keele N	★★★
Keele S	★★★
Leicester Forest East N	★★★
Leicester Forest East S	★★★
London Gateway	★★★★
Membury E	★★★
Membury W	★★★★
Michaelwood N	★★★
Michaelwood S	★★★
Newport Pagnell S	★★★
Newport Pagnell N	★★★
Oxford	★★★★
Sedgemoor N	★★★
South Mimms	★★★★
Telford	★★★
Warwick N	★★★
Warwick S	★★★★
Woodall N	★★
Woodall S	★★★

WESTMORLAND

Tebay N	★★★★
Tebay S	★★★★★

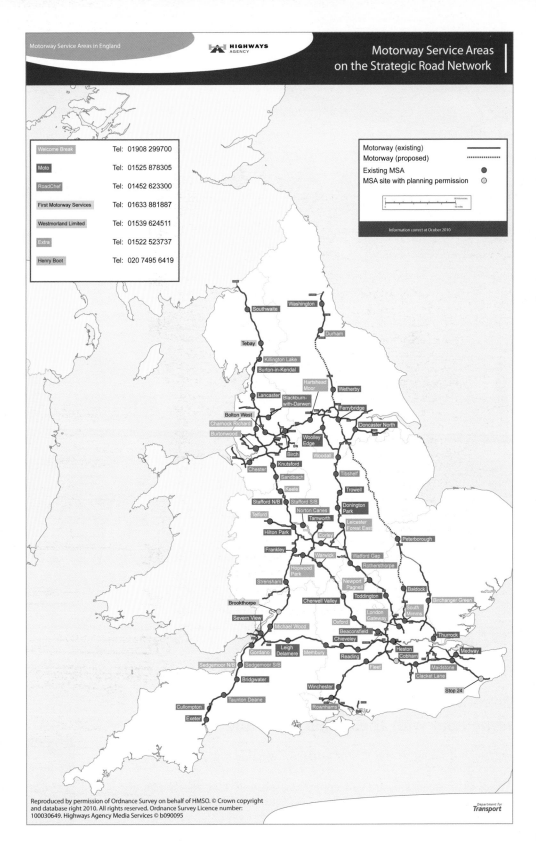

HIGHWAYS
AGENCY

Motorway Service Areas
on the Strategic Road Network

Welcome Break	Tel: 01908 299700
Moto	Tel: 01525 878305
RoadChef	Tel: 01452 623300
First Motorway Services	Tel: 01633 881887
Westmorland Limited	Tel: 01539 624511
Extra	Tel: 01522 523737
Henry Boot	Tel: 020 7495 6419

Motorway (existing)
Motorway (proposed)
Existing MSA
MSA site with planning permission

Information correct at October 2010

Reproduced by permission of Ordnance Survey on behalf of HMSO. © Crown copyright
and database right 2010. All rights reserved. Ordnance Survey Licence number:
100030649. Highways Agency Media Services © b090095

Department for
Transport

273

So much to see, so little time – how do you choose?

Make the most of your leisure time; look for attractions with the Quality Marque.

VisitEngland operates the Visitor Attraction Quality Assurance Scheme.

Annual assessments by trained impartial assessors test all aspects of the customer experience so you can visit with confidence.

For ideas and inspiration go to www.visitengland.com

Further Information

Advice and information

Making a booking

When enquiring about accommodation, make sure you check prices, the quality rating and other important details. You will also need to state your requirements clearly and precisely, for example:

- Arrival and departure dates, with acceptable alternatives if appropriate;

- The accommodation you need;

- The number of people in your party and the ages of any children;

- Special requirements.

Confirmation

Misunderstandings can easily happen over the telephone, so do request a written confirmation, together with details of any terms and conditions that apply to your booking.

Deposits and advance payments

In the case of caravan, camping and touring parks and holiday villages, the full charge often has to be paid in advance. This may be in two instalments – a deposit at the time of booking and the balance by, say, two weeks before the start of the booked period.

Cancellations

Legal contract

When you accept accommodation that is offered to you, by telephone or in writing, you enter into a legally binding contract with the proprietor. This means that if you cancel your booking, fail to take up the accommodation or leave early, you will probably forfeit your deposit and may expect to be charged the balance at the end of the period booked if the place cannot be re-let. You should be advised at the time of the booking of what charges would be made in the event of cancelling the accommodation or leaving early, which is usually written into the property's terms and conditions. If this is not mentioned you should ask the proprietor for any cancellation terms that apply before booking your accommodation to ensure any disputes are avoided. Where you have already paid the full amount before cancelling, the proprietor is likely to retain the money. However if the accommodation is re-let, the proprietor will make a refund to you which normally excludes the amount of the deposit.

Remember, if you book by telephone and are asked for your credit card number, you should check whether the proprietor intends to charge your credit card account, should you later cancel your reservation. A proprietor should not be able to charge your credit card account with a cancellation fee without your consent unless you agreed to this at the time of your booking. However, to avoid later disputes, we suggest you check whether this is the intention before providing your details.

Avoiding peak season

In the summer months of June to September, parks in popular areas such as North Wales, Cumbria, the West Country or the New Forest in Hampshire may become full. Campers should aim to arrive at parks early in the day or, where possible, should book in advance. Some parks have overnight holding areas for visitors who arrive late. This helps to prevent disturbing other campers and caravanners late at night and means that fewer visitors are turned away. Caravans or tents are directed to a pitch the following morning.

Other caravan and camping places

If you enjoy making your own route through Britain's countryside, it may interest you to know that the Forestry Commission operates campsites in Britain's Forest Parks as well as in the New Forest. Some offer reduced charges for youth organisations on organised camping trips and all enquiries about them should be made well in advance of your intended stay to the Forestry Commission.

Travelling with pets

Dogs, cats, ferrets and some other pets can be brought into the UK from certain countries without having to undertake six months' quarantine on arrival, provided they meet the requirements of the Pet Travel Scheme (PETS).

For full details, visit the PETS website at
w www.gov.uk/take-pet-abroad
or contact the PETS Helpline
t +44 (0)370 241 1710
e pettravel@ahvla.gsi.gov.uk
Ask for fact sheets which cover dogs and cats, ferrets or domestic rabbits and rodents.

There are no requirements for pets travelling directly between the UK and the Channel Islands. Pets entering Jersey or Guernsey from other countries need to be Pet Travel Scheme compliant and have a valid EU Pet Passport. For more information see www.jersey.com or www.visitguernsey.com.

Insurance

A travel or holiday insurance policy will safeguard you if you have to cancel or change your holiday plans both abroad and in the UK. You can arrange a policy quite cheaply through your insurance company or travel agent.

Finding a park

Tourist signs similar to the one shown here are designed to help visitors find their park. They clearly show whether the park is for tents or caravans or both.

Tourist information centres throughout Britain are able to give campers and caravanners information about parks in their areas. Some tourist information centres have camping and caravanning advisory services that provide details of park availability and often assist with park booking.

Electric hook-up points

Most parks now have electric hook-up points for caravans and tents. Voltage is generally 240v AC, 50 cycles. Parks may charge extra for this facility, and it is advisable to check rates when making a booking.

What to expect at holiday, touring and camping parks

In addition to fulfilling its statutory obligations, including complying with the Regulatory Reform (Fire Safety) Order 2005, holding public liability insurance and ensuring that all caravan holiday homes/chalets for hire and the park and all buildings and facilities, fixtures, furnishings, fittings and decor are maintained in sound and clean condition and are fit for the purposes intended, the management is required to undertake the following:

Prior to booking

- To describe accurately in any advertisement, brochure, or other printed or electronic media, the facilities and services provided;
- To make clear to guests in print, electronic media and on the telephone exactly what is included in all prices quoted for accommodation, including taxes and any other surcharges. Details of charges for additional services/facilities should also be made clear, for example breakfast, leisure etc;
- To provide information on the suitability of the premises for guests of various ages, particularly for the elderly and the very young;
- To allow guests to view the accommodation prior to booking if requested.

At the time of booking

- To clearly describe the cancellation policy to guests i.e. by telephone, fax, internet/email as well as in any printed information given to guests;
- To adhere to and not to exceed prices quoted at the time of booking for accommodation and other services.

On arrival

- To welcome all guests courteously and without discrimination in relation to gender, sexual orientation, disability, race, religion or belief.

During the stay

- To maintain standards of guest care, cleanliness, and service appropriate to the style of operation;
- To deal promptly and courteously with all enquiries, requests, bookings and correspondence from guests;

- To ensure complaints received are investigated promptly and courteously to an outcome that is communicated to the guest.

On departure

- To give each guests, on request, details or payments due and a receipt, if required/requested.

General

- To give due consideration to the requirements of guests with special needs, and to make suitable provision where applicable;
- To ensure the accommodation, when advertised as open, is prepared for the arrival of guests at all times;
- To advise guests, at any time prior to their stay, of any changes made to their booking;
- To hold current public liability insurance and to comply with all relevant statutory obligations, including legislation applicable to health and safety, planning and fire;
- To allow assessment body representatives reasonable access to the operation, on request, to confirm that the Code of Conduct is being observed, or in order to investigate any complaint of a serious nature notified to them

What to expect at holiday villages

The operator/manager is required to undertake the following:

Prior to booking

- To describe accurately in any advertisement, brochure, or other printed or electronic media, the facilities and services provided;
- To make clear to guests in print, on the internet and on the telephone exactly what is included in all prices quoted for accommodation, including taxes, and any other surcharges. Details of charges for additional services/facilities should also be made clear, for example breakfast, leisure etc;
- To provide information on the suitability of the premises for guests of various ages, particularly for the elderly and the very young;
- To allow guests to view the accommodation prior to booking if requested.

At the time of booking

- To clearly describe the cancellation policy to guests by telephone, fax and internet/email, as well as in any printed information given to guests;
- To adhere to and not to exceed prices quoted at the time of booking for accommodation and other services;
- To advise guests at the time of booking, or subsequently in the event of any change in what has been booked;
- To make clear to guests, if the accommodation offered is in an unconnected annexe or similar, and to indicate the location of such accommodation and any difference in comfort and/or amenities from accommodation in the establishment.

On arrival

- To welcome all guests courteously and without discrimination in relation to gender, sexual orientation, disability, race, religion or belief.

During the stay

- To maintain standards of guest care, cleanliness, and service appropriate to the type of establishment;
- To deal promptly and courteously with all enquiries, requests, bookings and correspondence from guests;
- To ensure complaint handling procedures are in place and that complaints received are investigated promptly and courteously and that the outcome is communicated to the guest.

On departure

- To give each guests, on request, details or payments due and a receipt, if required/requested.

General

- To give due consideration to the requirements of guests with special needs, and to make suitable provision where applicable;
- To ensure the accommodation is prepared for the arrival of guests at all times when the operation is advertised as open to receive guests;
- To hold current public liability insurance and to comply with all relevant statutory obligations including legislation applicable to fire, health and safety, planning, food safety and all relevant statutory requirements;

- To allow assessment body representatives reasonable access to the establishment, on request, to confirm that the Code of Conduct is being observed or in order to investigate any complaint of a serious nature notified to them.

Comments and complaint

Information

The proprietors themselves supply the descriptions of their establishments and other information for the entries (except ratings). They have all signed a declaration that their information conforms to The Consumer Protection from Unfair Trading Regulations 2008. VisitBritain cannot guarantee the accuracy of information in this guide, and accepts no responsibility for any error or misrepresentation.

All liability for loss, disappointment, negligence or other damage caused by reliance on the information contained in this guide, or in the event of bankruptcy or liquidation or cessation of trade of any company, individual or firm mentioned, is hereby excluded. We strongly recommend that you carefully check prices and other details when you book your accommodation.

Problems

Of course, we hope you will not have cause for complaint, but problems do occur from time to time.

If you are dissatisfied with anything, make your complaint to the management immediately. Then the management can take action at once to investigate the matter and put things right. The longer you leave a complaint, the harder it is to deal with it effectively.

In certain circumstances, the assessment body may look into complaints. However, it has no statutory control over establishments or their methods of operating. The assessment body cannot become involved in legal or contractual matters or in seeking financial compensation.

If you do have problems that have not been resolved by the proprietor and which you would like to bring to our attention, please write to:

England
Quality in Tourism, 1320 Montpellier Court, Pioneer Way, Gloucester Business Park, Gloucester, Gloucestershire GL3 4AH

Scotland
Quality and Standards, Ocean Point One, 94 Ocean Drive, Edinburgh EH6 6JH

Wales
VisitWales, Welsh Government, Rhodfa Padarn, Llanbadarn Fawr, Aberystwyth, Ceredigion SY23 3UR

Useful contacts

British Holiday & Home Parks Association

Chichester House, 6 Pullman Court,
Great Western Road, Gloucester GL1 3ND
t (01452) 526911 (enquiries and brochure requests)
w parkholidayengland.org.uk

Professional UK park owners are represented by the British Holiday and Home Parks Association. Over 3,000 parks are members, and each year welcome millions of visitors seeking quality surroundings in which to enjoy a good value stay.

Parks provide caravan holiday homes and lodges for hire and pitches for your own touring caravan, motor home or tent. On many, you can opt to buy your own holiday home.

A major strength of the UK's park industry is its diversity. Whatever your idea of holiday pleasure, there's sure to be a park which can provide it. If your preference is for a quiet, peaceful holiday in tranquil rural surroundings, you'll find many idyllic locations.

Alternatively, many parks are to be found at our most popular resorts – and reflect the holiday atmosphere with plenty of entertainment and leisure facilities. For more adventurous families, parks often provide excellent bases from which to enjoy outdoor activities.

Literature available from BH&HPA includes a guide to parks which have this year achieved the David Bellamy Conservation Award for environmental excellence.

The Camping and Caravanning Club

Greenfields House, Westwood Way,
Coventry CV4 8JH
t 0845 130 7631
t 0845 130 7633 (advance bookings)
w campingandcaravanningclub.co.uk

Discover the peace and quiet of over 100 award-winning club sites. Experience a different backdrop to your holiday every time you go away, with sites in the lakes and mountains, coastal and woodland glades or cultural and heritage locations.

The Club is proud of its prestigious pedigree and regularly achieves awards for spotless campsites, friendly service and caring for the environment – a guarantee that you will enjoy your holiday.

Non-members are welcome at the majority of our sites and we offer special deals for families, backpackers, overseas visitors and members aged 55 and over. Recoup your membership fee in just six nights and gain access to over 1,300 Certificated Sites around the country.

For more details, please refer to our entries listed at the back of this publication or if you require any more information on what The Friendly Club can offer you then telephone 0845 130 7632, or call to request your free guide to The Club.

The Caravan Club

East Grinstead House, East Grinstead,
West Sussex RH19 1UA
t (01342) 326944
w caravanclub.co.uk
The Caravan Club offers 200 sites in the UK and
Ireland. These include city locations such as London,
Edinburgh, York and Chester, plus sites near leading
heritage attractions such as Longleat, Sandringham,
Chatsworth and Blenheim Palace. A further 30 sites
are in National Parks.

Virtually all pitches have an electric hook-up point.
The toilet blocks and play areas are of the highest
quality. Friendly, knowledgeable site wardens are on
hand too.

Most Caravan Club Sites are graded four or five stars
according to The British Graded Holiday Parks Scheme,
run by the national tourist boards, so that you can be
assured of quality at all times. Over 130 sites are open
to non-members, but why not become a member and
gain access to all sites, plus a further 2,500 certificated
locations – rural sites for no more than five vans. Tent
campers are welcome at over 60 sites.

Join The Club and you can save the cost of your
subscription fee in just five nights with member
discounts on site fees!

Forest Holidays

Bath Yard, Moira, Derbyshire DE12 6BA
t 0845 130 8223 (cabins)
t 0845 130 8224 (campsites)
w forestholidays.co.uk

Forest Holidays, a new partnership between
the Forestry Commission and the Camping and
Caravanning Club, have over 20 camping and
caravan sites in stunning forest locations throughout
Great Britain in addition to three cabin sites. Choose
from locations such as the Scottish Highlands, the
New Forest, Snowdonia National Park, the Forest
of Dean, or the banks of Loch Lomond. Some sites
are open all year and dogs are welcome at most.
Advance bookings are accepted for many sites.

For a unique forest experience, call Forest Holidays
for a brochure on 0845 130 8224 or visit their website.

The Motor Caravanners' Club Ltd

1st Floor, Woodfarm Estate, Marlbank Road, Welland,
Malvern WR13 6NA
t (0) 1684 311677
e info@motorcaravanners.eu
w motorcaravanners.eu
The Motor Caravanners' Club is authorised to
issue the Camping Card International (CCI). It also
produces a monthly magazine, Motor Caravanner,
for all members. Member of The Federation
Internationale de Camping et de Caravanning (FICC).

The National Caravan Council

The National Caravan Council,
Catherine House, Victoria Road,
Aldershot, Hampshire
GU11 1SS
t (01252) 318251
w thencc.org.uk

The National Caravan Council (NCC) is the trade
body for the British caravan industry – not just
touring caravans and motorhomes but also caravan
holiday homes. It has in its membership parks,
manufacturers, dealers and suppliers to the industry
– all NCC member companies are committed
continually to raise standards of technical and
commercial excellence.

So, if you want to know where to buy a caravan,
where to find a caravan holiday park or simply need
advice on caravans and caravanning, see the website
thencc.org.uk where there is lots of helpful advice
including:

- How to check whether the caravan, motorhome
  or caravan holiday home you are buying complies
  with European Standards and essential UK health
  and safety regulations (through the Certification
  scheme that the NCC operates).

- Where to find quality parks to visit on holiday.

- Where to find approved caravan and motorhome
  workshops for servicing and repair.

Caravan holidays are one of the most popular
choices for holidaymakers in Britain – the NCC works
closely with VisitBritain to promote caravan holidays
in all their forms and parks that are part of the British
Graded Holiday Parks Scheme.

About the accommodation entries

Entries

All accommodation featured in this guide has been assessed or has applied for assessment under a quality assessment scheme.

Start your search for a place to stay by looking in the 'Where to Stay' sections of this guide, where proprietors have paid to have their establishment featured in either a standard entry (includes photograph, description, facilities and prices) or an enhanced entry (photograph(s) and extended details).

Locations

Places to stay are listed by town, city or village. If a property is located in a small village, you may find it listed under a nearby town (providing it is within a seven-mile radius).

Within each region, counties run in alphabetical order. Place names are listed alphabetically within each county, and include interesting county information and a map reference.

Map references

These refer to the colour location maps at the back of the guide. The first figure shown is the map number, the following letter and figure indicate the grid reference on the map. Only place names that have a standard or enhanced entry feature appear on the maps. Some standard or enhanced entries were included in the scheme after the guide went to press, therefore they do not appear on the maps.

Telephone numbers

Booking telephone numbers are listed below the contact address for each entry. Area codes are shown in brackets.

Prices

The prices printed are to be used as a guide only; they were supplied to us by proprietors in summer 2014. Remember, changes may occur after the guide goes to press, therefore we strongly advise you to check prices before booking your accommodation.

Prices are shown in pounds sterling, including VAT where applicable. Touring pitch prices are based on the minimum and maximum charges for one night for two persons, car and caravan or tent. (Some parks may charge separately for a car, caravan or tent and for each person and there may be an extra charge for caravan awnings.) Minimum and maximum prices for caravan holiday homes are given per week.

Prices often vary throughout the year and may be significantly lower outside of peak periods. You can get details of other bargain packages that may be available from the establishments themselves, regional tourism organisations or your local Tourist Information Centre (TIC). Your local travel agent may also have information and can help you make your booking.

Opening period

If an entry does not indicate an opening period, please check directly with the site.

Pets

Many places accept guests with dogs, but we advise that you check this with the proprietor before booking, remembering to ask if there are any extra charges or rules about exactly where your pet is allowed. The acceptance of dogs is not always extended to cats and it is strongly advised that cat owners contact the property well in advance of their stay.

Some establishments do not accept pets at all. Pets are welcome by arrangement where you see this symbol 🐾. The quarantine laws have changed and now dogs, cats and ferrets are able to come into Britain and the Channel Islands from over 50 countries. For details of the Pet Travel Scheme (PETS) please turn to page 277.

Payment accepted

The types of payment accepted by an establishment are listed in the payment accepted section. If you plan to pay by card, check that the establishment will accept the particular type of card you own before booking. Some proprietors will charge you a higher rate if you pay by credit card rather than cash or cheque. The difference is to cover the charges paid by the proprietor to the credit card company.

When you book by telephone, you may be asked for your credit card number as confirmation. Remember, the proprietor may then charge your credit card account if you cancel your booking. See details of this under Cancellations on page 276.

Symbols

The at-a-glance symbols included at the end of each entry show many of the services and facilities available at each property. You will find the key to these symbols on page 7.

Smoking

In the UK and the Channel Islands, it is illegal to smoke in enclosed public spaces and places of work. Smoking may be allowed in self-contained short-term rental accommodation, such as holiday cottages, flats or caravans, if the owner chooses to allow it.

If you wish to smoke, we advise you to check the proprietors smoking policy before you book.

Awaiting confirmation of rating

At the time of going to press some properties featured in this guide had not yet been assessed therefore their rating for this year could not be included. The term 'Rating Applied For' indicates this throughout your guide.

Looking for something else?

The official and most comprehensive guide to independently inspected, quality-assessed accommodation.

- B&Bs and Hotels
- Self Catering
- Camping, Touring and Holiday Parks

Now available in all good bookshops and online at

www.hudsons.co.uk/shop

Getting around

Travelling in London

London transport

Each London Underground line has its own unique colour, so you can easily follow them on the Underground map. Most lines run through central London, and many serve parts of Greater London. Buses are a quick, convenient way to travel around London, providing plenty of sightseeing opportunities along the way. There are over 6,500 buses in London operating 700 routes every day. You will need to buy a ticket or Travel Pass before you board the bus.

London's National Rail system stretches all over London. Many lines start at the main London railway stations (Paddington, Victoria, Waterloo, Kings Cross) with links to the tube. Trains mainly serve areas outside central London, and travel overground.

Children usually travel free, or at reduced fare, on all public transport in London.

Oyster cards

Oyster cards can be used to pay fares on all London Underground, buses, Docklands Light Railway and trams, however are generally not valid for National Rail services in London.

Oyster cards are very easy to use, you just touch the card on sensors at stations or on buses and you are charged the lowest fare available for your journey. You buy credit for your journey and when it runs out you simply top up with more.

Oyster cards are available to adults only. Children below the age of 11 can accompany adults free of charge. Children between the ages of 11 and 15 can travel free on buses and trams and at child rate on Tube, DLR and London Overground services, provided they have an 11-15 Zip Oyster photocard. You can purchase an Oyster card for a fee of £5, which is refundable on its return, at any underground station, one of 3,000 Oyster points around London displaying the London Underground sign (usually shops), or from www.visitbritainshop.com, or www.oyster.tfl.gov.uk/oyster

London congestion charge

The congestion charge is £11.50 daily charge to drive in central London at certain times. Check if the congestion charge is included in the cost of your car before booking. If your car's pick up point is in the congestion-charging zone, the company may pay the charge for the first day of your hire.

Low Emission Zone

The Low Emission Zone is an area covering most of Greater London, within which the most polluting diesel-engine vehicles are required to meet specific emissions standards. If your vehicle does not, you will be required to pay a daily charge.

Vehicles affected by the Low Emission Zone are older diesel-engine lorries, buses, coaches, large vans, minibuses and other heavy vehicles such as motor caravans and motorised horse boxes. This also includes vehicles registered outside of Great Britain. Cars and motorcycles are not affected by this scheme. For more information visit www.tfl.gov.uk

Rail and train travel

Britain's rail network covers all main cities and smaller regional towns. Trains on the network are operated by a few large companies running routes from London to stations all over Britain. Therefore smaller companies that run routes in regional areas. You can find up-to-the-minute information about routes, fares and train times on the National Rail Enquiries website (www.nationalrail.co.uk). For detailed information about routes and services, refer to the train operators' websites (see page 291).

Railway passes

BritRail offer a wide selection of passes and tickets giving you the freedom to travel on all National Rail services. Passes can also include sleeper services, city and attraction passes and boat tours. Passes can usually be purchased from travel agents outside Britain or by visiting the BritRail website www.britrail.net.

Bus and coach travel

Public buses

Every city and town in Britain has a local bus service. These services are privatised and managed by separate companies. The largest bus companies in Britain are First (www.firstgroup.com/ukbus), Stagecoach (www.stagecoachbus.com) and Arriva (www.arrivabus.co.uk), and run buses in most UK towns. Outside London, buses usually travel to and from the town centre or to the busiest part of town. Most towns have a bus station, where you'll be able to find maps and information about routes. Bus route information may also be posted at bus stops.

Tickets and fares

The cost of a bus ticket normally depends on how far you're travelling. Return fares may be available on some buses, but you would usually need to buy a 'single' ticket for each individual journey.

You can also buy your ticket when boarding a bus by telling the driver where you are going. One-day and weekly travel cards are available in some towns, and these can be purchased from either the driver or from an information centre at the bus station. Tickets are valid for each separate journey rather than for a period of time, so if you get off the bus you'll need to buy a new ticket when getting on another.

Domestic flights

Flying is a time-saving alternative to road or rail when it comes to travelling around Britain. Domestic flights are fast and frequent and there are 33 airports across Britain that operate domestic routes. You will find airports marked on the maps at the front of this guide.

Domestic flight advice

Photo ID is required to travel on domestic flights. However it is advisable to bring your passport as not all airlines will accept other forms of photo identification. Please be aware of the high security measures at all airports in Britain which include include restrictions on items that may be carried in hand luggage. It is important that you check the restrictions in place with your airline prior to travel, as these can vary over time and don't forget to allow adequate time for check-in and boarding on arrival.

Cycling

Cycling is a great way to see some of England's iconic scenery and there are many networks of cycling routes available across England. The National Cycle Network offers over 10,000 miles of walking and cycling routes details for connecting towns and villages, countryside and coast across England. For more information and view these routes see page 287 or visit Sustrans at www.sustrans.co.uk.

Think green

If you'd rather leave your car behind and travel by 'green transport' to some of the attractions highlighted in this guide you'll be helping to reduce congestion and pollution as well as supporting conservation charities in their commitment to green travel.

The National Trust encourages visits made by non-car travellers and it offers admission discounts or a voucher for the tea room at a selection of its properties if you arrive on foot, cycle or public transport (you may need to produce a valid bus or train ticket if travelling by public transport.).

More information about The National Trust's work to encourage car-free days out can be found at www.nationaltrust.org.uk. (Refer to the section entitled 'Information for Visitors').

Book your accommodation online

Visit our websites for detailed information, up-to-date availability and to book your accommodation online. Includes over 20,000 places to stay, all of them star rated.
www.visitor-guides.co.uk

Walkers and cyclists welcome

Look out for quality-assessed accommodation displaying the Walkers Welcome and Cyclists Welcome signs.

Participants in these schemes actively encourage and support walking and cycling. In addition to special meal arrangements and helpful information, they'll provide a water supply to wash off the mud, an area for drying wet clothing and footwear, maps and books to look up cycling and walking routes and even an emergency puncture-repair kit! Bikes can also be locked up securely undercover.

The standards for these schemes have been developed in partnership with the tourist boards in Northern Ireland, Scotland and Wales, so wherever you're travelling in the UK you'll receive the same welcome.

sus**trans**
JOIN THE MOVEMENT

Here are just some of the most popular long distance routes on the 12,000 mile Sustrans National Cycle Network. To see the Network in it's entirety and to find routes near you, visit **www.sustrans.org.uk**

Sustrans is the UK's leading sustainable transport charity working on practical projects to enable people to choose to travel in ways which benefit their health and the environment.

68 National Cycle Network Route Number
Long Distance Routes
1 Coast & Castles Cycle Route
2 Pennine Cycleway - North Pennines
3 Hadrian's Cycleway
4 Sea to Sea
5 Pennine Cycleway - South Pennines & the Dales
6 Derby to York
7 Hull to Fakenham
8 East of England
9 South Midlands Cycle Route
10 Thames Valley Cycle Route
11 Garden of England
12 Downs & Weald Cycle Route
13 Devon Coast to Coast
14 The Cornish Way
15 The West Country Way
16 The Severn & Thames

Map reproduced from Ordnance Survey material with the permission of Ordnance Survey on behalf of the Controller of Her Majesty's Stationery Office © Crown copyright. Unauthorised reproduction infringes Crown copyright and may lead to prosecution or civil proceedings.
Licence number 100020852 (2009)

Newcastle Tynemouth
Workington
Ravenglass
York
Kingston-upon-Hull
Manchester
Sheffield
Lincoln
Derby
Fakenham
Oxford
Bristol
London
Staines Croydon
Dover
Brighton Hastings
Padstow
Plymouth

N
W E
S

By car and by train

Distance chart

The distances between towns on the chart below are given to the nearest mile, and are measured along routes based on the quickest travelling time, making maximum use of motorways or dual-carriageway roads. The chart is based upon information supplied by the Automobile Association.

To calculate the distance in kilometres multiply the mileage by 1.6
For example: Brighton to Dover
82 miles x 1.6 =131.2 kilometres

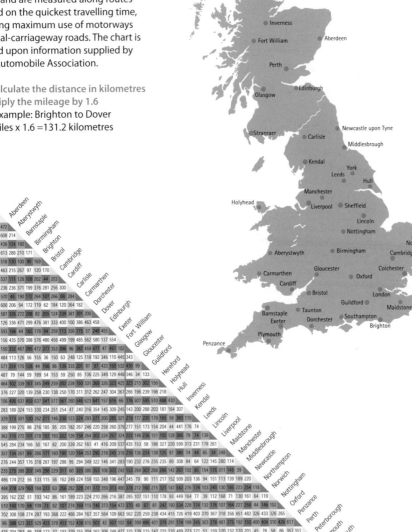

Chart place names (diagonal): Aberdeen, Aberystwyth, Barnstaple, Birmingham, Brighton, Bristol, Cambridge, Cardiff, Carlisle, Carmarthen, Dorchester, Dover, Edinburgh, Exeter, Fort William, Glasgow, Gloucester, Guildford, Hereford, Holyhead, Hull, Inverness, Kendal, Leeds, Lincoln, Liverpool, Maidstone, Manchester, Middlesbrough, Newcastle, Northampton, Norwich, Nottingham, Oxford, Penzance, Perth, Peterborough, Plymouth, Portsmouth, Preston, Salisbury, Sheffield, Shrewsbury, Southampton, Stoke-on-Trent, Stranraer, Taunton, Wick, York, LONDON

```
472
608 214
436 124 180
613 288 210 171
518 130 100 99 169
463 215 267 97 120 170
537 311 128 109 202 44 203
236 236 371 199 376 281 256 300
520 48 190 172 264 107 266 68 264
600 206 94 172 119 62 184 120 364 182
587 326 272 208 82 205 124 239 381 301 200
126 336 471 299 476 381 333 400 100 386 463 458
593 198 44 165 178 84 259 113 356 175 57 248 455
156 435 570 398 576 480 456 499 199 485 562 580 137 554
150 332 467 295 472 377 353 396 96 382 459 477 47 451 102
484 113 126 56 155 36 150 63 248 125 118 192 346 110 445 343
571 224 175 128 44 106 96 139 335 201 97 97 433 150 532 430 99
487 79 144 59 189 54 153 59 250 85 136 225 349 129 448 346 34 133
464 102 339 167 345 249 259 202 228 150 331 369 326 323 425 323 215 302 156
376 227 320 139 258 230 138 250 170 311 312 262 247 304 367 266 196 239 198 218
106 496 631 459 637 541 517 561 260 546 623 641 157 616 66 176 507 595 510 498 430
283 189 324 153 330 234 251 254 47 240 316 354 145 309 245 143 200 288 203 181 164 307
329 173 301 120 262 211 146 230 123 224 293 271 200 285 321 219 177 220 179 165 59 383 110
388 199 275 98 216 185 95 205 182 267 246 220 258 260 379 277 151 173 154 204 44 441 176 74
362 110 272 101 278 182 193 202 126 158 264 302 224 257 324 222 148 236 151 102 128 386 79 74 139
545 284 234 166 50 167 82 200 339 262 161 41 416 209 537 435 153 58 186 327 220 599 313 231 178 261
357 134 261 89 266 171 160 190 120 184 253 290 219 245 318 216 136 224 139 91 74 380 74 44 85 34 248
276 244 357 176 318 267 197 286 95 294 349 322 146 341 283 190 232 276 235 235 89 308 84 64 122 145 280 114
235 275 388 207 349 298 229 317 60 325 380 353 106 372 242 153 264 307 266 266 142 267 102 95 154 176 311 145 39
486 174 212 56 133 115 56 162 249 224 159 155 348 196 447 345 79 90 111 217 152 509 203 136 94 151 113 139 189 220
488 278 329 160 168 233 63 266 282 328 241 172 359 313 480 378 212 160 215 321 147 542 276 174 103 240 130 185 254 118
395 162 232 51 193 142 86 161 189 223 224 210 266 216 387 285 107 151 110 178 93 449 164 77 39 112 168 71 130 161 64 119
510 160 170 68 109 73 82 107 274 169 115 146 373 154 472 370 48 67 81 242 190 534 228 174 132 176 107 164 227 258 44 146 102
702 308 108 274 287 193 368 222 466 284 167 357 564 109 663 562 220 259 238 434 415 726 419 403 370 367 318 356 451 482 326 433 326 265
86 388 523 351 529 433 378 453 152 438 515 503 42 507 100 44 399 486 401 375 192 150 400 404 310 426 617
435 204 263 86 158 173 37 193 229 255 204 162 306 248 427 325 139 115 142 225 110 489 223 121 51 159 120 132 170 201 45 78 58 86 357 351
633 239 62 205 218 124 299 153 337 215 98 295 485 41 584 491 151 190 169 365 346 657 350 334 301 298 249 287 382 413 257 364 257 196 78 544 288
596 244 162 154 53 125 137 158 360 220 73 141 458 132 558 456 145 152 328 276 226 102 250 313 344 310 344 168 65 241 500 157 172
326 145 281 110 287 191 209 211 89 197 273 311 188 266 287 185 157 245 160 138 122 349 43 69 134 36 260 35 103 139 159 235 121 184 375 237 180 306 270
549 184 118 121 52 145 98 313 160 39 160 411 93 511 409 72 62 105 281 203 215 51 203 298 329 115 212 173 70 203 461 165 134 44 223
397 166 272 91 233 182 122 201 161 263 264 247 236 256 359 257 148 191 150 157 66 421 115 38 47 79 205 39 100 131 104 148 45 142 366 309 93 297 228 73 212
417 75 220 48 226 130 140 111 181 110 212 250 279 205 379 277 96 184 52 105 162 441 135 119 124 65 208 71 190 221 98 203 87 123 314 329 129 245 209 92 161 88
578 255 142 155 66 106 136 140 342 201 53 159 439 137 540 411 128 133 120 439 100 49 153 309 258 601 295 241 199 243 113 232 440 111 204 169 67 221 489 157 152 20 252 23 209 191
392 112 220 48 226 130 140 150 156 211 212 250 254 205 353 251 96 184 99 123 129 415 109 93 91 57 208 46 164 195 98 172 54 123 314 303 99 245 209 66 161 50 38 191
235 342 477 305 482 387 363 406 106 392 469 487 132 461 161 86 352 440 355 333 276 261 153 229 288 232 445 297 181 163 354 388 295 380 571 149 333 502 465 195 418 267 297 461 261
560 165 50 132 194 70 266 80 323 142 45 224 422 34 521 419 77 126 96 291 232 623 247 231 208 179 184 123 144 471 215 75 114 234 70 224 172 94 172 429
207 597 732 560 738 642 618 662 361 647 724 742 258 716 166 277 608 695 610 588 531 104 408 484 407 609 644 500 535 826 215 589 757 721 451 673 523 542 702 516 362 684
323 201 314 133 275 224 154 243 116 251 306 279 193 298 314 212 189 233 192 192 38 376 91 24 79 102 237 71 51 89 146 180 87 184 408 239 125 339 269 96 254 57 146 251 120 223 265 477
550 239 216 121 54 120 59 153 314 215 125 78 413 200 512 410 102 31 136 282 186 574 268 201 143 216 39 204 254 285 68 118 129 56 310 462 86 241 75 225 85 169 163 77 161 420 167 675 211
```

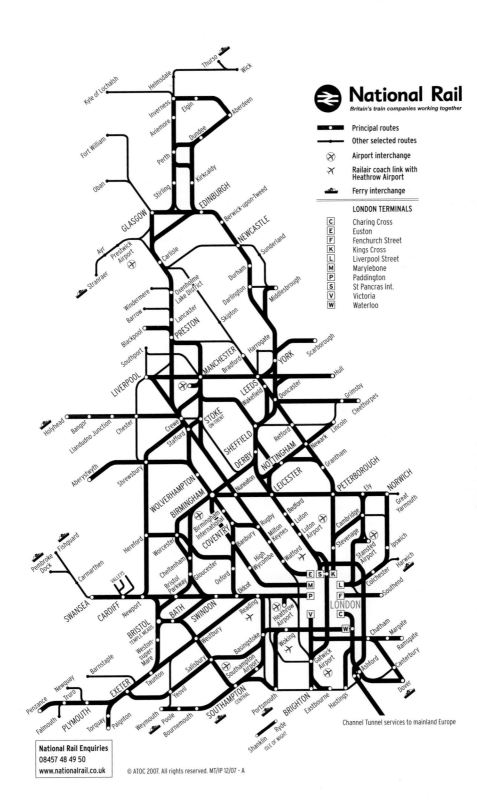

National Rail
Britain's train companies working together

	Principal routes
	Other selected routes
⊗	Airport interchange
✈	Railair coach link with Heathrow Airport
⛴	Ferry interchange

LONDON TERMINALS

C	Charing Cross
E	Euston
F	Fenchurch Street
K	Kings Cross
L	Liverpool Street
M	Marylebone
P	Paddington
S	St Pancras Int.
V	Victoria
W	Waterloo

Channel Tunnel services to mainland Europe

National Rail Enquiries
08457 48 49 50
www.nationalrail.co.uk

© ATOC 2007. All rights reserved. MT/IP 12/07 - A

Travel information

General travel information

Streetmap	www.streetmap.co.uk	
Transport for London	www.tfl.gov.uk	0843 222 1234
Travel Services	www.departures-arrivals.com	
Traveline	www.traveline.info	0871 200 2233

Bus & coach

Megabus	www.megabus.com	0900 160 0900
National Express	www.nationalexpress.com	08717 818 178
WA Shearings	www.shearings.com	0844 824 6351

Car & car hire

AA	www.theaa.com	0800 085 2721
Green Flag	www.greenflag.com	0845 246 1557
RAC	www.rac.co.uk	0844 308 9177
Alamo	www.alamo.co.uk	0871 384 1086*
Avis	www.avis.co.uk	0844 581 0147*
Budget	www.budget.co.uk	0844 544 3407*
Easycar	www.easycar.com	
Enterprise	www.enterprise.com	0800 800 227*
Hertz	www.hertz.co.uk	0870 844 8844*
Holiday Autos	www.holidayautos.co.uk	0871 472 5229
National	www.nationalcar.co.uk	0871 384 1140
Thrifty	www.thrifty.co.uk	01494 751500

Air

Air Southwest	www.airsouthwest.com	0870 043 4553
Blue Islands (Channel Islands)	www.blueislands.com	08456 20 2122
BMI	www.flybmi.com	0844 848 4888
BMI Baby	www.bmibaby.com	0905 828 2828*
British Airways	www.ba.com	0844 493 0787
British International (Isles of Scilly to Penzance)	www.islesofscillyhelicopter.com	01736 363871*
CityJet	www.cityjet.com	0871 663 3777
Eastern Airways	www.easternairways.com	08703 669100
Easyjet	www.easyjet.com	0843 104 5000
Flybe	www.flybe.com	0871 700 2000*
Jet2.com	www.jet2.com	0871 226 1737*
Manx2	www.manx2.com	0871 200 0440*
Ryanair	www.ryanair.com	0871 246 0000
Skybus (Isles of Scilly)	www.islesofscilly-travel.co.uk	0845 710 5555
Thomsonfly	www.thomsonfly.com	0871 231 4787

Train

National Rail Enquiries	www.nationalrail.co.uk	0845 748 4950
The Trainline	www.trainline.co.uk	0871 244 1545
UK train operating companies	www.rail.co.uk	
Arriva Trains	www.arriva.co.uk	0191 520 4000
c2c	www.c2c-online.co.uk	0845 601 4873
Chiltern Railways	www.chilternrailways.co.uk	0845 600 5165
CrossCountry	www.crosscountrytrains.co.uk	0844 811 0124
East Midlands Trains	www.eastmidlandstrains.co.uk	0845 712 5678
Eurostar	www.eurostar.com	08432 186 186*
First Capital Connect	www.firstcapitalconnect.co.uk	0845 026 4700
First Great Western	www.firstgreatwestern.co.uk	0845 700 0125
Gatwick Express	www.gatwickexpress.com	0845 850 1530
Heathrow Connect	www.heathrowconnect.com	0845 678 6975
Heathrow Express	www.heathrowexpress.com	0845 600 1515
Hull Trains	www.hulltrains.co.uk	0845 071 0222
Island Line	www.islandlinetrains.co.uk	0845 600 0650
London Midlands	www.londonmidland.com	0121 634 2040
Merseyrail	www.merseyrail.org	0151 702 2071
National Express East Anglia	www.nationalexpresseastanglia.com	0845 600 7245
National Express East Coast	www.nationalexpresseastcoast.com	0845 722 5333
Northern Rail	www.northernrail.org	0845 000 0125
ScotRail	www.scotrail.co.uk	0845 601 5929
South Eastern Trains	www.southeasternrailway.co.uk	0845 000 2222
South West Trains	www.southwesttrains.co.uk	0845 600 0650
Southern	www.southernrailway.com	0845 127 2920
Stansted Express	www.stanstedexpress.com	0845 600 7245
Translink	www.translink.co.uk	(028) 9066 6630
Transpennine Express	www.tpexpress.co.uk	0845 600 1671
Virgin Trains	www.virgintrains.co.uk	08450 008 000*

Ferry

Ferry Information	www.discoverferries.com	0207 436 2449
Condor Ferries	www.condorferries.co.uk	0845 609 1024*
Steam Packet Company	www.steam-packet.com	08722 992 992*
Isles of Scilly Travel	www.islesofscilly-travel.co.uk	0845 710 5555
Red Funnel	www.redfunnel.co.uk	0844 844 9988
Wight Link	www.wightlink.co.uk	0871 376 1000

Phone numbers listed are for general enquiries unless otherwise stated.
* Booking line only

David Bellamy
Conservation Award

2013/14 BRONZE 2013/14 SILVER 2013/14 GOLD

Parks wishing to enter for a David Bellamy Conservation Award must complete a detailed questionnaire covering different aspects of their environmental policies, and describe what positive conservation steps they have taken. The park must also undergo an independent audit from a local wildlife or conservation body which is familiar with the area. Final assessments and the appropriate level of any award are then made personally by Professor Bellamy.

Parks with a current 2013/14 Bellamy Award offer a variety of accommodation from pitches for touring caravans, motor homes and tents, to caravan holiday homes, holiday lodges and cottages for rent or to buy. Holiday parks with these awards are not just those in quiet corners of the countryside. Amongst the winners are much larger centres in popular holiday areas that offer a wide range of entertainments and attractions.

The parks listed on the following pages all have a detailed entry in this guide and have received a Gold, Silver or Bronze David Bellamy Conservation Award. Use the Index by Property Name starting on page 283 to find the page number.

For a free brochure featuring a full list of award-winning parks please contact: BH&HPA, 6 Pullman Court, Great Western Road, Gloucester, GL1 3ND
t (01452) 526911
e enquiries@bhhpa.org.uk
w bellamyparks.co.uk or ukparks.com

Hill Cottage Farm Camping and Caravan Park	Gold	Alderholt	South West
Highlands End Holiday Park	Gold	Bridport	South West
Wooda Farm Holiday Park	Gold	Bude	South West
Cofton Country Holidays	Gold	Dawlish	South West
Lady's Mile Touring and Camping Park	Gold	Dawlish	South West
Polruan Holidays Camping & Caravanning	Gold	Fowey	South West
Tudor Caravan Park - Slimbridge	Gold	Gloucester	South West
Atlantic Coast Holiday Park	Gold	Hayle	South West
Hele Valley Holiday Park	Gold	Ilfracombe	South West
Ross Park	Gold	Ipplepen	South West
Thorney Lakes and Caravan Park	Gold	Langport	South West
Whitemead Forest Park	Gold	Lydney	South West
Seaview International Holiday Park	Gold	Mevagissey	South West
Trevella Holiday Park, Caravan & Camping	Gold	Newquay	South West
Ladram Bay Holiday Park	Gold	Otterton	South West
Porlock Caravan Park	Gold	Porlock	South West
Trethiggey Touring Park	Gold	Quintrell Downs	South West
Tehidy Holiday Park	Gold	Redruth	South West
Stonehenge Campsite & Glamping Pods	Gold	Salisbury	South West

Trethem Mill Touring Park	Gold	St. Just in Roseland	South West
Woodovis Park	Gold	Tavistock	South West
Watergate Bay Touring Park	Gold	Watergate Bay Newquay	South West
Halse Farm Caravan & Tent Park	Gold	Winsford	South West
Meadowbank Holidays	Silver	Bournemouth	South West
Juliots Well Holiday Park	Silver	Camelford	South West
Harrow Wood Farm Caravan Park	Silver	Christchurch	South West
Oakcliff Holiday Park	Silver	Dawlish	South West
Langstone Manor Holiday Park	Silver	Tavistock	South West
Dulhorn Farm Holiday Park	Bronze	Weston-super-Mare	South West
Hurley Riverside Park	Gold	Hurley	South East
Shorefield Country Park	Gold	Lymington	South East
Whitefield Forest Touring Park	Gold	Ryde	South East
Hardwick Parks	Gold	Standlake	South East
Appuldurcombe Gardens Holiday Park	Gold	Wroxall	South East
Green Pastures Caravan Park	Silver	Ower	South East
Fen Farm Camping and Caravan Site	Gold	Colchester	East of England
Waldegraves Holiday Park	Gold	Colchester	East of England
Peewit Caravan Park	Gold	Felixstowe	East of England
Clippesby Hall	Gold	Great Yarmouth	East of England
Searles Leisure Resort	Gold	Hunstanton	East of England
Pakefield Caravan Park	Gold	Lowestoft	East of England
Sandy Gulls Caravan Park	Gold	Mundesley	East of England
Vauxhall Holiday Park	Silver	Great Yarmouth	East of England
Rivendale Caravan & Leisure Park	Gold	Alsop-En-le-Dale	East Midlands
Sandybrook Country Park	Gold	Ashbourne	East Midlands
Beech Croft Farm Caravan & Camping Park	Gold	Buxton	East Midlands
Darwin Forest Country Park	Gold	Matlock	East Midlands
Skegness Water Leisure Park	Gold	Skegness	East Midlands
Golden Square Caravan and Camping Park	Gold	Helmsley	Yorkshire
Holme Valley Camping and Caravan Park	Gold	Holmfirth	Yorkshire
Skirlington Leisure Park	Gold	Hornsea	Yorkshire
Cayton Village Caravan Park Ltd	Gold	Scarborough	Yorkshire
Otterington Park	Gold	South Otterington	Yorkshire
Sand le Mere Holiday Village	Gold	Tunstall	Yorkshire
Middlewood Farm Holiday Park	Gold	Whitby	Yorkshire
Northcliffe & Seaview Holiday Parks	Gold	Whitby	Yorkshire
Whitby Holiday Park - Touring Park	Gold	Whitby	Yorkshire
Willowbank Holiday Home and Touring Park	Gold	Ainsdale	North West
Wild Rose Park	Gold	Appleby-in-Westmorland	North West
Bassenthwaite Lakeside Lodges	Gold	Bassenthwaite	North West
Bay View Holiday Park	Gold	Carnforth	North West
Holgates Caravan Park	Gold	Carnforth	North West
Hollins Farm Caravan Park	Gold	Carnforth	North West
Lakeland Leisure Park	Gold	Grange-over-Sands	North West
Castlerigg Hall Caravan & Camping Park	Gold	Keswick	North West
Woodclose Park	Gold	Kirkby Lonsdale	North West
Eastham Hall Caravan Park	Gold	Lytham St. Annes	North West
Flusco Wood	Gold	Penrith	North West
Hillcroft Holiday Park	Gold	Ullswater	North West
Waterfoot Caravan Park	Gold	Ullswater	North West
Hill of Oaks Park	Gold	Windermere	North West
Park Cliffe Camping & Caravan Estate	Gold	Windermere	North West
Riverside Holiday Park	Bronze	Southport	North West
Waren Caravan and Camping Park	Gold	Bamburgh	North East
Seafield Caravan Park	Gold	Seahouses	North East
Belhaven Bay Caravan and Camping Park	Gold	Dunbar	Scotland
Linwater Caravan Park	Gold	Edinburgh	Scotland
Mortonhall Caravan and Camping Park	Gold	Edinburgh	Scotland
Tantallon Caravan and Camping Park	Silver	North Berwick	Scotland
Garreg Goch Caravan Park	Gold	Porthmadog	Wales

If you have
access needs...

Guests with hearing, visual or mobility needs can feel confident about booking accommodation that participates in the National Accessible Scheme (NAS).

Look out for the NAS symbols which are included throughout the accommodation directory. Using the NAS could help make the difference between a good holiday and a perfect one!

For more information on the NAS and tips & ideas on holiday travel in England, go to: www.visitengland.com/accessforall

National Accessible Scheme index

Establishments with a detailed entry in this guide who participate in the National Accessible Scheme are listed below. At the front of the guide you can find information about the scheme. Establishments are listed alphabetically by place name.

Mobility level 1

Lowestoft, East of England	**Pakefield Caravan Park** ★★★★	123
Whitby, Yorkshire	**Whitby Holiday Park - Touring Park** ★★★★	178

Mobility level 2

Ainsdale, North West	**Willowbank Holiday Home and Touring Park** ★★★★★	201

Hearing impairment level 1

Ainsdale, North West	**Willowbank Holiday Home and Touring Park** ★★★★★	201
Lowestoft, East of England	**Pakefield Caravan Park** ★★★★	123

Visual impairment level 1

Lowestoft, East of England	**Pakefield Caravan Park** ★★★★	123
Whitby, Yorkshire	**Whitby Holiday Park - Touring Park** ★★★★	178

OFFICIAL TOURIST BOARD POCKET GUIDE

Walkers & Cyclists Welcome

England's star-rated great places to stay and visit

The **OFFICIAL** and most comprehensive guide to England's independently inspected, star-rated guest accommodation specialising in Walkers and Cyclists.

Hotels • Bed & Breakfast • Self-catering • Camping, Touring & Holiday Parks

- Regional round ups, attractions, ideas and other tourist information
- National Accessible Scheme accommodation at a glance
- Web-friendly features for easy booking

www.visitor-guides.co.uk

Walkers Welcome & Cyclists Welcome

Establishments participating in the Walkers Welcome and Cyclists Welcome schemes provide special facilities and actively encourage these recreations. Accommodation with a detailed entry in this guide is listed below. Place names are listed alphabetically.

Walkers Welcome & Cyclists Welcome

Craven Arms, Heart of England	Greenway Touring & Glamping Park	155
Dawlish, South West	Lady's Mile Touring and Camping Park ★★★★	50
Dawlish, South West	Oakcliff Holiday Park ★★★★	51
Great Yarmouth, East of England	Clippesby Hall ★★★★★	119
St. Issey, South West	Trewince Farm Holiday Park ★★★★	47
Tavistock, South West	Langstone Manor Holiday Park ★★★★★	56
Ullswater, North West	Hillcroft Holiday Park ★★★★	196

VisitWales Walkers Welcome & Cyclists Welcome

Fishguard, Wales	Fishguard Bay Caravan & Camping Park ★★★★	252
St Davids, Wales	Caerfai Bay Caravan & Tent Park ★★★★	253

Families and Pets Welcome

Establishments participating in the Families Welcome or Welcome Pets! schemes provide special facilities and actively encourage families or guests with pets. Accommodation with a detailed entry in this guide is listed below. Place names are listed alphabetically.

Families and Pets Welcome

Dawlish, South West	Lady's Mile Touring and Camping Park ★★★★	50
Holmfirth, Yorkshire	Holme Valley Camping and Caravan Park ★★★	179
Windermere, North West	Park Cliffe Camping & Caravan Estate ★★★★★	197

Families Welcome

Dawlish, South West	Oakcliff Holiday Park ★★★★	51
Otterton, South West	Ladram Bay Holiday Park ★★★★	55
Slingsby, Yorkshire	Robin Hood Caravan Park ★★★★★	175
St. Issey, South West	Trewince Farm Holiday Park ★★★★	47

Pets Welcome

Bamburgh, North East	Waren Caravan and Camping Park ★★★★	216
Craven Arms, Heart of England	Greenway Touring & Glamping Park	155
Felixstowe, East of England	Peewit Caravan Park ★★★★	123
Ipplepen, South West	Ross Park ★★★★★	52
Scarborough, Yorkshire	Cayton Village Caravan Park Ltd ★★★★★	173
Seahouses, North East	Seafield Caravan Park ★★★★★	217
Skegness, East Midlands	Skegness Water Leisure Park ★★★	139
Ullswater, North West	Hillcroft Holiday Park ★★★★	196

Swimming Pools index

If you're looking for accommodation with swimming facilities use this index to see at a glance detailed accommodation entries that match your requirement. Establishments are listed alphabetically by place name.

🏊 Indoor pool

Ashbourne, East Midlands	**Sandybrook Country Park ★★★★**	136
Bridport, South West	**Highlands End Holiday Park ★★★★**	58
Carnforth, North West	**Holgates Caravan Park ★★★★**	199
Crediton, South West	**Yeatheridge Farm Caravan Park ★★★★**	49
Dawlish, South West	**Lady's Mile Touring and Camping Park ★★★★**	50
Dawlish, South West	**Cofton Country Holidays ★★★**	50
Dawlish, South West	**Welcome Family Holiday Park ★★★★**	51
Filey, Yorkshire	**Crows Nest Caravan Park ★★★★**	171
Filey, Yorkshire	**Orchard Farm Holiday Village ★★★★★**	172
Grange-over-Sands, North West	**Lakeland Leisure Park ★★★★**	195
Great Yarmouth, East of England	**Vauxhall Holiday Park ★★★★★**	120
Great Yarmouth, East of England	**Summerfields Holiday Park ★★★★**	120
Hastings, South East	**Shearbarn Holiday Park ★★★★**	86
Hemsby, East of England	**Hemsby Beach Holiday Park ★★★**	121
Hornsea, Yorkshire	**Skirlington Leisure Park ★★★★**	170
Hunstanton, East of England	**Searles Leisure Resort ★★★★★**	121
Kingsdown, South East	**Kingsdown Park Holiday Village ★★★★★**	84
Lydney, South West	**Whitemead Forest Park ★★★★**	61
Lymington, South East	**Shorefield Country Park**	83
Manorbier, Wales	**Manorbier Country Park ★★★★**	252
Matlock, East Midlands	**Darwin Forest Country Park ★★★★★**	137
Newquay, South West	**Hendra Holiday Park ★★★★★**	43
Newquay, South West	**Riverside Holiday Park ★★★★**	44
Otterton, South West	**Ladram Bay Holiday Park ★★★★**	55
Par, South West	**Par Sands Holiday Park ★★★★★**	45
Scarborough, Yorkshire	**Flower of May Holiday Park ★★★★★**	173
Seahouses, North East	**Seafield Caravan Park ★★★★★**	217
Selsey, South East	**Green Lawns Holiday Park (Bunn Leisure) ★★★★★**	86
Selsey, South East	**Warner Farm Camping & Touring Park ★★★★★**	87
Selsey, South East	**West Sands Holiday Park (Bunn Leisure) ★★★★**	87
Selsey, South East	**White Horse Holiday Park (Bunn Leisure) ★★★★**	87
Silloth, North West	**Stanwix Park Holiday Centre ★★★★★**	196

🏊 Outdoor pool

Index by property name

Accommodation with a detailed entry in this guide is listed below.

Index by place name

The following places all have detailed accommodation entries in this guide. If the place where you wish to stay is not shown the location maps (starting on page 254) will help you to find somewhere to stay in the area.

HUDSON's MEDIA LIMITED

Published by: Hudson's Media Ltd
35 Thorpe Road, Peterborough, PE3 6AG
Tel: 01733 296910 Fax: 01733 209292

On behalf of: VisitBritain, Sanctuary Buildings, 20 Great Smith Street, London SW1P 3BT

Editor: Deborah Coulter
Editorial Contributor: Neil Pope
Production team: Deborah Coulter, Rhiannon McCluskey, Rebecca Owen-Fisher

Creative: Jamieson Eley
Advertising team: Ben Piper, Matthew Pinfold, Seanan McGrory, James O'Rawe
Email: VEguides@hudsons-media.co.uk Tel: 01733 296913
Production System: NVG – leaders in Tourism Technology. www.nvg.net
Printer: Stephens & George, Merthyr Tydfil
Retail Sales: Compass – Tel: 020 8996 5764